THE GRAND EXPERIMENT

PATRONS OF THE OSGOODE SOCIETY

David Asper
Blake, Cassels & Graydon LLP
Gowlings
McCarthy Tétrault LLP
Osler, Hoskin & Harcourt LLP
Paliare Roland Rosenberg Rothstein LLP
Torkin Manes Cohen Arbus LLP
Torys LLP
WeirFoulds LLP

The Osgoode Society is supported by a grant from
The Law Foundation of Ontario.

The Society also thanks The Law Society of Upper Canada
for its continuing support.

LAW AND SOCIETY SERIES
W. Wesley Pue, General Editor

The Law and Society Series explores law as a socially embedded
phenomenon. It is premised on the understanding that the conventional
division of law from society creates false dichotomies in thinking, scholarship,
educational practice, and social life. Books in the series treat law and society
as mutually constitutive and seek to bridge scholarship emerging from
interdisciplinary engagement of law with disciplines such as politics, social
theory, history, political economy, and gender studies.

A list of the titles in this series appears at the end of this book.

THE
GRAND EXPERIMENT

LAW AND LEGAL CULTURE IN
BRITISH SETTLER SOCIETIES

Edited by

Hamar Foster, Benjamin L. Berger, and A.R. Buck

UBCPress · Vancouver · Toronto

Published for the Osgoode Society for Canadian Legal History by UBC Press

16 15 14 13 12 11 10 09 08   5 4 3 2 1

Printed in Canada on acid-free paper.

Library and Archives Canada Cataloguing in Publication

The grand experiment : law and legal culture in British settler societies / edited by Hamar Foster, Benjamin L. Berger, and A.R. Buck.

(Law and society, ISSN 1496-4953)
Includes bibliographical references and indexes.
ISBN 978-0-7748-1491-1

 1. Law – Great Britain – Colonies – History. 2. Law – Great Britain – History. I. Foster, Hamar, 1948- II. Berger, Benjamin L., 1977- III. Buck, A. R. IV. Osgoode Society for Canadian Legal History V. Series: Law and society series (Vancouver, B.C.)

KD5020.G73 2008   349.41   C2008-903338-8

Canadä

UBC Press gratefully acknowledges the financial support for our publishing program of the Government of Canada through the Book Publishing Industry Development Program (BPIDP), and of the Canada Council for the Arts, and the British Columbia Arts Council.

This book has been published with the help of a grant from the Canadian Federation for the Humanities and Social Sciences, through the Aid to Scholarly Publications Programme, using funds provided by the Social Sciences and Humanities Research Council of Canada.

UBC Press
The University of British Columbia
2029 West Mall
Vancouver, BC V6T 1Z2
604-822-5959 / Fax: 604-822-6083
www.ubcpress.ca

FOR JOHN PETER SOMERSET McLAREN

Legal historian, colleague, teacher, friend ... and unrepentant Morris dancer

CONTENTS

CONTENTS

PART 2: COURTS AND JUDGES IN THE COLONIES

CONTENTS

PART 2: COURTS AND JUDGES IN THE COLONIES

6   Courts, Communities, and Communication:
    The Nova Scotia Supreme Court on Circuit, 1816-50 / 117
    Jim Phillips and Philip Girard

7   Fame and Infamy: Two Men of the Law in Colonial New Zealand / 135
    David V. Williams

8   Moving in an "Eccentric Orbit": The Independence of Judge
    Algernon Sidney Montagu in Van Diemen's Land, 1833-47 / 156
    Stefan Petrow

9   "Not in Keeping with the Traditions of the Cariboo Courts":
    Courts and Community Identity in Northeastern British Columbia,
    1920-50 / 176
    Jonathan Swainger

PART 3: PROPERTY, POLITICS, AND PETITIONS IN COLONIAL LAW

10 Starkie's Adventures in North America: The Emergence of Libel Law / 195
    Lyndsay M. Campbell

11 The Law of Dower in New South Wales and the United States:
    A Study in Comparative Legal History / 208
    A.R. Buck and Nancy E. Wright

12 Contesting Prohibition and the Constitution in 1850s New
    Brunswick / 221
    Greg Marquis

13 From Humble Prayers to Legal Demands: The Cowichan Petition
    of 1909 and the British Columbia Indian Land Question / 240
    Hamar Foster and Benjamin L. Berger

Afterword: Looking from the Past into the Future / 268
John McLaren

Notes / 277

Selected Bibliography / 352

Contributors / 377

Index / 380

VIII

ILLUSTRATIONS

FOREWORD

The Osgoode Society for Canadian Legal History

IN RECENT years Canadian legal historians have shown an increasing interest in imperial themes and the comparative legal history of British colonies, and this book reflects that interest in comparing ourselves with other settler colonies. It examines the legal cultures of former British colonies, principally Canada, Australia, and New Zealand, although there is also some discussion of the United States and South Africa, and covers such topics as dower, prohibition, libel law, and the clash of colonial and indigenous legal regimes. Its themes are how local life and culture in selected colonies influenced, and was influenced by, the ideology of the rule of law that accompanied British colonialism, and it includes examination of the much-neglected question of the extent to which British courts took note of the decisions made by courts in the settler dominions. The volume is rich in empirical detail and ends with a reflection on the state and future of the discipline by Professor John McLaren.

The purpose of the Osgoode Society for Canadian Legal History is to encourage research and writing in the history of Canadian law. The Society, which was incorporated in 1979 and is registered as a charity, was founded at the initiative of the Honourable R. Roy McMurtry, formerly attorney general for Ontario and chief justice of the province, and officials of the Law Society of Upper Canada. The Society seeks to stimulate the study of legal history in Canada by supporting researchers, collecting oral histories, and publishing volumes that contribute to legal-historical scholarship in Canada. It has published seventy books on the courts, the judiciary, and the legal profession, as well as on the history of crime and punishment, women and law, law and economy, the legal treatment of ethnic minorities, and famous cases and significant trials in all areas of the law.

Current directors of the Osgoode Society for Canadian Legal History are Robert Armstrong, Attorney General Chris Bentley, Kenneth Binks, Patrick Brode, Brian Bucknall, David Chernos, Kirby Chown, J. Douglas Ewart, Martin Friedland, John Honsberger, Horace Krever, Ian Kyer, Gavin MacKenzie, Virginia MacLean, Roy McMurtry, Jim Phillips, Paul Reinhardt, Joel Richler, William Ross, Paul Schabas, Robert Sharpe, James Spence, Mary Stokes, Richard Tinsley, and Michael Tulloch.

The annual report and information about membership may be obtained by writing to the Osgoode Society for Canadian Legal History, Osgoode Hall, 130 Queen Street West, Toronto, Ontario, M5H 2N6. Telephone: 416-947-3321. E-mail: mmacfarl@lsuc.on.ca. Website: http://www.osgoodesociety.ca.

R. Roy McMurtry
President

Jim Phillips
Editor-in-Chief

ACKNOWLEDGMENTS

THE EDITORS would like to thank Lyndsay Watson and Rosemary Garton for their assistance in bringing this book to press and to acknowledge the financial support of the University of Victoria, Macquarie University, the Faculty of Law at the University of Victoria, and the Social Sciences and Humanities Research Council of Canada. We would also like to thank Professors W. Wesley Pue of the University of British Columbia and Robert Menzies of Simon Fraser University for organizing the 2005 "Law's Empire" Conference, which produced the idea for this book, and for their help in securing funding.

THE GRAND EXPERIMENT

INTRODUCTION

DOES LAW MATTER?
THE NEW COLONIAL LEGAL HISTORY

Benjamin L. Berger, Hamar Foster, and A.R. Buck

THE HISTORIAN E.P. Thompson eloquently expressed the awkwardness surrounding law, particularly the elusive notion of "the rule of law." He readily conceded that, "in a context of gross class inequalities, the equity of the law must always be in some part sham" and that, when transplanted to a colonial context, it could well become an instrument of imperialism. But he maintained nonetheless that "the rules and categories of law penetrate every level of society," and its forms and rhetoric "may, on occasion, inhibit power and afford some protection to the powerless." For his part, Thompson concluded that, if "law is no more than a mystifying and pompous way in which class power is registered and executed, then we need not waste our labour studying its history and forms." But he did, and we do. And we do it because — to quote Thompson one more time — "law *matters*."[1]

Talk of the "rule of law" is everywhere today, and scholarship about its nature and what it requires of societies that profess to enjoy it has loomed large in discussions about constitutional development and the international political order. What is it? Who has it? How can we create it? But the concept is no longer reserved for political philosophers and students of jurisprudence. The idea of the rule of law has found its way into the carefully prepared speeches of politicians, media commentary about world events, and, increasingly, everyday discussions about contemporary issues. In these uses, the concept has become closely associated with notions of constitutionalism, of human rights, and of stable democratic government, to be contrasted with dictatorial and oppressive forms of rule.

But the meaning or content of the rule of law is less clear, and the fog descended early. According to Albert Venn Dicey, the jurist whose name is most associated with the concept, the rule of law, at a minimum, includes three basic elements. The first is that no one may be subject to a civil or criminal penalty "except for a distinct breach of law established in the ordinary legal manner before the ordinary Courts of the land." The second is that no one is above the law and everyone is subject to "the ordinary law of the realm and amenable to the jurisdiction of the ordinary courts." And the third is that the general principles of the constitution are "with us the result of judicial decisions determining the rights of private persons in particular cases," not the product of a priori principles.[2] The third of Dicey's principles is peculiarly English, but the first two are widely accepted and have engendered debate about such issues as anti-terrorism legislation, Aboriginal rights, and administrative law in general.[3] Some have taken a different tack in approaching this protean concept, expanding upon and catholicizing, rather than critiquing, the formal Diceyan requirements. These scholars have imagined that the rule of law imposes robust substantive requirements amounting to a minimum degree of "equity" within the law.[4] The rule of law has even been deployed in Canada, for example, as an unwritten constitutional principle capable of invalidating legislation.[5]

But the ubiquity of the concept has not only made the definition of the rule of law elusive; its uniform rhetorical acceptance has often veiled the concrete realities of living under it. This rhetoric occludes the meaning of living within the culture of law's rule, including the dynamics of local power, economics, exclusion, resistance, and transformation that exist beneath the surface of even the most pristine and venerable traditions of the rule of law.[6] The rule of law thus matters deeply but hides much.

Thompson, a social historian, was criticized by some of his colleagues on the Left for this apparent privileging of law. But the situation is even trickier for legal historians, who cannot avoid such privileging without ceasing to *be* legal historians. For the most part, however, they have done so mindful not only of the value of the rule of law but also of its ideological function and its potential for what Thompson called "sham." In a number of ways, the chapters in this collection all take this lesson to heart, attempting both to show the way in which law is sham — meaning the way in which historical, economic, social, and local realities serve to shape and even distort the meaning of the rule of law at a given time in a given place — and the extent to which law matters.

One Canadian legal historian who has been engaged for years in the task of peeling away the veneer of the rule of law to reveal the messy ways in which all of this has "mattered" is John McLaren. Whether considering the manner in which the rule of law has interacted with religious cultures in Canada, with the historical injustices perpetrated by colonial legislatures, or with the realities of the administration of colonial law, John's work has consistently asked hard questions and offered illuminating answers about the nature of the rule of law in the British Empire.[7] John has also been a tireless advocate of the importance of this sort of legal history to legal education in these former colonies, a commitment that is strikingly demonstrated in the creation of a colonial legal history course at the University of Victoria that is a web-based joint venture with the University of British Columbia, the Australian National University in Canberra, and Macquarie University in Sydney.[8] Above all, John has been instrumental in making legal history a transboundary, comparative, contextually sensitive, and collective enterprise involving colleagues both inside and outside Canada.

This was acknowledged at the "Law's Empire" Conference at Harrison Hot Springs, British Columbia, in June of 2005. At the session titled "Themes in Comparative Colonial Legal History," scholars from Canada, the United States, New Zealand, and Australia collected to honour John McLaren and to build upon his contributions to legal history. The idea for this volume was born at that conference, a volume that would draw on the work of legal historians who have been in the vanguard of the comparative and contextual approach to our mutual legal past. In this way, we would honour not only John's contribution to the field but also his pioneering efforts to have legal historians in these various jurisdictions speak to one another and even, increasingly, to work together.

The essays that follow also reflect the exciting new directions in which legal history in the settler colonies of the British Empire has developed in the last two decades. Recent publications such as *Despotic Dominion: Property Rights in British Settler Societies; Masters, Servants, and Magistrates in Britain and the Empire, 1562-1955;* and *Law, History, Colonialism: The Reach of Empire* attest to the contemporary flourishing of legal history in these former colonies.[9] If more evidence is needed, one need look only at the scholarly journal *Legal History* (formerly the *Australian Journal of Legal History*) and the many volumes published by the Osgoode Society for Canadian Legal History and in the Law and Society Series of UBC Press. There clearly is a "new colonial legal history," and it is exemplified in this volume. No longer a narrowly construed doctrinal history for lawyers—although getting the law "right" is obviously critical—the "new" legal history has been particularly attentive to the social and cultural context in which legal institutions and actors have operated. As Keith Smith and John McLaren explain, this new legal history is focused on the "investigation of cultural factors, social forces and values, ideological and intellectual impulses and political and economic realities. In turn it takes account of the impact of law and legal culture on intellectual thought and on the community and life more generally."[10]

Set within this frame, the question is not simply what the law *was* but what the law *meant* to the communities that engaged and lived within it. This has involved close attention to the details of local culture, geography, biography, and politics, and how these have inflected and refracted the rule of law. It is in this sense that the chapters in this volume all reflect the profoundly contextual nature of this new colonial legal history. In fact, the notion of "contextual" colonial legal history echoes a distinction that has long been drawn between "internal" and "external" legal history generally. The former stays "in the box," concerning itself with matters purely legal; the latter addresses itself to the law and its relation to society. But as John McLaren and one of the editors of this volume wrote nearly fifteen years ago,

> [T]hese approaches should not be mutually exclusive. Legal history that neglects the wider context risks misunderstanding or ignoring altogether the forces that shaped both the legal rules and the events to which they were applied. But, equally, legal history that slights cases, statutes, regulations and the legal profession begs a crucial philosophical question by assuming without proof that the law, as a Marxist might say, is mere superstructure ... Whether one sees oneself as doing "legal" history or not, the institutions of the law and the activities of those who work within them cannot be divorced from broader cultural influences; but neither can these influences be treated as though the law were a mere appendage.[11]

The chapters that follow reflect this advice by treating the law as intimately connected to, influenced by, and expressive of its environment without relegating it to mere epiphenomenon, determined entirely by other forces.

They do so within a particular context, one that involves two more concepts that are very much on the minds of people today: colonialism and empire. George Orwell, reflecting in 1936 on an experience he had during his stint with the Burmese Colonial Police, reported that he had decided early on that imperialism—by which he presumably meant colonialism as well—"was an evil thing." But, he added, "I was young and ill-educated ... I did not even know that the British Empire is dying, still less did I know that it is a great deal better than the younger empires that are going to supplant it."[12] Recently, historian Niall Ferguson has gone Orwell one better. He concludes that the British Empire may even have been, on balance, a good thing and that if the American empire is to do as well it must first face up to the fact that it is one. He is also careful to point out that British successes were often due as much to luck as to planning. British ascendancy over Spain, for example, was apparently due to tardiness! Because it was a "latecomer to the imperial race, [Britain] had to settle for colonizing the unpromising wastes of Virginia and New England, rather than the eminently lootable cities of Mexico and Peru." So, instead of engaging in plunder, the colonists focused on establishing effective and durable institutions.[13] In the nineteenth century, the fundamentals of these institutions, however imperfectly realized on the ground, were among the things that the settlers, merchants, and their local governments had left behind in England: parliamentary supremacy, the rule of law, and the common law tradition generally.

Of course, one can conclude that the British Empire was a good thing only if one is comparing it to what other imperial powers did or might have done, not if one is trying to imagine how Britain might have done better or how a world untainted by imperialism might look. Many theorists approach this question from the latter standpoint and, as a result, colonialism has—apart perhaps from railways in India and the business about the rule of law—generally been regarded as having been, on the whole, a bad thing. Evidence of this, from the Battle of Omdurman to the massacre at Amritsar, is substantial. But in the countries whose legal history is addressed in this book—primarily Canada, Australia, and New Zealand, but also South Africa and the United States—the British Empire and the colonialism it engendered are inescapable historical facts.

Faced with this irreducible reality, legal historians have tended to eschew the more utopian approach of the theorists. Although, when they use the term "colonialism," an unmistakable odour definitely clings to it, they have chosen to examine its complex and often messy workings on the ground instead of engaging in abstract and wholesale condemnations. In particular, they have looked at how, and how well, the transplanted apparatus of the British legal system has adapted to its various new surroundings. Some have focused on how colonial and imperial law might have, for all its rhetorical splendour, facilitated a kind of plunder that differed from the Spanish variety: the evils of the slave trade, for example, or the appropriation of indigenous lands and resources. Others have looked at how, as Barry Wright puts it in Chapter 1, the "incomplete implementation of the British Constitution" in colonial societies led to opposition, legal repression, and, occasionally, rebellion. Some have even wondered whether an empire whose gubernatorial instructions were usually framed in terms of "peace, order, and good government" was as concerned with "law" as has been supposed.[14]

Nor have legal historians confined themselves to colonies, narrowly defined. British Columbia, for example, was a British colony until 1871, when it joined Canada. Was it a colony after that? Was Canada? If so, when did this status end? With the Battle of Vimy Ridge in 1917? With the *Statute of Westminster* in 1931? With Canada's separate declaration of war against Germany in 1939? What about when appeals to the Judicial Committee of the Privy Council were abolished in 1949? Or was it not until the passage of the *Canada Act* in 1982? A similar problem arises in connection with colonial status in Australia. Constitutionally, the Australian colonies threw off their colonial shackles with Federation in 1901. But did that mean Australia lost its colonial status entirely? Or did that status survive, only to end on the beaches of Gallipoli in 1915? Or after the fall of Singapore in 1942? In terms of law, did that colonial status end only in 1986 with the passage of the *Australia Act,* which abolished appeals to the Privy Council? Has it ended yet?

All of the contributors to this volume would no doubt agree that the colonial nature of the jurisdictions they discuss persisted long after each one ceased, formally, to be a colony. Most would go further and assert that patterns and structures dating from the colonial period continue to inform social, economic, and political relations in these jurisdictions today. This is certainly true with respect to the place of indigenous peoples, who are the subject of Chapters 3, 7, and 13. It also explains why two other essays—Chapters 5 and 9—reach well into the twentieth century. As Stevens, a character in William Faulkner's play *Requiem for a Nun,* famously remarked, "The past is never dead. It isn't even past."

A virtual corollary to this contextual turn in colonial legal history has been an increased interest in, and attention to, the comparative study of the rule of law in the former British Empire. In certain respects, the call to legal history as necessarily a comparative enterprise is not a new one. Well over a century ago, Frederic William Maitland announced that "[h]istory involves comparison and the English lawyer who knew nothing and cared nothing for any system but his own hardly came in sight of the idea of legal history ... [T]here is nothing that sets a man thinking and writing to such good effect about a system of law and its history as an acquaintance however slight with other systems and their history."[15] This admonition has particular force with respect to the history of the rule of law in British settler societies. No matter how parochial, the magisterial nature of the British rule of law and its imperial posture meant that there was a relatively uniform sense of the kinds of institutions of law and governance that ought to order these colonies — notwithstanding that they were separated not only by vast distances but also by substantial local, cultural, geographical, and political differences. This aspiration to homogeneity is a great boon to the colonial legal historian who, with a comparative lens in place, is able to see the influence of context so very much more clearly.

Although only some of the chapters in this volume are explicitly comparative, all reflect this second aspect of the "new" colonial legal history: an awareness of developments in comparable jurisdictions. Chapters 1, 10, and 11, explicitly comparative in nature, compare and contrast one jurisdiction's approach to an area of the law with that taken in another part of the common law "empire." Chapter 5 ranges over four jurisdictions, relating how courts in England utilized the jurisprudence of each, and Chapter 7 compares the role of two leading jurists in one colonial jurisdiction. But all the essays draw on a body of colonial or imperial legal history that is by definition transboundary in scope. Prohibition in New Brunswick (Chapter 12) and Aboriginal title in British Columbia (Chapter 13) — to take but two examples — simply cannot be properly understood otherwise.

This methodological commitment to context and comparison in the study of the legal history of British settler societies underlies the several themes that are developed in this volume, themes that illustrate the complex relationship between law and the environment in which it operates, from discipline on the high seas (Chapter 2) to the circuit courts of Nova Scotia (Chapter 6) and the Tasmanian judiciary (Chapter 8), and from the law of the fur trade in seventeenth-century Rupert's Land (Chapter 3) to perceptions of legal virtue in twentieth-century New Zealand (Chapter 7). All of these themes are, themselves, joined in their relevance to an appreciation of the broad concepts with which we began this introduction: colonialism and the rule of law.

One such theme is what might be called legal translation, that is, how different legal cultures, even very early on, received and translated common law doctrines in different ways.[16] The concept of legal culture, which the late Graham Parker discussed more than twenty years ago with respect to Canada, is of course central to how the common law was "translated" and forms the background to many of the chapters in this volume.[17] In two of them — dealing with the rule of law in colonial New South Wales (Chapter 4) and with legal traditions in the Cariboo and Peace River "countries" of British Columbia (Chapter 9) — it may even be said to move into the foreground, although this is of course a matter of degree. More specific examples of this theme of translation are to be found in Chapters 1 and 10, by Barry Wright and Lyndsay Campbell, who examine how the law of libel was adapted and transformed in Upper Canada, New South Wales, Nova Scotia, and Massachusetts, and in Chapter 11, in which Andrew Buck and Nancy Wright discuss the law of dower in New South Wales and the United States.

Another related theme is the importance of "local" histories. In Canada, British Columbia historian Tina Loo, invoking the work of anthropologist Clifford Geertz, drew attention some time ago to the importance of local understandings to how law is applied.[18] Some of the essays in this volume emphasize this as well. Jonathan Swainger, for example, wonders in Chapter 9 whether "localized notions of pragmatic sense" and the contributions of a particular judge created a regional legal tradition that, by the 1940s, clashed with modernity. In a way, Chapter 6, by Jim Phillips and Philip Girard, looks at the same phenomenon from the other end of the microscope, emphasizing as it does the transformation of the Supreme Court circuits in Nova Scotia from community event to government service. In Chapter 3, Janna Promislow puts a slightly different twist on this when she seeks to analyze a late twentieth-century Canadian judge's interpretation of late nineteenth-century Cree leadership by looking at how the Cree and the fur traders interacted in the seventeenth century. She concludes, in part, that "legal traditions are full of symbolism" and that if we fail to search the historical record for barely discernible local meanings, we "will miss important signals of political and legal authority." What seems just as clear when one reviews the historical record is that, whether it is a judge in Australia striking down statutes as repugnant to the laws of England, or one in British Columbia approving departures from the English norm due to "local circumstances," the law and its various local interpretations were important ingredients in the bubbling cauldron of colonial politics.

Related to this focus on local histories is the role of biography, and particularly judicial biography, in the legal histories explored in this volume. It is notable how prominently the relationship between the colonial judiciary and the rule of law figures in these essays, a theme that itself strongly reflects the interests and influence of John McLaren.[19] For example, in Chapter 8, Stefan Petrow presents a detailed portrait of an early Tasmanian judge whose personal foibles, he argues, have unfairly overshadowed his more positive attributes. In the same vein, David Williams asks his readers to reassess how we assign praise and blame in the law when, in Chapter 7, he contrasts the careers of two New Zealand jurists, the "famous" Sir William Salmond and the "infamous" Chief Justice Sir James Prendergast. For those who specialize in the history of indigenous rights in the British Commonwealth, Williams' discussion should be of particular interest. In Chapter 9, Jonathan Swainger profiles Judge H.E.A. Robertson. And although some might quarrel with the suggestion that a County Court judge in British Columbia in the first half of the twentieth century qualifies as "colonial," we think he does. Certain judges, moreover, make appearances in more than one of these studies, notably Chief Justice Francis Forbes in New South Wales, thus attesting to the transboundary nature of the colonial legal enterprise.[20]

A fourth theme apparent in this volume is what might be referred to as law "at the boundaries," that is to say, either at the outermost limits of the legal system or at least in its remoter backwaters. How the law operates in these regions may throw light not only on its performance at the margins but also on how lesser legal narratives may complement the dominant one — or undermine it by revealing the sham behind the rhetoric. Bruce Kercher's examination, in Chapter 2, of the "power of masters to ensure discipline at sea" is an excellent example of this sort of thing and reveals an asymmetry between master and seaman that others have documented in the master-servant relationship on land.[21] In Chapter 13, two of us also tread on this territory and look at the role of the Cowichan Petition of 1909 in the campaign to have Aboriginal title recognized in British Columbia in the early twentieth century. That the attempt failed says volumes about the reality behind the rhetoric of the rule of law at that time. What the apparent success of the late twentieth-century campaign for such recognition will amount to, in Canada and elsewhere, remains to be seen. But what cannot be doubted is that the rule of law exists in a state of tension with the interests of settler societies and their successors: it both legitimates the status quo and challenges it with principles that, instead of being put into practice, have often been allowed to moulder in old books. Responsible government, for example, was for settlers an indispensable boon; for indigenous peoples, it posed a considerable threat to any sort of respect for their Aboriginal rights and title. Indeed, where Aboriginal people are concerned, almost any example will do because colonialism, even when tempered by the rule of law, required indigenous people to choose sides. Does one fight for traditional rights or compromise with the new order?[22] Whether one is speaking about the law banning the potlatch in British Columbia or the Maori Land Court in New Zealand, the dilemma is the same.[23] Thompson would have understood this very well.

Finally, many of the chapters in this volume have to do with what may fairly be described as "constitutionalism"—not the formal consti-tutionalism of the "supreme" legal documents that guide so much law in contemporary liberal democracies but, rather, the more fundamental sense of the constitution as the way in which the legal order has been constructed in different parts of the world. As Karl Llewellyn put it, a "constitution" in the most meaningful sense of the word "may be summed up more or less adequately as the going scheme of government under which those who do it, do it; and those who get something out of it proceed about getting something out of it; and those who take it, take it—sometimes hard."[24] Viewed in this way, the chapters discussing the relationship between colonial forces and Aboriginal communities, such as Chapter 3, by Janna Promislow, on the particular ways in which these relationships were negotiated between Aboriginal groups and traders in Rupert's Land, and Chapter 13, on the Cowichan Petition of 1909, are quintessentially about constitutionalism in colonial legal history. This is also very much a theme of Chapter 12's examination of the prohibition phenomenon and the Constitution in New Brunswick in the 1850s. The issue of how the practices and attitudes of governance develop in colonial societies is perhaps most squarely addressed in Chapter 4's analysis of what its authors call "common law constitutionalism" in the early development of Australia.

The essays in this collection explore these analytically rich themes in a comparative context that, for better or worse, would not be possible were it not for the existence of the empire that George Orwell, looking forward as well as back, damned with such faint praise. And although we readily concede that it is difficult to read Victorian prose these days with the seriousness of our ancestors (knowing as we do just how much "sham" was involved in the colonial enterprise), it nonetheless seems fitting to end with the concluding words of that masterpiece of legal history, Pollock and Maitland's *The History of English Law*. Speaking of the fact that English and European law went their separate ways in the period covered by the book, the authors wrote,

> Which country made the wiser choice no Frenchman and no Englishman can impartially say; no one should be judge in his own cause. But of this there can be no doubt, that it was for the good of the whole world that one race stood apart from its neighbours, turned away its eyes at an early time from the fascinating pages of the *Corpus Iuris,* and, more Roman than the Romanists, made the grand experiment of a new formulary system ... Those few men who were gathered at Westminster round Pateshull and Raleigh and Bracton were penning writs that would run in the name of kingless commonwealths on the other shore of the Atlantic Ocean; they were making right and wrong for us and for our children.[25]

We no longer speak so unabashedly of empire or invoke "race" in this fashion. But, warts and all, the common law was a system unto itself and it did spread — through settlement, conquest, and treaty — across the globe.[26] This volume tells a part of that story, a story about the very phenomenon that so awed Pollock and Maitland. And if we are honest with ourselves, this story astonishes us still — even if we cannot view the reach of empire with the apparent equanimity of some of our predecessors.

Whether deconstructing ideology or simply documenting the regular workings of a colonial legal system, the essays collected here reveal, we believe, that Thompson was right: no history can be complete without taking the law and its practitioners into account. Law, in other words, does matter. And, thanks to the pioneering efforts of scholars such as John McLaren, the study of colonial legal history, in particular, has become an increasingly cosmopolitan undertaking, reaching across old imperial boundaries and engaging many in a common enterprise. As editors, we hope that this volume provides a context that not only enriches our understanding of that phenomenon but encourages others to join us in this rewarding task.

PART ONE

AUTHORITY AT THE BOUNDARIES OF EMPIRE

LIBEL AND THE COLONIAL ADMINISTRATION OF JUSTICE IN UPPER CANADA AND NEW SOUTH WALES, c. 1825-30

Barry Wright

IN THE past thirty or forty years, many historians have moved beyond the traditional narratives and accounts of empire, past the "culture cringe," to focus on local and national struggles. This has brought important, previously marginalized experiences into focus, but at the risk, perhaps, of parochialism. In the case of British colonies with received English laws, and the self-governing dominions that emerged from them, there are imperial legal networks that warrant further research and offer enormous scope for new comparative legal historical scholarship. There are similar legal and constitutional issues, common imperial policy responses, and initiatives that involved more than directives from London but were also informed, as Bruce Kercher has pointed out, by ideas circulating among British jurisdictions, facilitated by the intercolonial migration of legal and political personnel.[1] None of this is to suggest the displacement of history from "below" by history from "above," or the uncritical restoration of the Whiggish narratives about imperial policy reform and London's enlightened promotion of the rule of law or responsible self-government in the face of recalcitrant colonial elites. Rather, it is about a better understanding of context.

John McLaren's recent comparative overview of judicial controversies in colonial Australia and Canada illuminates the rich potential for contextualized comparative legal historical research.[2] This chapter elaborates his themes by way of a closer examination of parallel legal controversies around attempts to suppress political opposition and the independent press in the British North American colony of Upper Canada (present-day Ontario) and the Australian colony of New South Wales in the latter half of the 1820s. McLaren's study of the issue of judicial independence in both colonies in the first four decades of the nineteenth century highlights the prominence of the rule of law and related British constitutional claims. Such claims were used to challenge Upper Canada's ruling "Family Compact" and to contest its attempts to discredit and silence opposition. The New South Wales Governor's wide executive powers over the affairs of the convict colony, generally supported by the "Exclusives," triggered the same constitutional discourse as the "Emancipists," including former convicts, who struggled for rights and representative institutions. The courts in both colonies were a primary forum for political battles, and judges were at the centre of these conflicts. A study of attempts to suppress opposition and silence the press by seditious libel and related colonial legislation enables us to extend McLaren's comparative look at the judiciary to other contentious elements in the colonial administration of justice (prosecutions and the jury) and the opportunity to further explore the social and institutional pressures on local executives and their domination of law and politics.

Similarities in uses of the law to manage opposition and political expression, and contestation of these uses, not only reveal common legal and constitutional issues but also underscore the central place of law in the narratives of colonial political struggles, their emerging "public spheres," and imperial-colonial relations. Popular pressures from "below" and imperial pressures from "above" were important factors that influenced the course of events examined here. In Upper Canada the 1828 conviction of Francis Collins for seditious libel was the culmination of a series of prosecutions against opposition leaders and the press and was accompanied by the dismissal of Judge John Walpole Willis (who ended up on the New South Wales bench in 1837). Legislative Assembly demands for his reinstatement were petitioned to the British government along with related grievances, notably frustrated majority bills to repeal local legislated deportation powers over "seditious" aliens and recently arrived British subjects (the *Sedition Act,* 1804). During this same period, New South Wales saw the prosecutions of Robert Wardell (1827), Edward Hall (1828, 1829), and Attwell Hayes (1829), and legislative attempts to license the press (the *"Libel"* or *"Newspaper" Acts,* 1827, 1830) that included the punishment of banishment from the colony and other provisions that Chief Justice Francis Forbes (formerly Chief Justice of Newfoundland) refused to certify. The curbing of prosecutions and British legislative interventions (repeal of Upper Canada's *Sedition Act* in 1829 and disallowance of the New South Wales *Libel Act* in 1831) reflect common patterns of pressures from above and below. Both colonies experienced the broadening of politically engaged public opinion supported by an independent press and increasingly articulate concerns about executive domination of law and politics and departures from the British Constitution. By the 1830s the prospects of successful legal repression were much reduced, constrained by the development of colonial public spheres and supported by the ascendancy of liberal reform interests in the British government and more critical scrutiny of colonial affairs.

THE POLITICAL AND LEGAL CONTEXT

British Background and English Criminal Law

The English criminal laws adopted in Upper Canada and New South Wales included the offence of seditious libel, the primary means British governments used to manage oppositional political expression and published criticism of the state in the eighteenth century and the first two decades of the nineteenth century. The late seventeenth-century constitutional compromises did not resolve issues around the legitimacy of organized political opposition, freedom of the press, and political expression as governments attempted to stem the erosion of deference to authority, and reformers attempted to secure these liberties. Even until the 1820s, British governments tended to share Edmund Burke's view that growing popular engagement and debate about politics and public policy, particularly as expressed in the "republic of letters," was a dangerous revolutionary stirring of popular opinion. What governments characterized as serious threats to the existing order were perceived by political opposition, and increasingly by the engaged public, as legitimate challenges to privileged control over politics and public policy. The eighteenth-century elaborations of sedition and criminal libel laws were a response to fears of developing connections between organized opposition and emerging broader public opinion, a widening engagement with political matters by means of voluntary associations and their processes of deliberative democracy, increasing popular literacy, and a growing independent press.[3]

The common law offence of seditious libel was prosecuted for publications that criticized the state on the basis that they promoted discontent and disaffection, although there was no need to prove actual incitement of public disturbance. It derived from the political misdemeanour of sedition, expressed criticism of the Crown, government, or officials, and was punishable by fines, imprisonment, and the pillory. Prosecutions could be taken with relative ease, with no required proof that the accused caused violence or breach of the peace, unlike the more serious political offence of treason, which required proof of overt acts against the state and involved significant evidentiary and procedural protections for the accused after 1696. Advances such as the *Treason Act,* 1696, the *Habeas Corpus Act,* 1679, and the more general constitutional compromises of the period between parliamentary authority and the Crown were accompanied by the emerging convention of no prior restraint. Proactive press censorship was no longer feasible with the 1694 demise of print licensing and government monopoly over printing. Seditious libel was developed to fill the gap, becoming the most important form of the offence as reformers struggled against governments over the reach of post-publication sanctions.

The courts established the main elements of seditious libel, distinct from the criminal libel of defamation and the parliamentary privilege offence of contempt, by the second quarter of the eighteenth century.[4] These included a minimal burden of proof and judicial control over the most contentious questions. General verdicts were prohibited, and the issues to be decided by the jury were narrowed to the fact of publication and innuendo as suggested by the Crown. Conflicts between juries and judges were highlighted by the famous confrontations between Lord Chief Justice Mansfield and the libertarian defence counsel Thomas Erskine, who urged juries to resist instructions from the bench and use their verdicts as a measure of public opinion of oppressive laws and prosecutions.[5] These cases highlighted the uncertain status of liberties such as freedom of the press and political expression and underscored related legal concerns such as freedom of the jury's verdict, the need for further protections of judicial independence beyond security of tenure, and clearer articulation of the Crown's burden of proof. Fox's *Libel Act,* 1792, a "correction" of the common law that reiterated the powers of the jury to give a general verdict (including matters of intent and seditious inference), represented a partial reform advance. The offence nonetheless continued to have repressive utility, in the 1790s during the reaction to the French Revolution, and as a response to urban disorder in the period 1816-20.[6] However, by the 1820s governments had little confidence in securing compliant juries, and reformers began to advocate the defence of truth in all libel cases, achieved with Lord Campbell's *Libel Act,* 1843.[7]

Although the 1792 and 1843 legislative advances reduced the repressive utility of seditious libel, perhaps the most important check was the threat of jury acquittals, which in turn reflected wider currents in public opinion. These flowed from what Jürgen Habermas has described as the modern public sphere — the development of informed and politically engaged popular opinion through the eighteenth century, fostered by a growing independent press and processes of deliberative democracy outside established institutions, the legitimacy of which British governments began to recognize by the 1820s and 1830s.[8] James Fitzjames Stephen described the resulting transformation in terms of a shift from the traditional presumption that rulers are social superiors who are entitled to deference (and therefore it is wrong to criticize regardless of truth) to a Lockean presumption of popular sovereignty. Governments serve as agents of the people, exercising delegated authority, and could not demand deference but had to earn it (criticism is therefore a right, and only false or demonstrably harmful statements should be sanctioned).[9] The experience of these British struggles informed colonial resistance in the face of prosecutions for seditious libel and related local legislation. As we shall see, the British Constitution and the associated liberties thought to flow from it figured prominently in opposition rhetoric and criticism of colonial governments.

The American situation does not appear to have had much influence on the Canadian and Australian experiences; nor did the US serve as a particularly edifying example during this period. There were similar patterns of repression around an emerging public sphere. The celebrated colonial seditious libel case of John Peter Zenger (1735) did little to restrain similar measures against Loyalists and Quakers during the revolution. The US Bill of Rights and the First Amendment confirmed no prior restraint but did not eliminate seditious libel, despite the teleological impression left in many Whiggish constitutional histories. Jefferson's repeal of the 1798 federal alien and sedition legislation was accompanied by his active encouragement of state jurisdiction prosecutions for the common law offence against political opponents and the press. Despite geographic proximity, the American situation does not seem to have had a direct impact on Upper Canadian reformers (who tended to draw inspiration from British and Irish examples, and whose struggles for responsible government were not significantly republican in nature), or on broader public attitudes, apart from views possibly transmitted by non-Loyalist American immigrants. Despite distance,

Upper Canada and New South Wales had much in common in terms of the direct influence of British experiences and local colonial circumstances.[10]

The Colonial Background, Reception, and Colonial Institutions

Upper Canada, established in 1791, and New South Wales, established in 1788, differed significantly from each other. Nonetheless, these differences do not overshadow remarkable similarities and parallels between them, highlighted by events examined in detail here. In both colonies, the courts and the administration of justice occupy a central place in political battles, there is common reference to the British Constitution and the rule of law in opposition rhetoric and criticism of government practices, and governments encounter similar pressures from above and below, in the form of imperial supervision and the emergence of local popular public spheres.

Upper Canada was divided off the western part of the colony of Quebec to accommodate Loyalist refugees from the American Revolution. Although promised the image and transcript of the British Constitution, as Lieutenant Governor John Graves Simcoe put it, and granted an elected legislature, regular courts, and the full range of English law, avoidance of perceived mistakes made in the American colonies put a decidedly counter-revolutionary spin on these matters. The legislature was dominated by the appointed upper house, and the executive maintained tight control over office holding and the administration of justice. (Struggles for more accountable government culminated in the achievement of responsible cabinet government after rebellions in Upper and Lower Canada/Quebec in 1837-38, Lord Durham's influential 1839 report, and the electoral dominance of local reform moderates in the 1840s.) The first generation of government leadership had experienced, and therefore tended to regard criticism and organized opposition as a prelude to, revolution, a view reinforced by the French Revolution and the 1798 Irish Rebellion. American expansionism and the vulnerability of British North America's large, easily crossed border, highlighted by the War of 1812, and the related emergence of populist or Jacksonian democracy, reinforced official fears. Although the earliest manifestations of political opposition reflected inter-elite tensions, the emergence of an organized opposition party and a nascent popular movement in the decade before the war was influenced by Irish Whigs who had migrated after 1798, and drew parallels between the Irish and Canadian conditions of colonial rule and the incomplete implementation of the British Constitution. This development was met by the passage of the *Sedition Act, 1804*, and the silencing of the opposition leadership that included barrister William Weekes (killed in a duel), Judge Robert Thorpe (removed from the bench), and the editor of the colony's first opposition newspaper, Joseph Willcocks (prosecuted for seditious libel and imprisoned for contempt after parliamentary privilege proceedings). The post-war opposition was initially led by Scottish radical Robert Gourlay, who organized constitutional meetings to collect grievances and petition the British government, and whose acquittals in seditious libel trials led to his deportation under the *Sedition Act*. The resurgent opposition of the mid-1820s was accompanied by a broadening public sphere, increasing popular engagement with politics fuelled by a proliferation of independent newspapers, and was met by the measures discussed below.[11]

New South Wales was a convict colony, tightly controlled by the Governor's wide executive powers, and there was little scope for the expression of opposition, although, with the arrival of trained judges in the wake of the Rum Rebellion (1808), the courts soon became a key battleground. The *New South Wales Act, 1823*, checked the Governor's powers with the creation of an appointed Legislative Council (an elected element was introduced only in 1842, a full legislature equivalent to Upper Canada's in 1856) and a formal role for the Chief Justice in supervising colonial legislation. Although transported political convicts (English and Scottish radicals and United Irishmen) were an obvious potential source of opposition, the tight convict regimes limited opportunities for political organization and expression. Resistance, such as the 1804 Castle Hill uprising by Irish convicts, was quickly suppressed by military or police. The Rum Rebellion was a manifestation of inter-elite tensions between Governor William Bligh and John Macarthur's officers of the New South Wales Corps, who formed the nucleus of the Exclusives, a political grouping that grew with the arrival of free settlers. Free settler privileges and the disabilities of those with convict backgrounds were increasingly challenged in the 1820s by the Emancipists, a group including former convicts seeking equal rights and reformers seeking representative institutions and regular jury trials, using the rhetoric of the British Constitution and the rule of law. The emergence of independent newspapers fuelled the opposition and broadened engagement with it, prompting the legal responses examined here.[12]

The common law offence of seditious libel, along with Fox's *Libel Act,* 1792, formed part of the applicable laws in Upper Canada and New South Wales. The colonial reception of English law in overseas British territories acquired through conquest or discovery and occupation is a complex topic bound up with the imposition of an outside political and legal order. There were numerous colonial variations including, for our purposes, Upper Canada and New South Wales.[13] Upper Canada's situation was the more straightforward. The establishment of a legislature and courts in 1791 suggests that year as the "formal" reception date for the full (as opposed to partial and discretionary) application of English common law and legislation in effect at that time. Uncertainty stemming from the province's creation out of the former colony of Quebec (which acquired a legislature and regular courts in 1774) led to an Act passed in 1800 specifying September 1792 (when the legislature first met) as the relevant date, although confusion persisted, notably, for our purposes, over the applicability of the 1792 *Libel Act*.[14] The situation was more uncertain in New South Wales, with an extended period of "informal" reception where applicable English laws were subject to the wide executive discretion of the Governor. The *New South Wales Act,* 1823, confirmed the Chief Justice's function as councillor and his role in certifying local legislation (that it was not repugnant to English law but consistent so far as colonial circumstances would permit). Continued uncertainty about the status of English law led to the passage of the imperial *Australian Courts Act,* applicable to both New South Wales and Van Diemen's Land, which fixed a formal reception date at 1828.

In contrast to the liberalizing British legislation of 1792 and 1843, colonial legislative elaborations of the received sedition and libel laws were decidedly draconian, although subject to imperial review (disallowance or petition) and imperial legislation. Upper Canada's *Sedition Act,* passed in 1804 as permanent legislation, went further than similar temporary British, Lower Canadian, and US measures passed in the shadow of the French Revolution that extended executive powers around the entry and residency of aliens and their associates who engaged in political activity.[15] Aliens and recently arrived British subjects, not permanently resident in the province six months before proceedings were initiated, or who had not taken a provincial oath of allegiance, could be brought before a summary hearing to answer allegations of causing disaffection. Refusal to comply with an executive order to leave the province constituted an offence for which the accused could be held indefinitely, without access to *habeas corpus.* When the accused was tried and convicted, a sentence of deportation (immediately or after a further term of imprisonment) was confirmed, with further refusal to leave or return punishable by death.[16] The Act purged the province of over four hundred recent American immigrants during the War of 1812, but its most prominent target was Robert Gourlay, noted earlier.[17] As we shall see, repeal by way of petition to the British government in 1829 followed a decade of bills frustrated by the appointed upper house. The New South Wales legislation of 1827, amended in 1830, attempted to regulate the independent press by prior restraint, introducing a registration and licensing system with revocation upon a libel conviction or the Governor's discretion. It also introduced an onerous stamp duty as a secondary means of suppressing the press and added the penalty of banishment from the colony for further libel convictions. As discussed below, Chief Justice Forbes' refusal to certify the licensing provisions, on grounds that included conflict with established British constitutional convention, led to amendments in 1830, but the legislation was effectively disallowed months later by the British government.[18]

Accompanying these repressive colonial laws were issues around their administration. Heavy reliance by colonial governments on criminal prosecutions to fend off challenges and maintain authority was supported by greater executive domination of the administration of justice, resulting in expedients that would not be tolerated in nineteenth-century Britain. However, such domination was constrained because such practices evoked constitutional claims that, as E.P. Thompson observes in the context of the eighteenth-century English criminal courts, were a powerful means to contest repression.[19]

Neither colony benefited from the protections of judicial independence that had developed in Britain, where from 1701 judges held office according to good behaviour determined by Parliament rather than royal pleasure. Colonial judges could be removed at the instigation of executive councils (as was the case of John Walpole Willis in Upper Canada in 1828 and New South Wales in 1843) as well as being recalled. Colonial judges were usually at the centre of government, extrajudicial opinions before trials were routinely sought and given, and chief justices were leading executive and legislative councillors. These practices went well beyond acceptable conventions in Britain from the early nineteenth century (after Lord Chief Justice Ellenborough's controversial inclusion in the Ministry of All the Talents) and were formalized under the *New South Wales Act, 1823*. Chief Justice Forbes' role is central to the controversies examined here, and though his conflicts with the executive helped promote freedom of the press and separation of powers, they drew critical scrutiny from Colonial Undersecretary James Stephen in the shorter term. Forbes brought the issue of the powers of colonial judges into focus, and Stephen's concerns came to apply to partisan pro-government judges, notably Upper Canada's Chief Justice John Beverley Robinson. Although complaints about Robinson's conduct as Attorney General and role in Willis' removal to Parliament's 1828-29 Canada Committee did not deter his appointment as Chief Justice, they influenced Lord Goderich's 1831 attempt to end the practice of judicial appointments to governing councils. Robinson continued to defy the policy by playing a leading informal role in councils through to the aftermath of the 1837-38 rebellion.[20]

Executive influences extended to the organization of prosecutions and the local administration of justice. Upper Canadian law officers of the Crown effectively monopolized prosecutions and resorted widely to the prerogatives of *ex officio* informations (to bypass grand jury review of charges, leave "hanging threats" of prosecution to induce compliant behaviour, and add powers to change venue and pack juries) and *nolle prosequi* stays (to terminate private prosecutions potentially embarrassing to government). In New South Wales, where there was no obstacle of a grand jury, the absence of a regular indictment process resulted in routine use of informations. This was quite unlike English practice where private prosecutions predominated before the rise of professional policing and the prosecutorial prerogatives were regarded with suspicion as Star Chamber remnants.[21] The colonial executive's appointment powers over officials charged with the local administration of justice (justices of the peace, magistrates, sheriffs, constables) resulted in less autonomous parochial authority than in England.[22] In Upper Canada contention focused on the jury and, in particular (as in Ireland), on the sheriff's control over jury selection and the problem of pro-government jury packing. In New South Wales, there was a protracted struggle for the even more basic liberty of trial by a jury of peers, provisionally achieved in 1833, although military panels continued to be used in the criminal courts until 1839.[23] As we shall see in the cases examined here, military panels were urged to decide cases such as regular juries, but members' independence was almost invariably compromised by their commanding officers.

UPPER CANADA

My earlier study of sedition prosecutions in Upper Canada indicates nearly fifty cases, which, taking populations into account, exceeded English rates of the period, even during Pitt's "Terror" of the 1790s and the flurry of prosecutions between 1817 and 1819. The most significant and heavily punished cases, noted earlier, took place at ten-year intervals, prosecuted as seditious libel against opposition leaders associated with an independent press.[24] Joseph Willcocks was indicted for seditious libel in 1807, but concerns about a sympathetic jury led to conversion of the prosecution to an *ex officio* information and a related conviction secured by parliamentary privilege proceedings for contempt in 1808.[25] Robert Gourlay, twice acquitted by juries in seditious libel trials in 1818, was unable to contest his deportation the following year under the *Sedition Act,* and a well-managed seditious libel prosecution by *ex officio* information resulted in a ruinous conviction of his editor, Bartimus Ferguson.[26] The Francis Collins case in 1828 lies at the centre of events examined here. Although opposition and the independent press were primary concerns in all these cases, it was unclear how far the colony's public sphere had developed before the 1820s. There is little doubt that widely engaged public opinion had emerged by the time of Collins. Although he was convicted, his case greatly discredited the administration of justice in Upper Canada, resulting in the demise of heavy-handed use of seditious libel and imperial intervention to repeal the *Sedition Act.*

Although there were earlier attempts to establish an independent press, Willcocks' newspaper was the first associated with an organized opposition. Such newspapers saw phenomenal growth in the 1820s, increasing from three in 1819 (two in 1820, after the conviction of Gourlay's editor, Ferguson) to ten by 1830. Jeffrey McNairn's research on the development of public opinion in Upper Canada examines postal records that show high subscription rates, supplemented by the wide availability of newspapers at taverns and hotels, as well as at community reading rooms and libraries run by a growing range of voluntary associations. Subscription rates exceeded those of England outside of London, and estimates based on the second quarter of the nineteenth century suggest that provincial literacy rates approached 80 percent, well above those of English counties and towns. McNairn also illustrates the growing importance of voluntary associations (such as mechanics institutes, agricultural, literary, scientific, and constitutional societies, and the Masons) after the War of 1812. These organizations not only increased the availability of public information and newspapers but also debated public issues with elaborate rules for discussion.[27] Whereas the earlier sedition prosecutions were a response to organized political opposition and an independent press, the emergence of broader, politically engaged opinion by the 1820s deepened the challenges to privileged claims and control over politics and public policy. Effective defence use of constitutional and rule of law claims and the pivotal role of the jury were evident in the Willcocks and Gourlay affairs, but they had wider popular resonance by the time of Collins.

The 1820s saw a growing public sphere that reflected a shift in public opinion from deference to government to an expectation of free discussion of public measures. Government concerns extended even to the King's Printer, leading one editor of the *Gazette* to be called to the bar of the House and reprimanded for his accounts of parliamentary debates and political reporting, and his successor's loss of appointment for portraying reform too positively. Three independent newspaper editors — Hugh Thomson of the *Upper Canada Herald,* William Lyon Mackenzie of the *Colonial Advocate,* and Francis Collins of the *Canadian Freeman* — became a particular concern for their political commentary. Parliamentary privilege proceedings for contempt were taken against Thomson.[28] The dumping of Mackenzie's press into Lake Ontario by young Tory hooligans, many of whom were law students, along with other incidents of "rough justice" unprosecuted by the Crown and suggesting official complicity with violence against selected reform targets, gave rise to a Legislative Assembly inquiry into the administration of justice and public prosecutions.[29] It heard testimony from the recently arrived Judge Willis, who made much of colonial departures from English practices, questioned their constitutionality, and repeated these charges at the assizes. A related series of articles by Collins revealed yet more about government legal abuses and linked the law officers of the Crown to unprosecuted criminal acts.[30]

Attorney General Robinson expressed caution in contemplating a legal response:

> Within a few Years Two Newspapers have been established in this Town, under the Conduct of Men [Collins and Mackenzie] of much less responsible Stations in Society than the editors of Public Journals commonly are ... I always regretted the Tendency which such Publications might have in misleading the Opinions of

People ... and perhaps a Sense of this ought to have induced me, for the sake of the Province, to attempt to put them down by Law ... [but] I feared to call the Papers into Notoriety, and to protract their Existence, by the political Excitements which Prosecutions for Libel usually occasion.[31]

The growing controversy surrounding the Attorney General's partisan conduct compounded matters and explains his reluctance to resort to the expedient of an *ex officio* information, although he was willing to conduct prosecutions by regular indictment upon the Lieutenant-Governor's request or any individuals libelled. As the Home District assize opened on 7 April, the grand jury returned a true bill on the indictment against Collins and another against Mackenzie.[32] Robinson's caution did not, however, extend to anticipating Willis' presence. Just before the trials commenced, Willis permitted Collins to air concerns about Robinson and to lay private charges for alleged acts by government supporters.[33] A furious Robinson withdrew the Collins case to the next assize in October, declaring subsequent press conduct would determine whether the Collins or Mackenzie cases proceeded.

During the summer, the Executive Council recommended Willis' removal and suspended him on the pretext of his challenge to the constitutionality of the King's Bench.[34] A third seditious libel indictment was issued in Kingston when Hugh Thomson of the *Herald* wrote: "This high handed measure plainly shows that judges who hold their appointments during pleasure may not give an opinion contrary to the will of the Executive, without running the risk of being dismissed."[35] The Mackenzie and Thomson indictments were dropped, but Robinson proceeded against Collins when the autumn assize opened on 13 October. Collins tried to postpone the case, pointing out that, in the confusion of the spring assize, he had not been formally arraigned. When this was confirmed, Robinson demanded and won an impossibly high security for Collins' good behaviour, prompting Collins to opt for immediate trial to avoid imprisonment.[36] The jury acquitted, but the Attorney General brought new charges on different evidence — Collins' recently published remarks on Robinson and Judge Hagerman during the trial itself.[37]

The Crown's third crack at Collins came on 25 October before Justice Sherwood (whose son and brother-in-law faced Collins' criminal charges at the spring assize). Collins' counsel, John Rolph, attempted to raise the defence of truth, claiming that the Attorney General had indeed stated a falsehood in court, and at the end of arguments moved for an immediate acquittal because Robinson refused to read the alleged libels to the jury.[38] Robinson and Judge Sherwood attempted to steer the jury clear of these matters, but the jurors struggled with their verdict, and while they were deliberating, Sherwood left the bench to be replaced by Hagerman (who was allegedly libelled). The jurors gave a verdict of guilty on the libel against the Attorney General only, which Hagerman rejected, instructing them to give a general verdict including the libel on him.[39] The jury eventually complied, and Sherwood returned to sentence Collins to a year's imprisonment and crippling fines, a sentence that the British law officers later declared twice as severe as comparable English cases.

Collins' sentence was challenged by petition to the British government that accompanied a number of other grievances concerning the local administration of justice.[40] Reformers had won an unprecedented number of seats in the 1828 elections, and the Assembly petitioned Willis' dismissal, concerns about executive manipulation of the judiciary and public prosecutions, as well as the upper house's repeated refusal to accept jury reform and *Sedition Act* repeal bills passed by majorities. These matters were considered by the previously mentioned British parliamentary committee, the first of a series of committees on the Canadas in the 1830s. The most immediate result was remission of Collins' sentence and imperial intervention to uphold the eighth bill to repeal the *Sedition Act* in 1829.[41] As noted earlier, Robinson's involvement did not prevent his appointment as Chief Justice, although his continuing political influence drew scrutiny from the Colonial Office in the decade that followed. Willis successfully challenged his own removal on procedural grounds, and his judicial career continued in other colonies.

The Collins affair marked the end of seditious libel prosecutions against the press in Upper Canada. With the exercise of the Crown's prosecutorial authority under intense public scrutiny, the *ex officio* prerogative was no longer a feasible option, and there was little confidence in securing compliant regular juries. The government had failed to marginalize government criticism; on the contrary, repressive proceedings attracted precisely the attention and notoriety Robinson feared. The shift away from seditious libel in Britain in the 1820s is mirrored in Upper Canada in the 1830s, including local legislative debate about the truth defence (later adopted with Campbell's *Libel Act*). A seditious libel prosecution against Mackenzie was contemplated by the Crown law officers in March 1832, but the Executive Council, concerned about public attention and a jury, deemed it politically inexpedient. Instead, Mackenzie was repeatedly expelled from the Assembly for contempt to prevent him from sitting as an elected member, although such privilege proceedings were no longer taken directly against the press.[42] Even private actions for defamatory libel against the press were questioned if perceived to be a front for government interests, as seen in the 1834 acquittal of George Gurnett, editor of the *Courier*. By the 1830s Upper Canada's public sphere had developed to the point that deference to privileged control over politics was dramatically weakened, and public policy and repressive control of political expression were effectively constrained. As the editor of the *Christian Guardian* put it, "public opinion is the true supporter of the press — and public opinion is the proper and only effectual corrector of its licentiousness."[43] The acceptable standards for political expression were to be set by informed public opinion, not by the government or the Crown prosecutor. For the public, the only legitimate limits on political expression became deliberate falsehoods or advocacy of violence, a development that Robinson and other more astute government leaders were obliged to accept. Prosecuting oppositional political expression served only to put government under the critical scrutiny of the provincial public and the imperial government.[44]

New South Wales

From 1824 to 1831, a similar combination of pressures from below and above determined the course of events in New South Wales.[45] The Emancipist struggle for open and accountable institutions broadened into a clash between an emerging public sphere and the quasi-military colonial order. In the absence of representative government, and with legislative councillors sworn to secrecy about proceedings, it is not surprising that many of these conflicts took place in the courts and involved the independent press, an essential forum for broadening engagement with colonial public affairs. As Brendan Edgeworth puts it, "[i]f there was no political forum in which the most important deliberations on matters of public significance in the colony could be the focus of genuine public debate, all that was left was the press."[46]

The *Sydney Gazette,* the sole newspaper for the first quarter century, reflected official perspectives (like its sister in Upper Canada, censored by way of the King's Printer's contract) but did regularize access to information about government and opened the way to broader engagement with politics and public policy. The *Australian,* the colony's first independent newspaper aimed at reform-oriented free settlers, was established in 1824 by Emancipist leader William Charles Wentworth and edited by Robert Wardell. They had met in London in 1819 and together returned to Australia with a printing press (also becoming the first two barristers admitted to the New South Wales Supreme Court—Wardell sought but failed to be appointed Attorney General). The *Monitor* followed in 1826, edited with evangelical zeal by Edward Smith Hall, and appealed directly to convict readers, urging them to assert their rights as full British subjects. Governor Brisbane had a benign attitude toward the press, ignoring calls to discipline it by way of libel prosecutions. Brisbane's replacement, Governor Darling, arrived in 1825 with warnings about the dangers of the press underscored in imperial instructions from Lord Bathurst. As criticism of government mounted, Darling turned to seditious libel prosecutions and prior restraint through licensing legislation. Conflict with Chief Justice Forbes over the legislation and the conduct of trials was quickly brought to the attention of the British government. Just as Darling's campaign to silence the press and opposition criticism began to encounter local success, the political tide had turned at the imperial level. Pressures from below frustrated Darling's repression, but it was ended by intervention from above.

Brisbane did nothing to oppose Wentworth and Wardell and allowed the editor of the *Gazette* a freer hand as the *Australian* began to outstrip its circulation. The Exclusives placed higher hopes in Darling. Bathurst's warnings raised the possibility of a legislative response and also appeared in instructions to Lieutenant-Governor George Arthur in Van Diemen's Land. Arthur (who became Lieutenant-Governor of Upper Canada during the 1838 rebellion crisis) quickly enacted compulsory licensing and stamp duty legislation, with revocation upon a libel conviction and a wide range of other grounds. Darling hesitated, refusing to act on repeated requests from John Macarthur and Archdeacon Scott to direct the Attorney General to prosecute the editors of the *Australian* and later the *Monitor* and even the *Gazette.* Although, in the absence of legislation, the common law offence of seditious libel was readily available, supported by *ex officio* informations, he had little confidence in the abilities of Attorney General Saxe Bannister. This became evident in the first seditious libel prosecution, taken in August 1826 against Hall of the *Monitor* (for criticism of government intrusions into "ancient rights"), which the

Governor suspended as the case unravelled. In October Saxe Bannister urged a seditious libel prosecution against Wardell for the manner in which the *Australian* reported his resignation as Attorney General. Darling sensibly ignored the call since the libel occurred after Saxe Bannister had left office. A private prosecution for criminal defamation before Justice Stephen failed, as did another before Chief Justice Forbes against the editor of the *Gazette* (Robert Howe, for his description of the ideal qualities of a non-partisan attorney general). The government's restraint emboldened the press, and as public criticism intensified over the months, Darling contemplated his options.[47]

Darling's treatment of army deserters Thompson and Sudds (the latter died in custody) led the *Australian* and the *Monitor* to question the legality of the Governor's actions and raise the larger legacy of the brutal treatment of convicts. Darling, however, continued to lack confidence in his Crown law officers and received a negative advisory opinion from the judges on prosecutions. Returning to his original instructions, Darling concluded that proactive legislation was the best option.[48] The Van Diemen's Land legislation sent to him by Arthur, and already certified as consistent with English law by Chief Justice Pedder, provided a ready-made bill.

The government's purported surprise at Chief Justice Forbes' objections to Darling's legislation, and the prevailing view that his actions were politically motivated, are cast into doubt in a recent biography by John M. Bennett. Forbes enjoyed good relations with Governor Brisbane, who welcomed the colony's first Chief Justice, but Forbes fully recognized the awkwardness that might arise by his inclusion in councils and role in certifying local legislation, which made him a sort of super Lord Chancellor, or "justiciar" as Bennett puts it. He expressed reservations to James Stephen about the mixture of legislative and judicial functions, and the potential pressures on his independence that arose from the 1823 arrangements, concerns that proved well founded as relations with Darling deteriorated.[49] Nearly a year before he was asked to review the legislation, Forbes signalled to Darling that he would not hesitate to use his powers to refuse local measures. When Darling first proposed legislation based on Bathurst's instructions in Executive Council in October and November 1826, Forbes reiterated that he could refuse to certify a bill he found inconsistent with English law, and in December 1826 he expressed clear reservations about measures founded on Arthur's legislation.[50] As Bennett puts it, "[n]o legal precedent was created by Pedder's certificate and instructions from the Colonial Office to a Governor that he submit specific legislation could not, as a matter of law or practice, enliven the automatic issue of a certificate."[51]

The Licensing and Stamp Duty Bills were formally submitted to the Chief Justice in early April 1827, and his lengthy opinion two weeks later carefully outlined objections and declared an unwillingness to certify a number of the provisions.[52] Citing Blackstone and Chief Justice Lord Ellenborough as authorities, Forbes noted that prior restraint by way of a licensing system for newspapers was contrary to the laws of England from 1695. A local legislature had assumed unrestricted powers to suppress the established constitutional liberty of the press. Moreover, the Governor's power to revoke a licence would make him a judge in his own cause. The applicable common law should provide ample correctives against a licentious press. The imperial instructions could not be intended to encourage local legislation but merely envisaged, if prosecutions under the common law proved insufficient, a recommendation from the New South Wales Legislative Council that the imperial Parliament consider enacting such a law.[53] Although Forbes was willing to certify the Bill to introduce a stamp duty on newspaper sales in principle, when the Governor assented to the Bill with a prohibitive amount subsequently added, he retracted his approval on the basis that the real object of the proposed tax was the silencing of newspapers, not legitimate revenue.[54]

The *Australian* broke details of the Bill, and the other newspapers, including the *Gazette,* criticized the measures. The *Australian's* commentary was similar to Forbes' confidential opinions, and, suspecting a leak, Darling began sending complaints against the Chief Justice to the Colonial Secretary, who also received a flood of newspapers, letters, and petitions seeking British intervention.[55] The Exclusives initially had the upper hand in this paper war, as Undersecretary James Stephen quickly came to the conclusion that Forbes was "a troublemaker who, inflated with Benthamite ideas of man and society, strained Acts of Parliament to suit his own notions of colonial government" and that "the Chief Justice is the idol of the Newspapers ... whereas the Governor is the object of their unremitting hostility."[56] However, Forbes' position on the legislation was vindicated early in 1828 when the law officers in London, agreeing with his ruling that the first six clauses of the licensing legislation were repugnant to the laws of England, upheld the *Stamp Act* levy for legitimate revenue only, not the suppression of the press.[57] As the British political tide turned in the 1830s, Stephen moved beyond impulsive criticism of Forbes and began to confront the larger problem of colonial judicial independence.

With the frustration of Darling's legislative strategy, the government's only option was to return to libel prosecutions. Forbes himself had noted the absence of such proceedings as one of the grounds for rejecting the licensing system. Prosecutions were fraught with risks, given the public attention whipped up, the competence of the Crown law officers, and deteriorating relations with the Chief Justice. Balanced against this were the surviving certified provisions (the reporting of ownership and authorship, the prompt delivery of all newspaper issues to the Colonial Secretary, the possible sentence of banishment for repeated libel convictions), and the ready availability of the *ex officio* expedient that favoured the government's hand.[58]

The first cases went against the government. Wardell's libel prosecution in June 1827 for an article criticizing abuses in the quarter sessions court collapsed on technical grounds, and Forbes touched the nerve of the colony's lack of trial by jury by urging the military panel to deliberate as if it were a regular English jury of peers. Wardell was back in the courts in September on new charges of seditious libel stemming from commentary that suggested improper motives and conduct on the part of the Governor. Wardell made much of Forbes' prior direction that the panel should conduct itself as a regular jury, and Forbes permitted him wide scope in conducting his own defence, resulting in a "hung" military panel and acquittal. A third prosecution in December 1827 for the *Australian's* publication of a letter critical of the Governor again resulted in a hung panel.[59] The Crown law officers blamed the latitude given to Wardell in his jury addresses and Forbes' charges to the panel. At the end of 1827, the Judges wrote to Darling that "[w]e do not think that the cases selected for prosecutions in this Colony would have been deemed of sufficient importance to have demanded State prosecution in England" and expressed concern about possible defamation in the *Gazette's* reporting.[60]

Darling encountered greater success in 1828 and 1829, although the first foray against Hall in July 1828 failed when the Chief Justice ruled that charges of violating upheld provisions in the 1827 legislation were inapplicable, since the *Monitor's* change in format from newspaper to magazine took it outside the terms of the Act.[61] A dispute with Archdeacon Scott over access to a pew resulted in Hall's successful civil action, but his attack on Scott and his political associates in the *Monitor* negated the victory. It drew an *ex officio* information for seditious libel by a government emboldened by the arrival of a third more compliant Supreme Court Judge, James Dowling.[62] Hall conducted his own defence with rather less skill than the barrister Wardell, and Dowling's summing up emphasized the Court's responsibility to curb press licentiousness.[63] Hall's conviction led to more seditious libel prosecutions before Dowling. The *Gazette's* resurrection of the Sudds affair, in the attempt to clear Darling, prompted Attwell Hayes, the new editor of the *Australian,* to attack the Governor's fitness for office. Although Hayes was skilfully defended by Wentworth, the latter's petition to the British government, calling for Darling's impeachment and indictment for murder, undermined his advocacy, and Hayes was convicted. Wentworth then attacked the selection, legality, and constitutionality of a military "jury." Although this resonated with the Chief Justice's earlier charges to panels, and Wentworth helped spark the struggle for trial by jury over the coming years, all three Supreme Court Judges upheld the conviction.[64] Hayes received six months' imprisonment. His fines were paid by public subscription, and he continued to edit the *Australian.*

Meanwhile, the campaign continued against Hall, who had not been deterred by his conviction and lenient sentence. He was convicted in April 1829 on two charges of seditious libel (against the Governor and the Commandant at Port Macquarie) and received fifteen months of imprisonment. Like Hayes, Hall continued to edit his paper, resulting in another set of trials on four charges of seditious libel in December 1829, a further cumulative sentence of two years, and crippling fines for violating earlier recognizances for good behaviour.[65] Darling also exercised his executive powers widely, revoking convict assignments in March 1829 of an *Australian* journalist and the foreman printer of the *Monitor,* in defiance of a Supreme Court ruling that called into question his unfettered discretion in such matters.

Although the Colonial Secretary had warned both Darling and Forbes of the possibility of recall in 1828, the Governor's dispatches complaining of the press, opposition, and Forbes were unrelenting and continued after Wentworth's impeachment petition. Just as Darling seemed to have won his battle against the local press in 1829, he began to lose the war at the imperial level. The Colonial Office concluded that he was mishandling the situation, and political change, with the fall of the Tories under Wellington and the rise of the Whigs under Grey, was decisive.[66] In January 1830 the colonial government enacted an amended version of the newspaper legislation, with the uncertified sections removed but with the banishment provision strengthened by making the punishment automatic rather than a matter of judicial discretion. However, the British government had just repealed a discretionary banishment provision originating in the 1819 *Six Acts,* rendering the colonial provision repugnant to English law, and the legislation was disallowed in January 1831. Colonial Secretary Goderich informed Darling that prior restraint of the press would not be permitted, that the existing common law was more than sufficient, and that it should be used circumspectly. Hall was released from prison in February, two years early, and Darling was recalled later in the year.[67]

The repressive measures against the press by Darling and the Exclusives had failed to curb opposition and the emerging colonial public sphere. The authoritarian politics of the colony could not be reconciled with open political expression and popular engagement with public affairs or the formation of public opinion, judgment, and criticism. As in Upper Canada, the colonial governing elite could not turn back these local developments, especially with the liberal reform ascendancy at Westminster and Whitehall.[68]

CONCLUSION

The similar legal, constitutional, and political issues in Upper Canada and New South Wales in the 1820s demonstrate the rich potential for comparative legal historical research within the nineteenth-century British Empire. To be sure, there were important points of difference. A colony dominated by the management of transported convicts was quite distinct from one created to reward Loyalists. Although the courts were an important site of struggle in both colonies, the existence of an elected legislature in Upper Canada meant that such struggles occurred in a wider range of institutional sites and moved more quickly from interelite conflicts to a broader base. Judges proved to be a greater obstacle to government ambitions in New South Wales than in Upper Canada. As John McLaren notes, judges brought into New South Wales from elsewhere in the empire were more "varied in their political and social philosophies and their attitudes towards colonial conditions," whereas Upper Canadian judges were drawn largely from local elites.[69] Equally capable, Francis Forbes was an independent-minded outsider, John Beverley Robinson a consummate insider.

Despite such differences, the similar issues and patterns around the emergence of opposition, an independent press, and libel prosecutions speak to the common importance of law in the politics of the period. The centrality of the courts, highlighted some time ago by H.V. Evatt, has been recognized more recently by Canadian historians. A related element, noted by McLaren and others, is the prominence of claims associated with the rule of law and the British Constitution in opposition rhetoric. Events in both colonies not only brought the problem of judicial independence to the fore but also illuminated related issues concerning prosecutions and the jury. Executive domination over the colonial administration of justice nonetheless proved an uncertain advantage when challenged forcefully by way of these formal legal and constitutional claims.

The events examined here show a pattern of determined colonial governments "winning key battles but losing the war" when faced with similar pressures from below and above. Governments encountered increasing resistance in the 1820s in their attempts to manage opposition and critical political expression in the face of a proliferating independent press and emerging colonial public spheres. This tide could not be turned back, with political ascendancy of reform in London, a more open ear to colonial grievances, closer supervision of colonial political and legal affairs, and the increasing influence of utilitarian ideas in the Colonial Office. Through a combination of pressures from below and above, routine prosecutions for seditious libel and related measures were rendered moribund, a setback to the colonial elites and an important step toward pluralistic political cultures and democratic advances in Canada and Australia. Unfortunately, the offence was not eliminated altogether, and in situations of crisis, later governments supported by compliant public opinion could and did make use of it well into the twentieth century.[70]

The nonetheless significant advances achieved by the 1830s would not have been possible without the contestable potential of law and the increasingly effective use of formal constitutional and legal claims to check colonial governments. Their discursive prominence in colonial political and legal struggles and their effectiveness suggest the validity of Thompson's assertion about how such formal claims check the repressive potential of the law.[71] Habermas' concept of the public sphere, the colonial emergence of popular deliberative democracy outside established institutional politics, and the key role of the press in developing public opinion helps to make further sense of the social meanings of these proceedings.[72] The role of the jury as a barometer of emerging public opinion, its reform a preoccupation in Upper Canada, and its very implementation a key struggle in New South Wales certainly warrants further research. So too, the imperial networks, beyond critical re-examination of the political and bureaucratic pressures of imperial reconfiguration to include the impact of political and legal personnel and ideas circulating between the colonies. Upper Canada and New South Wales were not isolated back-waters but were connected to larger developments, and their remarkably parallel and contemporaneous experiences are suggestive of the rich potential for further comparative research.

CHAPTER TWO

THE LIMITS OF DESPOTIC GOVERNMENT AT SEA

Bruce Kercher

IN 1829 a passenger named Thompson suffered brutal treatment following an argument with the master of a ship called the *Faith*.[1] The ship
was off the Cape of Good Hope at the time, at about 40 degrees south,
on its way to Sydney. The master, Willet, had Thompson put in irons,
threatened to kill him, and then placed him in a small box on deck.
About five feet long, three feet high, and two feet wide at the bottom,
it was full of cockroaches and other vermin. The bottom was lined with
mud and the only light came through chinks between the boards, which
also let in water when the ship dipped. Attached to a chain, handcuffed,
and in leg irons, Thompson remained there for another five or six weeks,
being fed only musty biscuits and whatever the sailors had left over in
the forecastle. When the ship arrived in Sydney, Thompson staggered
out as if drunk, wearing a long beard because he had not been shaved.
When he sued in the Supreme Court of New South Wales, he received
the astonishing sum of £500 in damages.

Although Willet's response to his passenger's conduct was extreme,
this kind of case was not unusual during the first half of the nineteenth
century. This chapter is based on a study of ninety superior court cases,
most of which were decided during this period. They were heard in
England (sixteen cases), the United States (ten), and two Australian colonies, New South Wales (fifty-two) and Van Diemen's Land (twelve). An
increasing quantity of nineteenth-century case law is being placed online,
allowing full text searches by researchers in any location. That facility was
used for this chapter.[2] Among the cases examined here, passengers won
all but two of their actions, both in New South Wales. The primary concern of this chapter is the power of masters to ensure discipline at sea.

The most elaborate cases concerned the long voyages between Europe and the Australian colonies, which allowed plenty of time for resentments to simmer. Many of them involved steerage passengers who argued with the ship's master or officers, and who were handcuffed in response. As Thompson found, however, even cabin passengers could be treated roughly. Most actions brought by passengers were for civil assault or false imprisonment, with only the occasional criminal prosecution for assault.

CREW MEMBERS SUE

Masters usually treated their crews more brutally than they did passengers. But crew members were less successful in litigation, winning fewer damages actions and receiving less in damages.

Not all of these cases were brought by lower-class seamen, and not all of them were civil actions. At worst, a ship's master could be criminally liable for assault or even murder. In one case, a naturalist and ship's doctor on a scientific voyage, who had stated that the ship's master was a delusional lunatic, was ordered to be tied to a capstan and flogged. He was not flogged, but he was imprisoned in his cabin. The Supreme Court of Van Diemen's Land, which found the master guilty of assault and false imprisonment, sentenced him to two months in jail plus a fine of £50.[3]

Of course, the ultimate crime committed by masters at sea was murder, though at most only manslaughter was proved in the cases studied here. Just short of murder was a prosecution under *Lord Ellenborough's Act,* involving what would later be called attempted murder.

THE LAW AND MASTERS' DISCIPLINARY POWERS

In common law countries, there were two sources of the law governing masters at sea: the common law itself and the civilian maritime laws in admiralty. At the simplest level, civil actions for violence brought by passengers and sailors against ships' masters were just trespass actions at common law, simple actions for assault and false imprisonment. But the assault and imprisonment took place at sea, bringing admiralty into the jurisdictional picture. Maritime law is at root common to all of Europe.

This chapter is primarily concerned with tort actions, where there was concurrent jurisdiction in common law and admiralty. Although admiralty was under attack by common lawyers from the fourteenth to the nineteenth century, its powers over torts committed at sea were apparently never seriously challenged.[4] Of the cases studied here, the common law courts heard all of those in England and the colonies (except for one admiralty action in England), whereas in the United States they were all brought in admiralty.[5]

English law was received into colonial law only if it was applicable or suited to the circumstances of the colony. The statutory phrase of 1828 applicable to some of the Australian colonies stated that English law was received "so far as the same can be applied."[6] These rules on the formal reception of law raised no special problems for the law as it affected ships' masters. Local statutes may have differed from those in force in England, but the general reception of admiralty law was never in doubt. Nor was there any difficulty with the reception of the common law torts of assault and false imprisonment. The Australian colonies also had Admiralty Courts, as did the United States before and after the revolution.[7] Admiralty Courts were usually established in the maritime colonies, among the earliest being at Newfoundland where maritime law dominated for centuries.[8]

When English law travelled to new colonies in the eighteenth and nineteenth centuries, it came to be applied in novel ways in the new places. Frontier conditions made the applicability of the inherited law problematic if not impossible on many detailed points. Even the most determinedly English of colonial lawmakers found that variations were necessary.[9] For this insight into the contested nature of colonial law, we owe much to the career of John McLaren. His publications and especially his brilliant Ozcan comparative legal history course were constantly alive to differences among the colonies. The history of the British legal empire is a history of variation, pluralism rather than centralized law.[10]

As a result, we might have expected considerable variation in the formal law affecting the obligations of care of ships' masters to their crews and passengers. Becoming the master of a merchant ship was subject to no strict qualifications; in many instances, a principal requirement was access to capital so as to become a part owner of the vessel.[11] Ships varied in size, purpose, and location, and their masters varied just as much. Given all this, one might well expect that, even at the level of formal legal principle, the law governing the whaling masters of Salem, Massachusetts, would have differed from that applying to the masters of chartered convict ships voyaging from Britain or Ireland to Australia, or those of colonial-built sealing ships in Sydney or Hobart, or those of the great merchant vessels sailing from England.

But such was not the case — the basic law concerning discipline at sea remained the same across the English-speaking world, and it changed little throughout the decades. Whether in common law or admiralty, the formal law governing the disciplinary powers of masters at sea was quite uniformly expressed by the judges. This was not so in statute law, however. There was considerable variation across the empire in master and servant statutes, though less so in statutes governing employment at sea.[12] The imperial *Merchant Seamen Act, 1835* stated that it did not apply to ships registered in British colonies that had Legislative Councils.[13] The colonies took advantage of that invitation to legislate.[14]

The basic rule on discipline at sea was rooted in paternalism. Across the common law world, judges often referred to masters of ships as being like stern but fair fathers whose obligations applied equally to both passengers and crew. Another image was of the ship at sea as a small government, the master being sovereign. In *Fuller v. Drake,* 1827, the New South Wales Chief Justice Francis Forbes said: "A ship at sea resembled a small Government, at the head of which was the master, answerable, however, to the laws of his country for the proper execution of the powers with which he was invested." The master's power was necessary because he was in charge at sea, with responsibility for all the lives and property on board.[15] As a result, Forbes said, the law "delegated to him a power to enforce his orders by the infliction of such chastisement as parents or masters of families were permitted to exercise, because there were no means of obtaining relief by application to the Civil Law." Although it was necessary to maintain the authority of ships' masters, the risk was that a master might be too passionate, too eager to punish. So the law looked with a "jealous eye at the conduct of the master." This was especially important on a convict ship, where drunkenness of the crew could have such dangerous consequences. But even that behaviour did not necessarily justify immediate physical punishment, Forbes thought.

This was "disciplinary paternalism," Marcus Rediker has argued, essential in the eighteenth century at a time of transition to capitalist labour relations.[16] Through the cases in this study, however, we can see that it lasted until well into the nineteenth century, as did the very strict hierarchy at sea, on which it was based. It is also apparent from reading the case law that the law played a greater role in restraining brutal masters than Rediker claims. He overstates it in asserting that "most checks, such as they were, came not from the law, but from the seamen themselves."[17] The colonial judges, at least, were often sympathetic to sailors, who also won the majority of their actions across all jurisdictions.

As for passengers, Forbes said in *Merrett v. Kenn,* 1826, that a master was bound to protect officers, crew, and passengers as well as to maintain the subordination of all three. If a passenger were insubordinate, he or she could be placed in custody if a spirit of mutiny was also present. In one way, passengers differed from crew members: the courts made no mention of flogging them.

As Chief Justice Pedder of the Van Diemen's Land Supreme Court put it in *R. v. Dillon,* 1827, the master's power was not a despotic one but was to be exercised "with caution, moderation and justice." Pedder told the Court that the image of the parent over a child, or master over an apprentice, came from a book by Lord Chief Justice Abbott.[18] Abbott also wrote that except in emergencies, the master should take advice of the officer immediately below him and punish only on evidence. This, too, appears in a number of judgments. Pedder was concerned that the master should not use his power as an excuse to gratify his own resentments.

Under this rule of necessity, the greater the risk to the ship from the actions of the passenger or seaman, the greater the master's physical response could be. A violent attempt to take the ship by force might well justify great force, even firearms, but the courts looked carefully at the justification for such actions. Simple disobedience of orders was not sufficient for such lengths, as Pedder pointed out in another case.[19]

The same kinds of statements were made in English case law.[20] The English cases state that the duty of obedience to a master's orders also applied to passengers, and this might include working the ship in an emergency or even fighting a battle.[21]

Unlike most of the cases in the British jurisdictions, those in the United States were heard under admiralty procedures. The most important difference in these cases was that the judge heard the case alone, rather than with a jury. But there was little difference in substantive law, which used familiar paternalist language.[22] When there was no jury, judges tended to be more explicit about the basis on which damages were assessed, as were these American courts and the court in the only English case heard in admiralty. The American courts referred to punitive or vindictive damages as well as compensation.[23]

So the formal law in all of these courts was essentially the same: the master was entitled to use corporal punishment against crew members who disobeyed his orders, to put down dissent with the lash, iron confinement, and limited food. Passengers could be restrained but not flogged. Masters ought to impose these penalties only after consultation with other officers except in emergency, but that was not a strict legal obligation. This was the formal code of the sea, as much in force in France before the middle of the nineteenth century as in America or England and its colonies.[24] No doubt the context allowed some variation in practice: what was necessary on a convict ship at risk of being seized might have been very different on a whaling or passenger vessel. In all cases, however, the law of the land allowed the masters to have a large amount of leeway in deciding the law of the sea: what offences deserved punishment and what punishment was appropriate. It allowed them to be accuser, judge, setter of penalties, and enforcer.

The Custom of the Sea: Despotic Government

In broad terms, then, there was little variation in formal law between America, England, and the British colonies about the disciplinary powers of masters at sea. But what did that mean in detail? What did the masters think they could do in response to what kinds of actions by crew members or passengers? How did the law respond to their assertions of right implicit in their actions, and what response was there by the victims of the masters' violence? Through the case law, we can go some way toward reconstructing the details of the unwritten disciplinary code of the sea and the ways in which the various parties played a role in its creation and amendment. The formal legal statements give few specifics regarding attitudes at sea, but the surviving records of litigation provide much of what is missing.

We cannot know from these cases what proportion of disciplinary matters at sea led to litigation. Access to justice was a less serious problem in the relatively informal colonial courts than in England. This changed over time, as barristers replaced convict attorneys and the formalities of England replaced the frontier courts' informalities. At all times, litigation had its costs, especially for illiterate sailors. Only the more serious cases are likely to have been litigated, but they give us strong hints about the interaction of formal law and customary practices.

Passengers

All of the actions brought by passengers included a claim for false imprisonment. None of the passengers studied here was flogged, though some were kicked or punched. The custom, then, appeared to be to restrain or imprison passengers when the master felt that their conduct endangered the ship or was likely to lead to a breakdown of discipline.

The Court endorsed this particular practice in only one case, by finding for the defendant. In that case (*McDowall v. Middleton,* 1827, New South Wales) the plaintiff was a surgeon on a convict ship. Both he and the master had written instructions from admiralty to keep the crew away from the convicts, but that was the source of their conflict. After a disagreement concerning their relative duties and access to a privy, the master knocked down the surgeon and confined him to a cabin over his refusal to obey orders. Surprisingly, the jury found for the master. But a surgeon on a convict ship was in an ambiguous position, being neither a paying passenger nor an ordinary sailor.

In the other civil cases brought by passengers, the plaintiff won damages, ranging from 40 shillings to £500. This meant that, in all of these cases, the masters thought they had a right to restrain their passengers but failed to convince the Court. The judges did state that physical restraint was available to masters but only in cases of necessity. The masters' views regarding the use of imprisonment, much more liberal than the law allowed, were often quite brutal, as the following examples show:

- A passenger in dispute with another refused to be quiet, so the master handcuffed him, chained him to a beam, gagged him, caused him to be hit on the head, threw drink at him, hit him with the drinking vessel, kicked him down stairs, and chained him down below (£100).[25]
- After a passenger refused to come away from the crew's forecastle, the master abused, punched, knocked down, and kicked him, telling him that he would not get more than £10 in Sydney, where judges and everyone were convicts (£250).[26]
- An argument over cards led a passenger to say that the ship was merely a floating hotel. The master ordered that the passenger be put in irons (verdict for the plaintiff).[27]
- A first-class passenger on a ship from Melbourne to London complained about the food and provisions, the master in turn complaining that the passenger insulted him by holding his hand to his nose. The

master forced the plaintiff into his cabin and to remain there for seven days, until he apologized (the Court awarded £25 damages, holding that justification required proof that a reasonable man would have believed the ship to be in danger).[28]

Passengers on some ships even enforced their own code. Cabin-class passengers sometimes held trials of steerage passengers for offences such as stealing, and confined guilty passengers in custody, limiting them to bread and water.[29]

Crew Members

Both the law and the unwritten code of the sea allowed greater brutality toward seamen than passengers. Masters assumed a right to flog their crew when discipline demanded it, but they often went too far and were required to pay damages:[30]

- A sailor complained that he was too ill to work. The master called him a d____d son of a b___h, dragged him out of bed and onto deck, and struck him with a thick rope, saying that he could strike anyone he liked with a rope of that thickness (£10 damages).[31]
- After arbitrarily dismissing the second officer, the master ordered him to sweep the decks. Upon his refusal to do so, the master knocked him down twice and beat him while he was down (£80).[32]
- A crew member was confined in heavy irons for fifty days in hot weather, then put ashore at Batavia (US$270).[33]
- The master of an East India ship in private trade badly treated a quarrelsome cook (a "man of colour") without hearing his defence or consulting with other officers, including kicking, collaring, and hitting him about the head before flogging him (£100).[34]
- On a whaling ship, a crewman who refused to work was hit and then, during the nights, confined in irons for four months (£50).[35]

The masters were more likely to be supported by the courts when they punished the crew than when they inflicted imprisonment on passengers. Here was the analogy with apprenticeship or the navy, and here flogging was allowed when the courts thought it necessary. The following actions resulted in a finding of not guilty of assault. That is, in these cases, the master's actions were found to be justified at law.

- After the master put one crew member in irons, the rest of the crew refused to work until he was released. The master began flogging them one by one until they conceded.[36]
- A quarrelsome seaman may have struck the master. The master kicked him while he was tied up, after which he fell seven feet and received three dozen lashes. The master consulted with officers before ordering the flogging.[37]
- A drunken crew member was struck by the master, then put in irons and flogged.[38]

Seamen's Version of the Code

Sailors generally accepted that their masters had a right to use physical punishment to retain order at sea. John Nicol, a sailor in both the navy and merchant ships from 1776 to 1801, often showed sympathy to those flogged, but he did not complain that flogging itself was wrong.[39] Flogging was just as common on naval vessels, where many sailors spent part of their working lives, moving back and forth from there to the merchant fleet. Greg Dening has calculated that over 20 percent of the naval sailors on Pacific explorations were flogged, with William Bligh the least violent of naval captains. Those sailors, too, generally accepted the punishment.[40] But sailors on the merchant ships frequently showed that they disagreed about the appropriateness of a particular punishment or its circumstances. They expressed this through disobeying orders or by litigation once they reached land.

Some cases involved uproar or rebellion at sea, an extreme way in which seamen tried to enforce their views of the limits of punishment. This included collective as well as individual action.[41] What sailors might have called a strike was seen, in the language of the law, as revolt. Beyond that was mutiny, a violent seizing of the ship. According to Pedder C.J., the term "mutiny" did not apply to "civil transactions."[42] The correct terms in law were either revolt or piracy.

Sometimes the crew joined together to resist the punishment of one sailor. For example, in the English case of *Lamb v. Burnett,* 1831, one seaman was flogged four days after his offence, the master having been absent in the meantime.[43] Others in the crew then refused to obey orders as a form of resistance to this punishment. Four judges in the English Court of Exchequer found that the crew had no right to do such a thing. As Baron Garrow put it, nothing could be more dangerous than the crew deciding the limits of discipline aboard ship. They had no right to constitute themselves as a court of appeal. A state of mutiny existed on board, he said, and the master was entitled to use moderate correction to put it down. As shown below, they might have been subjected to a much greater legal penalty for revolt.

On occasion, people went much further than Baron Garrow might have imagined, by making themselves into an alternative source of authority at sea. The best example of this among "passengers" at sea occurred in New South Wales. In 1826 some convicts being taken to Norfolk Island managed to seize the ship. They sailed for New Zealand and, while en route, created their own government at sea, electing their own officers and establishing a guard dressed in soldiers' uniforms. The convict in charge wrote some "regulations ... for the purposes of subordination in the ship." They also created a council of seven to try their fellow prisoners for misdemeanours. The council sentenced one of them to undergo a period in irons for some unnamed misdemeanour. The custom of the sea demanded discipline on board ships, even in circumstances as extreme as this. All of this — the election, the regulations, the egalitarianism — followed the traditions of Atlantic piracy a century before.[44] This was true piracy. The contrast with the hierarchy of the navy or merchant fleet could not have been starker.

IMBALANCE OF REMEDIES

It is unrealistic to talk of the formal law as the sole tool enforcing the code of the sea. Both masters and sailors had a practical way of enforcing their views of the code while the ship was still at sea, a form of self-help. Masters could flog crew members or imprison dissenting passengers. Crewmen of a particularly brutal master could refuse to work. Passengers alone were essentially restricted to waiting until the ship reached shore, where they could sue.

A serious imbalance existed between the risks implicit in self-help by sailors and those faced by masters. The legal position of seamen was a specialized, and often harsher, version of that of other workers, part of the great sweep of master and servant laws across the empire.[45] Those laws varied from one time and place to another, particularly in the degree of punishment applied to recalcitrant workers. Some of them even authorized magistrates to order the flogging of disobedient seamen, just as convicts were flogged by order of magistrates in the Australian colonies.[46]

Few classes of servants were treated more harshly than seamen, because the judges consistently enforced the notion of discipline at sea, which usually meant flogging by the master.

When sailors took self-help remedies, usually through an individual or collective refusal to work, they did so at immense personal risk. This included flogging at sea, the loss of their income, and criminal penalties, as shown below. Since the law disapproved of any notion of self-help for seamen, the only lawful course they had was to put up with the master's abuse at sea until reaching a port where they could sue for assault and seek to have their contract cancelled for improper treatment.[47] Seamen had a legal right to disobey unlawful orders, but doing so risked a flogging by the master.[48]

Masters rarely risked more than an action for damages for excessive flogging or imprisonment. The criminal law of assault or murder was rarely invoked against them. Sometimes they also left sailors ashore in foreign ports, with nothing to live on and no obvious way to get home. This had two potential benefits for the master: he could get rid of a troublesome crew member, and if he could show that the man had left the ship voluntarily, the seaman forfeited his wages or profits. However, a potential criminal penalty on the master meant that it was a high-risk strategy to abandon a sailor. Some masters were prosecuted under a statute that prohibited them, on pain of fine or imprisonment for misdemeanour, from leaving crew ashore against their will.[49] There were two prosecutions of this kind in New South Wales, neither of them resulting in a conviction.[50]

Loss of Wages or Profits

One of the greatest risks for a dissenting seaman came from the entire contract rule, under which a sailor received no wages or profits from a voyage unless he completed all of it. For example, if sailors in London signed the ship's articles for a return voyage to Sydney and deserted once they arrived in Sydney, they were unable to recover their wages for the trip out. It is here that shipboard discipline intersects with the general principles of master and servant law. The entire contract rule was a matter of contract law applicable to workers of all kinds though unevenly applied and also with statutory backing.[51] An English piracy statute of 1700 declared that if a seaman deserted a ship before completing the whole voyage, he was to forfeit all wages earned to date.[52] This was replaced by new legislation in 1823 and then in 1835, but the principle of loss of wages remained.[53]

The same loss of income would have applied if a sailor refused further work while the ship was at sea, and this was seen as an abandonment of the contract. Seamen could lose their share of the profits of a voyage for actions less than desertion. In *Jackson v. Cooper*, 1831 (New South Wales), the plaintiff lost his share of the oil obtained on a south seas voyage because he had acted "mutinously in contravention of the articles he had signed." His only actions listed in the newspaper account of the case were that he had told the master "that he had had navigation knocked into his head with a *mallet*," and the chief mate that he was a damned liar.

The New South Wales Admiralty Court was less strict than this rule appears on first sight. In one case, a master dismissed a seaman and claimed total forfeiture of wages earned between London and Sydney, because the sailor went ashore in Sydney for three hours without permission. The articles in this case were very harsh: they stated that if a seaman quit the ship for one hour without permission, the master would be entitled to dismiss him and forfeit the wages. In the Court of Admiralty, Forbes C.J. held that the forfeiture of entire wages was too great a loss for such a breach of articles. His was a court of equity, he said, one that protected a seaman against harsh clauses he did not understand.[54]

In none of these cases did a sailor lose the wages or profits of a voyage specifically as a result of his response to ill-treatment. Nevertheless, they do demonstrate that this was a possible consequence of such a self-help remedy. The law's policy of preventing desertion could have the effect of keeping seamen at work for harsh masters.

Direct Sanctions against Refusal to Serve

Most of the statutory sanctions against refusal to work applied to desertion rather than disobeying orders once a ship was at sea. But some of the statutes touched on disobedience, too. Under imperial statute law, sailors who refused to proceed on a voyage they had agreed to undertake were liable to thirty days' confinement in a house of correction. Under the same legislation, the rate of lost pay short of desertion was two days' pay for each twenty-four hours of absence. The same rate of forfeiture applied to neglect of service.[55] Some colonial statutes made refusal to work an offence punishable by imprisonment, with a longer jail term for insubordination or inciting insubordination.[56]

A more punitive approach in New South Wales began well before a colonial legislature commenced in 1824. Under New South Wales port regulations from 1810 onward, deserting seamen could be ordered to work alongside convicts and suffer up to thirty-one lashes, whereas under revised regulations those who were guilty of contumacious disobedience and very disorderly conduct could be ordered into government work until their ship left port. These penalties were usually applied to unruly convicts but here spread to free sailors. The same applied in Van Diemen's Land.[57]

Common law and maritime law, civil and criminal law, and sailors' and masters' versions of customs all fed into each other, each version of law or right interacting with and sometimes influencing the others. Michael Quinlan gives an 1848 example from Tasmania of the interaction of some of these laws and practices. Seven seamen were sentenced under the *Police Act, 1838* (Van Diemen's Land) to sixty days at hard labour for refusing to work. They complained of harsh treatment by the master, which led to a dangerous illness by one seaman who had been confined in irons. Not even statements by passengers in support of the sailors were enough for their defence. The shipping firm claimed that they were simply attempting to coerce the ship into paying the local higher wages.[58]

Revolt and Piracy

When the refusal to do duty spread beyond one seaman to the entire crew, the situation was much more serious. In 1700, the English legislature extended the meaning of piracy to include "make, or endeavour to make a Revolt in the Ship." Revolt alone became piracy. In effect, this meant that a strike on board ship was from then onward a capital offence. This Act, which initially was to be in force for only seven years, was subsequently made perpetual.[59]

The harshness of this statutory provision is shown by *R. v. Blandford,* 1841 (New South Wales). The *Brothers,* carrying emigrants, was lying off the Cape of Good Hope on its way from England to Sydney when the crew refused to weigh anchor. The passengers helped the master do so, and even after that point the crew remained insubordinate. Once the ship arrived in Sydney, the sailors were charged with two criminal offences—revolt and insubordination on the high seas. Their primary defence was that the master had used excessive punishment. They claimed he had no right to construct stocks on board or to place them in irons for three days without allowance for toilet breaks. They also claimed that the ship was short-handed. Justice Burton criticized the harshness of the statutory offence of revolt under which the prisoners were charged, stating that it required that insubordination was sufficient for a capital conviction. He thought that punishment much too harsh for the crime and told the jury that he would recommend a pardon if it found the men guilty. Remarkably, Burton dictated a verdict for the jury, leaving it to its discretion as to whether to deliver it. The jury's decision was almost as instructed: it found that the seven prisoners did refuse to obey orders and did commit revolt, but whether this revolt lay within the meaning of the statute, the jury was not "apprised." This is all the more remarkable because Burton was usually anything but sympathetic to those who broke the law. He did, however, have a strongly developed Christian conscience. His colleague Justice Dowling showed similar sympathy in another case, complaining that English courts were too strict.[60]

Some juries were also merciful of their own initiative. In *R. v. Fox,* 1825 (New South Wales), the seamen of a whaling ship went on strike and refused to take in the whales because the master had stopped supplying them with grog. They were charged with "mutiny" (presumably revolt) and conspiracy, but the jury found them guilty only of the lesser conspiracy charge, on which the judge sentenced them to remain in prison for two more weeks in addition to the confinement they had already suffered.

When faced with widespread opposition at sea, masters sometimes realized that physical coercion would not make mutinous men submit to discipline. Thus, they returned the ship to port, where the men were prosecuted. This occurred in the whaling case of *R. v. Higgins,* 1833 (New South Wales), in which six men had refused to work because they were not being supplied with meat. They were charged with the capital offence of revolt. During their trial, Burton J. told the military jury that he

> was of opinion that many of these cases of mutiny and revolt originated in the improper conduct of the Captain; a British sailor — he meant one who could and would do his duty if justice was done him, would generally do justice. Sailors must be protected from the illtreatment of Captains, and Captains from mutinous conduct of sailors. If the sailors had felt themselves aggrieved when they came into any port, they would be protected by the laws. One

> owes to the other protection, and the other implicit obedience.
> The Captain has the power of a Sovereign on board his vessel, and
> the character of a parent, the most honorable of the two, and the
> seamen owe to him the most implicit obedience. A revolt is the
> throwing off that obedience, or in the real statutary [sic] sense of
> the term, the duty a sailor owes to the master, disobedience of or-
> ders, and refusing to do work, as much as when the subject sets
> himself in and against his Sovereign.

Burton added that revolt could not be legally defended on the grounds
that its intent had been to redress alleged grievances. A revolt required
the throwing off of lawful authority, and the jury must decide whether
this had occurred or whether the master had dispensed with the services
of the six sailors. The jury pronounced all six of the prisoners guilty.
Burton found that he was not required to sentence them to death, so he
ordered them sentenced to death recorded. This was a formal sentence
of death, but one in which the judge indicated an intention that it be
commuted to transportation or lesser punishment.[61] Burton told the
sailors that they had been adjudged to be "pirates, felons and robbers."
Exaggerated as that description appears to be, it does show the great risk
of self-help for seamen.

So, if a ship's crew members chose to respond to an abusive master
by going on strike, they did so at peril of their lives. But in fact, none of
the sailors found guilty of revolt in New South Wales was hanged. In
each case of this kind, the trial judge recommended mercy, apparently
under the belief that the law was much too harsh. Execution was restricted
to cases where the prisoner was found guilty of piracy in its original
sense of carrying away a ship on the high seas. Although some convicts
were executed for stealing a ship in order to escape from a penal colony,
only a minority of those convicted of this offence were hanged.[62]

Murder and Attempted Murder

In the most extreme cases, the relationship between seamen and masters
ended in murder or attempted murder. There was no such crime as
"attempted murder" in the early nineteenth century, but to some extent
Lord Ellenborough's Act provided for its prosecution. This Act made a
capital crime of attempting to shoot a person with a gun. The cases
studied here yielded one example of this: in 1832, Henry Smiley was

convicted under the Act for having tried three times to shoot his ship's master, the gun failing to discharge each time. He was sentenced to a year's imprisonment.[63]

And finally, there is the case of *R. v. Hibbill, Harris and Smith,* 1836 (Van Diemen's Land), the ultimate example of taking the code of the sea too far. The three crew members of the *Industry* threw its master, Captain Bragg, overboard when the ship was three hundred miles west of New Zealand, in the Tasman Sea. They claimed that he had threatened to deal with them severely when the ship reached New Zealand, by handing them over to the Maori, who, they feared, would have eaten them. Theirs was claimed to be an act of self-defence, then, but that carried no weight in the Supreme Court of Van Diemen's Land, where Montagu J. "denied that there was anything which could discover in the Captain's conduct to justify such apprehension." The three men were hanged and dissected, the uniquely cruel fate of those convicted of murder.[64]

CONCLUSION

The custom of the sea concerning discipline was a matter of negotiation between masters, sailors, passengers, and the law. Its limits were ill-defined. As Geoffrey Rush's character said in the first *Pirates of the Caribbean* movie, "the code is more what you call guidelines than actual rules." The formal law provided only the broadest guidelines, leaving details to negotiations among those at sea. But what is certain is that the law supported the masters' views of the custom to a much greater extent than those of the sailors and passengers and with much greater force.

When a master flogged a sailor or confined a passenger for the remainder of the voyage, he usually justified it by reference to the safety of the ship. No one on board had a right to restrain him even if he were mad; he truly was a sovereign at sea. The law accepted the important point that there be just one master. If the master went too far in his disciplinary actions, as many of them did, little could be done lawfully until the ship reached port. The usual sanction imposed on masters who overdid their discipline was merely an obligation to pay damages. Only rarely were they held criminally liable and then only for the most extreme actions.

Like masters, sailors sometimes tried to force their version of the custom of the sea through self-help, but in doing so they were less violent than the officers on board ship. Usually, they merely disobeyed orders, individually or collectively. Despite their lack of violence, the law was very much more severe on seamen than masters when they went beyond the limits of the law in expressing their versions of the code of the sea. One major difference in this instance was that, though a master could legitimately use self-help remedies at sea, the law's recognition of the shipboard hierarchy meant that a sailor's attempt to follow suit was not usually considered lawful. Only if the master's order was illegal could a sailor disobey it without legal sanction, but judging an order to be illegal was risky. Even when a sailor had lawfully disobeyed an order, the master very probably would have had him flogged.

So, when a sailor challenged the master's authority, the risks were much greater than those faced by an over-zealous master. Sailors could lose the income of months of work, and they faced imprisonment and even capital punishment for disobedience. The Australian colonial courts saw the injustice in the latter and softened the punishment. But the fundamental difference remained. To face a capital trial, a master would have to murder a seaman. Sailors could risk the same eventuality simply by refusing to obey orders they thought unreasonable, illegal, or in breach of the understood customs of the sea.

The code of the sea had multiple influences, including statute law, the common law, the practice of masters, and the expectations of passengers and crew. It was like a multi-part dance, in which each partner had a role to play. But the roles were uneven: one participant was wearing heavy boots supplied by the formal law, whereas the others had bare feet.

CHAPTER THREE

ONE CHIEF, TWO CHIEFS, RED CHIEFS, BLUE CHIEFS

NEWCOMER PERSPECTIVES
ON INDIGENOUS LEADERSHIP IN RUPERT'S LAND
AND THE NORTH-WEST TERRITORIES

*Janna Promislow**

IN 1995 a case came before the Federal Court of Canada in which the Sawridge First Nation from Slave Lake, Alberta, attempted to assert an Aboriginal right to control its membership.[1] Justice Muldoon concluded that any such right was "emphatically extinguished" by clear acts of Parliament, a conclusion that he reinforced through historical evidence combed from treaty negotiation records.[2] Justice Muldoon's decision was thrown out the following year after the Federal Court of Appeal found a reasonable apprehension of bias in his judgment,[3] but his interpretation of the evidence from the Treaty 6 record in particular nevertheless merits our attention.[4]

Much of the evidence cited by Justice Muldoon was drawn from the reports kept by Treaty Commissioner Alexander Morris, Lieutenant-Governor for Manitoba and the North-West Territories. Morris was the lead Crown negotiator for Treaties 3, 4, 5, and 6, which were negotiated with primarily Cree, Assiniboine, Ojibway, and Saulteaux peoples in the 1870s. In pursuing these numbered treaties, the Canadian government believed it was clearing the way for peaceful settlement of the West in accordance with long-established British principles.[5] Treaty 6 was concluded in 1876 with First Nations who lived across what is

* My thanks are due to Kent McNeil, Susan Drummond, and the editors of this volume, whose insightful comments and subtle suggestions have substantially improved this chapter. I would also like to acknowledge that this research has been supported by the Social Sciences and Humanities Research Council of Canada. Last, but certainly not least, I would like to thank John McLaren for opening my eyes to the intrigues of comparative colonial history and for his constant encouragement of my studies.

now south-central Alberta and Saskatchewan. Morris' preparations for the negotiation of this Treaty included commissioning Methodist missionary Reverend McDougall to visit the Indians of this region the year before Morris planned to arrive. McDougall's purpose was to "tranquillize" the Indians by informing them of the government's intention to negotiate a treaty, an issue that was causing some concern in the region.[6]

Justice Muldoon cited Reverend McDougall's report to Morris about his mission as evidence of the extinguishment of self-government rights. In this report, McDougall described the reception of the Governor's message and also conveyed several requests from the Plains Cree regarding the upcoming negotiations. Among those requests was the following: "We would further ask that our chiefships be established by the Government. Of late years almost every trader sets up his own Chief and the result is we are broken up into little parties, and our best men are no longer respected."[7] Taken without attention to the interpretive dimensions of language, historical context, and the personality and interests of the narrator, these words imply that Plains Cree leadership and government was in total disarray before the negotiation of Treaty 6.

Justice Muldoon pursued this ostensibly straightforward interpretive route, bolstering his conclusion with further choice quotes from Morris' treaty record. For example, he cited Morris' report of the following speech to the Willow Indians, a band of Plains Cree: "One of you made a request that if he were accepted as a Chief, he should have a blue coat. I do not yet know who the Chiefs are. To be a Chief he must have followers. One man came forward as a Chief and I had to tell him unless you have twenty tents you cannot continue as a Chief."[8] These passages evoke the colonial milieu of Treaty 6, a milieu marked by a long interaction between colonial authorities and indigenous communities during the fur trade that affected the legal and political institutions of both societies.[9] The complexities of these interactions, however, are not conveyed on the face of these passages. Instead, they leave a strong impression that at the time of Treaty 6, Plains Cree chiefs were dependent on colonial recognition for their political authority. In *Sawridge,* Justice Muldoon saw these passages as demonstrating that the Cree leaders lacked self-defined political authority, implying a further lack of control over the definition of the political unit. In his view, this constituted conclusive evidence that any right of control over membership was extinguished at the time of the Treaty, as a condition of making it. According to him, not only had the ancestors of the First Nations who brought this challenge surrendered control over their membership, but they had themselves acknowledged the absence of control and requested the assistance of the Dominion government.[10]

Many problems, some historical and some legal, can be ferreted out of Justice Muldoon's decision. Given that it was overturned, its significance lies not in its legal implications but, rather, in what it reveals about the problem of political recognition across cultural divides and the interpretation of such problems in historical contexts, particularly when self-government rights are at stake. The significance of the *Sawridge* decision, then, is understanding what to make of Justice Muldoon's finding of radical discontinuity in Plains Cree political life and how such interpretations of the historical record come to be constructed.

In using the *Sawridge* case as a window on the complexity of colonial interactions around political authority, this study builds on socio-legal approaches to colonial legal history that John McLaren and his colleagues and admirers have pioneered in Canada, Australia, and New Zealand over the last three decades. In addition to being the engine behind much of this scholarship, McLaren's work demonstrates how situating historical legal doctrines, actors, and debates in their full social and political contexts produces a richer understanding of law and legal processes.[11] This chapter intends to emulate this fine McLaren tradition by situating the dilemmas of leadership and political community implicated by the Treaty 6 record in a more complete historical picture than is apparent from the discussion in *Sawridge*. It is thus an effort to correct the impression left by Justice Muldoon's interpretation of the Treaty 6 passages cited earlier — to answer his interpretation of the history with more history by asking how it came to be that the Plains Cree would ask for government assistance in "establishing" their chiefs.

Pursuing this question necessitates looking beyond the Treaty 6 record into the colonial relationships that preceded and shaped the Treaty negotiation. This quest takes us into the practices used by the Hudson's Bay Company (HBC) and other European traders to encourage indigenous people to take part in the trade; it also involves examining the relationships between these men and their indigenous trading partners. The investigation will not, however, pursue direct connections between players who negotiated treaties and the participants who shaped relations during the fur trade. Such connections are difficult to make because, although many participants in the treaty negotiations are named and identified, most of the Indians who traded with the HBC in earlier eras are not named in the written record.[12] Moreover, though European traders identified the band and kinship ties, geographic residence, and larger national or tribal affiliations of their indigenous trading partners to the best of their knowledge, their knowledge was frequently incomplete and left something to be desired. As a result, this inquiry attempts a goal that is less ambitious than tracing the history of a particular group of Plains Cree from their fur trade relations to their treaty negotiations. Its aim is to portray general patterns to situate the Treaty 6 episodes discussed earlier and to set a backdrop against which we can imagine continuity in Cree governance structures, even in the face of colonial interference and disruption.

This discussion highlights the methodological concerns that shape interpretive projects of this sort. Ethnohistorical studies and approaches will be relied on to deconstruct the conclusions reached in *Sawridge* and to rebuild the picture, a process that exposes the sources upon which narratives of interference and disruption have been grounded.[13] This attention to how narratives of colonial relations are constructed demonstrates that even confident historical interpretations are permeated by ambiguities that strike at the foundations of our understandings of these relations. Although these ambiguities are often the point of debate and intrigue for historians, this chapter will turn the question back to *Sawridge* and invite the reader to consider the different purposes served by historical interpretation when undertaken by judges, particularly in the course of determining Aboriginal rights claims.

The starting point for these explorations is recognizing that Justice Muldoon's interpretation of Plains Cree governance from the Treaty 6 record is, from a certain perspective, unremarkable. It is simply a recent addition to a long-standing colonial tradition of confusion around indigenous political forms that runs the gamut from misapprehension to manipulation. Examples from other treaty histories illustrate this. For instance, the Crown entered into the Robinson-Huron Treaty with the Ojibway in 1850 to settle their respective land rights north of Lake Huron. One Ojibway Chief became a signatory to the Treaty even though his territory was on the American side of the border.[14] Similarly, in 1921, Treaty Commissioner H.A. Conroy concluded Treaty 11 negotiations at Fort Simpson with "Old Antoine," while the spokesperson selected by the people themselves, "Old Norwegian," went to eat lunch.[15] The *Indian Act* codified the tradition, producing legendary disruptions and distortions in Aboriginal governance and citizenship practices, lead-ing to cases such as *Sawridge*.[16] And the tradition is being reproduced in contemporary settings, in which comprehensive treaties between the Crown and particular First Nations and Métis peoples are contested by other nations who assert that they also have rights and jurisdiction in the same region but have been excluded from the negotiations.[17] Whether arising from innocent misconceptions or intentional interference, the failure on the part of colonial administrations to grasp and respect the dimensions of indigenous political life is ongoing.

The problem of political recognition is also a theme that animates colonial history more generally. The history of North America (and beyond) is replete with examples of mixed success on the part of colonial authorities in their attempts to recognize and gain influence over indig-enous leaders. The historiography of this issue, mixed as it is with other aspects of colonial encounter, once portrayed contact as having a fairly immediate and disruptive impact on indigenous societies and their forms of social and political organization. The force of European culture and its technology was portrayed as pervasive. Inherent in such narratives were the classic dualisms of savage and civilized, heathen and Christian, nature and society, all of which fed a presupposition of superiority on the part of those who recorded the encounter as well as many who later interpreted that record. With the advent of the "new Indian history," however, the story has become much more complex.[18] Although narra-tives of disruption and devastation implying radical cultural (and political) change remain, they are told alongside stories of resistance and continuity. A key theme in this shift has been an emphasis on individuals and their significance as cross-cultural mediators.[19] Through these individuals, we begin to see past the macro-level shifts in behaviour brought on by contact and technological change to how things looked on the ground and how individuals drew from centuries-old logic to grapple with new situations.

Taking these common themes back to the relations that set the stage for Treaty 6, our exploration begins with the story of a Chief named The Bearded from the early years at York Factory, an HBC trading post located in present-day northern Manitoba. Although these events predate the Treaty 6 negotiations by almost two hundred years, several parallels exist between them. Occurring very close to the point of first contact in the York Factory region, this story contradicts histories that portrayed European contact as disruptive of previously "pristine" and static structures of leadership and governance amongst the Cree.[20] Instead, a more subtle narrative emerges, one that not only recognizes the influence of Europeans as new trading partners and allies but also leaves room for adaptive and even renegade behaviour by individuals manoeuvring in a world of indigenous politics that remained beyond view. This account will be followed by a brief and more generalized examination of HBC practices regarding the recognition of leaders among their Cree trading partners before returning to the late nineteenth century to revisit the negotiation of Treaty 6.

ONE CHIEF, TWO CHIEFS:
RADISSON, THE BEARDED, AND THE SETTLING OF YORK FACTORY

In 1682, the French and the English extended their colonial rivalry into the area that eventually included York Factory, one of the most significant HBC establishments in the early fur trade (see Maps 3.1 and 3.2). Their interests in securing this location were fairly obvious. With two large rivers—the Nelson and the Hayes—merging to flow into Hudson Bay, it was ideally situated for Cree, Assiniboine, and other inland peoples to travel to the coast to trade furs, giving the European traders unparalleled access to desirable inland furs without having to travel into these unknown territories themselves. Moreover, the access to Hudson Bay from the Atlantic was also convenient for transport of goods and supplies between Europe and North America. Eventually, the English secured their claim to this region from the French through the Treaty of Utrecht in 1713, but the trading post changed hands several times in the preceding thirty years, with both the French and the English attempting to establish their presence there in 1682-83.

In the process of competing for the York Factory region, the HBC and French traders followed what was by then fairly standard colonial patterns in dealing with the indigenous peoples of the area. There is no report of the diplomatic efforts undertaken by the HBC officers who first landed there, but we do know that the company instructed its officers to settle "leagues of friendship" with the peoples who inhabited these lands and later claimed that they had done so.[21]

The record left by the French is more detailed. Their team was led by Pierre Esprit Radisson, an experienced trader well schooled in the arts of diplomacy among Algonquian peoples through his earlier experience

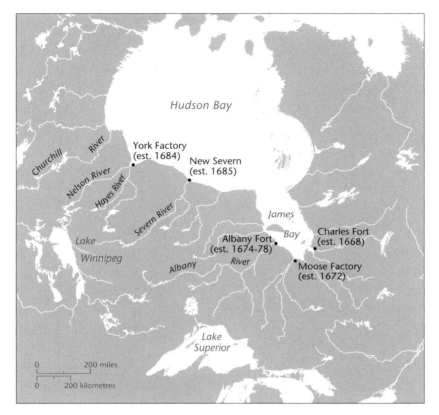

MAP 3.1 Early trading posts of the Hudson's Bay Company
Cartographer: Eric Leinberger

in the Great Lakes and a key player in the HBC's earliest explorations of Hudson Bay before he switched teams to lead the French efforts in the York Factory region. Radisson left a journal documenting this mission, and his report confirms adherence to French practices of gift-giving and establishing kin relations with the local populations.[22] He describes making contact with the Swampy Cree people inhabiting the Hayes River basin shortly after arriving in the York Factory region in 1682.[23] Soon after contact was established, Radisson participated in a small gathering during which he and the leader of the Hayes River Cree made speeches, exchanged gifts, and smoked pipes of tobacco. Through this process, Radisson was adopted by the Hayes River Chief as his son, and

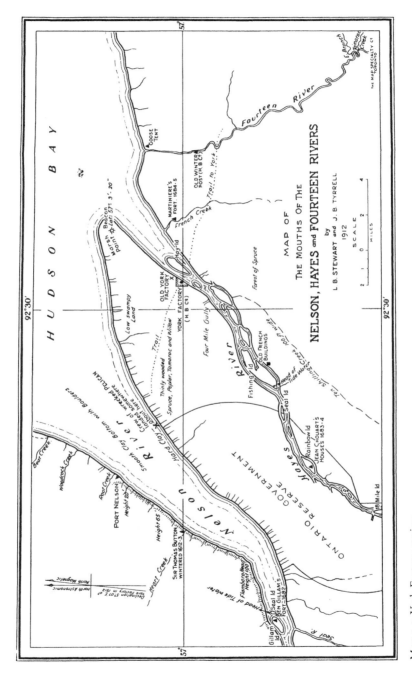

MAP 3.2 York Factory region
Published with the permission of the Champlain Society

he himself promised to protect the Chief and his kin as if they were his own.[24] Radisson believed that this ceremony gave him and his men permission to build a trading house in the Chief's territory and to conduct commerce there.[25]

Radisson makes it sound so easy. He arrives and in no time manages to establish an alliance and adoptive relationship with the most important person in the region. But how did Radisson know that he had the right man? By his own account, upon landing in unfamiliar territory, he located the Chief via the simple expedient of asking the first group of Indians that he met.[26] By some happy coincidence, the first person he asked was the Hayes River Chief himself, who, after appropriate words and ceremonies were exchanged, immediately granted Radisson the permissions he sought. It was also convenient that the Hayes River people were eager to form an alliance with Europeans such as Radisson and his men. These people were well aware of the existence of the Europeans and their goods — particularly their guns — through their allies and kin networks. Their more southerly Swampy Cree relatives in western James Bay had already been in contact with European traders for almost a decade, and their Ojibway neighbours around the Great Lakes for the better part of a century. This prior knowledge of Europeans and their guns is confirmed by Radisson's report that, upon learning of his intention to establish a trading house and enter into a trade and alliance with them, one of the elders of the Hayes River people said: "Young men, you have no longer anything to fear. The sun has become favourable to us, our enemies will fear us, since here is the man whom we have been seeking since our fathers were born."[27] But none of these dimensions of the encounter helps us understand whether Radisson had formed this important relationship with the right man. Indeed, some incidents he reports from the following year give us pause.

After establishing a relationship with the Hayes River Cree, Radisson went back to Europe and left his nephew, Jean Baptiste Chouart, in charge of the fledgling French trading house they had built near the mouth of the Hayes River.[28] Shortly after Radisson left, a different group of Cree from the New Severn River, located to the south of the Hayes, were travelling near the French trading house. These people had already formed a trading relationship with the English who, since 1674, maintained a presence at the mouth of the Albany River in James Bay. Aware of these prior associations, the French were nevertheless keen to attract new customers. They greeted the New Severn people, told them of their purposes in seeking trade, and invited them to come to the trading house to smoke tobacco with them. Upon arriving at the French trading house, one of the party left and returned two days later. He, too, was greeted with tobacco, as was the custom of the land, but he came with unfriendly intentions. He took the unarmed Chouart aside and informed him that "[he] was worthless because [he] did not love the English and that [he] had not paid by presents for the country [he] inhabited to him who was the chief of all the nations and the friend of the English at the head of the bay."[29] After proclaiming himself "chief of all the nations," this man escalated his insults until the exchange degenerated into a scuffle. Chouart was injured but, by his report (through Radisson), was still able to gain the upper hand. The scuffle attracted the attention of the other New Severn people and Frenchmen at the fort, and Chouart was told that the man he held was an English mole to whom gunpowder and other goods had been promised if he succeeded in killing all the Frenchmen at the fort. The moment passed, and Chouart, in a show of generosity (again, by his report), permitted all the New Severn River Cree to leave.

When the Hayes River people learned of this incident, they were not satisfied to leave the dispute unresolved and the plot against their allies unanswered. They called the New Severn people back to the French trading house for a council and feast to "learn the merits of the case." Instead of diffusing the tensions, however, the meeting simply worsened the dispute. Insults were traded until the man who had described himself as a chief to Chouart was assaulted and killed on the spot.[30] The Hayes River Cree went on to attack the nearby English post, escalating tensions throughout the region and beyond. With the threat of retaliatory attacks readily apparent, the French convinced several Hayes River Cree to stay with them throughout the winter for security. When the rivers were once again passable in spring, Chouart reported that "several detachments of friendly nations arrived to relieve us," including some from much further south.[31] The rivalry between the French and the English was thus taken up by their respective allies among the indigenous nations. Less apparent from this narrative, however, is how this rivalry might have been overlaid onto pre-existing or latent rivalries among the indigenous nations.

It was to these tensions that Radisson returned in the summer of 1684, with the surprising news that he was in the service of the English once again.[32] Radisson then had the delicate task of converting his loyal Hayes River and other allies into friends of the English and enemies, or at least "strangers," to the French. During this process, he had a conversation with his adoptive father, the Hayes River Chief from whom he had originally received permission to settle in the York Factory region on behalf of the French. According to Radisson, the Hayes River Chief had learned "that the chief of the nation which inhabits the upper part of the river New Severn, named The Bearded, and one of his sons, who were his relations, had been killed when going to attack those among the Indians who had felt it their duty to maintain the Frenchman [Chouart] who had been wounded by an Indian gained over by the English."[33] In this recounting, the New Severn Chief—identified as "The Bearded"—and his son are differentiated from the man who was "gained over" by the English and who proclaimed himself to Chouart as "chief of all the nations."[34]

Perhaps the man who described himself in this manner was the leader of a different band of New Severn people or was a rival of The Bearded. Perhaps he was not a leader at all and was hoping his association with the English would help establish him as one. Or perhaps, in spite of the Hayes River Chief's report (delivered via Radisson), this man was The Bearded himself, or a different son, or another relative. We cannot be certain. But if we take Radisson's second-hand recounting as a reliable report of events, what we do know is that there were overlapping, if not competing, claims of authority regarding whose permission was required by the Europeans wanting to establish a presence in the York Factory region. Equally interesting for our purposes is that, though we cannot assess the strength of the claims to this authority, the Hayes River Chief's identification of The Bearded as kin and fellow Chief nonetheless indicates that political authority was established and recognizable among the Cree, if not their European trading partners.

There is one final postscript and one more player to add before closing this tale. Captain Geyer, the HBC's bayside governor, was also in the York Factory region during the summer of 1684, continuing construction of the company's fort.[35] Anxious to introduce the Hayes River Chief to him, Radisson called Geyer to meet him and the Chief before he sailed back to England. Introducing the Chief to Geyer was a measure that would confirm Radisson's renewed connection with the English and reassure the Chief that he too would benefit from the relationship with the English and their continued alliance. The meeting with Geyer, however, did not go well. Radisson suggested that Geyer give some presents to his adoptive father. He emphasized that such presents were necessary for two reasons: first, to demonstrate respect for the Hayes River Chief's authority in the region in which they were building the English fort; and second, to fulfill a promise of gifts that Radisson had made the previous year, which would both confirm their relationship and preserve his reputation. Geyer bristled at Radisson's suggestion. As Radisson explains, Geyer

> took this in bad part and was irritated even against the chief, without any reason, unless it was that he was my adopted father. I learned afterwards that he was annoyed because on my arrival I had not given any presents to a common Indian, who served him as a spy, and was son of the chief called "The Bearded," which would have been a horrible extravagance; for besides the Governor being inferior to me, I was not obliged to acknowledge his favourite, and I have never made presents except to the chiefs of these nations.[36]

Radisson's words, which show his disdain for the company's bayside Governor, also reveal his concern that Geyer's conduct should uphold his honour in the relationships he had formed while acting for the French. We might also say that Geyer was similarly concerned or perhaps simply disliked Radisson and did not want to recognize his authority and superior knowledge of Hudson Bay. In any event, it is unlikely that either of these men took kindly to entertaining the other's allies. To do so would not only acknowledge the rival officer's authority, but might also imply that he himself had been wrong—that he had not identified the "right" leader or leaders to work with in the first place.

Although this tale of political conceits has only one narrator—Radisson—it nonetheless provides three different versions of related events, offering a number of claims regarding both the identity of the regional Cree leaders and the scope of their authority. First, Chouart, through Radisson, reported the New Severn Cree man's claim to being "chief of all the nations" and the person to whom presents were owed. Second, the conversation between Radisson and the Hayes River Chief identified The Bearded as the New Severn Chief and implied that, although loyal to the English, this Chief and at least one of his sons were not involved in the original incident concerning Chouart. And third, the report from Radisson's dealings with Geyer indicates that one of The Bearded's sons was an English spy, increasing the probability that the individual who described himself as "chief of all the nations" had also been a son of the

New Severn Chief. Further, the disagreement between Radisson and Geyer about who properly merited their respects in establishing their trading presence in the York Factory region may have indicated overlapping or competing indigenous claims or simple ignorance on the part of the Europeans. The reports are nevertheless consistent that there was a New Severn Chief known as The Bearded who died in the ensuing hostilities. What else can we know? Did the Hayes River Chief have the authority to grant Radisson permission to establish the French trading post, or did Radisson also require permission from The Bearded? How extensive was the influence of these two Chiefs, and to what extent was it bolstered by their newly formed connections with the French and the English, respectively? What were the contours of the relationship and the reciprocal obligations between the New Severn Cree and the Hayes River Cree? And what of other relationships formed and tested through this tale: between adopted sons and fathers, between chiefs, their sons, and their larger kin relations?

If we trust Radisson's account, the Hayes River Chief was the right man with whom to curry favour in trying to establish a foothold in the region where York Factory was eventually built. The Bearded was a neighbouring Chief, to whom they owed no special favours in respect of building on that land, and Geyer was foolish to assume that The Bearded's son automatically carried the mantle of Chief through his father. If we continue along this line and assume for the moment that the man who claimed to be "chief of all the nations" was The Bearded, this claim was a renegade one. If he was not The Bearded, its renegade quality is even more obvious. It was a claim that pushed the status quo, at least as assumed by Radisson and his entourage. It constituted a power grab, either by a person who already had some power or by one who was more audaciously seizing the moment to get some. But this interpretation of the claim follows only if Radisson's assessment of the Hayes River Chief and his authority was correct. The possibility that Radisson's assessment was wrong requires that we consider a different backdrop for this story, a status quo in which the man claiming to be chief actually was the more powerful figure or in which the Europeans required permission from more than one chief to establish their trading houses. Alternatively, the Europeans might also have arrived in the midst of a power struggle that rendered the scope of the Chiefs' respective authorities unclear.

There are more reasons to trust Radisson's reporting and analysis than to distrust them. His narrative of the events of 1682-84 was at least in part a self-serving account to confirm his renewed loyalties to the HBC and underscore his accomplishments for the company, thereby securing his importance to it in future. This aim might have affected his writing style, but it would not have affected his judgment and actions during the events he described. Radisson was one of the most knowledgeable traders in North America, with many years of experience in Indian country, including periods of adoption and captivity among the Iroquois.[37] His nephew Chouart also had many years of experience in Indian country. If any European traders could distinguish an Indian chief on sight, whether by comportment, clothing, or other distinguishing marks, it would probably have been these two. Thus, in spite of a well-earned reputation for hyperbole and a healthy ego, Radisson was likely to have understood the political dynamics of his new acquaintances and was among the most able narrators of this era.[38]

The reliability of narrators is always questionable, however, even when we deal with someone as knowledgeable as Radisson. Their limitations are particularly apparent when we begin to probe the extent of their knowledge. Radisson may have understood how to greet and make alliances with Algonquian peoples such as the Swampy Cree of the Hudson Bay lowlands. And he quite probably understood the qualifications of a chief, along with the privileges and obligations of this office. However, he could not have known the lay of the land with respect to rivalries and disputes between the nations of the lowland Cree and others. When he wrote his narrative, he had not been in the region long enough to discover these dynamics. What he knew of these matters would have come from the Hayes River Cree, a group that had already tied its trading future to him and vice versa. There is no neutral informant or any final answer to historiographic questions of continuity: did the Europeans create new rivalries among the Cree and new leaders to lead them, or did their arrival simply reignite old fires? On these issues, the record is silent.

RED CHIEFS, BLUE CHIEFS: HBC TRADING CAPTAINS, CREE CHIEFS, AND SYMBOLS OF AUTHORITY

Radisson clearly had a good understanding of his indigenous trading partners and knew how to work in their country. This knowledge and skill was highly valued in the fur trade, as the ability to know and be respected by indigenous traders meant stronger relationships and, ultimately, more furs. But not every trader had Radisson's know-how. Some

HBC traders were better than others at knowing and working with their Indian trading partners. Over time, some of the individual wisdom was consolidated through the institutional practices of the HBC, but the success of individual traders applying these practices remained variable.

One such company practice was the appointment of trading captains. During the first century of its presence in North America, the HBC stayed firmly planted on the coast of Hudson Bay. Most of the furs it acquired were brought to it by Plains Cree and other inland peoples who made an annual or biennial trek down the rivers in large trading parties. From this fixed geographic position, trading post factors had very little scope to influence inland peoples and their participation in the trade. One of the few tools available to the factors was recognizing trading captains. Bestowed upon the leaders of large trading parties, this recognition nurtured relationships with resourceful and influential (or so the factors hoped) leaders, encouraging them to bring more people, or at least more furs, down to the Hudson Bay coast to trade. Once at the fort, these leaders represented the inland fur producers and members of the trading party in discussions of price and other dealings with the HBC. Company factors hoped that recognizing a special relationship through the trading captain system would convince their trading partners to remain loyal to them and not to do business with the French (and later, Canadian) competition.[39]

The HBC also depended upon local populations to assist it with hunting and other activities associated with daily subsistence. Local leaders were instrumental in organizing the labour force necessary to undertake bigger seasonal activities, such as the spring and fall goose hunts, and were therefore also recognized as trading captains. The relationships between these local leaders, their kin, and the company often moved beyond such services, becoming close and multi-faceted. They were, as we saw in Radisson's narrative, allies who gave the company permission to be on their land. They were also frequently the fathers of the women who married senior company officers according to the "custom of the country," bringing the officers into their kin networks and fostering more integrated relations between the company and the local peoples.[40] In addition, these local leaders also served as HBC ambassadors, greeting leaders from other nations in the course of their seasonal travels and inviting them to the trading post on the company's behalf. In fostering these relationships, the HBC was also implicated in the enmities and rivalries of these local peoples.

Recognition as a trading captain meant receiving gifts and material symbols of the relationship implied by this status. In a system that quickly became standardized across HBC trading posts, the captains received gifts of tobacco, liquor, food, a special coat that was either red or blue, and other clothing when they arrived at the forts to trade. They received further gifts of tobacco, guns, cloth, and brandy when they left.[41] Local trading captains received similar gifts at the gathering accompanying the spring goose hunts and at least some tobacco, food, and brandy when they visited the forts at other times. In material terms, these gifts expressed the HBC's rudimentary understanding of the institutions of Cree leadership, the central feature of which was that, except in times of war, Cree leaders maintained their status without coercive force, relying instead on their persuasive abilities, their wisdom, and their generosity.[42] These characteristics signalled the leader's merit as a hunter and diplomat, as someone capable of acquiring wealth. But wealth was valued only as something that would be shared rather than accumulated. The HBC gifts played into the dynamics of Cree leadership, at least as the HBC understood them. The coats served to distinguish a captain's status, whereas the other gifts could be distributed among his trading party and his constituency to confirm and maintain it.[43] By giving the captains tobacco to distribute to other nations upon their departure, HBC factors promoted their ability to demonstrate generosity to other people and nations away from the fort, thereby again reinforcing their status as leaders. The more "productive" trading captains — those who brought more furs to the company — were rewarded with larger quantities of gifts and promises of more to come, again reinforcing their influence among their own people.[44]

To return to questions of continuity and disruption, the key to understanding the implications of this system for indigenous political forms and governance lies in the manner and scope of its application. First, we must question how well the HBC men knew the Cree communities they dealt with. As in the story of The Bearded, we must consider the scope of our narrators' knowledge and factor in an appropriate margin of error. For example, one of the best-known observations regarding Cree governance is from the journals of Andrew Graham.[45] Graham spent approximately twenty-five years on the west coast of Hudson Bay and benefited from the tutelage of James Isham, one of the most respected and successful factors York Factory ever saw. Both were known to have taken country wives. But Graham never travelled inland himself, culling his observations from his experience among the local peoples and from other men who had made the journey into Indian country. And though both Isham and Graham left rudimentary trading vocabularies in Cree and other languages, it is remarkable that no pidgin language, no *lingua franca,* ever developed through the contact between the HBC and the Swampy Cree or inland peoples. That there was no Chinook of the northwest is indicative of limited contact between trading post factors and their trading partners.[46] Given these parameters, the development of more than a tourist's acquaintance with the lives and political systems of their indigenous trading partners was very much a matter of individual initiative and skill in getting the required information through other sources.[47]

Second, though most of the HBC's interests aligned with recognizing trading captains who already had a following, the implementation of this strategy depended on the ability of individual factors to identify such persons, a skill that was not universally well developed. As a general rule, the company needed trading captains who had influence over others. Due to this, it sometimes found itself dealing with leaders whom, had circumstances permitted otherwise, it would not normally have chosen for such a role. Daniel Francis and Toby Morantz discuss an example from Richmond Fort (1749-59) on the eastern coast of Hudson Bay whereby "Shewescome, an Indian the postmaster deemed an 'idle lazey fellow,' was maintained as a captain because 'he has so Great a Sway over the Natives here I am Obliged to be very kind to him, for what he says is a Law with them.'"[48] On the other hand, there were interests and situational factors, including less knowledgeable and talented HBC officers, which would have led to the appointment of captains who would not otherwise have attained leadership status in their communities.[49] For example, HBC factors were under pressure from the company to encourage Aboriginal hunters to change their hunting objectives from food to furs, a change the company believed would increase the productivity of its trading posts. Bestowing the title of "captain" and its associated presents was the primary means by which HBC factors could encourage this transition, and it was probably applied indiscriminately by at least some HBC men. Competition with rival French traders was also a significant motivation for recognizing trading captains who were otherwise not recognized as leaders by their communities. Finally, the HBC was not alone in its interest in forming trading captain relationships. Trading captain status was meaningful to the local and trading party leaders in part because it gave them the tools they needed to seek or reinforce their leadership status within their own communities. Consequently, the institution of trading captain presented an opportunity to stake out or expand a leadership role, an opportunity that would appeal as much, if not more, to ambitious or potentially rebellious individuals as to well-established leaders. One need only reflect on the story of The Bearded to consider how this potent mix of colonial and local interests might play out.

In the context of this system of recognition and rewards, and the circle of generosity it created, the line between the recognition of existing Cree leaders and the creation of new ones was easily crossed. Trading captains may or may not have been men who were, or would otherwise become, recognized as leaders in their communities. However, the appointment of leaders who might otherwise not have been recognized as such does not necessarily equate to the subversion or disruption of a whole system of governance and politics. In fact, the HBC's choices of leaders and forms of recognition relied on Cree institutions and practices and may have in some cases served to reinforce rather than detract from them.[50] Thus, though it is important to recognize that the institution of trading captain had some impact on leadership in Aboriginal communities and probably had disruptive impacts in specific cases, conclusions that HBC practices caused discontinuities in Cree leadership structures and resulted in "puppet" leaders lacking legitimacy in their own communities are unwarranted, at least on a general level.

In the last quarter of the eighteenth century, the company began to establish trading posts inland, finally engaging its Canadian competitor, the Northwest Company, directly. With this move the competition between the two trading companies heightened until they merged in 1821. Deeply connected to the company's efforts to outdo its competitors, the practice of recognizing captains fell away after this merger. However, this formal end to the institution of captain did not end the HBC practice of recognizing important leaders and "principal men." In spite of Governor Simpson's best efforts to rationalize the company's practices and cut away all the fat that had accumulated through the years of competition, trading post factors were never able to completely abandon the annual or sometimes semi-annual giving of gifts and special tokens of recognition to the leaders of their trading partners.[51] The negotiation of the numbered treaties on the prairies thus occurred against this backdrop of long-standing practices of political recognition.

THE LESSONS OF HISTORY: REVISITING THE *SAWRIDGE* CASE

The numbered treaties include provisions regarding the distribution of medals and suits of clothing for Indian chiefs and headmen. To a modern reader, these provisions seem archaic and appear to support interpretations of treaty history that portray the Indians as victims who gave away their land for trinkets. However, if we keep in mind the events of the early 1680s in the York Factory region and the HBC practice of recognizing trading captains, the historic significance of these provisions comes into focus. Rather than demonstrating victimhood, they take their place in a long history of recognition in which the newcomers acknowledged Cree and other Aboriginal leaders through gifts, coats, and symbolic gestures.[52] It was a process that influenced and disrupted local politics, including the selection of particular leaders in some cases, but that certainly did not supplant the political modalities underlying the recognition of those leaders.

If we take this longer view in revisiting the excerpts from the Treaty 6 record cited in the *Sawridge* judgment, the Plains Cree's request for the Dominion government to establish their chiefships is still troubling but less mysterious. The Treaty 6 context included the collapse of the buffalo herds.[53] The conditions of scarcity rendered special relationships with the company, or its more recently arrived American competitors, more important than ever since these relationships were a medium through which indigenous peoples accessed relief and support for hunting and trapping from the European traders. In these conditions, the Plains Cree who asked that their "chiefships be established by the Government" undoubtedly did not mean to imply that they had no system of government but, rather, that they would like the Dominion government to regulate the destructive forces wrought by the combination of American competition in the fur trade and scarcity on a scale never before experienced. They understood that the interests created by these conditions had the potential to splinter their communities, but such comprehension cannot be equated with the disappearance of a system of governance as a *fait accompli*. And yet, this is precisely the conclusion drawn by Justice Muldoon in the *Sawridge* decision.

Muldoon's literal interpretation of the Plains Cree's request is also problematic on a number of other fronts. Drawing on the interpretive lessons from Radisson's narrative of events in the early 1680s, we can query whether Muldoon treated Reverend McDougall's report with sufficient appreciation of the factors that shaped and limited McDougall's vision. Little probing is required to conclude that he does not. For one, Justice Muldoon's conclusions assume that all Plains Cree were looking for colonial recognition and assistance in sorting out internal leadership problems. He does not consider who made the requests relayed by Reverend McDougall or on whose behalf they were voiced. Digging just a bit deeper into the record confirms that taking this request as representative of the views of all or even most of the Plains Cree is problematic. A consideration of the whole report submitted by Reverend McDougall reveals that the group of Cree who asked the government to establish their chiefships was primarily composed of people whom the Reverend considered moderate, reasonable in their demands, and inclined to co-operate with the government's designs. For example, McDougall expressed relief that the troublemaker Big Bear — the famous Plains Cree Chief who resisted the treaty until 1882 and was jailed for his part in the Northwest Rebellion of 1885 — and his followers were a "very small minority" in this larger group.[54] In his report, he further marginalized Big Bear's influence by describing him as "a Saulteaux, trying to take the lead in their [the Plains Cree] council," a statement presuming that Big Bear's non-Cree ethnic origins diminished his legitimacy as a Cree leader.[55] Although this assumption certainly reveals McDougall's views on the subject, it provides no insight into the institutions of leadership as understood by the Cree themselves.[56]

Like Radisson's assertions regarding the Hayes River leader's importance and the correctness of his own decision to deal with him, McDougall's attempts to downplay the significance of Big Bear's influence demonstrate his eagerness to establish the success of his mission and to please Lieutenant-Governor Morris. But simply probing the record regarding his motives and bringing a longer history of colonial relations and ethnographic sources to bear on his assertions reveals that the Plains Cree held differing opinions concerning the treaties. The request conveyed by Reverend McDougall did not represent the wishes of all Plains Cree, even though a majority did accept the treaty the following year.

Further comments from the Treaty 6 record cited in the *Sawridge* judgment can also be productively revisited at this juncture. The beginning of this chapter quoted Treaty Commissioner Morris' report of the Treaty 6 negotiations. In it, Morris told the Willow Band of the Plains

Cree that a chief must have a following of twenty tents in order for the government to deal with him as a chief. In this instruction, we see the old HBC concern that a man possess a certain amount of influence to be recognized as a leader. Contrary to Justice Muldoon's interpretation, however, this concern can be seen as a reflection of the persistence of Cree political institutions rather than a sign of their breakdown. As discussed earlier, Cree political community and leadership was flexible, decentralized, and held together by non-coercive means. In this system, the influence of a Cree chief varied over his lifetime.[57] The Cree did not need a numerical definition of chiefhood; the government did. Moreover, the top government negotiators did not come equipped with the wisdom and experience of Radisson, Isham, or Graham that was necessary to understand these institutions of leadership. Morris, for instance, had been a lawyer and parliamentarian in Upper Canada and a judge in Manitoba before his appointment to negotiate the treaties. Although Morris was informed and accompanied by HBC men in the negotiations, his view of Cree political institutions was probably coloured — if not confined — by his background and class. Even if he understood that Cree leadership was dynamic and flexible, these characteristics would appear to confirm the inferiority of Cree society and signal the administrative headaches and obstacles involved in bringing order to the "chaos" of the North-West Territories.[58] To grapple with Aboriginal governance structures, Morris and his successors introduced rigid, distorting means of control such as the *Indian Act,* but such measures were not present during the fur trade. Morris' comments thus mark a new era in the influence of the colonists on Aboriginal leadership, not because the underlying desire to identify influential leaders had changed, but because of the new legal tools used to address it.

Lastly, Morris also referred to a request made by a chief for a blue coat. The colour of a coat may seem a trivial matter, but in fact it was a potent signifier. In a section not quoted in the *Sawridge* judgment, Morris reported responding to this request as follows:

> The color of your Chief's coat is perhaps a little thing; red is the color all the Queen's Chiefs wear. I wear this coat, but it is only worn by those who stand as the Queen's Councillors; her soldiers and her officers wear red, and all the other Chiefs of the Queen wear the coats we have brought, and the good of this is that when

the Chief is seen with his uniform and medal every one knows he is an officer of hers. I should be sorry to see you different from the others, and now that you understand you would not wish it.[59]

As noted above, coats were an important element of the "outfits" that were given to captains upon their arrival at the trading post. Andrew Graham's report describes the coats as being red or blue, but he makes no mention of any significance attaching to which colour a captain received. Morris, however, imbues only red coats with the symbolism of the Queen and, in particular, with being an officer of the Queen. Interestingly, his reply was not immediately accepted by the Cree in these negotiations. Instead, a second Cree Chief, known as Kah-mee-yis-too-ways or the Beardy, voiced a similarly worded request for a blue coat: "I want from my brother a suit of clothing in color resembling the sky so that he may be able when he sees me to know me."[60] To this second request, Morris again responded, "I cannot give the Chief a blue coat: he must accept the red one and he must not suffer so small a matter as the color of the coat to stand between us."[61]

These extracts come from a larger conversation in which relief and assistance with preserving and managing the buffalo were clearly much more pressing concerns for the two Cree Chiefs mentioned here. In the end, both the Beardy and the first Chief, Say-sway-pus, accepted the treaty, indicating a pragmatic willingness to put symbolism aside for the sake of preserving their peoples' livelihoods. Nevertheless, the insistence of the Cree Chiefs and the potential symbolism of coat colour remain unexplained. Did the Cree Chiefs reject the notion of becoming officers of the Queen? Did blue have a particular symbolic meaning for the Willow Cree? Did these Chiefs want to be distinguished from the other Chiefs taking treaty? Or perhaps they sought a particular symbol of the treaty, with the colour of the sky embodying a promise that would satisfy the Beardy's insistence that the treaty payment "exist as long as the sun shines and the river runs."[62]

As usual, the documentary record presents a number of mysteries that cannot be solved, at least not without assistance from Cree people, ethnographies, and other resources far removed from the documents themselves. However, instead of assuming such mysteries to be trivial matters, thereby dismissing their importance to our understanding of history and the treaties, we should stop and take note. Legal traditions are full of symbolism, and we miss important signals of political and legal authority when we pass over such details without considering what these strange little notes in the record might reveal. Moreover, we should be skeptical that a narrator such as Morris would catch the meaning of these requests himself.

CONCLUSION

The path travelled in this chapter took us from events around the 1876 negotiation of Treaty 6 to some of the earliest colonial encounters on the west coast of Hudson Bay in the late seventeenth century. The intervening two centuries were very roughly filled in by briefly canvassing the HBC practice of recognizing trading captains during the fur trade. This journey demonstrates that, from day one of the colonial encounter and in varying degrees, Cree political structures have been understood and misunderstood by European newcomers. It demonstrates that not only is continuity to be found in the political institutions of indigenous peoples but also in newcomer confusion. This continuity of confusion is itself enough to raise doubts about Justice Muldoon's conclusion that Plains Cree leadership and governance were in disarray by the time of the treaties. Finally, this journey highlights the ambiguities that permeate colonial history and interpretations of Native-newcomer relations. It is this ambiguity that must be carried forward and considered when judicial interpretations of history are poised to determine—and, very often, deny—the rights of Aboriginal peoples.

In the end, the identification of general themes cannot answer questions raised in a particular case. In such cases, attention to ambiguities invites new questions to match every question answered. These questions act as place holders for what we do not, and possibly cannot, know. They serve to remind us that we cannot always distinguish renegade from representative in historical narratives, that we need to factor the incompleteness of our knowledge into the interpretive process and the conclusions we reach, particularly when Aboriginal rights are implicated. Once we acknowledge the incompleteness of our knowledge, we must also acknowledge that a secure foundation for Aboriginal rights rests on more than a history built like a house of cards.

CHAPTER FOUR

RHETORIC, REASON, AND THE RULE OF LAW IN EARLY COLONIAL NEW SOUTH WALES

Ian Holloway, Simon Bronitt, and John Williams

[A] cluster of ideas known as the rule of law provided the major
institutions, arguments, vocabulary and symbols with which the
colonists forged the transformation. The rule of law served as a
fund of English ideas about political ordering, as the instrument
with which to accommodate these traditions to the unlikely
circumstances of the penal colony of New South Wales, and
as a means of incorporating the newer democratic ideas of the
nineteenth century.

— DAVID NEAL, *The Rule of Law in a Penal Colony*

ACCORDING TO David Neal, the rule of law was a pivotal concept that
transformed early colonial New South Wales from its unfree penal origins
to a free society, paving the way for representative government in the
mid-nineteenth century.[1] Our purpose is to critically interrogate this
claim.

In his discussion of the "ancient constitution," Glenn Burgess makes
the deceptively simple, though powerful, point that "[i]n the past people
thought differently."[2] He continues: "It is always tempting to interpret
ideas from the past in ways that make them more like our own than they
really were. No matter how frequently we remind ourselves of the differences between the past and the present, our very habits of mind encourage us to abridge them. The study of past ideas must always be in
part a process of defamiliarization."[3]

If Neal is right and the rule of law was a "transformative" device, have
legal historians sufficiently questioned whether they are "defamiliarizing"

themselves with the here and now in order to understand the past? If we accept Neal's point that the rule of law was transformative, the next obvious questions are when, and how, did the people in colonial New South Wales start to think like us? Modern constitutionalism is arguably the bridge between the past and contemporary legal norms.

For New South Wales, the architect of that link was Chief Justice Francis Forbes and the Supreme Court over which he presided. This chapter will argue that the rule of law as an institutional mechanism has in fact been overstated. Rather, the rule of law as a mindset or culture was a far more significant link to colonial New South Wales. The upshot of this conclusion is that the rule of law was much less uniform in its reception in colonial Australia than has previously been articulated.

Returning to David Neal, we see that he is clearly sensitive to the importance of historical context in understanding the rule of law, for he notes that the concept today, which is most associated with the constitutional scholarship of A.V. Dicey in the late nineteenth century, has "different connotations from those which it had for seventeenth and eighteenth-century English people."[4] Having stressed the importance of historical contingency, Neal's subsequent discussion of this "fund of English ideas" nevertheless draws heavily on contemporary concerns about political legitimacy and authority. In particular, Neal refers to the importance of the separation thesis (that refutes natural law claims on the conceptual interrelatedness of law and morality) and the theory that law conforms to the following three liberal tenets, namely, "general rules laid down in advance, rational argument from those principles to particular cases, and, at least in a developed form, a legal system independent of the executive for adjudication of disputes involving the general rule."[5] It follows from this conception that the purpose of the rule of law is to constrain the exercise of arbitrary power, and to this end, Neal agrees with E.P. Thompson's claim that it serves as an "unqualified good."[6] It is through this liberal positivist lens that Neal then turns historical attention to the key institutions of colonial justice, namely, the courts, the magistracy, policing, and jury.

But is Neal's focus on the rule of law useful in unpacking colonial understandings of justice and legality? Is there not a danger of falling into the trap of "forensic history," a history that deploys historical events to justify a predetermined belief system? In this context, this predetermined belief system constructs the historical pedigree and enduring value of key liberal tenets inherent within the rule of law. The question for interrogation here is whether these tenets in fact loomed large in determining the conferral of legal rights on convicts and subjecting executive power to legal constraint. Or, as may in fact be the case, the modernist project associated with the rule of law mindset cannot be said to be fully formed in colonial Australia until after the arrival of lawyers such as Francis Forbes in the early 1820s.

Our discussion here resonates with the historical debate over the significance of the rule of law in the system of criminal justice in eighteenth-century England. On the one hand, the rule of law is presented by some scholars as a pivotal concept, providing authority and legitimacy for the exercise of state power and paving the way for representative and democratic systems of government. On the other hand, the rule of law is presented as an ideological tool, serving only to legitimate or mask oppressive systems of governance and class oppression.[7] Our contention is that neither approach — which contains both instrumental and symbolic dimensions — is satisfactory. Both approaches, which focus on the *rules of law applied by the courts,* limit our understanding of colonial law and justice. This obscures the critical role of common law *culture* and the values that shape the belief systems of the individuals (litigants, public officials, lawyers, and judges) participating in the colonial justice system. Moreover, the focus on the rule of law diverts attention away from the role of non-judicial institutions and actors responsible for interpreting and applying the law.[8] As pertains to the present day, the bulk of legal ordering was administered within colonial society without recourse to litigation and authoritative adjudication before the courts. Ironically, though the adherence to formal legal norms is one example of the existence of the rule of law, its wilful disregard or "judicious" application to the circumstances of New South Wales — as in the case of the attainder doctrine discussed later in this chapter — may shed light on the common law mind and colonial legal culture.

To illustrate how the rule of law "lens" limits our understanding of colonial law, we will investigate the landmark decision of *Kable v. Sinclair* and the civil legal status of felons in New South Wales (for a verbatim transcript from *Kable,* see Appendix 4.1).[9] Through its retelling by Neal and Bruce Kercher, *Kable* has assumed an iconic status in Australian legal history.[10] The story concerns two luckless First Fleet convicts, Henry and Susannah Kable, whose possessions were "lost" during their transportation to Botany Bay. The recovery against the shipmaster for failing to deliver their belongings in the first civil suit in the colony is valorized as a triumph of rule of law values. As Sir Victor Windeyer, High Court Justice and legal historian, succinctly put it, "[t]he proceedings of the Court were a vindication of the rule of law."[11] After discussing the case, Neal specifically notes the importance of equality before the law:

> Early New South Wales shows one more thing about the rule of law: that its use as an instrument of power is not confined to rulers. Susannah and Henry Kable demonstrated that. This is not just the point that the rule of law acts as a constraint on the power of rulers, that is a shield against oppression. In early New South Wales, rule of law ideas served as a sword, not just a shield, for a variety of people battling over partition of power in a relatively open setting.[12]

In a similar vein, John Braithwaite uses *Kable* to construct a powerful narrative of reintegration in the "Convict Republic." As a leading criminologist in the field of restorative justice, Braithwaite enthusiastically embraces Neal's account, retelling the Kables' story as one of "hope": "[M]ost significantly, hope from the fairness of a Governor and a Judge Advocate who believed that unless convicts enjoyed the protection of the rule of law from the predations of their military jailers, a convict colony could not survive."[13] But hope in the law is *not* the same as the rule of law.

Braithwaite contends that this early demonstrated commitment to procedural justice in an otherwise harsh legal system such as that of New South Wales not only constrained abuses of power by public officials, but also assisted convicts in realigning their identities to those of law-abiding citizens (especially in the case of Tasmania).[14] Braithwaite is careful to point out that the rule of law often failed to live up to its rhetoric. This was most evident in relation to Aboriginal people. The occasional royal proclamation and judicial exhortation to treat Aboriginals as British subjects who fell under the protection of the King's peace did little to overcome the practical difficulties in accessing the courts of justice or experiences of blatant racism at the hands of police, magistrates, judges, and jurors.[15] As Neal concedes, the rule of law provided "cold comfort" to Aboriginal people, who, figuratively and legally speaking, were rendered outlaws.[16] By comparison, those who had suffered felon attaint, the true outlaws, were able to access a legal system that recognized and vindicated their rights and interests.

Kable established that convicts were amenable both to the benefits and burdens of the law and, more importantly, that others present in the colony (whether military personnel or civilians) could not act with legal impunity against convicts. But can *Kable* really be viewed as an expression of the rule of law (as Neal and Braithwaite contend) given that, strictly speaking, the common law of England provided no such civil remedy for felons under sentence because of the doctrine of attainder? That is, a conviction for a felony at common law would render an individual dead in the eyes of the law. This "gap" between the common law of England and colonial practice may be understood in several ways. This deviation of the "law in action" from the "law in the books" resonates with contemporary law and society research. However, it is important to appreciate that the gap is not some remediable derogation from legality. Rather, it represents something more fundamentally constitutive about colonial law.[17] Some view the gap as exemplifying the innovative, dynamic aspects of colonial legal systems: indeed, these adaptive aspects of colonial law conformed with William Blackstone's view that British settlers took with them only those laws of England applicable to the local circumstances of the colony.[18] Kercher's own research has focused on how colonial legal innovation and ingenuity overcame the civil incapacity caused by felon attaint, promoting the legal security of commercial transactions by enabling free wives of convict husbands to assume property rights over their spouses' services.[19]

The landmark significance of *Kable* in terms of the rule of law can be overstated. Without diminishing its historical importance or practical impact as the first civil suit in Australia, we argue that the decision by Judge-Advocate Collins did *not* affirmatively establish, in derogation from English common law, that convicts under sentence had standing to sue or be sued.[20] The legal obstacle to the Kables' suit presented by felon attaint would have been well known to everyone involved in the case, including the Judge-Advocate. But to have denied the suit on the ground of felon attaint would effectively have closed the Court for business.[21] The Judge-Advocate avoided civil disability by viewing the plaintiffs as settlers, rather than as convicts, for the purpose of this litigation. It is unclear who drew up the "beautifully written" statement of claim, as the Kables were illiterate. However, the initial description of the plaintiffs as "New Settlers of this place," which was mysteriously crossed out, implies an awareness of the civil incapacity of felons. These deliberate silences around the legal status of convicts and the attaint attaching to them laid the foundations of access to justice under colonial law — though it was a foundation resting on an undoubted legal fiction that would stand unchallenged for many decades.[22] It was the judicial invocation of this legal fiction (a traditional trope of the common law) rather than a commitment to the rule of law or convicts' rights that marks the beginnings of colonial justice in New South Wales.

Viewed from this *procedural* perspective, *Kable* seems much less of a triumph for the rule of law. Adopting this perspective, Neal's formative and influential monograph could perhaps be retitled *Legal Fictions in a Penal Colony*. Rather than derogating from the common law of England, the Judge-Advocate simply resorted to the customary practice and culture of the common law. The centrality of *procedure* to the common law — in particular, the idea of procedural fidelity to legal form — by necessity fostered the development of legal fictions and presumptions. *Kable* employed a legal fiction to overcome an apparent legal disability. This was necessary to establish the authority of law and, as a matter of expediency, to provide a functional forum for resolving disputes.

Legal fictions have a venerable history: they are a customary forensic device used in almost every compartment of the common law. The criminal law of the seventeenth and eighteenth centuries was replete with legal fictions to temper the harsh operation of the "Bloody Code": juries would be encouraged to resort to "pious perjury" in larceny cases, returning verdicts of guilty though finding the property to be worth less than forty shillings, thereby avoiding a sentence of capital punishment.[23] In relation to the civil disabilities flowing from felon attaint, the practice (not precedent) represented by *Kable* was eventually transformed into a presumption against civil incapacity. When these arguments were raised in the courts many years later, Chief Justice Forbes took the view that the law presumed all litigants were free, not felon, until and unless that free status was formally refuted by incontrovertible evidence of the proof of sentence (requiring documents from England that could never be practically obtained). This procedural burden, as John Hirst has demonstrated, proved to be an exceedingly useful device. For instance, in an 1838 case before Justice Willis, the Attorney General, who was cross-examining a witness, asked him "what were you sent out for?"[24] As Hirst notes, "Judge Willis refused to allow the question on the grounds that a witness was not required to degrade himself. The attorney-general disputed the matter and the judge referred to a recent unanimous ruling of the full court that a witness was not required to answer whether he had been in the pillory."[25]

In the colonial context, the common law's commitment to procedural fidelity operates as a two-edged sword, sometimes working to retard rather than advance convicts' rights and the Emancipist cause. An example of the former occurred in 1820, when the colony went into uproar over the decision of Justice Field to disallow a suit by leading Emancipist Edward Eagar on the basis that his prior convict status had not been properly expunged by his pardon. Eagar's pardon had been granted by the Governor of New South Wales but executed in an incorrect form without the embossment of the Great Seal.[26] This inconvenient decision posed a substantial threat to commercial interests in the colony, throwing into doubt Emancipist rights to hold property, enforce contracts, and give evidence in court. Not surprisingly, this led to an immediate petition to London and the passage of retrospective remedial legislation in England.

Our attention to the importance of *legal culture* rather than the rule of law rests on developments in legal history over the past two decades. Legal historians are increasingly aware that formal legal sources — embodied in the surviving fragments of common law and statute — can be understood only by studying the personalities, prevailing ideas, and values of the legal community who created and applied these laws. A.W.B. Simpson has attempted to articulate this perspective into a general theory of law. Disputing the positivist model of law as a "rule-book" or "system of rules," Simpson offers an alternative concept in which "the common law is best understood as a system of customary law, that is a body of traditional ideas received within a caste of experts."[27] Focusing attention on the customary aspects of law and the "caste of experts" — which includes lawyers and judges — reveals the wider role of legal culture in understanding how law is applied and developed over time. Early decisions in New South Wales are firmly rooted in the rhetoric and customary practices of "British justice." To be sure, traditional ideas about justice may be embedded in formal legal rules expressed in decision and legislation. But they are also found in other forms (expressed as principles, maxims, customs, conventions) as well as being informed by the wider education and ethics of the legal profession. A significant component of this culture is formalism, which is reflected in the traditional common law priority attached to procedural justice or "due process of law."[28]

It is important to be clear about the implications of the "law as culture" perspective. It does not regard law as something separate from social structures and practices: instead, it sees law as part and parcel of those structures and practices. So, law regulates social behaviour not as a set of rules that is imposed from the "outside" but, instead, by being internalized in that behaviour — we see ourselves as law sees us, and the demands that law makes come to seem obvious and natural to us. This approach therefore emphasizes the ideological and expressive (or rhetorical) nature of law and the ways in which law is important in shaping and reinforcing certain social, economic, and political relationships. Understood in this way, law in the colonial context could never be a mimetic of the law as practised in the Royal Courts in London.

THE COLONIAL INHERITANCE: RECEPTION OF A LEGAL DYNAMIC

Our central thesis is that it is incorrect to speak of the uniform reception of English law in Australia. Indeed, in the case of New South Wales, it is a patent nonsense to say that English law was received in 1788. This is what Blackstone said *ought* to have happened, but clearly it did not. But what *did* happen — though in 1824, not 1788 — was that a court was created with all of the authority of the English common law courts.[29] This meant not that the substantive law in New South Wales would be the same as in England, for it never had been, but that the legal *dynamic* would be the same. To put it another way, Australia did not receive English law, but it received — and this serves as the foundation stone of today's Australian constitutionalism — English *legal culture*.

Implicit in this thesis is the definitional issue: how we define the "rule of law." The argument is that when we talk about law in the common law world, we are not actually talking about rules. Rather, we are talking about a way of thinking about power and the way that power is shared within society. This, of course, was a common phenomenon within England itself. The "ancient constitution" was an undated document that linked the rights and duties of the past to the present. It was, as J.G.A. Pocock suggested, the birthplace of the "common law mind."[30] As Burgess suggests, the link to the past for seventeenth-century lawyers was a means to legitimate the present: "The law of England was good law not because it was old but because it was rational. The theory of the ancient constitution was an explanation for this rationality, and consequently it was also a justification of the law and the constitution. The rational was *ipso facto* good."[31] Thus, this chapter represents one aspect of a rather larger intellectual quest: to discover the place of liberal ideals and Whiggish rhetoric in the establishment of constitutional government in New South Wales.[32]

A SETTLED COLONY WITH UNSETTLED LAWS?

It is trite — notorious, even, in some quarters — that Australia was deemed to be *terra nullius* and, consequently, a settled colony within the British Empire. The colony was first claimed by the British Crown in 1770 (by Captain James Cook), but the first permanent European settlement was not established until 1788. What is perhaps less well known is that the colony was established because the American colonists had succeeded in their revolution, and Britain needed another place to send her convicts. So, the colony of New South Wales was established as a penal settlement in January 1788. On 26 January of that year, there was first a formal ceremony in which the Union flag was raised and a salute fired.[33] Then, on 7 February, the whole population of the colony was assembled and royal letters patent were read, which formally instructed Captain Arthur Phillip of the Royal Navy to go about the duty of creating a penal establishment.[34]

Because this was a settled colony — as distinct from a conquered or ceded one — the accepted law governing the basis of the legal order was as set out in Blackstone's *Commentaries,* specifically the Introduction to the first volume. In describing which countries were subject to the laws of England, Blackstone wrote: "For it hath been held, that if an uninhabited country be discovered and planted by English subjects, all the English laws then in being, which are the birthright of every subject, are immediately there in force. But this must be understood with very many and very great restrictions. *Such colonists carry with them only so much of the English law, as is applicable to their own situation and the condition of an infant colony.*"[35]

It is equally trite (though we suggest, erroneous) to Australians that the basis of the understanding by which Australia and other so-called settled colonies received English law was a literal reading of Blackstone. Generations of law teachers throughout the Commonwealth have recounted how, instantly upon the formal establishment of a permanent settlement, different parts of the globe came to be governed by the English common law. As Brennan J. (as he then was) of the High Court of Australia put it in *Mabo v. Queensland (No. 2),* the landmark case in which the concept of Aboriginal title was recognized for the first time as existing in Australian common law, "English colonists were, in the eye of the common law, entitled to live under the common law of England, which Blackstone described as their 'birthright.'"[36]

That New South Wales fell into the juridical class (if not historical class) of settled colony was confirmed by the Judicial Committee of the Privy Council in the 1889 *Cooper v. Stuart* decision.[37] In *Cooper v. Stuart,* it was accepted by Their Lordships that Blackstone's prescription about the reception of English law was governing. Speaking through Lord Watson, the Board stated:

> The extent to which English law is introduced into a British Colony, and the manner of its introduction, must necessarily vary according to circumstances ... The Colony of New South Wales belongs to [the class of settled colony] ... In so far as it is reasonably applicable to the circumstances of the Colony, the law of England must prevail, until it is abrogated or modified, either by ordinance or statute. The often-quoted observations of Sir William Blackstone appear to their Lordships to have a direct bearing upon the present case.[38]

Thus, a legal ambiguity was established from the very beginning of the colony of New South Wales. As the Crown claimed sovereignty over the lands, the actual detail of the rights of indigenous and non-indigenous alike were dependent upon the practised vagaries of a Blackstonian formula of what law applied and when.[39]

FORBES C.J. AND THE RIGHTS OF ENGLISHMEN

In fact, however, for the first few decades after settlement, little more than lip service was paid to the actual implementation of Blackstone's view of colonial transplantation and legal propagation. Elsewhere, Ian Holloway has written about the struggle to have the colonial executive acknowledge that it actually was bound by law.[40] It was not until 1824, when the present Supreme Court of New South Wales was established, that the real debate over the nature of the rule of law began to take place in Australia.

The first Judge of the new Supreme Court was Chief Justice Francis Forbes. Much has been written about him, so a few general biographical words should suffice for present purposes.[41] Forbes was born in Bermuda, and though he was educated in England (he was a member of Lincoln's Inn), nearly all of his professional practice took place in the colonies. Between 1810 and 1817, he served as the Attorney General and King's Advocate of Bermuda. In 1817 he was appointed Chief Justice of Newfoundland, where he served until 1822.

In that same year, Forbes went to England where he played a role in the drafting of the *New South Wales Act,* the colony's first written Constitution. In 1823 he was appointed Chief Justice of New South Wales, an office in which he served until 1837. He was knighted shortly after his retirement, and he died in Sydney in 1841. Our understanding of Forbes' views and motivations is assisted greatly by the fact that he was a prolific correspondent. In particular, Forbes wrote regularly to Sir Robert Wilmot-Horton, the Under Secretary for War and the Colonies from 1821-28, and much of this correspondence is still extant.

Australians are not much given to celebrating a mythology of heroism (except when it comes to sporting stars and horses), but it is arguable that Forbes occupies the same place in Australian history as does the great Chief Justice John Marshall in American history. In fact, Forbes actually resembled Marshall in some of his personal habits — he was, for example, said to have been rather informal in his dress.[42] But more importantly, it was to Forbes that fell the project of educating what we now understand to be the political branches of government in the principles of the Constitution.

To put it another way, it was Forbes who gave the values of the Glorious Revolution life in the Australian setting. After his appointment as Chief Justice, the substance of English law was not only received in bits and pieces, but doctrines, and statutes even, had things read in and read out of them, so as to tailor them to the colonial setting in a way that exceeded any reasonable reading of Blackstone. In large measure, this was as a result of Forbes' influence. As Kercher has put it, for Forbes "the reception of English law did not so much mean the reception of strict rules as of a general common law technique and advocacy of British freedom."[43]

What emerges from a review of the Forbes judgments is a clear picture of a judicial pragmatist at work. Forbes was not a legal ideologue. Rather, he was what one might call an *essentialist.* The picture that emerges from his judgments is of a man deeply concerned with the preservation of what today are sometimes referred to as "deep rights," but who was willing to allow ultimate results in individual cases to be shaped by particular circumstance. His was an *instrumental* view of the rule of law, rather than a doctrinal view. As Alex Castles once put it, "Forbes aspired to a style of law-making role which he may well have regarded as necessary in a colonial situation where other law-making bodies may not have had the capacity nor the ability to come to terms with local conditions."[44]

Among Forbes' first cases in New South Wales was the so-called civil jury case, *R. v. Magistrates of Sydney.* Castles has described this case, which established the right to empanel civil juries at quarter sessions, as the "first major constitutional case in Australian history."[45] In reality, however, *R. v. Magistrates of Sydney* was just one of a series of four cases concerning the introduction of civil juries in New South Wales, along with *R. v. Sheriff of New South Wales, R. v. Wentworth, Campbell and Dunn,* and *R. v. Cooper.* Prior to these cases, the undoubted birthright of Englishmen to trial by jury was considered impractical within a society comprised largely of felons. The combined effect of "Forbes' experiment" was to establish trial by jury (including the grand jury) for quarter session proceedings.[46] Paradoxically, more serious matters heard before the Supreme Court, consistent with the relevant legislation, continued to be tried before a military panel of seven. The jury experiment was largely successful, demonstrating the political value of the institution (with the grand jury's investigative powers revealing the unlawful punishments meted out by the colony's magistrates in 1825). However, the experiment was short-lived, terminated by imperial legislation. Nonetheless, as students of Australian colonial history know, these events stimulated and sustained the political struggle for the right of trial by jury, which was one of the most fiercely waged battles in the first half century of settlement.

Castles has written that the dispute in *R. v. Magistrates of Sydney* satisfied what he described as "the basic requirements of great constitutional cases." The litigation was instigated to further a broader political campaign (by the so-called Emancipists—freed convicts), and it was accompanied by sharp reporting in a partisan press.[47] In his words, the jury litigation was "the focal point of bitter and often vituperative comment, which reflected the highly charged political atmosphere in which the decisions were handed down."[48]

For present purposes, what is striking about the judgment in *R. v. Magistrates of Sydney* is the extent to which Forbes relied upon the power of emotive rhetoric. As the ultimate justification for his view, he offered the fact that a right to jury trial existed in *Magna Carta:* "It would not merely be against the express language of *Magna Charta* to try free British subjects without the common right of a jury, but against the whole Law and Constitution of England."[49]

The Idea of Rhetoric in Legal Argumentation

To some, this reference in Forbes' judgment to the Great Charter of 1215 might be reminiscent of the sort of rhetoric that Greg Marquis has written of in the case of the Canadian Maritime provinces of Nova Scotia, New Brunswick, and Prince Edward Island. In a wonderful article published some years ago, Marquis discussed the development of a political culture in the Maritimes in more or less the same period.[50] Writing (of the Maritimes) that, "[d]uring this period, the civil and religious struggles of 17th century England, although distorted by an idealized philosophy of history and the demands of partisanship, were very much alive in the colonial mind," he added that

> members of the Maritime political class drew on a variety of intellectual traditions to develop and legitimate their beliefs. Law and history were the most important sources of metaphor and example ... The plain language of politics, however, came from England. Its history, real and mythical, provided a collection of folk tales and folk heroes accessible to the unsophisticated ... Rather than seeing themselves as residents of an imperial backwater, Maritime British Americans took solace in a thousand-year history that was elevated to a form of civil religion ... The presumed antiquity of English legal and political institutions, which produced in the 17th century a school of thought known as the Ancient Constitution, lent prestige to local political questions.[51]

One can make many of the same observations about political debate in New South Wales. In his book *Public Law and Political Theory*, Martin Loughlin notes that we often tend to overlook the importance of Henry Hallam's work in the eighteenth century when considering early nineteenth-century thinking about constitutionalism.[52] We are not aware whether Forbes' library contained a copy of Hallam, but his judgments are replete with Hallam-like Whiggish references to *Magna Carta* and the other elements of the "ancient constitution." In the Australian setting, this use of Whiggish rhetoric contains the seed of a subtle yet profound shift in jurisprudential thinking about the reception of English law that we have for the most part overlooked in our study of the process of reception.

In an interesting book entitled *Rhetoric and Philosophy in Hobbes' "Leviathan,"* Raia Prokhovnik divides political argumentation into two categories: rhetoric and logic.[53] Both, she says, are means of connecting ideas, or giving meaning to something by linking it to something else whose meaning is familiar and accepted. "Logical reasoning," she says, involves definition. And "definition," she adds, is a means of telling us about a thing itself—about its intrinsic nature. "Rhetoric," in contrast, involves the process of *association*. With identification, the focus of attention is not on the thing itself but, rather, on the marks of identity that relate this thing with other things. In rhetoric, the process of argument is to consider whether something can be identified—and consequently understood—by its relations with something else. In an attempt to understand the dynamics of legal culture in a settled colony such as Australia, Prokhovnik's dichotomy can be a most useful one—especially given that, until relatively recently, people here considered themselves British people who happened to live in the Antipodes.

The Repugnancy Doctrine
versus the Blackstonian Formula for Reception

To reiterate, New South Wales was deemed to be a settled colony. Hence, the reception doctrine was in principle governed by Blackstone's *dictum,* viz. that "all the English laws then in being, as [were] applicable to their own situation and the condition of an infant colony [were] immediately there in force." To use Prokhovnik's classification, the Blackstonian formulation (noted earlier) required people to engage in the process of logical reasoning to determine which laws had been received. The process of determining which laws were "applicable to ... the condition of an infant colony" involved considering the colony's intrinsic nature—in this particular case, as a penal colony.

But with the passage of the *New South Wales Act* in 1823, this was to change. Whereas reception had been determined through the process of logical reasoning, the new law implicitly facilitated a shift to a rhetorical style of reasoning. Section 19 of the *New South Wales Act* provided that a bill could not come into force unless the Chief Justice had certified that it was "not repugnant to the laws of England, but is consistent with such laws, so far as the circumstances of the said colony will admit." Bruce Kercher has said in his book *An Unruly Child: A History of Law in Australia* that the "repugnancy provision," as it is commonly known in Australia, "was an implicit statutory statement that the law of New South Wales and Van Diemen's Land was that of England, as far as possible."[54] This is true, but it seems to us that the provision contains something deeper, as well.

As noted, Prokhovnik said that rhetorical argumentation involves the process of association—on the marks of identity that relate something with other things. In rhetoric, the process of argument is to consider whether something can be identified—and consequently understood—by its relations with something else. In our view, with its double-headed repugnancy requirement, section 19 of the *New South Wales Act* required that colonial law be understood in the first instance *not* by considering New South Wales' status as a penal colony (as the Blackstonian formula required) but, rather, by considering her as an offshoot of the British polity in the British Isles.

Forbes as Rhetorician—The *Newspaper Acts Opinion*

Let us look at an example of Forbes at work. Earlier, we quoted Kercher to the effect that for Forbes, "the reception of English law did not so much mean the reception of strict rules as of a general common law technique and advocacy of British freedom."[55] The tool that Forbes used in the course of his project was very much a rhetorical one. We offer one case in illustration of this—the *Newspaper Acts Opinion* of 1827.[56]

The status of the press had long been a matter of some controversy in New South Wales. Governors Brisbane and Darling had both been of the view that newspaper reports were often libellous, and in July 1812, Lord Bathurst, the Colonial Secretary, had suggested in a dispatch to Brisbane that it might be appropriate to impose some controls in a form similar to the licensing legislation that existed in England.[57] Eventually deciding that he could stand no more, Governor Darling introduced Licencing and Stamp Duties Bills into the Legislative Council, which, in April 1827, were transmitted to Forbes for his certification in accordance with section 29 of the *New South Wales Act*. Darling's Bills were based on ones that had previously been introduced in Van Diemen's Land and that had been certified by Chief Justice John Pedder. In Van Diemen's Land, relations between Governor Arthur and Chief Justice Pedder were as close "as Forbes was distant from Darling."[58] John Bennett surmised that, "[w]hether from ignorance, from an excessive zeal to accommodate Arthur's wishes, or from a combination of the two, Pedder gave his s. 29 certificate to the newspaper Bills perfunctorily."[59]

Forbes, however, refused to certify the Licencing Bill on the grounds that it was repugnant to the basic common law freedom of the press. In language that, with only slight alterations in manner of expression, one could imagine having come from the Australian High Court in the early 1990s, he said: "By the laws of England, the right of printing and publishing belongs of common right to all His majesty's subjects, and may be freely exercized like any other lawful trade or occupation. So far as it becomes an instrument of communicating intelligence and expressing opinion, it is considered a constitutional right, and is now too well established to admit of question that it is one of the privileges of a British subject."[60]

In Forbes' view, the licensing requirement amounted to a prior restraint on this freedom, which was fatal. In a long letter to his English correspondent Wilmot-Horton, he amplified his reasoning. Interestingly, in the course of so doing, Forbes made reference to a form of what we now understand as the proportionality doctrine of constitutional law:

[A]n unrestrained press is not politic or perhaps safe in a land where one half of the people are convicts, who have been free men; yet I must not leave out of the account that the other half of the people are free, and that, *as an abstract right, they are consequently entitled, as of birth-right, to the laws and institutes of the parent state.* It is a mixed question, and requires to be carefully examined; if you take away the freedom of public opinion upon matters of government, you take away a legal right; necessity you will say justifies it; then the limit of that justification is the necessity which compels it; it should go no further; a question then naturally arises whether all the means of restraint, which the law of England has provided, have been tried in this colony without success. The answer is at hand, they have not.[61]

This language of birthright, of course, is Blackstone's language. But the really interesting aspect of the case is that the reasoning was quite different from Blackstonian reasoning. Blackstonian reasoning would have required Forbes to look in the first instance at New South Wales' status as a penal colony and to ask whether free press laws were applicable to its needs. Instead, though, Forbes chose not to look at the colony's status. Rather, he engaged in an act of comparison, which allowed him to say that Englishmen in New South Wales should enjoy the same rights as Englishmen in England. This is an important and early reiteration of the liberal value of equality before the law in the colonial context.

R. v. Farrell, Dingle and Woodward

Let us now consider one other case, *R. v. Farrell, Dingle and Woodward,* in which Forbes' use of the rhetorical style was significant. It is actually one of the few cases from the Forbes era to have been reported in a conventional way, but Bruce Kercher's report is both fuller and annotated. Importantly, it also contains a summary of the arguments made by counsel.[62]

The case—or at least the point it established—is reasonably well known to students of the era. The question to be decided was the extent of the application of the felony attaint rule in New South Wales. The convict stain was difficult to remove. For those who had been convicted, sentenced to death, and had their punishment commuted to transportation to New South Wales, this did not put an end to the attainder. As was held in *Bullock v. Dodds,* even if felons served their sentence and returned to England without receiving a pardon, they continued to labour under the incapacities associated with the attainder.[63] At common law, someone who had been convicted of a felony was henceforth disqualified from acting as a witness. The theory was that someone who was not qualified to sit on a jury could not appropriately inform one.

In late 1828, George Farrell, James Dingle, Thomas Woodward, and William Blaxstone robbed the Bank of Australia. In the words of Dowling J., "the plan was executed with a degree of cunning, contrivance and perseverance, scarcely paralleled in the history of human villainy."[64] Perhaps it is a sign of how jaded we have become, but the plan does not seem to today's reader to be a particularly inspired one. Basically, the robbers dug a tunnel under the bank, came up under the vault, and made off with £12,000.

The authorities seemed to have little luck in catching the robbers, until one of them—ironically named Blaxstone—happened to be convicted of a separate offence and transported from New South Wales to Norfolk Island. After this, he was brought back to Sydney to act as a witness to yet *another* crime, at which time he agreed to give evidence against his colleagues for the bank robbery.

At the trial of the three — Farrell, Dingle, and Woodward — Blaxstone was to be the star prosecution witness. But counsel for the accused objected to his testimony on the basis of the felony attaint rule. What is interesting is to compare the style of argumentation between the Crown and the accused on this point, and to compare the approach taken by Forbes C.J. in dissent with that of Stephen and Dowling JJ. in the majority.

The defence presented its argument in rhetorical terms — by means of association. The essence of the defence case (on this point) was that since English law did not permit felons to testify, and since New South Wales was an English colony that employed English common law — a tenet of which was that the liberties of Englishmen should be taken away only according to the due process of law — *ergo* the felony attaint rule should apply. In other words, the tactic employed by the defence was an associative one: by drawing a link with the familiar — the rights of Englishmen — the defence sought to establish the appropriate outcome in the case.[65]

The Crown, in contrast, employed a logical, definitional, style of argumentation. It reasoned that given New South Wales' constitution as a penal colony, to employ the felony attaint rule would be to disqualify three-quarters of the population from ever giving evidence. It used this factor to found an argument of necessity. It hearkened back to Blackstone's assertion (the legal scholar, not the bank robber) that only so much of the law was received as was applicable to the circumstances of the infant colony. Thus, it argued that the definition of New South Wales' population led one to conclude that the felony attaint rule ought not to have been received (in response to which, the defence argued that a cardinal principle of the law of criminal evidence could *not* have not been received in any English colony).

Dowling and Stephen JJ.
The majority judges, Dowling and Stephen JJ. (whose judgment was read by Dowling J.), adopted the logical argument of necessity posited by the Crown. Dowling J. noted that the state of the law in New South Wales had reflected the historical fact that "to all intents and purposes

it [New South Wales] has been treated and regarded as an extensive gaol, and most, if not all, the laws and regulations for its government have been founded on that footing. In no sense of the word has it been, nor can it have been considered as a free Settlement and Colony of Englishmen."[66] In this "degraded situation," it was not possible to administer the municipal laws of England as they would have been applied in England. That said, Dowling J. was frank in the expediency that the judiciary had to employ in establishing a working legal system:

> They have been compelled to lay down principles, and adopt resolutions, which would perhaps startle a lawyer in Westminster Hall, but which they have been driven to resort to in order to meet the exigencies of society, and adopt the principles of British law as far as they were practicable, consistently with the heterogeneous state of the community. A very anxious and responsible duty has thus been cast upon the Judges of this Court. They could have been well pleased, if it were practicable by legislative authority, to declare beforehand what rules and maxims of the common law of England were and what were not applicable to the territory of New South Wales: but as such a legislative declaration might be productive of the greatest inconvenience the Legislature has been pleased to leave a wide discretion to the Judges, to mould the principles and rules of the common law, to the actual state of society, to which the Jurisdiction of this Court extends.[67]

Faced with the alternatives of rigid application of the common law or expediency, Dowling and Stephen JJ. chose the latter.

Forbes C.J.
Forbes C.J. rejected the Crown's argument and found himself in dissent. Like the defence, he employed the rhetorical, associative style. In defining the issue, for example, he said:

> To determine this most delicate and important question, we must look to the spirit of the law of England, and satisfy ourselves whether the rule of law, which excludes witnesses, *propter delictum,* be merely a rule *positivi juris,* admitting of a total deviation, without injury to the abstract principles of justice?—or, whether it be a rule founded in reason, and only admitting of a deviation, upon

grounds of extreme necessity, and not sanctioning a departure any further than such necessity will justify.[68]

Throughout his judgment, Forbes referred to the essential principles of English law—and there was even the familiar reference to *Magna Carta*. (The felony attaint rule, he said, was "laid in the foundations of the constitution. It is declared by *Magna Carta,* that no free man shall be interrupted in his person or his property, except by the judgment of his peers or by the law of the land.")[69] He also acknowledged the separation of powers concern. He said that to waive the felony attaint rule by judicial fiat would "raise up a most frightful responsibility in the bosom of judges."[70] Note again, Forbes' articulation of proportionality, the idea that any qualification to a principle of English law must be proportionate. Also, his appeal to founding the rule on reason (natural law) is significant.

CONCLUSION

These are but two cases of the many we have read that bear out the analysis. But—one can fairly ask—so what? Why are they of any importance at all? In our view, they are significant precisely because they laid the foundation of constitutionalism in Australia. As specific holdings, they have largely been forgotten, but they nonetheless served to establish a tradition of (common law) constitutionalism that has not been forgotten. That is why we feel it appropriate to think of Forbes as the Australian John Marshall. Interestingly, Bennett has contrasted Forbes with another Chief Justice of the United States: John Jay.[71] In doing so, he highlighted the fact that Forbes' commitment to the judicial function was greater than Jay's. Like that of Marshall, the educative role of Forbes in basic constitutionalism can be seen through his actions. As Hirst has expressed it, by way of contrast to Governor Darling, "Forbes was a liberal: he was determined to uphold the independence of the court: and was proud to have been the instrument by which a ramshackle colony had been brought under control of the full might of the English law."[72]

Yet, having said this, we add the interesting observation that this constitutional foundation was an odd one. The rhetorical connections Forbes sought to make were really quite non-contemporary. Forbes was making associations not with the rights of his English brethren in England. By his references—so frequently to *Magna Carta*—he was drawing rhetorical comparisons with Stephen Langton. The fact is that in England by this time, the so-called *Six Acts* of 1819, which followed the Peterloo riots and which placed quite significant limitations on the freedom of the press, were still in force.

Moreover, *R. v. Farrell* places the limits of the rhetorical style right on the table. It was one thing (and *is* one thing, for the style of argumentation is not dead) to speak in rhetorical terms about the rights of Englishmen as the foundation of the legal order. But the fact is—as the Crown pointed out in its argument—that had the argument succeeded, the administration of justice would in a practical sense have ground to a halt, for most cases would not have been able to proceed for lack of evidence.

Nonetheless, the fact that the working Constitution—the Australian colonial version of the rule of law—came to be based so solidly on this sort of a Whiggish rhetorical foundation says something about the social setting in which the legal argument was made. To borrow from Dicey, "liberty is never so highly prized as when it is contrasted with the bondage of our neighbours."[73] Forbes' critics, such as the constitutional historian A.C.V. Melbourne, argue that when disputes arose between the Chief Justice and the Governor—such as in the *Newspaper Acts Opinion*—Forbes misunderstood his role. Melbourne concluded that

> [t]he Governor and the Chief Justice were alike at fault. Darling was harshly intolerant of criticism, and Forbes failed to realize that, in this respect, the Act of 1823 had conferred upon him a political rather than a judicial obligation. Unlike the Governor, he was inclined to sympathize with the emancipists. It is to be feared that occasionally he allowed his sympathies to cloud his judgment, and that he gave a narrow interpretation to his duty in order to protect the interests he was prone to favour. His decisions may have been quite sound in law but politically they were often indiscreet.[74]

Forbes' alleged lack of political acumen, if that is what it was, was in reality a claim for greater (and workable) divisions of power. Acting like a judicial officer schooled in constitutionalism makes the distinction between Pedder and Forbes on this point.

In Forbes' New South Wales, there was a daily reminder of the fact that the state was founded upon the principle of lack of freedom. For those who possessed it, liberty—as enshrined in the rhetorical version of *Magna Carta*—must have seemed like the real jewel in the crown.

In a related way, there was also the governmental setting in which legal argument was made. This was a time of constitutional transition in the colony. The period of Forbes' tenure as Chief Justice may be conceived as the Australian version of the Glorious Revolution—in the sense that it marked the end of claims to autocratic power in the Crown. At the same time, these cases stand out as signposts of a profound change in the position of the legal apparatus vis-à-vis political conflict. Rather than being the subject of the conflict, as they had been in the first three decades of settlement, during Forbes' tenure, the courts came to be the forum in which the conflict was played out. As Bruce Kercher has put it, "[t]he great political contest of the Forbes years, between emancipated convicts and the exclusives ... was largely conducted in the language of law."[75] In a constitutional sense, few things surely can be as important as this.

APPENDIX 4.1:
COMMENCING WRIT IN *KABLE V. SINCLAIR*

Sydney Cove   To Davd Collins
County of Cumberland   Esqr
to wit   Judge Advocate in and
                                       for the Territory of New South
                                       Wales etc etc etc

Whereas Henry Cable and his wife, ~~New Settlers of this place~~, had before they left England a Certain parcel shipped on Board the Alexander Transp t Duncan Sinclair Master, Consisting of Cloaths and several other Articles suitable for their present Situation, which were Collected And Bought at the Expence of many Charitable dispos'd Persons for the Use of the said Henry Cable, his wife & Child—Several Applications has been made for the express purpose of obtaining the said parcel from the Master of the Alexander now lying at this port, and that without effect (save and except) a small part of the said parcel Containing a few Books,—the residue And remainder, which is of a more Considerable Value still remains on Board the said Ship Alexander, the Master of which, seems to be very Neglectfull in not Causing the same to be Delivered, to its respective owners as aforesaid—Henry Cable and Susannah Cable his wife most humbly prays you will be pleas'd forthwith to Cause the said Duncan Sinclair, Master of the Alexander aforesaid, to Appear before you to shew Cause why the Remaining Parcel is not duly and Truly delivered in that ample and beneficial a manner as is Customary in the delivering of Goods—And also humbly prays you will on Default of the Parcel not being forthcoming take and use such Lawfull and Legal means for the recover or Value thereof, as your Honour shall think most expedient.

Sined by the hands of the said
Henry Cable and Susannah Cable
his wife this the First Day of July in
the year of our Lord 1788.

his
Henry X Cable
mark

her
Susannah X Cable
mark

CHAPTER FIVE

SOMETIMES PERSUASIVE AUTHORITY
Dominion Case Law and English Judges, 1895-1970

Jeremy Finn

Every student of the law of Australia, Canada, New Zealand, or South Africa—a group of former British colonies that, with some degree of anachronicity, will be collectively referred to here as "the Dominions"—is familiar with the enormous influence of English judicial precedent on the decisions of local judges.[1] There has, however, been no discussion of the reverse process—the manner in which English lawyers and English courts made use of case law from the Dominions. This chapter surveys some aspects of that question, looking at the use by English lawyers and judges of case law precedents from the courts of the Dominions between 1895 and 1970. It first considers the extent to which Dominion law was cited in the English courts over the period and in different areas of law, and explores some of the ways in which the participants in the English legal process may have gained their information about Dominion decisions. Lastly, it provides some hypotheses about the changing nature of the English perception of Dominion case law and what may have influenced those changes.

It must be emphasized at the outset that Dominion cases were cited in only a tiny fraction of even that small element of the cases in the English courts that came to be recorded in any law report. However, as the frequency of Dominion citations increased (to perhaps 10 percent of those in the official law reports in the late 1960s), we are dealing with both an interesting example of the transmission of legal information between legal systems and a significant contribution to English legal and judicial thinking as evidenced in the leading law reports. The importance and intellectual impact of Dominion case law cannot therefore be measured solely by statistics.

CITATION DATA

Methodology

This study looks at the use of Dominion authority in cases before the English High Court, Court of Appeal, and House of Lords between 1895 and 1970 that are reported in the "official" law reports—Appeal Cases, Queen's (or King's) Bench, Chancery, and Probate—published by the Incorporated Council of Law Reporting. The study is restricted to these reports partially because it was possible to make electronic searches of the data and partially because it is possible to determine from the report whether a particular case was first cited by counsel or by the judge(s).[2] Unfortunately, the citation study may somewhat under-represent citation of Dominion cases by counsel, as on occasion, especially during the two world wars and their immediate aftermath, even the official reports did not report the argument. This is unavoidable but probably not material, given the relative infrequency of judicial references to Dominion law in those periods.

The cases sampled exclude decisions of the House of Lords in Scottish cases, as Dominion precedent, based as it was on English law, was clearly less relevant there. More importantly, the study deliberately excludes the citation of Dominion authority in the Privy Council and the citation of Privy Council cases in domestic English decisions. The influence of Privy Council decisions on English law is largely unexplored territory, but the inquiry is too broad to be pursued here. Nor has an attempt been made to consider English use of decisions from non-self-governing colonies, though on casual inspection instances of this from jurisdictions other than India appear to have been very rare.[3] Only a single case was found where reference was made to both Dominion and Indian case law.[4]

The dates for the study were selected as encompassing the first known report, from 1895, in which an English case cited a "Dominion" suit, and the apparent development of a practice among many English lawyers that, in full-dress legal arguments before the House of Lords, counsel would canvass relevant Dominion authority.[5] The practice had apparently gained some traction in the lower courts as well.[6] An indication of this developing trend is that, though for most of our period, little discernible correlation exists between the number of citations and the court in which the case was being heard, we find that for the period 1966-70 there are more House of Lords cases (fifteen) that cite three or more Dominion cases than for the Court of Appeal (six) and first instance courts (seven) combined. In earlier periods, or where only one or two Dominion cases were cited, no obvious correlation of any kind emerges.

Citations by Actor and Frequency

Over the seventy-five years under study, 283 decisions were recorded in the official law reports where counsel, or the judge, or both referred to at least one Dominion case as a precedent. A number of these decisions represent different stages of a single suit as it proceeded through the courts.[7] The data are set out in Table 5.1.

Two different points must be made. First, we must consider which of the legal actors was citing the Dominion case. Overall, we see an increase in the absolute number of cases where Dominion cases cited by counsel are mentioned in the judgments, but in the final fifteen years, for reasons that are not clear, there is a higher proportion of cases where counsel's references to Dominion law were not reflected in the judgment.[8] More striking is the increased number of cases in which the judge or judges referred to Dominion litigation that had not been cited by counsel, a phenomenon returned to below.

Second, we must consider the frequency with which counsel or judges referred to more than a single Dominion precedent in the course of the argument or the judgment. Such multiple citations may be taken as a reasonable indication of substantial effort by counsel or judges to understand, and to derive assistance from, relevant Dominion law. As Table 5.1 shows, this occurred in only a relatively small percentage of the total number of cases, but it was a rapidly increasing percentage over the period under study.

Citations by Dominion Court

An obvious parallel question arises. Which Dominion courts were being cited? The data for the 515 references to Dominion decisions appear in Table 5.2.[9]

There are some striking features of these data, particularly the extraordinary and increasing preponderance of references to Australian law,

TABLE 5.1

Citation numbers by person citing, multiple citations, and year						
PERIOD	1895–1910	1911–25	1926–40	1941–55	1956–70	TOTAL
N=	4	15	29	45	190	283
Judge and counsel	2	9	16	32	105	164
Judge alone	–	2	2	4	15	23
Counsel alone	2	4	11	9	70	96
Multiple citations (3+)						
Cited	–	2	2	6	46	56
Judge and counsel	–	1	2	6	27	36
Judge alone	–	–	–	–	2	2
Counsel alone	–	1	–	–	17	18

TABLE 5.2

Dominion cases cited in English courts						
PERIOD	1895–1910	1911–25	1926–40	1941–55	1956–70	TOTAL
N=	5	24	39	71	376	515
HCA*	–	4	10	13	92	119
Other Aust.	4	5	11	22	112	154
SCC**	–	5	5	8	10	28
Other Can.	–	3	6	18	90	117
New Zealand	1	6	3	8	50	68
South Africa	–	1	4	2	22	29

*   High Court of Australia

** Supreme Court of Canada

most especially to High Court of Australia decisions. This is further discussed later in this chapter. By contrast, there are relatively few decisions of the Supreme Court of Canada. The dominance of Australian cases and the primacy of the High Court of Australia are even more marked on inspection of the figures for the last decade of the study. In that time, 186 different cases were cited; 96 of these were Australian, 54 from the High Court. By comparison, over the same period, 52 Canadian decisions were cited, only 5 from the Supreme Court of Canada. The number is rounded out with 25 New Zealand decisions and 13 from South Africa.

The pattern over time must also be considered. The last fifteen years of this study dominate the statistics, with 184 individual suits, well over two-thirds of the total. In the first thirty years of our sample, there were often no Dominion citations at all. Such blank years occurred even as late as 1947, and only in 1925 were there more than two cases where Dominion precedents were cited. In 1934, however, the tally rose to seven — for entirely unknown reasons — a level matched in 1939, 1952, 1953, and 1955. Citations became much more frequent in the last years: for example, in 1963 and 1970, twenty decisions cited Dominion case law, and more than forty Dominion cases were cited in each of 1963, 1968, and 1970.

Citations by Area of Law

There are some interesting features of the areas of law in issue in the cases that cited Dominion authority. By far the most common area was the law of torts — personal wrongs — with fifty-nine cases, or almost a quarter of the whole sample. The bulk of these were concerned with one or another aspect of personal injury litigation, but among the other tort cases, ten involved the law of defamation. Next came the somewhat overlapping areas of conflict of laws or private international law (twenty-six cases) and family law (twenty-four). In third place was the broad field of contract, commercial law, insurance, and company law (thirty-four cases) to which may be added thirteen cases on intellectual property (mostly concerning copyright). Next largest was criminal law and evidence, with twenty-eight cases. Four other areas reached double figures — wills and trusts (fourteen); taxation (thirteen), constitutional and administrative law (thirteen), and statutory interpretation (ten). It is notable that, in the 257 cases in our sample, only 6 involved land law, a figure that can only partially be explained by the often significantly different, Torrens-Title influenced, Dominion land laws.

Other Reports

Some assurance that these data from the official reports give a reasonably accurate picture can be gained from a brief inspection of the first thirty years of the *All England Law Reports* (1936-65), which indicates a pattern broadly consistent with that in the official reports. These volumes include only a small number of cases — thirty — in which Dominion authority was cited by a judge (the series does not give counsel's argument) that do not appear in the official reports. None of these referred to three or more Dominion cases, nor did any contain citations from more than one Dominion jurisdiction. More than half the references were to Australian cases (eighteen), with fourteen of those referring to decisions of the High Court of Australia. Of the remainder, surprisingly, nine referred to one or more New Zealand cases, only two to Canadian law, and one to a South African decision. Dominion decisions were also occasionally reported in specialist series published in England and were thus more readily accessible to English lawyers. In consequence, they may have been more frequently cited.[10]

Issues for Discussion

Several issues raised by the data require more detailed consideration. How did English lawyers and judges find the relevant Commonwealth law that was advanced for discussion? *How did judges make use of the Dominion law cited?* Why was there such a marked shift in the frequency with which Commonwealth authority was cited in the latter years of our sample? Lastly, what inferences can we draw about the impact of Dominion law on lawyers, judges, and legal developments in England?

Sources of Information

English lawyers and judges, as might be expected, derived the vast bulk of their information about Dominion case law from a range of published material. However, before we consider that material, it is convenient to examine a subsidiary conduit for information.

Privy Council Decisions or Other Earlier Litigation

Perhaps surprisingly, the English profession only rarely had recourse to Dominion precedents that had been canvassed in decisions of the Privy Council determining appeals from a Dominion. The most notable example of the use of such Dominion decisions is *Bullock v. Unit Construction Co Ltd,* a tax case, where at first instance the judge applied *dicta* from a Privy Council case that itself had adopted a *dictum* of Dixon J.'s in the High Court of Australia in *Koitaki Para Rubber Estates Ltd v. Federal Commissioner of Taxation.*[11] In the Court of Appeal and the House of Lords, the discussion focuses not on the Privy Council decision but on Dixon's judgment in *Koitaki*. There is also one suit where a judge cited a Dominion case with which he became acquainted through sitting in the Privy Council.[12] More significantly, in ten cases where counsel cited Privy Council decisions, judges subsequently relied on passages from the lower court decisions in the matter. In one of these, the House of Lords preferred the lower court view to that of the Privy Council.[13]

English and Empire Digest

The principal resource for lawyers seeking Dominion case law precedents was the multi-volume reference work called the *English and Empire Digest* (the Digest). This listed, under more than a hundred headings, all of the decisions of the English courts on particular areas of law and any Scottish, Irish, Dominion, or colonial cases dealing with the same issues or that had mentioned the English decisions. The first edition, of forty-four volumes, was launched in 1919 and completed by 1929, although there were various volumes of indexes and supplements. A second series was launched in 1950, although the fifty-first and final volume was not published until 1967. The Digest therefore provided reasonable, if not total, assurance that any extant Dominion precedent could be discovered by those motivated to look. Evidently, not all were, as even in the 1960s judges at first instance could use a perhaps coded phrase along the lines of "the industry of counsel enabled us to be referred to [a named Dominion case]," thus indicating that counsel rarely carried out a careful search for relevant Dominion law when arguing cases at that level.[14]

The impact of the Digest cannot be precisely established, but of the fifty-seven Dominion references in the years 1919-49 (from commencement of the first edition to initiation of its successor), thirty-six are cases where the Digest reference would have been published prior to the citation of the case. Thus, we may reasonably hypothesize that a person involved in the litigation had consulted the Digest—and perhaps a textbook or other aid as well. Of the remaining twenty-one cases, six predated the publication of the relevant Digest volume and a further six do not appear there at all. In the remaining nine, the report indicates some alternative source for the reference.

Of course, the Digest would assist only where the lawyer or judge had access to the relevant law reports. Unfortunately, it is not clear when the major English law libraries began to hold copies of Dominion law reports, although we do know that the *New Zealand Law Reports* were not available in London until 1905.[15] It must have taken much longer for barristers to have convenient access to such reports.[16] As late as 1966, a judge sitting in Bristol could say of counsel's references to an article in the *Harvard Law Review* and to a Canadian case, "unfortunately that article and that case have not been available; no doubt there would have been considerable difficulty in obtaining them."[17] However, we may surmise that from at least the 1950s judges had ready and speedy access to Dominion reports, as several instances exist of judicial references to decisions of appellate Dominion courts after counsel had canvassed only the lower court decisions.[18] This alone does not explain the increase in citations.

Law Dictionaries

A small number of Dominion references seem to have been made because counsel or judges had recourse to legal dictionaries or similar books in which authors had assembled judicial definitions of terms (usually, but not always, words or phrases used in statutes) that could then be used in the interpretation of other statutes or documents. A paradigm of such usage is provided by *Moriarty v. Regent's Garage and Engineering Co,* where McCardie J. determined that a company director's fees were not "salary": "The same view has been taken in New Zealand, for I find in *Bedwell's Australasian Judicial Dictionary,* under the word 'salary,' a useful extract from the judgment of Williams ACJ in *In re Industrial Conciliation and Arbitration Act 1908* (1909) 28 NZLR 933, 940."[19]

Curiously, the most elaborate of these reference works, the five-volume *Words and Phrases Judicially Defined* published between 1943 and 1946, appears to have been rarely used by counsel or judges in locating Dominion references.[20] During its first twenty years in use, only four English cases cite Dominion authorities listed in the book, though many more appear there.

Textbooks

It appears that, over the whole of the period, the most common source of information as to Commonwealth law was provided by the authors of textbooks that cited Commonwealth decisions. For the most part, such texts were English, but on occasion works of Commonwealth authors are cited—as with texts on the law of torts by John William Salmond and, several decades later, John Fleming and reference to an essay in an Australian work on international law.[21]

Legal Journals

Despite the fact that at least one leading English academic, Edward Jenks, had taught law at the University of Melbourne for six years before retiring to England, references to Dominion law in English legal journals before 1940 are rare indeed.[22] However, after that, we see a steady increase in the number of cases in which counsel, and/or the judge, drew on legal journal articles for relevant Dominion case law, as with *Gold v. Essex County Council,* where references to cases from Canada and New Zealand were derived from an article in the *Law Quarterly Review.*[23] In the 1960s other articles in the same journal, apparently by British writers, drew attention to Dominion decisions that were later cited by counsel to English courts.[24]

A most interesting development in the later years of our sample is that English lawyers and judges began to draw regularly upon academic writings by Dominion authors. There were only two references to journals published in Commonwealth jurisdictions: one was to an *Australian Law Journal* report of an address by Sir Owen Dixon; the other was to an article by Colin Howard, whose views were canvassed in *Connelly v. DPP.*[25] In addition, one case referred to an American article that cited Dominion decisions.[26]

More frequently, and therefore probably more importantly, there are a number of cases where the most plausible explanation for the citation of Commonwealth materials in the English courts is that counsel and judges had recourse to articles by Commonwealth authors in leading English legal journals. Although this seems to have first occurred in the 1930s, it was not common practice until the 1950s and 1960s.[27] Two examples may suffice. The first was a case involving misprision of felony—an offence of failing to inform authorities of offending by others—where both the Court of Appeal and the House of Lords extensively discussed Canadian and Australian cases that had been the subject of *Criminal Law Review* articles by Australian writers.[28] Similarly, *Sweet v. Parsley,* a case on offences of "strict liability," made regular reference to an article by Colin Howard discussing the relevant Australian law.[29]

JUDGES AND THE USE OF DOMINION LAW

Rules of Precedent and Their Effect

English judges were often not free to adopt decisions from overseas. The High Court was bound by the decisions of the Court of Appeal and of the House of Lords, the Court of Appeal by decisions of the House of Lords and, with narrow exceptions, by earlier decisions of its own, and, until 1966, the House of Lords was bound by its own previous decisions. Thus, Dominion authority could be really influential only where there was a new and undecided point, where the English law was uncertain, or where a court could change its views. Further, under the prevailing doctrines of judicial precedent, any decision of a Dominion court could at most be what lawyers call "persuasive authority," that is, a decision that an English judge could choose to apply in his judgment if he approved the reasoning and the result.[30] The higher in the judicial hierarchy the Dominion decision was—and the greater the reputation of the judges involved—the more persuasive the case would be. Thus, English judges could validly ignore or dismiss Dominion authority as being contrary to settled English law, as involving significant different statutory provisions, or being influenced by purely local considerations. Even where judges did consider the cited overseas authority to be both relevant and correct, they not infrequently resolved the case before them primarily on the basis of English precedents, only later canvassing overseas decisions before expressing pleasure that the decision on the English law accorded with that reached by a Dominion court.[31]

Use of Dominion Case Law

Despite these constraints, English judges often found no, or no determinative, English precedent and were ready to look to Dominion precedents. This was particularly likely to be the case in the latter third or so of our sample. One facet of this is the increasing willingness to adopt Dominion decisions on the interpretation of essentially similar statutory wording.[32] However, Dominion decisions overall had more impact on points of common law or public policy. A simple example is provided by two cases—*Attorney-General v. Clough* and *Attorney-General v. Mulholland*—where it was alleged that journalists who had written stories about a spy scandal were in contempt of a royal commission when they refused to reveal their sources.[33] Not surprisingly, in each case the

Attorney General relied heavily—and successfully—on *McGuinness v. Attorney-General of Victoria*, a High Court of Australia decision that had held such refusal was indeed a contempt.[34]

Other examples of this acceptance of Dominion authority can be found, though more rarely, in earlier decades, as when the Probate Division and the House of Lords had adopted the views of the Supreme Court of Canada that at common law a plaintiff could not claim damages for death of a human being.[35] Similarly, a New South Wales decision was relied on in a later refusal on public policy grounds to allow a prisoner to sue in tort for injuries allegedly caused by a warder.[36] On occasion, the debate over Dominion decisions spilled over several years and a number of cases. This can be seen in the gradual resolution of a dispute as to the appropriate standard of proof of "matrimonial offences"—or fault-based grounds for divorce such as cruelty and adultery—where English judges noted regularly, and sometimes with apparent regret, that the High Court of Australia had refused to follow a decision of the English Court of Appeal. In 1966 the House of Lords determined to adopt the Australian decision, not that of the English Court of Appeal.[37] Dominion decisions were not always so well received—the English courts consistently refused to adopt an Australian decision setting an employee-friendly test for determining whether contributory negligence would bar an action against an employer for negligence.[38]

Independent Research by Judges

In a significant number of lawsuits, the judge(s) cited and, in some instances, applied Dominion cases not cited by counsel. A simple example is *In re Callaway, Callaway v. Treasury Solicitor,* where Vaisey J. relied on a New South Wales case not mentioned by either counsel.[39] Where a judge in a lower court did engage in some independent research and in consequence canvassed a Dominion decision, it was natural that the Commonwealth case would then be discussed on appeal and in later cases on the same point.[40]

Sometimes judges may have been prompted by dissatisfaction with the comprehensiveness of counsel's argument; in other cases it may simply have been that relevant authorities were later drawn to their attention by journal articles—or in one unusual case, by a reference from an English academic.[41] In others, however, judges may have been seeking out Dominion case law that supported their stance on a matter of some controversy, as in *National Provincial Bank Ltd v. Ainsworth,* where the House of Lords overruled a number of Court of Appeal cases that had recognized the so-called deserted wife's equity—a claim in equity to an interest in a matrimonial home where title was held by the husband alone, and the wife could not prove cash contributions to the purchase price or mortgage payments.[42] Lords Upjohn and Wilberforce both referred to relevant Australian cases not cited by counsel, stating this was desirable as the House of Lords was reversing the Court of Appeal on a point of significance.[43]

It is notable, too, that occasional remarks in the early 1960s indicate that the English judges thought counsel should be readier to look to the Commonwealth courts for relevant precedents. Most significant here is Diplock L.J.'s comment in *Letang v. Cooper* that a Victorian decision on the limitation period point was "yet another illustration of the assistance to be obtained from the citation of relevant decisions of courts in other parts of the Commonwealth."[44]

Citing the High Court of Australia — The Dixon Factor

As indicated earlier, a remarkable feature of the citation of Dominion authority in English courts is the highly dominant position of the High Court of Australia. In part, this may have sprung from regard for what was seen as collectively a very strong bench, described indeed by Lord Denning as a court with a higher reputation than the House of Lords itself.[45] But a major element was an apparent and extraordinary regard for the judgments of Sir Owen Dixon, quondam Justice of the High Court and then Chief Justice of Australia. The reports contain laudatory judicial statements concerning Dixon, "a man," as one judge remarked, "whose judgment commands the greatest respect, not only in Australia and this country, but I venture to think throughout the world."[46] In a bigamy case, the judge remarked that "[t]he matter came before a High Court of Australia which included Latham CJ and Dixon J, who has earned a world-wide reputation as a common lawyer which is outstanding in the twentieth century. The decisions of the High Court of Australia even when so constituted may be persuasive only—but how persuasive they are."[47]

Judges cite Dixon's *dicta* or judgments, with attribution, in at least twenty-five cases in the official law reports. That is at least five times as many as any other Dominion judge, and no other judge of a Commonwealth court is mentioned in such complimentary terms. Curiously, perhaps, all but three of these references came late in Dixon's long career or after his retirement. Indeed, all but three — and all of the laudatory ones — came after Dixon received an honorary doctorate from Oxford in 1958, an event surrounded by vigorous socializing with leading English figures (many of whom Dixon already knew).[48] Almost invariably, judges cited Dixon with approval. Indeed, in one case, both Devlin J. at first instance and the Court of Appeal adopted Dixon C.J.'s reasoning in a dissenting judgment in preference to the majority of the High Court.[49] Dixon was also the only Dominion Judge whose extrajudicial pronouncements were cited in the House of Lords in the sample period.[50]

CONCLUSION

As we have seen, Dominion decisions are increasingly cited in the English courts over our seventy-five-year period, with a remarkable acceleration in that frequency over the latter decades. Why is this and why did it take so long for citation of Dominion cases to become commonplace, albeit far from universal? Clearly, citation practices were not controlled solely by the availability of convenient reference works: had they been, the significant time lag between the full publication of the *English and Empire Digest* and the rise of Dominion citations in the 1930s would not have occurred. Nor was the citation solely a function of counsel's readiness to put forward Dominion precedents — or we would not see significant independent judicial references. Perhaps the best explanation is that, before Dominion case law could be widely invoked, two developments must occur: first, information regarding it must be effectively communicated to the English bar and judiciary, and second, legal professionals must come to perceive that research into, and citation of, Dominion law was worthwhile. The first was realized when discussion of Dominion authorities in legal journals and a wider range of textbooks improved awareness of their range and quality. The latter was slower, perhaps, to develop but clearly well established by the late 1950s. Once these preconditions were established, an overall increase in citation of Dominion cases was highly likely.

The extraordinary frequency of citation of High Court of Australia decisions may have resulted from the unforeseen creation of an effective feedback system. As the perception grew that decisions of that Court, and of Dixon in particular, were likely to be given weight by the judges, counsel would be moved to seek and cite them. Judges who regularly heard such citations would be increasingly likely to mention them in their judgments — thus encouraging yet more reference to such authority by counsel. The lack of any equivalent recognition of a dominant judicial figure may have relegated Canadian case law to a very poor second place.

As this chapter shows, careful analysis of case law citation patterns, particularly of case law from different jurisdictions, can tell us much about the transmission of legal information between jurisdictions and the development of legal cultures within a jurisdiction. Let us hope that such studies become more common.

PART TWO

COURTS AND JUDGES IN THE COLONIES

CHAPTER SIX

COURTS, COMMUNITIES, AND
COMMUNICATION
THE NOVA SCOTIA SUPREME COURT ON CIRCUIT,
1816-50

*Jim Phillips and Philip Girard**

THE NOVA Scotia Supreme Court (NSSC) went on circuit—travelled
to communities outside the capital of Halifax—for the first time in 1775,
following the passage of the *Supreme Court Circuit Act* of 1774.[1] The circuit
initially took the Court to just three locations—Annapolis, Cumberland,
and Kings Counties—but over the years more were added: Hants County
in 1781, and the Colchester and Pictou Districts of Halifax County and
Lunenburg County between 1802 and 1805 (see Map 6.1).[2] In 1816
Queens, Shelburne, and Sydney Counties were included, so that the
circuit covered the entire mainland, with the judges going to some locations annually and others twice a year.[3] Cape Breton was added in 1821,
after the island ceased to be a separate colony and was re-annexed to
Nova Scotia.[4] Thereafter the circuit continued to expand as population
increases led to new counties being carved out of existing ones and/or
divided into districts for judicial purposes: Yarmouth, for example, was
included in 1834 as a district of Shelburne and as a new county from
1836.[5] Expansion also took place in the sense that some locations previously visited annually received a second visit each year. In 1841, when
the inferior civil courts were abolished, the Supreme Court's circuit
itinerary saw it go twice a year, in the spring and the fall, on four circuits.[6]

* We thank Daniel Girard and Rachel Kent for excellent research assistance, and Ben
Berger and Hamar Foster for their comments on a previous draft. A version of this
chapter was presented to the Toronto Legal History group in 2007, and we thank its
members for their valuable suggestions. Financial support for the research was provided
by the Osgoode Society for Canadian Legal History and the Social Sciences and Humanities Research Council of Canada.

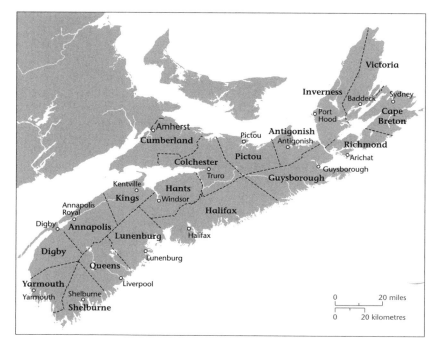

MAP 6.1 Nova Scotia Supreme Court circuit
Cartographer: Eric Leinberger

One went to the south shore, to Lunenburg, Liverpool, Shelburne, and Yarmouth County (alternately Yarmouth and Tusket); one went to the northwest, to Windsor, Kentville, Annapolis, and Digby; one went to the east, to Truro, Amherst, Pictou, and Antigonish; and one went to what, as we shall see, the judges regarded as the far east — Guysborough County and Cape Breton Island (Sydney, Arichat, and Port Hood). This system remained essentially in place until Confederation in 1867, with just one change — the addition of Victoria County on Cape Breton, with the Court sitting at Baddeck as of 1851.[7]

Canadian legal historians have long been cognizant of the central role that courts and the judiciary should occupy in the development of the field, although the emphasis has tended to be on the evolution of legal thought or the fine-tuning of legal doctrine. John McLaren, for example, has illustrated the importance of deep-seated judicial notions of the rule of law that could transcend even personal ethnic chauvinism.[8] But we know relatively little about curial administration and the role played by courts in what might broadly be termed colonial governance. Circuit courts—the equivalent of the English assizes—were much employed in both British North America and the new American republic in the late eighteenth and nineteenth centuries, although they had not been a significant element of judicial organization in the American colonies prior to the revolution.[9] In the newly created United States they were used both as a nation-building device—for its first few decades, even the judges of the United States Supreme Court went on circuit—and as a way to achieve a degree of judicial uniformity.[10] In British North America circuit courts also brought formal state law to the hinterland, while simultaneously "showing the flag"—asserting British sovereignty and the primacy of the common law in sparsely populated outposts of empire. This certainly seems to have been a major function of the circuits undertaken by Matthew Begbie, British Columbia's first Chief Justice, who rode extensively around the interior of the colony in the 1860s, applying English law while also reporting on the prospects for settlement and resource exploitation.[11]

Despite the circuits' importance, with a few notable exceptions historians have paid little attention to them, effectively treating them as a minor corner of the history of judicial administration, a device to bring legal services to the hinterland. The best-known analysis placing them in a broader context is Douglas Hay's account of the ways in which the majesty of the English assizes helped to cement the power of rural elites and to inculcate habits of deference among the governed.[12] The circuit played this role in mid- to late eighteenth-century Nova Scotia also, but not in the changed circumstances of the nineteenth century, when the significance of the loyalty issue faded.[13] The NSSC on circuit nonetheless played an important part in the lives of many people within the legal system and outside of it, and this chapter examines the operation of the circuits from two perspectives: that of the communities visited and that of the visitors—principally the judges who took journeys to all parts of the colony, but also the lawyers who accompanied them. In the process we offer assessments of the Court's role, and perceptions of it, from a variety of perspectives. The judges on circuit were the only senior central administration officials to regularly visit the hinterland. To some degree, therefore, they were agents of central government. The evidence suggests little objection to this role across the colony and, indeed, a general enthusiasm for the Court's visits. The NSSC on circuit offered communities a more "professional" judicial system than that provided by local courts, as the assizes later did in British Columbia, and indeed it eventually displaced, in 1841, county-level courts staffed largely by lay judges.[14] Yet this change was not wholly welcome, for some communities prior to 1841 clearly preferred the alternatives to the NSCC on circuit. The judges themselves held their own views, often strongly expressed, about circuit organization, and their attempts to influence policies on a number of issues—judicial fees and salaries, circuit frequency, and whether the circuits should be staffed by one or two judges—involved them profoundly in colonial politics, especially during the 1830s, Nova Scotia's "age of reform." The circuit, therefore, was not simply about judicial administration: it is a lens through which broader themes—central-hinterland relations, professionalization, and reform politics—can be viewed.

The Circuit Court and Local Communities

The relationship between the Supreme Court on circuit and the communities it visited was multi-faceted and at times contradictory. The judges on circuit were agents of central government, although they played this role in a more utilitarian manner than the English assize judges of the eighteenth century. Although in the 1770s the origins of the circuit were clearly grounded in a desire to use the Court to propagate both respect for the law and loyalty to the political system from which it sprang, and though such ideas seem to have persisted into the early years of the new century, by 1815 loyalty to the Crown was not at issue.[15] But the Halifax authorities still desired fealty to the established order and Tory politics, and did not hesitate to use the NSSC on circuit to promote what they regarded as good government. The judges sent in reports on local justices of the peace (JP), advised on appointments to the local Inferior Courts of Common Pleas (ICCPs), certified that road- and bridge-building money had been spent appropriately, selected annually the list of persons who could be appointed sheriffs of each county, and generally reported on local conditions and politics.[16] In these tasks they were joined, after 1823-24, by the divisional chief justices of the lower courts, whose place in the system is discussed in more detail later in this chapter.[17]

This is not to say that the NSSC on circuit entirely lacked those features of the English assizes that contributed to the "majesty" of the law. It certainly sought to reproduce the pomp and majesty of the mother country's assizes, as David Bell has pointed out: "At the courthouse they [the judges] were met by the sheriff, the county constables carrying staves of office embellished with a gold crown ... Sometimes a special sermon preached by a local divine brought further solemnity to the occasion."[18] But this was a majesty somewhat tempered by colonial conditions, as it was in Lower Canada. There too authorities sought to use the majesty of courtrooms, robes, and wigs to impress the populace with British justice, but the reality all too often involved stinking courthouse privies, ill-heated courtrooms, and jurors deliberating in alehouses.[19] As discussed below, the NSSC judges often arrived late, bedraggled, and in bad humour, and for much of this period held court in relatively makeshift facilities. Before 1810 few counties had built courthouses, and court might be held in the market building, a shop, or a private home.[20] Until 1816, when Antigonish built its own courthouse, court was held in the Presbyterian church, with the nearby kitchen of one Mr. Symonds used as a jury room and the school house used as a retiring room for the grand jury. Even these arrangements were relatively luxurious compared to those at Pictou, where the jury could only retire to a nearby field (in the summer at least) to consider its verdicts. The first generation of county courthouses, constructed mainly in the 1810s and 1820s, could not have been terribly impressive; almost all had jails attached, and all but a few were wooden buildings already in disrepair twenty years later.[21] Many of these were torn down (or had burned down) by the 1850s and 1860s, at which time they were replaced by much more solid and architecturally ambitious structures, a number of which are still used as courthouses today.

Shifting the focus to the local communities themselves reveals plenty of evidence that the Supreme Court visits were seen as desirable and beneficial. They were in part, of course, simply a public service, the Court's presence in a particular county or district meaning that litigants did not need to travel either to Halifax or a distant county seat to pursue their cases. It also meant economic activity, work for lawyers, and fees for those who provided lodgings not just for the judges but for their accompanying retinue of lawyers and clerks, and for the magistrates, jurors, litigants, and witnesses who came to town. And it was an occasion for social and recreational events made possible by the presence of people from outlying areas. In 1849 Thomas Chandler Haliburton, himself successively a divisional Chief Justice of the ICCP and a Judge of the NSSC, wrote that court sessions were the centre of attraction for the whole county. The vicinity of the courthouse was a sort of fair, where people assembled to transact business or to amuse themselves. Horse-swapping or racing, wrestling and boxing, smoking and drinking, sales or auctions, and games of various kinds occupied the noisy and not always sober crowd.[22] When a man was killed by a runaway horse during a horse race in Windsor in 1841, his death was witnessed by a large crowd of "persons from all parts of Hants ... who were called to Windsor to attend the business of the Supreme Court."[23]

Communities also gained prestige from their inclusion on the circuit. As it became apparent that the declining town of Shelburne was being outstripped as the principal centre of the county by Yarmouth, changing the location was mooted—an alteration that would "mortify the pride of poor Shelburne."[24] Four years later, when the choleric Judge James Stewart fulminated against having had to travel to Shelburne in 1829, by then a town "without inhabitants, without money, and of course, without Law," he also recognized that removal from the circuit was not possible because the assemblymen for the area would resist strenuously.[25]

The circuit's desirability can be gauged from lobbying for inclusion on the itinerary and from the less frequent disputes over where in a county the Court should sit. In 1826, for example, the inhabitants of Guysborough petitioned for a meeting of the Court in the town. The Sydney County circuit went only to Antigonish (then named Dorchester), some thirty-four miles away.[26] The petition was unsuccessful, but Guysborough got its court in the wholesale reform of 1834, discussed later. Similarly, in 1839 the inhabitants of Digby lobbied successfully for a second meeting of the Court in their town.[27] As well as pressing for additional locations, some communities asked for the Court to be moved within the county.[28] The most long-drawn battle over location within a county was that between the inhabitants of Amherst and River Philip in Cumberland. The Cumberland circuit had met at Amherst from 1775, but this was changed to "some suitable place near the bridge at Duncan's, on the River Philip" in 1816. This turned out to be River Philip (now Port Philip), on the coast of the Northumberland Strait. Fourteen years of petitioning ensued, from both sides, before the Court was moved back to Amherst in 1830, and lobbying continued after that for a couple of years.[29]

Against this evidence that communities saw the circuit as desirable there are some contrary indications that suggest it had its drawbacks also. Lobbying to change the court dates was common, inhabitants frequently complaining that their timing caused inconvenience to local economies. This problem was exacerbated by the fact that litigants, jurors, and witnesses might be required to attend not just the Supreme Court but also the sittings of the ICCP and sessions for the county. Typical is a petition from Pictou County in the late 1830s, asking to alter the timing of the circuit because of the "great and wasteful drawbacks" consequent on "attending on the Supreme and Inferior Courts four times in each year."[30] Inhabitants — especially those from rural areas who lived many miles from the county courthouse — also complained about being called for jury duty, which entailed both time away from gainful pursuits and expensive and difficult travelling on the colony's often rudimentary roads.[31]

More fundamentally, it is clear that though litigants in some places welcomed the chance to take their cases to a higher tribunal, leading to full dockets and long, busy days for the judges on their short stays in each community, elsewhere there was a marked preference for the county-level ICCPs.[32] These courts had an almost co-extensive civil jurisdiction with the NSSC and were manned by local JPs with no legal training, although from 1823-24 all county benches were presided over by a legally trained "first justice."[33] Judges often complained of arriving to find a near empty docket, making the circuit "a useless pursuit," as Stewart said of Shelburne in 1829.[34] Cape Breton Island was also notorious for light dockets. Stewart, in one of his common outbursts against having to travel there (discussed in more detail later), complained in 1826 that when the judges arrived "not a cause, civil or criminal, may require their attendance."[35] Two years earlier there had been "very little business in either Sydney or Arichat."[36] When cataloguing the hard work he had put in as Cape Breton ICCP Chief Justice from 1823 until his post was abolished in 1841, John George Marshall asserted that "nearly all the Civil Actions were brought and prosecuted in that Court [the ICCP]" and, indeed, that in one seven-year period only one civil suit was brought in the NSSC in Cape Breton.[37]

This anecdotal evidence of preference for the ICCP in some areas is supported by two Assembly investigations in the 1830s, part of the long-running debate on reform of the judicial system that culminated in the abolition of the ICCPs in 1841. Reports presented in 1838 and 1841 made it clear that the court system as a whole was underused. Between 1832 and 1836 there was an annual average of only 43 civil trials on circuit in all counties, exclusive of Halifax and Cape Breton Island, whereas the ICCPs conducted 37 trials a year. In 1838 and 1839, there were 210 civil trials in all the hinterland counties and 45 in Halifax. All of the Halifax trials took place in the NSSC, but of the 210 other suits nearly half—106—were tried on circuit, the other half in the county ICCPs. As importantly, the relative popularity of each court was not evenly distributed across the colony. Some counties, such as Guysborough and the Cape Breton Island counties of Cape Breton, Richmond, and Inverness, saw much more litigation in the ICCP, whereas others, such as Cumberland and Hants, had residents who preferred to litigate in the NSSC on circuit.[38]

The debates over judicial reform that animated the Assembly throughout the 1830s similarly reveal ambivalence about the circuit in some communities. The years immediately prior to the 1841 abolition of the ICCPs saw a broad consensus on the need to do something to reduce the cost of the judicial system by eliminating some judicial posts, but no clear agreement on how to do that. Some legislators wanted to see the ICCPs abolished, some to reduce the number of NSSC sittings on the circuit (which would allow a reduction in the number of NSSC judges). In 1835, for example, one member for Cumberland, Alexander Stewart, presented petitions asking for a reduction in the number of ICCP sittings, whereas another member from the county, James Morse of Amherst Township, presented other petitions for the abolition of the fall circuit. Neither proposal was accepted.[39]

Thus the picture is complicated. In some areas, litigants clearly preferred the NSSC, perhaps expressing a preference for the higher "quality" of adjudication they could get from the colony's legal elite, whereas others opted for a hearing before local men. Explanations of the phenomena are not easy to find. We should be wary of a simple dichotomy between professional and lay judges; the very fact that after 1823-24 the ICCPs were presided over by trained judges may have made them popular. The colony's best-known legal author, Beamish Murdoch, who believed that the division system had improved the quality of adjudication in the ICCPs, had no doubt that it had also led people "to withdraw the greater part of the business from the higher to the lower court."[40] Cost must have been a factor for some; it was considerably cheaper to go to the ICCP. As stated in an amendment moved by Lawrence Doyle to an 1836

Bill that would have eliminated one of the ICCP sessions in Cumberland, such a change "has a tendency to increase the Expenses of Law by transferring the business to the Supreme Court."[41] Doyle represented Arichat Township, on Cape Breton Island. Cost was generally a concern of many reformers and country members of the Assembly — often one and the same — who fought hard to eliminate the fees taken by the NSSC judges on circuit, succeeding in 1838.[42]

Cost alone does not explain litigants' preferences, however, nor is it likely that the class status of litigants or the type of action taken to court was generally responsible for the choice of venue. All of these factors applied throughout the colony, and as we have seen, use of the courts varied substantially by locality. There were other benefits to local justice. The Doyle amendment noted earlier also mentioned another reason some people preferred the ICCP — fewer ICCP sessions would "concentrate in the Town of Halifax much of the business which could more conveniently be done in the County."[43] He was perhaps referring to a preference for local lawyers to get the business and for local men to have a say in disputes about their neighbours. The divisional chief justices may have known the law, but there is evidence that the laymen they sat with were not mere cyphers.[44] Again, however, there is no evidence that local judges were necessarily better in one place than another.

The best explanation for why some litigants preferred the ICCPs to the NSSC on circuit is geographical. The ICCP was clearly the preferred forum in counties far away from Halifax, such as Guysborough and the counties of Cape Breton Island, and in those closer but to which travel was very difficult, such as Lunenburg and Queens on the south shore. Conversely litigants used the NSSC more when they lived closer to Halifax and/or in places through which the itinerant judges enjoyed better travelling conditions — such as Cumberland, Annapolis, Kings, and Colchester (as both a district of Halifax County and a county in its own right after 1835). Perhaps there was more distrust of outsiders in the more remote locales, or perhaps the NSSC was seen as an unpredictable forum when furthest away from Halifax. The judges sometimes arrived late or did not get there at all, and, as we shall see below, they not infrequently arrived tired, angry, and irritable at the privations of the journey.[45]

Not surprisingly the abolition of the ICCPs in 1841 meant much more work for the NSSC on circuit. William Blowers Bliss experienced the change immediately, finding an unusually large amount of business before him on the south shore summer circuit of 1841, and within a year the judges asserted that "[o]ur duties have of late been much increased ... by the abolition of the Inferior Court."[46] A decade later the eastern circuit involved "four weeks in succession and 8 or 9 hours in Court every day."[47] Yet even after the abolition of the ICCPs there were still periods of light dockets, caused not by curial competition but by a lack of business. In 1850 Bliss held a "very short court" at Digby in which he "did nothing." In the later 1850s there was again very little work for the Court at Shelburne, "this dead and abandoned place of the old American Loyalists."[48]

THE JUDGES AND THE CIRCUITS

Nobody was more interested in the circuits, of course, than the judges themselves. There were five of them to do circuits from 1816, four between 1836 and 1840, and five after 1841.[49] They all complained a lot about their workload and the difficulties of travelling. There is no question that the requirement to travel the circuit could be an onerous one, as was also the case with the US Supreme Court judges in this period.[50] James Stewart's circuit workload for the fourteen years in which he travelled them, 1816-29, averaged about fifty days a year.[51] In the late 1830s William Blowers Bliss did fifty-six days a year. After the abolition of the ICCPs Bliss did sixty-seven a year from 1841 to 1847, while his new colleague T.C. Haliburton, appointed in 1841, averaged eighty-three. In 1847 Haliburton put in a full 114 days or almost four months. In 1850 four of the Court's five Judges, Edmund Dodd, William Desbarres, Bliss, and T.C. Haliburton, did a total of 330 days. And all this had to be undertaken in the spring, between the late-May end of Easter Term in Halifax and the beginning of Trinity in July, and in the late summer and early fall, before Michaelmas Term convened in late October. Complaints about having to put in this kind of work were common. T.C. Haliburton called the circuits "severe labour," and Bliss, who often found himself bored, "cheated away many a weary mile on my lonely Circuits by a recurrence to my own compositions."[52]

These figures alone do not tell the whole story. Another problem for some of the judges was that the workload was unevenly, sometimes very unevenly, distributed. Although there is some evidence that the puisne judges could act collegially in trying to divide the work, ultimately circuits were allocated by seniority, which always meant that the chief justice did least and the more junior judges more.[53] Between 1836 and 1840, for example, Chief Justice Halliburton and Lewis Martin Wilkins Senior (appointed in 1816) did twenty-eight and twenty-five days a year, respectively, while William Hill and Bliss, appointed in 1833 and 1834 respectively, did sixty-three and fifty-six. This pattern holds true throughout the period covered by this chapter. In some respects, this system made sense — circuit travel could be arduous, and the more senior judges were often literally very senior and not up to its rigours. The Associate Circuit Judge Peleg Wiswall, for example, was frequently too infirm to do more than visit Annapolis and Horton, stations close to his Digby home, after 1833.[54] He managed only nine days of circuit work the year before his death in 1836. The aging Lewis Wilkins Senior, who had done seventy to eighty days a year in the 1820s, was down to an average of twenty-five by the later 1830s, and did not ride the circuit at all in his final five years on the Court prior to his death in 1848.

Age certainly affected the ability to travel of the two Chief Justices whose tenure covers the entire period of this chapter — Sampson Salter Blowers, Chief Justice from 1797 until 1833, and Brenton Halliburton, 1833-60 — and they also took full advantage of their status. Blowers claimed no circuit expenses at all from 1807 until his retirement in 1833 at the age of ninety. He did do the spring Court at Windsor — an easy journey — on a number of occasions but never went further than that, and he may have thought it unnecessary to ask for expenses because he spent his summers at his Windsor farm in any event.[55] Halliburton did a good deal of circuit work until the late 1840s, but practically nothing after 1851 until his death in 1860. He was not shy about his right to rest on his laurels. In 1833, the year he became chief, he cheerfully agreed to take on the onerous Cape Breton circuit but noted that he intended "to attend the Circuit Courts as frequently as I can now in order that I may remain home with a better grace when I shall feel it necessary to do so."[56]

Before 1834 the judicial workload problem was even greater, because of a rule that required two judges to travel each circuit.[57] Its effect can be seen from the fact that between 1830 and 1833 the number of "man-days" put in by the four judges who actually did the circuits averaged 224 a year, but this dropped to 178 for the 1834-39 period. It took a decade or so of intense lobbying by the judges, supported by their friends on the Council, to have the two-judge rule changed. The 1834 Act that affected this originated in Council, evoked much heated debate, and passed the Assembly only on the speaker's tie-breaking vote.[58] The opposition to changing the two-judge rule was symptomatic of the strong anti-judicial sentiment in the Assembly in the 1830s. Reformers and country members objected to the cost of the judicial establishment generally, to the fees collected by the judges, and to their political influence, especially the presence of the chief justice on the Council. In this atmosphere some assemblymen would oppose anything put forward to lighten the workload of the judges. Others took the view that if they had to pay for what they saw as a bloated judicial establishment (four NSSC judges, one associate circuit judge, one master of the rolls, four divisional chief justices of the ICCPs), they should get good service. They argued that a one-judge circuit would concentrate too much power in the hands of one man, and that, should the judge become sick during his journey, communities with an annual circuit would be deprived of any visit for that year. Excessive delay would be the result, or excessive expense caused by having to litigate in Halifax.

Two factors probably persuaded some assemblymen to vote for the Bill. One was the argument that, if the circuits were reduced to one judge, the number of judges could be reduced and the expense of a salary saved. The other was the sense that the judges worked hard to evade the rule in any event. If assemblymen believed the law was being deliberately evaded, the extensive correspondence of Peleg Wiswall with his colleagues confirms this. The statute stipulating two judges had an escape clause — that so long as two judges set out, only one was needed to complete the circuit if the other could not continue due to "sickness or unavoidable accident."[59] There were certainly occasions on which this happened legitimately. But the judges were frustrated with what James Stewart called "our foolish law," which required that "a judge must not be sick or disabled until after the commencement of the circuit."[60] They wanted to be too sick to go beforehand. Thus they planned single-judge circuits that formally complied with the rule. In 1828, for example, they agreed that Blowers and Stewart were to take the western spring circuit although they knew that "[t]he Chief's health will not admit of his going beyond Windsor" and thus Stewart would have to carry on alone. With Halliburton in the United States, Wilkins and Wiswall were left to travel east. Nobody, least of all Wilkins, thought Wiswall was up to it, but Wilkins thought it important that he make a formal attempt: "[I]n my opinion," he said, "if you go from your house to the wharf it is a setting out under the law and then in the most scrupulous construction of the Act all will be right."[61] On another occasion, he arranged to meet Wiswall at Pictou, but then advised him that if he did not want to make the whole journey, "all you have to do when you reach Horton is not to be *quite so well.*"[62] That the judges were quite willing to flout the law may have persuaded some assemblymen that they might as well give up their cherished two-judge rule. Moreover, the fact is that the Court was in a difficult position when one of the five judges was absent from the colony and another too old and frail to travel. Four judges was the minimum required to do the circuits. The other solution to the problem—appointing more judges—was even more unpalatable to reformers.

The other major issue for the judges was travelling conditions, which never ceased to be a matter of complaint. Some of this was certainly justified. At the beginning of our period there were only about 150 miles of the network of so-called great roads, running from Halifax to Annapolis and Halifax to Truro. But even these were of stone and gravel, uncomfortable to travel at the best of times and occasionally practically impassable. They were traversable only by horseback and crude wagons. Stagecoaches could not operate on them at all until the late 1820s, and in the 1840s the stagecoach journey from Halifax to Annapolis along the Great Western still took three days. In the early nineteenth century it had taken three days also to get to Pictou; with the introduction of a stagecoach from 1829 on the "Great Eastern," it took a mere seventeen hours. By 1850 there were about a thousand miles of great road linking Halifax with the major centres of Windsor, Truro, Amherst, Annapolis, Yarmouth, and Pictou, but they were still susceptible to damage and poor drainage.[63]

In fact, despite the primitive state of the roads, the eastern and western circuits were actually not that bad, especially the latter. There is plenty of evidence that at times they permitted a pleasant summer sojourn in the countryside. William Blowers Bliss took his wife and eldest daughter with him to Horton in 1831, and he thought they "both derived some benefit from the excursion." In 1818 James Stewart started out for Antigonish, where the Court was scheduled to meet on the first Tuesday in September, early enough in August that "I may have ... time to get there in comfort" even though it was a "rough circuit." It could not in truth have been that rough, for his wife, a friend named Mrs. Black, and two of Mrs. Black's children were going as well, "so that we shall travel with Society around us."[64]

The real problem with the circuits was what Bliss called their "striking inequality."[65] In this respect the Nova Scotia circuits resembled those of the US Supreme Court, which varied greatly in distance and difficulty. The third circuit, encompassing Pennsylvania and New Jersey, was easiest, the seventh — Kentucky, Ohio, and Tennessee — much more difficult.[66] In Nova Scotia the south shore and the Cape Breton run received the lion's share of the criticism. Judges still rode horseback on the south shore circuit in the 1830s. Lewis Wilkins was twice injured from long days in the saddle, getting a "pain in the knee" in 1831 and a presumably more embarrassing "injury in his scrotum" in 1824.[67] James Stewart was wont to refer to the south shore circuit as "the vile shore circuit."[68] In 1839 Bliss complained after going all the way to Shelburne and back in a cart that he was "burnt fly bitten jolted to a jelly and sore and weary, for the road, part of the way at least, is scarcely navigable."[69]

Travel conditions were hardest on the Cape Breton circuit. Indeed problems with extending the circuit to the island after its annexation in 1820 were anticipated, both by the judges and the islanders themselves. The former's attitude was captured by Stewart, who saw the bill extending the circuit as giving "a vast increase of labour, expense and peril to us unfortunate Judges."[70] For their part, Cape Bretoners would rather have had their own Supreme Court judge, but the Council rejected a request to that effect and instead introduced the divisional chief justice system on the island, a year before it was established for the mainland.[71]

Experience bore out Stewart's worries about "labour, expense, and peril." Until 1830 the judges went overland all the way, on very poor roads, little more than tracks. Before making the trip in 1823 Wilkins noted that he and his colleague Peleg Wiswall "should allow ourselves at least 15 days to perform the journey"; he instructed Wiswall to "bring a good wagon as the road is poor and the way very bad."[72] From 1830 the Assembly made an annual grant of £40 for the judges to be conveyed to Sydney by sea, but they still had to travel within the island by rough track or lake boat and to return from Arichat overland.[73] Brenton Halliburton claimed that in the 1820s he "frequently passed whole nights in an open boat on the Bras D'or Lakes, in my endeavour to reach the places where the Court was to be opened at the time appointed by law."[74] The 1841 *Judiciary Act* provided that the Lieutenant-Governor could "procure such necessary and comfortable conveyances ... as he shall think fit and proper" for the circuit, but the judges were not happy with the vessel provided.[75] A year later all five of them importuned the Lieutenant-Governor for better travelling arrangements: the roads, they said, were such that one could travel only on horseback, and the journey was a total of 250 miles "with scarcely a House in which the most wretched accommodation can be obtained, or even a shelter for the night." Overall, the journey "is one of much suffering and exposure, to which from many causes, we are quite unequal."[76]

The judges' comments on the Cape Breton circuit reflected these difficulties. James Stewart went there in the first year it was on the circuit and then stated that "I would make any sacrifice pecuniary or otherwise rather than undertake a Circuit beyond the confines of Antigonish." In 1829 the aging Stewart—he was sixty-four and would die the following year—told Wiswall that the Cape Breton circuit would "always be out of the question" for him.[77] Even before he was appointed to the bench, but was expecting it, Bliss said that "there is nothing that affrights me more than the prospect of a long lonely circuit to the Eastward of this Province and to Cape Breton." Brenton Halliburton, who did the circuit three times in its first four years, and on many other occasions in the 1820s, was scathing about it: "I by no means wish to repeat my visit to that Island, oftener than my tour of duty calls upon me to do so."[78]

The antipathy to travelling to the island spilled over into general denunciations of everything to do with it. Cape Breton was "a vile little island," a "waspish island that frets all of us," "a devil of a place"—all this from Stewart.[79] More than once the judges expressed the view that, as Halliburton put it, "I wish the malcontents had their own Island again with all my heart."[80] Although the roads were gradually improved and the judges made increasing use of steamers, they continued in their dislike of the circuit. Nobody more wholeheartedly supported some islanders' attempts in the 1840s to have the 1820 annexation declared illegal. As Bliss told his brother Henry, an English lawyer and counsel for the Cape Breton separatists, "I wish you success with all my heart, for I desire most earnestly never again to go to that Island."[81]

LAWYERS ON CIRCUIT

For Bliss, as for most of the judges, circuit travel had been part of their professional lives from their early years as lawyers. Before about 1820, when there were very few lawyers outside Halifax, travelling the circuit was an ideal way of getting new clients. Afterward, as the number of lawyers grew rapidly and every county settlement of any size welcomed at least one lawyer, there was less need for metropolitan lawyers to service the circuit and more competition among those who did.[82] Harry King, a young lawyer just getting established in Windsor, noted when the Court arrived in 1830 that the town was "swarming with lawyers, and I fear those who come from afar to share our moderate fees will return empty away."[83] Bliss' own experience as a circuit lawyer had been frustrating, as he wrote resignedly to his brother Henry in 1824: "[T]he circuit empties the purse instead of replenishing it."[84] The main benefit was "a pleasant ride and a breath of fresh air." By 1829, however, a note of pride crept in as he related to Henry his experience in prosecuting nine cases at Annapolis, including trials for rape, burglary, and murder: "I am, what would be called in England ... the leader of our circuit, and generally get a fee of some kind in most of the causes which are tried. I am the more pleased at this because it gives me practice and this is essential to give confidence and facility in speaking, and tact and skill in the management of a cause."[85] Persistence at the circuits did have some benefits, then: the possibility of attracting prosecutorial and other fees and practice at presenting cases. But in 1831 Bliss returned to the theme of poverty while on the western circuit: "[L]ittle business and less pay to be divided among nearly a dozen, can now hold not much of a pecuniary inducement."[86] Being a "leader" did not help if there were no cases set down for trial, as often happened.[87]

Some lawyers, however, seem to have done very well on the circuit. William Young, who travelled the eastern circuit regularly from 1829 until at least 1842, often recorded net profits of £50 and £60 from the two-week trip; his 1841 excursion brought in £177.[88]

Bliss' rather bleak view of the circuit lawyer's life was probably shaped by his experience in England, where the financial rewards for successful barristers were more attractive and the nature of the work more "elevated" owing to the division of labour between attorneys and barristers. An English barrister would have disdained the constant "scribbling" (drafting documents) that was an essential part of the North American lawyer's daily grind, and Bliss duly reported to his brother that "I shall never feel inclined to kill myself with scribbling—and no one pays here for any other services."[89] But it is possible that William Bliss emphasized the negative in letters to his brother, himself a barrister in England, in order to cater to Henry's snobbish tendencies. A much more positive account of the same circuit travelled by Bliss can be found in Harry King's letters to his fiancée Halli Fraser. When the western circuit visited Windsor in May 1830 King revelled in the camaraderie: "Never was seen a more jovial convivial mess. I have dined with them every day since yesterday week except when they dined with us. And I assure you our dinner was very nicely prepared and of the best materials fish flesh & fowle in abundance ... The party was a very gay one and it was about 4 o'clock when we left the tables [Court not having ended until 9:00 p.m.]."[90] When he followed the circuit to Horton the next week, however, his enthusiasm had dimmed somewhat: "Bliss & Lewis Wilkins were pleasant enough when I got them together—but the business of the court was so great that we never sat down to dinner till 8 o'clock and then we were all tired of sitting in court all day listening to dry details of evidence."[91] King always enjoyed the hospitality in Lunenburg, where he was "received by my brethren very cordially so much that it is well worth my while to frequent that Circuit." He boasted to Halli that he had gone to four balls in the five nights he spent in the town.[92] In general King praised the "delightful ... harmony that exists among the members of the profession on circuit," but occasionally some lawyers did not fit in. Whether this resulted in actual ostracism or just occasional rudeness and teasing is not clear. When on the western circuit in 1831, King remarked that "there was only one among us that we did not like & that was lawyer Hall of Kentville. Larry Doyle made some verses upon him & the other practitioners at Horton ... in which he designates them as Hortontotts—by no means an inaccurate appellation."[93]

CONCLUSION

The period from the end of the Napoleonic Wars until the achievement of responsible government in Nova Scotia would often be looked at in retrospect as a golden age. Politically the province was untroubled by the rebellions that shook the Canadas, even if the reform movement did begin to introduce new societal divisions. Culturally the "intellectual awakening of Nova Scotia" and the rapid growth of newspapers, voluntary associations, and social movements such as temperance introduced a new dynamic of "improvement" to provincial society. Economically Nova Scotia was characterized by "excessive expectations," but the elite who elaborated the societal myths tended to be insulated from the effects of such underperformance.[94] The period covered by this chapter, beginning with the completion of the mainland circuit system in 1816, was also the heyday of the NSSC on circuit. Although the Court was often not all that busy at particular locations, its mere presence was considered important, an affirmation that the town in question was still "on the map." Civil suits were much more common than criminal proceedings, and business that might be routine legally, such as the signing of default judgments, was important in economic terms to local residents. The circuits fit perfectly into the seasonal rhythms of a society highly dependent on agriculture and fishing. The arrival of the Court was rather like a fair, as jurors and witnesses from the surrounding area, and judges and lawyers from Halifax, came to town. Occasional instances of serious crime might lend an ominous air to some assizes, but most were untroubled in this respect.

Change began to come with the growth of the legal profession and the arrival of the railway in the 1850s and 1860s. With the rapid growth of a more decentralized bar, it made less sense for Halifax lawyers to accompany the Court to towns already well supplied with lawyers. And if a litigant wanted Halifax counsel the lawyer could arrive by train without staying on for the rest of the circuit. The rich collegial life described so enthusiastically by Harry King in the 1830s would become a subject for nostalgia by the 1880s.[95] With the decline of both grand and petit juries over the same period, part of a general lessening of lay participation at all levels of the justice system, the circuit became less a notable community event and more a government service whose impact was restricted to the immediate participants.[96] But for the first half of the nineteenth century at least, it was much more than that.

CHAPTER SEVEN

FAME AND INFAMY
Two Men of the Law in Colonial New Zealand

David V. Williams

THIS IS a book on comparative and contextual colonial legal history. My contribution to it is a brief tale of colonial legal history and biography from New Zealand. It concerns two prominent lawyers, both of whom served in a number of leading roles in the state legal system of the Colony of New Zealand, founded in 1840 and restyled the Dominion of New Zealand in 1907: Sir James Prendergast (1826-1921) and Sir John William Salmond (1862-1924). My research and writing interests focus on indigenous customary rights and how those rights are handled in the legal systems of British colonial states. During the latter half of the nineteenth century, following the signing of the Treaty of Waitangi in 1840, the Colony of New Zealand developed from a sparsely populated territory dominated politically, economically, and militarily by independent Maori social formations to a society dominated in all respects by European settlers — most of whom were British. Maori people were a steadily diminishing population until the turn of the twentieth century, by which time they were living marginalized lives in communities largely confined to remote rural regions. Despite their differing reputations today, both of the men of law whom I discuss had similarly strong views on the vital importance for the European settlers of the colony that its superior courts should firmly reject as non-justiciable any claims to land based on Maori customary rights. For both of them, it was imperative that matters of Native title should be left to the political conscience of the Crown and Parliament in determining what was just.

A Symposium in 2006 to Honour the "Famous" Man

One of these men — Sir John William Salmond — is considered "famous" (see Figure 7.1). He was praised and honoured in his lifetime, and, in August 2006, Victoria University of Wellington held a centennial

FIGURE 7.1 John William Salmond, 1924, attired as a Justice of the Supreme Court (now High Court) shortly before his death.

S.P. Andrew Collection, Alexander Turnbull Library, Wellington, NZ (F-18546-1/1)

symposium to recognize his contributions to law and scholarship not just in New Zealand but also throughout the common law world. The publicity for that symposium included these remarks:

> The Hon. John Salmond was a prestigious jurist and Judge who spent time at Victoria University Law School as a professor of law in 1906. The Salmond Symposium proposes to look into the finer details of Salmond's work. As a teacher of Law at Victoria University College he was very highly regarded by students and the profession alike for his personality and ability to express the complexities of the law.
>
> The Hon. John Salmond's prominence is by no means restricted to Victoria University or New Zealand. He was born in England, and is widely known there for his work, as well as in other Commonwealth countries. The Salmond Symposium is an opportunity for those in the legal arena today, to share their thoughts on the significant contribution which Salmond made as both a jurist and Judge.[1]

The Salmond Symposium, subtitled "Developing a New Zealand Jurisprudence," was held in the John Salmond Room at the Law School and was preceded by an inaugural public lecture in the Salmond Lecture Series presented by the noted legal historian Professor A.W. Brian Simpson, Charles F. and Edith J. Clyne Professor of Law at the University of Michigan. Simpson's lecture, which was well attended by members of the judiciary and other notables of New Zealand's capital city, discussed the influential intellectual contributions made to the common law world by Salmond's *First Principles of Jurisprudence,* which formed the basis for successive editions of *Salmond on Jurisprudence.*[2]

But No Symposium in 2007 for the "Infamous" Man

In my contribution to the 2006 Salmond Symposium, I playfully offered the possibility of a follow-up conference to be held in 2007: "This symposium will be followed in 2007 by a Prendergast Symposium in the Sir James Prendergast Room in the Law Faculty. The Symposium will be preceded by the Inaugural Prendergast Lecture to honour the best known of all of New Zealand's Chief Justices on the 130th anniversary of his judgment in that most well known of all New Zealand cases on the legal status of the Treaty of Waitangi: *Wiremu Parata v. Octavius Hadfield* (1877)."

I went on to offer a warning, though, that it may not always be such a good idea to name buildings or rooms after a famous colonial chief justice. By way of example, I mentioned the name-change of the building in which Professor John McLaren worked as Lansdowne Professor of Law at the Law Faculty of the University of Victoria, British Columbia.[3] The building was originally named after Sir Matthew Baillie Begbie, an exact contemporary of Prendergast. He served as Chief Justice of British Columbia from 1870 to 1894 and, like Prendergast, played a role in the executive and legislative branches of government in addition to his appointment to the judiciary. The *Dictionary of Canadian Biography Online* article concerning him mentions but discounts "the accusation frequently levelled at Begbie that he was hard, inflexible, and bloody-minded—a 'hanging judge.'"[4] In discussing UVic's buildings, the university website omits to mention any reasons for replacing the name Begbie. I rather suspect, though, that Begbie, like Prendergast, was "a man of his times" and that his reputation in modern times has been somewhat dented, perhaps unfairly in both instances, by current disquiet about the nature of colonial justice.

The purpose of this chapter is to problematize the historical treatment of Salmond (revered) and Prendergast (reviled). My argument will be that, in regard to the positions taken by both men on the issue of recognition for customary indigenous rights in the common law of New Zealand, Salmond is as deserving as Prendergast of opprobrium. Equally, Prendergast, although not exactly deserving of praise for his contributions on this topic, has been unjustifiably vilified by comparison. It is worth reporting that, though there was of course no Prendergast Symposium in 2007, there was indeed a symposium on the issue of recognition for customary indigenous rights in the New Zealand common law. The "In Good Faith" Symposium was held "in recognition of the 20th anniversary of the Court of Appeal's landmark decision interpreting the principles of the Treaty of Waitangi: *New Zealand Maori Council v. Attorney-General* [1987] 1 NZLR 641."[5] I can only speculate that judges, lawyers, and legal scholars are more comfortable discussing contemporary legal thinking on the legal rights of indigenous peoples than they are in coming to terms with colonial legal history denying the existence of such rights. Meanwhile, if one wants a lightning rod for expressing discontent about the colonial past, one need only invoke the "infamous" and "notorious" decision of Prendergast C.J. in *Wi Parata v. Bishop of Wellington.*[6]

SALMOND

Salmond was a solicitor in a small South Island rural town when he wrote his first academic publications. He became a professor of law at the University of South Australia, Adelaide, where the law library is named after him, then briefly at Victoria University of Wellington. He went on to become counsel to the Law Drafting Office, Solicitor-General for ten years, and then a Judge sitting in the Supreme Court (now restyled the High Court) and the Court of Appeal. His awards and honours include the Ames Prize in 1911 from the Harvard Law School for the most meritorious English-language legal publication in the preceding four years. This prize was awarded for his *Law of Torts*—which went on, under successive editors, to a twentieth edition published in 1992. He was awarded the Swiney Prize by the Royal Society of Arts in 1914 for his *Jurisprudence*—another well-read text that went on to a twelfth edition, published in 1968.[7] He is the subject of a captivating sympathetic biography by the legal scholar Alex Frame.[8]

For me, however, Salmond is "famous"—or "infamous"—because he drafted the Native Land Bill that was enacted by Parliament in 1909. Though its details have been much amended over the years, the 1909 Act remains the most important influence on the structure of the *Te Ture Whenua Maori Act 1993 (Maori Land Act 1993),* which continues to govern the administration of Maori freehold land under the auspices of the Maori Land Court. This Court was first established as the Native Land Court in 1864 and was renamed the Maori Land Court in 1947. Under the 1993 Act, the Court administers the remnants of Maori-owned land—about 5.6 percent of the land area of New Zealand. The 1909 Act ably codified the pre-existing legislative bedlam of laws on Native land. That was a considerable achievement. It also ensured that any alleged failure by the Crown properly to extinguish Maori customary title could not be relied upon by Maori litigants to impeach titles to land held by settlers or by the Crown under Crown grants and *Land Transfer Act* titles. Salmond's drafting took great trouble to ensure that the Crown's radical title to land, all freehold titles to land derived from the Crown, and, indeed, even Crown adverse possession rights after ten years, were immune from attack in any legal proceedings. If Maori customary title had been extinguished according to the Crown's version of the matter, then extinguished they were, and courts were to be deprived of any jurisdiction they might otherwise have to inquire into such matters. One can observe Salmond's precision and his drafting style — a good deal less prolix than that of his nineteenth-century predecessors — by reading the relevant provisions of the *Native Land Act 1909,* which were as follows:

84. Save as far as otherwise expressly provided in any other Act the Native customary title to land shall not be available or enforceable as against His Majesty the King by any proceedings in any Court or in any other manner.

85. A Proclamation by the Governor that any land vested in His Majesty the King is free from the Native customary title shall in all Courts and in all proceedings be accepted as conclusive proof of the fact so proclaimed.

86. No Crown grant, Crown lease, or other alienation or disposition of land by the Crown, whether before or after the commencement of this Act, shall in any Court or in any proceedings be questioned or invalidated or in any manner affected by reason of the fact that the Native customary title to that land has not been duly extinguished.

87. The Native customary title shall for all purposes be deemed or have been lawfully extinguished in respect in all land which during the period of ten years immediately preceding the commencement of this Act has been continuously in the possession of the Crown, whether through its tenants, or otherwise howsoever, as being Crown land free from the Native customary title.

100. In respect of any area of customary land the Governor may, at any time and for any reason which he thinks fit, by Order in Council prohibit the Native Land Court or the Appellate Court from the proceeding to ascertain the title to that land or to make a freehold order in respect thereof: and no freehold order made in breach of any such prohibition shall be of any force or effect.

PRENDERGAST

The other man—Sir James Prendergast—is considered "infamous" (see Figure 7.2). An English barrister who emigrated to New Zealand in 1862, Prendergast became Attorney General, at that time a non-political role equivalent to the contemporary role of the Solicitor General administering the Crown Law Office. He served as Attorney General for ten years

FIGURE 7.2 Sir James Prendergast, c. 1886
Alexander Turnbull Library, Wellington, NZ (F-79213-1/2)

from 1865 until he was appointed the third Chief Justice of New Zealand in 1875. He was the first Chief Justice to be appointed by a New Zealand ministry rather than by the Colonial Office, and he served in that role until 1899. In a long retirement devoted to his love of farming matters, he became the first President of the Manawatu and West Coast Agricultural and Pastoral Association. As Chief Justice, he presided over significant reforms in the structures of the judicature, in the procedural rules of the courts, in the consolidation of the criminal law, and in ordering the affairs of the legal profession.[9] Yet any praise of his long record of service as Attorney General and then as Chief Justice is usually somewhat muted because he is now so well known—"perhaps unfairly" in Peter Spiller's opinion—for his "notorious" dismissal of the Treaty of Waitangi as "a simple nullity" in the judgment reported in *Wi Parata v. Bishop of Wellington.*[10]

The 1877 dismissal of the Treaty of Waitangi is now considered a grossly offensive heresy in many quarters. The Treaty was signed in 1840 at the outset of British colonial rule by the chiefs of many Maori tribes at the instance of Lieutenant William Hobson, appointed in 1839 by the Colonial Office as Consul and Lieutenant-Governor to the British settlements in progress in New Zealand.[11] It has had a checkered history in the annals of New Zealand, but after 1987 it became conventional and (for a while in the 1990s) almost uncontroversial to state that the Treaty of Waitangi is "the founding document of New Zealand," "a constitutional document," "simply the most important document in New Zealand's history," "essential to the foundation of New Zealand" and "part of the fabric of New Zealand society," and "of the greatest constitutional importance to New Zealand."[12]

If doing Google searches on James Prendergast and John Salmond is the test, then it is abundantly clear that Prendergast is much, much better known to the world than Salmond. Googling for the words "a simple nullity" comes up with 160 entries in 0.17 seconds, and virtually every single one of them refers to the phrase used by Prendergast—almost always prefaced by the words "notorious" or "infamous." Prendergast's dismissal of the Treaty of Waitangi is noted in academic papers, blogs, political commentaries, Waitangi Tribunal reports, school-teaching resources, Canadian political science course materials, Maori tribal resource websites, and so on, even, indeed, the New Zealand government's own Treaty of Waitangi information website.[13]

One contemporary legal scholar, Grant Morris, has made a serious attempt to discuss Prendergast's wider contributions. Morris has written a Ph.D. thesis and papers on those contributions. The "simple nullity" statement, as Morris notes, has effectively taken on a life of its own and is cited — with polarizing effect — in the current debate on the place of the Treaty in modern New Zealand society. Morris argues, however, that the debate and commentary on the case has largely omitted to consider Prendergast as a man of his times and background and as an important part of a small legal community.[14] Morris' "man of his times" comment is echoed by J. Bassett and J.G.H. Hannan: "He was, rather, a man of his times in his inability to conceive of the Maori people as deserving the recognition accorded to 'civilised' nations."[15]

Generally, though, Prendergast is condemned from pillar to post by academic and non-academic alike. His most recent detailed slating by an academic is contained in several articles published in New Zealand academic law journals by a scholar from the School of Policy, University of Newcastle, Australia.[16]

John McLaren has written on rogue colonial judges and described the process for getting rid of a recalcitrant or maverick judge by "amoval" at the instance of the colonial executive, and in several exceptional cases by a petition from a colonial legislature to the Privy Council in London praying for a judge's removal from office.[17] Prendergast was never in danger of such treatment. An element of the transition in New Zealand from Crown colony status to a colony governed by responsible ministries was the enactment of the *Supreme Court Act 1858*. Prior to that, the chief justice and judges of the Supreme Court held their offices "during Her Majesty's pleasure" and would have been subject to "amoval." Section 3 of the 1858 Act stipulated, however, that judicial tenure should be *quamdiu se bene gesserint* (during good behaviour), in line with the tenure of English superior court judges as established by the *Act of Settlement 1701*.[18] Section 4 of the 1858 Act required an address from both Houses of the General Assembly to remove a judge from office, and Prendergast was never in danger of that disgrace. On the contrary, it is only in contemporary retrospect that Prendergast's views are considered offensive. In settler circles at the time, his views on Maori rights were not at all surprising and would have been widely supported. Indeed, as late as 1966, the Prendergast entry in *An Encyclopaedia of New Zealand,* published by a government department, made no mention at all of the *Wi Parata* case and offered this assessment of the man: "There have been better Chief Justices than Sir James Prendergast, but he brought to the Judiciary a forthrightness and disciplinarian attitude when the Bar badly needed guidance and direction. Scorning any attempt at well-rounded periods, or even figures of speech for display, he went straight to the point, frequently to the point of bluntness. His vigorous personality was reflected in many uncompromising judgments and opinions which, whether right or wrong, were always interesting."[19]

The lack of specific comment on *Wi Parata* in a 1966 biography, and the citation of that case without adverse comment by the Court of Appeal in a 1963 judgment on the extinguishment of Maori customary rights over foreshore land, seem very strange when compared with the plethora of adverse critical comment now associated with Prendergast's "a simple nullity" remark.[20] This dramatic sea change in the direction of legal discourse is no doubt useful evidence for Michael Belgrave's excellent analysis of the reinvention and remaking of the Treaty of Waitangi by lawyers and policy-makers that began in the 1970s and continues to the present.[21] In short, Prendergast was not always "infamous."

THE FACTUAL CONTEXT OF THE "NOTORIOUS" REMARK

In 1848 the *rangatira* (chiefs) of the Ngati Toa tribe yielded rights to a block of tribal customary land known as Witireia—the modern spelling is Whitireia—to the Bishop of New Zealand, the Right Reverend George Augustus Selwyn. This transaction would have been a *tuku rangatira* (chiefly gift reciprocal arrangement) or a *tuku whenua* (land gift reciprocal arrangement) in Maori customary law. Under such a law, the land would be returned to the rangatira and tribe from whom it had been granted when the uses for which it had originally been yielded ceased.[22] The purpose of the transaction was for the Anglican Church to establish a school for the education of Ngati Toa children. No school was ever established at Whitireia (which is at Porirua, near Wellington, the modern capital of New Zealand). In 1877 the principal rangatira of Ngati Toa, Wiremu Parata, instituted proceedings for declarations that the land remained Native land, and that it was now held by the Bishop of Wellington (as successor to the Bishop of New Zealand) in trust for the Ngati Toa tribe. A Crown grant had been issued in 1850 by the Governor, Sir George Grey, to the Bishop of New Zealand "for the education of children of Our subjects of all races, and of children of other poor and destitute persons, being inhabitants of Islands in the Pacific Ocean." Pursuant to this Crown grant, the Bishop owned the land under a trust to carry out the educational charitable purposes identified in the grant. The demurrer filed by the Attorney General, the second defendant, submitted that a grant from the Crown could not be declared void for a matter not appearing on the face of the grant. The plaintiff's action failed without counsel for the Bishop or for the Attorney General even being called on to argue the case.[23] The judgment of the Supreme Court (the superior court of first instance — renamed since 1980 as the High Court) was delivered by Prendergast C.J. for himself and Richmond J. The Court refused to go behind the Bishop's title, based as it was on a Crown grant issued by the Governor of the Colony, and refused to consider whether the customary entitlements of Ngati Toa had been properly and lawfully extinguished prior to that grant. The particularly "infamous" and "notorious" passage referred to the "existence of the pact known as the 'Treaty of Waitangi'" and then stated: "So far indeed as that instrument purported to cede the sovereignty — a matter with which we are not here directly concerned — it must be regarded as a simple nullity."[24]

There were other memorable quotations in the judgment that were of more relevance to the outcome of the case than the "infamous" *obiter dictum*. The *Native Rights Act 1865* had bestowed a jurisdiction on the Supreme Court that might have enabled Native persons to call in question any Crown title in reliance on Maori custom, but the Chief Justice avoided that "most alarming consequence" by asserting that "[t]he Act speaks further on of the 'Ancient Custom and Usage of the Maori people,' as if some such body of customary law did in reality exist. But a phrase in a statute cannot call what is non-existent into being."[25]

United States and New Zealand case law on the doctrine of Aboriginal title was discussed in the judgment, and the Chief Justice noted "the well-known legal incidents of a settlement planted by a civilised Power in the midst of uncivilised tribes." He concluded that, "[h]ad any body of law or custom, capable of being understood and administered by the Courts of a civilised country, been known to exist, the British Government would surely have provided for its recognition ... But in the case of primitive barbarians, the supreme executive Government must acquit itself, as best it may, of its obligation to respect native proprietary rights, and of necessity must be the sole arbiter of its own justice."[26]

On the facts of the case as pleaded, no school had been established at Whitireia because the tribe in the area had diminished greatly from about a thousand in 1848 to a total of some thirty or forty persons in 1877. The Court's view was that, if the establishment of a school was not practicable, the *cy près* doctrine should operate so that the property would be used to support some other charitable object similar to that originally intended by the donor. Under no circumstances whatsoever would the land revert to Ngati Toa, because "we are of opinion that in law the Crown is to be regarded as the donor, and not the Ngatitoa tribe."[27]

"Wiremu" Rather Than "Wi"

My fictitious promotion of a Prendergast Symposium in 2007, quoted earlier, refers to this 1877 case as *Wiremu Parata v. Octavius Hadfield*. The case, of course, was actually reported as *Wi Parata v. Bishop of Wellington* and is almost always referred to as the *Wi Parata* case. In the nineteenth century, many Maori who converted to Christianity as adults took a Christian baptismal name as their first name. That was the situation for the plaintiff. He was born Te Kakakura Parata and later baptized with the Christian name Wiremu (William). Wi is an affectionate diminutive of Wiremu — akin to Will or Bill in English usage. The oddity is that the law reporter at the time and everyone else since then has used the diminutive version of his name.[28]

And Who Was the Bishop of Wellington?

Most people do not know even the name of the Bishop who was the first defendant. The Bishop of Wellington in 1877 was the Right Reverend Octavius Hadfield, who had been a missionary to the Maori (including Parata himself) at Waikanae and Otaki in the lower North Island of New Zealand from 1840 to 1870 prior to his consecration as Bishop. He had been fiercely disliked by most European settlers in the 1860s, and he was contemptuously dismissed as the "political parson." In 1860 and 1861, Hadfield bravely and very publicly defended the right of Wiremu Kingi as rangatira of the Te Atiawa tribe to forbid the sale of tribal lands at Waitara to the Crown.[29] Kingi's defiance of the government led to the outbreak of war in Taranaki between the Crown and the Maori.[30] Hadfield, who had ministered to Kingi when the latter lived at Waikanae prior to returning to Waitara in 1848, wrote three pamphlets in which he criticized the New Zealand government and supported the Maori appeal to the Colonial Secretary in London. He staunchly defended this unpopular stand at the bar of the House of Representatives.[31] It may be observed, incidentally, that a major reason why no church school was ever built at Whitireia was that so many of the Taranaki allies of Ngati Toa had, like Kingi and his Te Atiawa people, left the Wellington area and returned to their ancestral homelands further north in Taranaki. It is worth mentioning these facts to emphasize that the episcopal defendant in the 1877 litigation certainly was not a man whose primary concerns were with the property of the church; nor was he exclusively concerned with the interests of the British settlers who comprised the majority of the adherents to his church. In any case, the Ngati Toa case was chiefly directed at the second defendant, the Attorney General, to impugn the government's actions in issuing a Crown grant over tribal land without the knowledge or consent of the tribe.

WHY IS PRENDERGAST TREATED AS A JUDICIAL PARIAH?

The odd aspect of the infamy of Prendergast's "simple nullity" phrase in relation to the Treaty of Waitangi is that, in my view, the phrase itself is a long way from being the most objectionable feature of his judgment. What I find truly objectionable in the *Wi Parata* judgment is the monistic legal positivism that rejects the very existence of Maori customary law as a system of law and relegates Aboriginal title rights to the moral, non-justiciable sphere of the executive government. In refusing to countenance the possibility of giving effect to the *Native Rights Act 1865,* the judgment warned, as noted earlier, of a "most alarming consequence" if that Act rendered any Crown title liable to be called into question. Prendergast C.J. stated: "The Act speaks ... of the 'Ancient Custom and Usage of the Maori people,' as if some such body of customary law did in reality exist. But a phrase in a statute cannot call what is non-existent into being." In his vigorous questioning of the plaintiff's counsel, Richmond J. expressed incredulity that Maori title should revive once a Crown grant had been issued: "What an unheard of thing it is that a Maori tribe should come in again by the Maori title, in consequence of the expiry of a trust contained in a Crown grant." And again: "We are asked to allow the native title to spring up again."[32] This outright dismissal of Maori custom as a source of law is a matter that I have pursued elsewhere in research and writings on the importance of legal pluralism within

Aotearoa New Zealand.[33] I have long advocated the importance of legal pluralism to understand the role of law in society, and I prefer the more far-reaching and open-ended version of legal pluralism that holds that the concept of law "does not necessarily depend on state recognition for its validity."[34] I have argued that the state legal system can and should accommodate Maori adherence to Maori customary law. The desire for that law to be respected, moreover, can be seen as a fundamental right of indigenous people and in my view flows from a proper interpretation of the Treaty of Waitangi itself.[35]

On the other hand, the precise context for the phrase "a simple nullity" in Prendergast's judgment is more complex than is usually allowed for, and it needs to be given more careful analysis than it usually receives. As noted earlier, the words leading into the phrase are: "[s]o far indeed as that instrument purported to cede sovereignty—a matter with which we are not here directly concerned—it must be regarded as a simple nullity."[36] Paradoxical as it may appear, I have heard that proposition advanced, in near enough to the same words, by some of the more radical Maori advocates of Maori sovereignty who insist that Te Tiriti o Waitangi—the original Maori text of the Treaty—is the only valid version and that it did *not* cede sovereignty to the British Crown. The cession of sovereignty "absolutely and without reservation" is abundantly clear in the English-language Treaty, but, it is said, in Article 1 of the original Treaty text, the giving of *"kawanatanga"* (governorship) can by no means be construed as a cession of sovereignty, and, moreover, the retention of *"tino rangatiratanga"* (unqualified authority) in Article 2 can be read as an affirmation of continuing Maori sovereignty.[37] This line of argument has been relied on by a significant number of Maori litigants in recent years, often advanced in conjunction with an assertion that the independent sovereignty of the Confederation of Chiefs declared in 1835, and arguably affirmed by the "rangatiratanga" guarantee of Te Tiriti o Waitangi, still subsists to the present. No court will accept the argument, of course, but that does not deter some Maori nationalists from continuing to rely on it. Paul McHugh has noted some twenty-one cases, mostly unreported, between 1994 and 2001 in which Maori litigants have challenged Crown sovereignty in respect of a wide range of issues and argued for the continued existence of an independent Maori sovereignty.[38]

In a sense, the Treaty as "a simple nullity" is not all that different from "the Treaty is a fraud"—the frequently shouted slogan of some Maori nationalist groups in the 1970s. It is abundantly obvious, of course, that

Prendergast C.J. did not have that view in mind in 1877. His position was that "nothing could exceed the anxiety displayed" by the British government "to infringe no just right of the aborigines," and he asserted that, regardless of the Treaty, the Crown owed a duty to act "as supreme protector of aborigines, of securing them against any infringement of their right of occupancy." In carrying out that protectorate obligation, the acts of the Crown "are not examinable by any Court."[39] Still, I am not quite sure why people are so upset with Prendergast's logic, unless they themselves accept that the Treaty indeed *was* a valid cession of the sovereignty of Maori tribes or nations to the British sovereign.

Moreover, though it derives from a rather different perspective, I would argue that the current legal orthodoxy of the Privy Council on the legal status of the Treaty of Waitangi is not all that far distant from continuing to categorize the Treaty as a simple nullity. The leading case, a 1941 Privy Council decision, insisted that the Treaty must be incorporated into municipal law in order for it to be cognizable in New Zealand courts: *Te Heuheu Tukino v. Aotea District Maori Land Board*.[40] If the Treaty can be accorded legal status in New Zealand law only by Parliament's incorporation of all or part of it into an act, then the Treaty in itself remains in essence a nullity in New Zealand law. This is so, even though, in an international law forum, Professor Roscoe Pound and other members of the Anglo-American Claims Tribunal in the 1925 case of *William Webster* did recognize the Treaty of Waitangi as an international treaty and, indeed, as a valid cession of sovereignty. That tribunal considered, but rejected, the claims of a United States citizen that his property rights in New Zealand, said to have been justly acquired from the Maori prior to 1840, were unjustly expropriated by the British Crown colony government after 1840.[41]

The reasoning in *Te Heuheu*, requiring statutory incorporation of the Treaty of Waitangi for it to have legal effect, was doubted in *obiter dicta* and in extra-curial comments by Cooke P. in the late 1980s. The then President of the New Zealand Court of Appeal (later ennobled as Lord Cooke of Thorndon when appointed a Lord of Appeal in the United Kingdom's House of Lords) observed of *Te Heuheu* that "by past standards it could have been called the leading case on the Treaty of Waitangi" and that it "represented wholly orthodox legal thinking, at any rate from a 1941 standpoint." He acknowledged that the Maori owners who lost the *Te Heuheu* appeal "had cause to feel a sense of injustice."[42] In 1994 the Privy Council actually reaffirmed the 1941 decision, disregarding

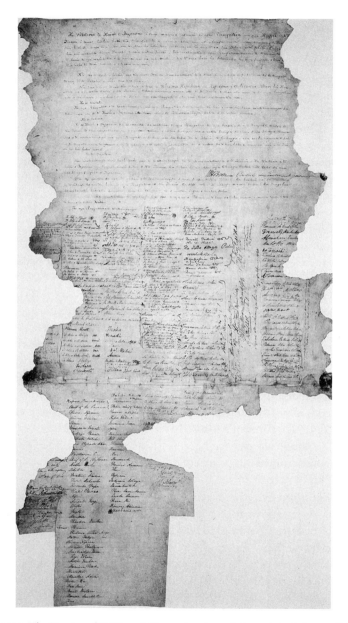

FIGURE 7.3 The Treaty of Waitangi. Reproduction of the original sheet of the Treaty, as signed at Waitangi in 1840, but in its current rather damaged condition. Archives New Zealand/Te Rua Mahara o te Kāwanatanga, Wellington Office, NZ (IA 9/9)

Cooke P.'s hints of his preference for the case to be overruled, and it remains "wholly orthodox legal thinking" to this day. The Privy Council did accept that the Treaty is "of the greatest constitutional importance to New Zealand," but its advice reaffirmed the necessity of statutory incorporation in order for the Treaty to have domestic law significance (see Figure 7.3).[43]

Rather than incorporate the Treaty itself into domestic law, Parliament has chosen on numerous occasions since 1975, and especially since 1986, to require that account should be taken of "the principles of the Treaty of Waitangi." Superior court judges since 1987 have creatively invented a number of "principles" based on good faith and partnership between the Crown and the Maori in attempting to interpret those words.[44] I would observe, though, that the texts and the context of the historical Treaty itself have been near to invisible in the crafting of those so-called principles of the Treaty. For the present, therefore, it would not be unfair to contemporary legal orthodoxy, in my opinion, to assert that it still treats the Treaty of Waitangi as "a simple nullity." If we are to cast stones at Prendergast for his 1877 views, we ought equally to deplore the almost total lack of consideration for the Treaty, especially the Maori text, Te Tiriti o Waitangi, in contemporary legal discourse as well.[45]

There are those, such as Mai Chen, who have argued that the Supreme Court, created in 2003 as the final appellate court for New Zealand upon the abolition of appeals to the Privy Council, might just possibly overrule *Te Heuheu* in the way that the Court of Appeal was prepared to overrule *In re Ninety Mile Beach* and *Wi Parata v. Bishop of Wellington* in the Marlborough Sounds case in 2003.[46] Rules of precedent would certainly allow that to be a possibility, but it would require something of a seismic shift in judicial thinking about New Zealand's constitutional norms for that possibility to come to fruition.

SO WHERE DID SALMOND STAND ON ALL THIS?

Salmond's position in 1909 seems nearly identical to that of Prendergast C.J. and Richmond J. in 1877. In a memorandum accompanying his draft of the Native Land Bill, Salmond wrote: "In its origin [the Treaty of Waitangi] was merely a moral claim, dependent on the goodwill of the Crown, and not recognisable or enforceable at law."[47]

In *Wi Parata,* Prendergast C.J. had put the matter in words to the same effect, but more bluntly and crudely (as a "man of his times" would, perhaps): "But in the case of primitive barbarians, the supreme executive Government must acquit itself, as best it may, of its obligation to respect native proprietary rights, and of necessity must be the sole arbiter of its own justice."[48]

Richmond J. (a man of the same times, but less blunt) wrote the judgment for a full bench of the Court of Appeal, including Prendergast C.J., in 1894 in *Nireaha Tamaki v. Baker*.[49] The 1894 litigation was one of a significant number of late nineteenth-century and early twentieth-century attempts by Maori litigants to challenge titles to land that had been acquired, they said, without proper extinguishment of pre-existing Maori customary rights. Richmond J. expressly affirmed the reasoning of *Wi Parata* in his short-shrift rejection of the argument that the courts had jurisdiction to consider such matters. "The plaintiff comes here," he wrote, "on a pure Maori title, and the case is within the direct authority of *Wi Parata v. Bishop of Wellington*." He went on: "The Crown is under a solemn engagement to observe strict justice in the matter [of Native territorial rights], but of necessity it must be left to the conscience of the Crown to determine what is justice. The security of all titles in the country depends on the maintenance of this principle."[50] That last sentence of Richmond's judgment was echoed by Salmond in his 1909 memorandum: "This Bill provides that the native customary rights shall not be enforceable by any legal proceedings either against the Crown or against grantees from the Crown — a principle which is essential to the security of the title of all Crown land and private land in the Dominion."[51]

Salmond went on to note that the purely moral nature of the Treaty in relation to the Crown had been doubted by the Privy Council in 1901 when reversing the Court of Appeal's *Tamaki* decision, but he added: "Whether by virtue of its legislative recognition [the Treaty] has now become a legal right enforceable against the Crown has never been decided, and was left an open question by the Privy Council in *Nireaha Tamaki v. Baker*."[52] It is hard to understand how Salmond arrived at that conclusion. The words used by Lord Davey in the Privy Council were as follows: "[It] was said in the case of *Wi Parata v. Bishop of Wellington*, which was followed by the Court of Appeal in this case, that there is no customary law of the Maoris of which the Courts of law can take cognizance. Their Lordships think that this argument goes too far, and that it is rather late in the day for such an argument to be addressed to a New Zealand Court. It does not seem possible to get rid of the express words of ss. 3 and 4 of the Native Rights Act, 1865."[53] The Court of

Appeal in 2003 had no difficulty in treating those remarks as an effective overruling of *Wi Parata,* but Salmond's position in 1909 was a very different one.[54] He was determined to characterize the Privy Council's advice as *dicta* only, thus leaving the issue of the Treaty's status following partial legislative recognition as an "open question." The importance of his restrictive distinguishing of *Tamaki* was that it enabled Salmond to affirm the continuing validity of the earlier Supreme Court decision in *Wi Parata:* "However this may be, it is settled that when land in New Zealand has once been granted by the Crown the validity of the title so obtained cannot be questioned on the ground that the antecedent Native customary title to that land had not been lawfully extinguished: *Wi Parata v. Bishop of Wellington.*"[55]

Salmond's starting point, of course, was the radical title of the Crown to all land in the Dominion. This is why his 1909 Bill in its definition section (section 2) — re-enacted in all acts based on it until 1993 — began from the position that "[c]ustomary land, since it has never been Crown-granted, belongs to the Crown." This is a legal proposition based on the radical title of the Crown that would doubtless have met with some astonishment if presented to chiefs at Waitangi in 1840 or at any time since then, and it is no longer the law.[56] Final appellate judicial committee for the British Empire though the Privy Council may have been, no hints of its *Tamaki* doubts about *Wi Parata* are to be detected in the privative clauses drafted by Salmond (set out at the beginning of this chapter as enacted in sections 84-87 and 100 of the *Native Land Act 1909*). Rather, Salmond's drafting was designed to embed firmly in statute law the important judicial doctrines espoused by Prendergast and Richmond in *Wi Parata.*

Of course, even if — contrary to his understanding of the Privy Council ruling — *Tamaki* could be said to have fully vindicated the entitlement of the Maori to assert title based on customary rights in ordinary court proceedings, Salmond knew that that would avail the Maori plaintiffs nothing. The supreme Diceyan pillar of the Westminster common law constitution — the colonial Crown-in-Parliament — had been extremely quick to assert its powers to pass retrospective legislation in 1901. As soon as the *Tamaki* Privy Council's decision became known in New Zealand, an Act was passed that emphatically reasserted the Crown's title to the particular block of land in issue in the litigation: it deemed the Native title to be fully extinguished, and it provided for payment of legal costs incurred by the "former owners" only on their discontinuance of the further legal proceedings that had been launched by Nireaha Tamaki to implement the Privy Council's decision.[57] More generally, a year later, section 2 of the *Land Title Protection Act 1902* declared that no Native Land Court order that had subsisted for over ten years could be called into question in any court. One Maori member of the House of Representatives, Hone Heke, complained bitterly, but to no avail, that this Act denied the Maori the right to bring cases to the Supreme Court and that this violation of due process was a breach of the third article of the Treaty of Waitangi.[58] A little later, further litigation initiated by the redoubtable and ever-persistent Nireaha Tamaki was explicitly discontinued, and future proceedings by him or on his behalf in relation to the land claimed by him to be Maori customary land were permanently barred.[59] That might be viewed these days as a sorry legislative record of retrospectively depriving a litigant of the fruits of his success in the final appellate court of the empire and then completely denying him due process in further litigation. How, then, did Salmond deal with concerns raised by a Maori member of the House of Representatives in 1909 about his privative clauses to prevent the courts inquiring into Maori customary title rights?

Apirana Ngata was a relatively young man in 1909. He had represented the Young Maori Party in Parliament since 1905 but was already very well known as the first Maori to graduate in law from the University of New Zealand and to be admitted to the bar. He went on to serve as a minister in several government ministries and as a Member of Parliament right through until 1943. In 1909 he had just been appointed a member of the Executive Council "representing the Native Race."[60] In that capacity, he played an advisory role in the drafting of the 1909 Bill, and he did raise concerns about the privative clauses. Salmond's personal explanation to Ngata of these clauses is quoted by Salmond's biographer, Alex Frame: "The intention is that when a dispute arises between Natives and the Crown as to the right to customary land, the dispute shall be settled by Parliament and not otherwise. The Native race will have nothing to fear from the decision of that tribunal, and to allow the matter to be fought out in the Law Courts would not, I think, be either in the public interest or in the interests of the Natives themselves."[61] However, the Maori minority of just four members, in a House of Representatives comprising eighty members, had little political leverage in 1909. None of the privative clauses queried by Ngata were modified in any way during the course of the debate and the enactment of Salmond's Bill.

Concluding Comment

What Salmond's drafting of the Native Land Bill 1909 achieved was a clarity of enactment to protect the Crown from any possible impeachment by Maori litigants of Crown-derived titles to land. Salmond consolidated the parliamentary nullification of the Privy Council outcome in *Tamaki* and drafted a generalized incorporation of the *Wi Parata* doctrines into New Zealand statute law. So Salmond's achievement was that, with crystal clarity, he dispelled any suggestion that the Treaty of Waitangi ought to be directly or indirectly incorporated into the law relating to Maori land. For Salmond, as for Prendergast, the legal mechanisms chosen by the Crown for extinguishing Maori customary rights were not to be matters for judges to consider. Salmond's avowed intent and purpose as counsel to the Law Drafting Office in 1909 was to incorporate the "infamous" *Wi Parata* judgment into the statute law of New Zealand. This is a historical fact that deserves to be better known than it is.

CHAPTER EIGHT

MOVING IN AN "ECCENTRIC ORBIT"

The Independence of Judge Algernon Sidney Montagu in Van Diemen's Land, 1833-47

Stefan Petrow

IN HIS comparative article on the rule of law in colonial New South Wales and Upper Canada between 1788 and 1840, John McLaren examined the role of an independent judiciary in preserving rights and "resisting corruption and arbitrariness."[1] Judges had fought hard for their independence during the constitutional struggles of the seventeenth century, and the principle had been enshrined in the *Act of Settlement 1701*.[2] Especially in New South Wales, McLaren argues, lieutenant-governors tended to ignore the rule of law, and this created tensions with the judiciary when a more English-style court system was introduced in the 1820s.[3] An adherent of English judicial traditions, Chief Justice Francis Forbes consciously kept himself "detached" from the executive and special interests and asserted the principle of "the supremacy of the law."[4] Although the independence of all judges can be influenced or compromised by the desire for high salaries, indebtedness, "bribes, pensions or promotion," English and colonial judges differed in at least one key respect.[5] Whereas English judges enjoyed life tenure subject to good behaviour and could be dismissed only by "a modified form of impeachment" (a vote to remove by both Houses of Parliament), colonial judges held office at the Crown's pleasure and "could be — and were — dismissed at will by the British government."[6] Those removed included John Walpole Willis in New South Wales in 1843, Benjamin Boothby in South Australia in 1867, and the subject of this chapter, Algernon Sidney Montagu, in the penal colony of Van Diemen's Land in 1847.[7]

Montagu's eccentric behaviour and independent mind attracted the attention of colonial newspapers. In January 1848, the *Hobart Town Courier*, commenting on the end of Montagu's judicial career, suggested that he "moved in an eccentric orbit." He sometimes "terrified by those motions," but "he occasionally delighted us by the brilliant light which he cast around his path. Fresh, vigorous, and original, his intellect always commanded respect, and not infrequently admiration." His mind possessed "a wild and vigorous caste, but he did not check its luxuriance."[8] The *Launceston Advertiser* thought eccentricity was "the leading and guiding principle" of Montagu's judicial proceedings and that eccentricity was "based upon a quick and ready talent — a clear perception of right and wrong, and ... a most powerful, deep and prevailing love of justice." As "a disciple" of Jeremy Bentham and Lord Campbell, Montagu was "a zealous reformer of the law's abuses — independent *almost* to a fault — no respecter of persons — and ... no worshipper of those who dwell in high places."[9]

These assessments capture the essence of Montagu's behaviour on the bench.[10] He was eccentric, which meant that he regularly deviated from what was usual or customary or expected of a judge. As the *Colonial Times* reflected, Montagu wished "to do everything differently to what any one else would do."[11] He was independent, which meant that he did what he thought was right based on his own interpretation of the law, but, a more negative attribute for a judge, he did not think of the consequences of his actions.[12] His impartiality was another strength, but he lost control and became petulant on occasions when his authority or dignity was challenged or from prejudices against certain individuals. His petulance was directed at suitors and their counsel as well as his only colleague, Chief Justice Sir John Pedder, and anyone who questioned or disagreed with his actions or directions.[13] He often vented his spleen at the press and government too. To preserve his independence, Montagu kept himself socially secluded and openly displayed "his own personal scorn towards the colonial race."[14] Despite his egregious behaviour and his tendency to get into debt, which opponents claimed impaired his independence, he ended his judicial career with the status of a martyr because colonists thought he had been illegally amoved by dictatorial Lieutenant-Governor William Denison for standing up for their rights.[15]

Montagu's career shows the fragility of judicial tenure in colonial societies when it conflicted with the political and economic objectives of government and challenged the power of the Lieutenant-Governor. We can sum up the situation thus. When Montagu supported government, his foibles, deficiencies, and even his indebtedness were overlooked or merely incurred reprimand; however, when he defied government, even when upholding the rule of law, he made himself dispensable. In what follows, I deal with his appointment as Attorney General and Puisne Judge. I then consider his stormy relations with the press, his propensity to impose severe sentences, his lack of respect for jury verdicts, his differences with Pedder, his disputes with executive government, and his indebtedness. I end by examining his amoval.

APPOINTMENTS AS ATTORNEY GENERAL AND PUISNE JUDGE

Algernon Montagu was born at Cambridge, England, in 1802.[16] His ancestors included many well-known lawyers, and his father, Basil Montagu, was a legal writer and a leader of the law reform movement in the early nineteenth century. Montagu was educated privately and was admitted to Gray's Inn in November 1817. He was called to the bar in February 1826. Despite his youth and limited legal experience, Montagu applied for the position of Attorney General in Van Diemen's Land. Patronage arising from his father's connections secured him the position, which he took up in October 1828. Although at first overwhelmed by the "arduous" work, Montagu won acclaim as Attorney General.[17] The *Colonial Times* especially approved of his honourable refusal to retain a private practice. He knew that he could not "serve two masters—either he must serve his country, or his private employers."[18] By deciding to serve his country, Montagu suffered financial loss. By not accepting private practice, he had little chance of becoming acquainted with "any Gentlemen at the Bar" and led an isolated life.[19]

Higher office became a possibility in 1830, when the colonists demanded a second judge because they thought it impolitic to leave the administration of justice in the hands of Chief Justice Pedder alone.[20] The *Colonial Times* criticized Pedder for his "want of decision."[21] Pedder felt the weight of responsibility in making decisions on his own, and a second judge would enable him to decide more quickly and save suitors from paying expensive legal fees. Although Lieutenant-Governor George Arthur and Pedder did not see the need for a second judge, the colonists prevailed and the new charter of justice provided for the appointment.[22] The first choice was Alexander Macduff Baxter, the Attorney General of New South Wales, but he proved to be a drunkard and insolvent, and was unacceptable to Arthur: he never assumed office.[23] Highly satisfied with his contribution as Attorney General, Arthur appointed Montagu as acting Puisne Judge until the Colonial Office confirmed the appointment.[24] Montagu was sworn in on 29 November 1833 under his new commission.

THE PRESS

A major source in assessing Montagu's judicial tenure is the newspapers. Many newspapers existed during the convict period, and they often commented on the actions of the government and the judges.[25] Sometimes newspaper comment was positive. For example, the *Colonist* thought Montagu's "independent character" made his appointment as Judge a popular one.[26] As Montagu had shown himself to be "a firm, honest, and determined" Attorney General, the *Colonial Times* was convinced that he would be "an independent, upright and humane Judge and that he will never forget to temper justice with mercy."[27] Early signs proved the *Colonial Times* to be right. At both Hobart Town and Launceston, Montagu dispensed justice "swiftly" with "energy and impartiality."[28] But soon newspapers were condemning Montagu's odd behaviour and severe sentences, as we shall see. Consequently, Montagu came to hold journalists and newspaper owners in low regard. In 1835 Montagu sentenced Gilbert Robertson, owner of the *True Colonist,* to twelve months' imprisonment and a £50 fine for publishing "a false, scandalous and seditious libel" on Captain John Montagu, the Colonial Secretary but not a relative. Claiming the colony was *"press ridden,"* Montagu declared that the "licentious and degraded state of the Press is one of the worst features in this Colony."[29] In January 1837 he denounced the press for publishing "anything likely to inflame the public mind" and bringing the Supreme Court and the administration of justice into "contempt."[30] He considered the reports not to be "impartial—they contain only one side of the question," whereas explanations from the bench were "invariably not reported at all."[31]

At times the press incurred Montagu's wrath for unfairly dragging his name before the public. One example occurred in 1841, when Gilbert Robertson successfully defended himself against a charge of libel by the Attorney General Edward Macdowell. During the case, Montagu reportedly said that he had tried "to live apart from strife and squabble, like a hermit" and condemned the editor of the *Courier* for mentioning him by name. The *Courier* took this charge lightly. It claimed the right to comment on the opinions and actions of judges where they had, as

Montagu often did, prostituted "the sacred seat of justice to personal feeling and animosity" and committed "illegal and capricious acts," which were "nothing short of an arbitrary and tyrannous exercise of power."[32]

SEVERE SENTENCES

As the *Courier* indicated, Montagu presided in a series of cases that threw doubt on his suitability for judicial office. The main point at issue was the severity of his sentences. When Montagu became a judge, he declared that he would "make the Supreme Court *dreaded*" and an "object of terror": he was true to his word.[33] Two cases stand out.

The Thomas Lewis Case

In 1833 Magistrate William Thomas Lyttleton convicted an assigned convict, Samuel Arnold, of cattle stealing and sentenced him to capital punishment.[34] After the trial and outside the courthouse, Thomas Lewis overheard Lyttleton say in the presence of three others that someone other than Arnold had been the offender, meaning Arnold's master and Lyttleton's fellow magistrate William Bryan. After being told of Lyttleton's allegation, Bryan asked his friend Lewis to challenge Lyttleton to a duel on his behalf. Lyttleton declined and asked the Attorney General Alfred Stephen to intervene. Bryan was one of Lieutenant-Governor Arthur's most implacable opponents, and the Lieutenant-Governor seized this opportunity to attack one of his circle. In 1834 Stephen prosecuted Lewis for attempting to incite Lyttleton to commit a breach of the peace by delivering a challenge to a duel.[35] Lewis defended himself. Montagu constantly interfered with Lewis' cross-examination of Lyttleton on his provocation of Bryan and fined Lewis £10 for casting aspersions on Stephen for being "the bearer or sender" of a similar challenge to Roderic O'Connor. After the military jury returned a guilty verdict, Montagu sentenced Lewis to eighteen months' imprisonment and fined him £150. Whether Montagu's behaviour and severe sentence were motivated by a desire to ingratiate himself with Arthur or whether he was truly disturbed by what he denounced as the intimidation of a magistrate remains open to conjecture, but he found himself at the centre of a legal storm. Lewis' friends, including Bryan, later "insulted" Montagu in the streets by calling him "a second Jeffreys," a reference to the bullying and over-bearing seventeenth-century English Judge.[36]

Lewis described Montagu's "arbitrary" and "oppressive" behaviour as "illegal and unconstitutional" and charged that he had deprived him of "a fair, open and impartial trial."[37] Lewis' charges were submitted to the Executive Council, the Lieutenant-Governor's "advisory body" on policy and constitutional matters.[38] It found the charges groundless, but on the advice of Pedder, a member of the Executive Council, recommended that Arthur use his discretion to reduce the sentence. Arthur was willing to grant some leeway to Lewis if he desisted from reflecting on Montagu's "integrity" or bringing "contempt upon the administration of justice." The Colonial Office sought advice from its law officers, who objected to Montagu's actions. Lewis had the "right" to ask questions in his own defence and "have all the circumstances fully disclosed." Lewis was entitled to show that he had not committed a crime and that his behaviour was "sanctioned by the example of persons holding the highest station in society." The Colonial Office felt that Lewis had been "unfairly tried" and "sentenced to a punishment of almost unexampled rigour." It rebuked Arthur for placing conditions on the remission of Lewis' sentence. Although Lewis might have demanded his release "in terms of undue warmth and of indecorous reproach" to Montagu, he had "a perfect right" to seek mitigation of his severe punishment. The Colonial Office directed that Arthur release Lewis from prison and remit or repay with interest the fines of £150 and £10.[39] Lewis later sought compensation, and after long discussion the Legislative Council settled on the amount of £2,068 6s. 8d., which was sanctioned by the Colonial Office.[40]

The press supported the Colonial Office. According to the *Colonist*, Montagu's "very extraordinary and unprecedented conduct" proved "the danger of entrusting the administration of justice into the hands of rash impetuous men, whose passions are not tempered down by years and experience."[41] As Lewis was "totally ignorant of the legal fashions of pleading and defence," the *Independent* thought that Montagu should have given him more latitude in court and that a small fine "would have answered the ends of Justice."[42] The *Colonial Times* agreed with four members of the Legislative Council that Montagu had been guilty of dereliction of duty and was unfit to hold judicial office. It called for "the spontaneous, loud, and eloquent voice of the people" to demand Montagu's recall.[43] This did not occur, but Montagu lost much public respect by his partisan and oppressive conduct in the Lewis case and was dubbed by the press "Mad Montagu."[44] However, his severity was not blunted.[45]

The Sidney Stephen Case

In December 1842 Pedder and Montagu removed leading barrister Sidney Stephen from the bar of Van Diemen's Land. Stephen had accepted a bill of exchange as payment for his professional services as a barrister and contacted the client directly instead of going through his Attorney Fisher. When Stephen attempted to obtain his payment in court, both Judges condemned his unprofessional behaviour. In passing judgment, Montagu spoke of the "honor, integrity, candour and unquestionable intelligence" that judges expected of barristers. But when judges found evidence of "trickery, in withholding facts, or in misstating circumstances ... all confidence [was] destroyed." Montagu warned that he would strike off the rolls any attorney who "took up an action for costs, or made himself a partisan for the purpose of annoyance or expense." As Stephen had indulged in "trickery, deception and falsehood" and "grossly unprofessional conduct," he "consigned" him to "a moral tomb" and invited him to "lift the lid if he can." One experienced but anonymous court reporter declared that he "never heard any thing so frightful. It was petrifying!" Although Stephen had notched up over twenty-five years of honourable practice, the Vandiemonian bar did not defend him. Stephen appealed to the New South Wales bar, which ruled that he was "entitled to the confidence of his professional brethren" and should be allowed to practise.[46]

Fortified by the support of the New South Wales bar, Stephen appealed to the Privy Council, which reversed the Tasmanian Judges' decision in March 1847.[47] The Privy Council severely reprimanded Montagu for his language and declared that Stephen's "private character and professional conduct were unimpeached." In January 1850, as part compensation for his treatment, Stephen was appointed by royal warrant Puisne Judge in New Zealand. The high cost of appeals to the Privy Council deterred many suitors, and only one other appeal, the case of *Tetley v. Sherwin* (see the next section), was made from Van Diemen's Land before 1850. In both cases the eminent Lords of the Privy Council found against Pedder and Montagu.

JURIES

Montagu suspected the verdicts of juries and said so frequently. For example, in May 1834, he declared that, as political factors too often

influenced juries, he would look closely at their findings.[48] This "prejudice" toward juries, typical of Arthur's regime, was interpreted by the
Colonist as "hostility to public liberty" and "an inclination to support
power."[49] The *Colonist* denounced any attempt to dictate to juries as
Montagu was wont to do.[50]

Montagu's disdain for juries was evident in the case of *Tetley v. Sherwin,*
which involved the question of agency.[51] Tetley applied to the agent of
the Van Diemen's Land Insurance Company, Isaac Sherwin, to insure a
ship, and Sherwin duly wrote for the policy. He received the policy and
waited for Tetley to pay the premium, but before payment was made the
ship was "lost." The policy could not therefore be "perfected," and Tetley
sued Sherwin. In four separate trials, the juries decided in favour of
Tetley: the Judges granted new trials because they deemed that the juries
had not understood that the contract had not been "perfectly completed
and therefore was rendered void."[52] Montagu criticized Vandiemonian
juries for "deviating from the Judges from the love of their own independence" and for frequently making up their minds before the trial
began. As the case involved a question of honesty and was based on "the
custom universally recognized by all mercantile men at home," the *Hobart
Town Advertiser* thought a jury, which was mainly composed of mercantile
men, not the Judges, should decide the issue. The *Colonial Times* felt that,
in this case, justice was being thwarted by the law, which was "an abomi-
nable corruption and destructive phantom."[53]

The Judges refused a fifth trial because the juries were too set against
the defendant; this refusal opened the door to an appeal to the Privy
Council.[54] Sherwin hoped that a favourable decision in the Privy Council
would persuade the jury in Van Diemen's Land to find in his favour. In
the event, the Privy Council refused the application on the ground of
the low monetary value at stake.

DIFFERENCES WITH PEDDER

In *Tetley v. Sherwin,* the Judges agreed with each other, but there were
other cases when they disagreed and presented contrary judgments. In
part, this was due to their differing personalities.[55] Where Pedder was
indecisive, Montagu made quick decisions. Where Pedder was long-
winded, Montagu was succinct. Where Pedder tended to be "mild" in
his sentencing, Montagu was "severe." Where Pedder adhered to ancient
forms and procedures, Montagu favoured the adoption of new ones.[56]

Moreover, the Judges were bound on occasion to have varying interpretations of legal issues, and, as no final judgment could then be given, this brought the system of justice into disrepute.[57]

This became a live issue in the 1840s, when barristers, attorneys, merchants, and landowners regularly petitioned Lieutenant-Governors Franklin and Eardley-Wilmot to appoint a third judge.[58] One petition stressed that when the Judges differed, "injustice" and expense — but not a resolution of the dispute — were the result.[59] The only way to remove "uncertainty in the administration of justice" was to appoint a third judge. The Colonial Office refused to sanction the appointment for various reasons.[60] One was Montagu's view that there was not enough work for three judges, and therefore the expense was not justified. Another was the small number of cases in which the Judges differed: they heard hundreds of cases concurrently but, between 1833 and 1840, had differed on six occasions only; from 1840 to March 1844, they had disagreed on five occasions.

One area of judicial difference was over Pedder's "pertinacious adherence to the strict formalities of practice," which worked against the ends of justice.[61] John Bennett argues that Montagu was concerned "less with the administration of justice" than with "undermining" Pedder, but it is more accurate to say that he saw Pedder as an obstacle to reform.[62] Montagu, more willing than Pedder to adopt new forms, was eager to dispense with practices, such as special pleading, that were "inimical" to "substantial justice."[63] Under section 22 of the *Australian Courts Act 1828,* the Judges were required to certify that laws passed by the Legislative Council were not repugnant to the laws of England.[64] This was another area over which Pedder and Montagu differed. Where Pedder tended to sanction colonial laws passed by the Legislative Council, Montagu tended to find fault with them or to find them repugnant to English law. "His instinctive reaction," Kathleen Fitzpatrick notes, "to any proposition put before him was dissent," but in a penal colony some brake was needed on rash legislation and Montagu's interventions benefited the community.[65] The *Austral-Asiatic Review* thanked Montagu for refusing to certify laws to which "the slightest doubt can exist." He was "a watchful guardian" against laws that could be construed to oppress the people.[66]

One example of Montagu's intervention involved the *Road Act,* where self-interest was also a motive. In August 1838 he spoke at a meeting in the Richmond district, protesting against a proposed road at Kangaroo Point that was to be opened through his property.[67] He attended the meeting "as one of themselves — as a landholder" — and not in his "official character." He wanted the road to be permanent so that he could with confidence build fences for his stock. In the past, he had lost two hundred acres of his "best pasture land" because people pulled down his fences "claiming right of way." He feared that the Commissioners, armed with legal power, would "compel" him to allow a road to be carried through his property "against his will." *Bent's News* praised Montagu for his "patriotic conduct" in identifying himself with "the interests of the people."[68]

When public protest proved ineffectual, Montagu used his official position to invoke the repugnancy clause against the *Road Act 1840*. He listed detailed objections to various clauses.[69] He showed that the Act enabled encroachment on private property and pointed out inconsistencies in the description of roads that rendered the Act "void for uncertainty." Attorney General Macdowell thought Montagu had made a case for repugnancy between different sections of the Act but was not justified in "certifying against it," because he did not show that the Act was repugnant to the laws of England.[70] Nevertheless, amendments were made and the Act was passed.[71]

The Colonial Office wearied of Montagu's constant objections. In September 1842, Secretary of State Stanley regretted that Montagu's objections to local legislation had been found by the British government's law officers "in each successive case without any apparent doubt ... to be untenable." Montagu's "unfounded objections" tended "needlessly" to embarrass the Legislative Council and "seriously to impair the respect with which it is so desirable that Judicial opinions should be received."[72] Stanley directed Eardley-Wilmot to persuade Montagu to be "more circumspect" in commenting on local statutes. This advice went unheeded.

DISPUTES WITH EXECUTIVE GOVERNMENT

Montagu's temper often got the better of him, and he vigorously defended himself if he thought his dignity had been impugned. No one was safe from his unpredictable outbursts, not even members of the executive. The most famous disagreement was with Attorney General Alfred Stephen in a series of courtroom eruptions in June and July 1836. When Stephen applied for a criminal information in the case of *Moore v. Rowlands,* Montagu said "he cared no more" for Stephen than for "the meanest person in the Colony" and accused Stephen of having slandered him in the press. He challenged Stephen to "either avow or retract to his face on that Bench" what he had "said or written against him."[73] Stephen denied writing to the newspapers or slandering him. Pedder was willing to grant the application, but Montagu was not. Stephen applied again on 17 June but failed, and the application was disposed of on 24 June.

Stephen thought Moore deserved to have his day in court and prosecuted the case in his private capacity in July. He alleged that Montagu brought the case on early "without reasonable notice" to protect his friend and lawyer Rowlands and to prevent Stephen himself from making adequate preparation. Montagu responded that the Court could not wait on Stephen's *"Royal Pleasure,"* that Stephen should obey Montagu's "commands," and that Stephen was "not his superior ... either in public or private life." Montagu felt that Stephen deserved "no more compliance or courtesy from him" than if he *were a convict in the prisoner's dock"* and that he deserved to be treated *"like a Cur and a Dog."* Finally, on 8 July, Montagu told convicts awaiting trial that Stephen had, in not giving their cases full consideration as grand jury for the colony, neglected his duty and *"done them great injustices."*[74] In England, the grand jury comprised between twelve and twenty-three respectable men who decided whether the accused should stand trial, but respectable men were scarce in the penal colony of Van Diemen's Land, and it was thought prudent to devolve this crucial power to one man, the Attorney General.[75] Stephen asked Arthur to uphold "the sacred character of the Bench, which scenes like these degrade" and to preserve "that confidence in the Administration of Justice, which strong and unfounded charges — made from that Bench against an important Minister of Justice — must inevitably destroy." In making his statements before a hundred people, Montagu "displayed an infirmity of mind or temper," which had "deprived his Court of every claim to respect."[76]

Montagu's lengthy reply of seventy-six pages did not reach Arthur until 29 August, and he tried to muddy the waters by alleging misbehaviour on Stephen's part. Montagu accused Stephen of dereliction of duty by not giving criminal cases his full and personal consideration as grand jury. He claimed that Stephen's behaviour in court had "for a long time been improper and calculated to bring the Judges and the administration of Justice into disrespect." Montagu catalogued Stephen's insults, which he felt "justified the severity of my language." Stephen would eat his lunch while the Court was in session, treating it like "a Chop House." Montagu described Stephen "carving meat, mixing vinegar etc, eating with a knife and fork and throwing himself back in his Chair" and noisily drinking "some wine or spirits" out of a bottle. He often addressed the jury and the Court with "his mouth *half full*." At times when the Judges delivered their judgment, Stephen left the courtroom and if the judgment went against him he questioned its correctness inside and outside the court. He belittled the Vandiemonian judges in comparison with those in New South Wales. In various places, Stephen had spoken disparagingly of Montagu, said his judgment was "liable to be warped by the humour and temper" he was in, and insinuated that he was corrupt and even insane.[77]

When Stephen displayed the same kind of provocative behaviour in June and July 1836, Montagu lost control, admitting that his language toward Stephen was "too violent in the two sentences particularly complained of." But he put a different construction on his words than did Stephen. In the first, he said "that the same courtesy and kindness with which I should treat every person, Counsel, Suitors and Prisoners in the Dock I should extend to him and no more." In the second, he could not recall the exact words used, but his meaning was "that I felt I had been treated with the contempt or neglect of a Cur or a Dog, that I would not bestow upon Mr. Stephen the treatment of a Cur or a Dog, although I thought his conduct richly merited it." Montagu wanted Stephen to be punished for insulting and slighting the Judges when they were discharging their "arduous and responsible duties."[78] Subsequently, Montagu traced Stephen's animosity to a threatened prosecution for compounding a felony, which Montagu had initiated when he was Attorney General. Stephen then threatened to *"crush"* Montagu.[79] Another possible cause was the Lewis case. While Montagu received the blame, Stephen's part was "lost sight of altogether."[80] Stephen had ordered Lewis' prosecution, had been "the prosecutor's private Counsel and influential adviser," had "bearded" Lewis in court, and had supported Montagu's sentence.

Arthur and the Executive Council investigated all charges during the last four weeks of his governorship. Arthur found the experience "painful." He thought the trouble began with Stephen's habit of attributing in conversation "any peculiarity of manner or mode of proceeding" by Montagu to "*a state of mind* for which I believe there is not the slightest foundation." In a small community such as Hobart Town, "such expressions would reach the ears of the party concerned," and this caused Montagu's "violent language." After carefully weighing the voluminous evidence, Arthur and the Council thought both men deserved the "strongest disapprobation," but Arthur was in a quandary about the most suitable punishment as both had strongly supported his government.[81] Moreover, he was about to leave the colony and did not want to cause a problem for his successor. He therefore opted to let the Colonial Office decide on the punishment.

Secretary of State Glenelg concluded that Montagu was more to blame than Stephen. Although Glenelg agreed with the Executive Council in absolving Montagu from "any corrupt or unjust exercise of his judicial functions," he remarked that Montagu was "lamentably deficient in temper, self-possession and moderation, qualities indispensable to the wholesome and satisfactory administration of justice." There was no justification for his violent and intemperate language, which was "unbecoming" and "reprehensible" in a judge. But Stephen was not blameless. He should have tried harder "to avoid giving needless offence" and as a member of the bar shown the bench "the utmost deference." As Attorney General, Stephen had an even greater duty "to exercise the greatest caution and self-control in abstaining" from giving the Judges cause for complaint or "to lessen the estimation in which they ought to be held by the public." Giving due weight to Arthur's high opinion of "the talents and services" of both men, and expecting them "to abstain from any approach to further misunderstanding," Glenelg declined to impose sanctions on them. But if the issues were raised with him again, he would advise Her Majesty to take action to prevent a "recurrence of conduct and of scenes in open Court which a Judge cannot be concerned in without serious detriment to the public interests."[82] Glenelg's decision confirmed the *Launceston Advertiser*'s view that Montagu's father had influence with ministers and that the colonists would be forced to retain an "incompetent" Judge, whose "distinction ... rests upon his freaks and eccentricities."[83] The animus between Montagu and Stephen continued until the latter's move to New South Wales in 1839.

Montagu fell out with government after the bushranger and criminal Lawrence Kavanagh, sentenced to death for robbery, was reprieved by Lieutenant-Governor Eardley-Wilmot in 1843. Montagu contended that Eardley-Wilmot was "incompetent or unworthy" of being "entrusted with the exercise of the Royal prerogative of mitigating" sentences passed by judges.[84] Consequently, Montagu declined to pass appropriate sentences on criminals because the executive would mitigate those sentences. In 1844 a gang of armed "desperadoes" committed a series of crimes and were convicted of two charges of robbery with violence.[85] This was a capital offence, but Montagu ordered that the lesser sentence of death recorded be applied to them.[86] Montagu stated that, as other prisoners had been convicted of capital crimes but had been reprieved by the government, he "conceived that justice in its administration should be sure and equal." The *Hobart Town Courier* concurred with Montagu and criticized "the too frequent suspension of capital punishment"—"the wholesale amnesty"—of prisoners who had committed offences of "the worst die."[87] The public warmly endorsed his stand.[88]

Montagu also increasingly criticized the convict system after it changed from assignment to settlers to probation in work gangs in the early 1840s. His prejudices against probationer convicts came out very strongly in August 1847, when he instituted a private prosecution in the Hobart Town Police Office. Suspecting one Nuttall of illegally seizing his stock, he charged him with a breach of the *Impounding Act* and vigorously cross-examined one defence witness James Reeves, a transported convict. When the defence counsel said Reeves' evidence was "very natural," Montagu replied "very natural" for probationers, but not for "honest men." Montagu threatened Reeves with prosecution if he found he was lying. The Chief Police Magistrate regularly twitted Montagu about his conduct. When Nuttall was fined £5 and costs, Montagu donated his part of the fine to the Infant School.[89]

The most probable reason why Montagu spoke so strongly against the probation system was its deleterious effect on the economy. Montagu had invested much money in laying out his property at Rosny, seeking, as he remarked, to "accumulate an independence for myself and my children."[90] Before the advent of the probation system, he had been offered up to ten thousand guineas for his land, but that system "destroyed" the market, and he could not sell his land for £2,500. He told Lieutenant-Governor William Denison that his twenty years "hard struggling in my arduous office" had been "destroyed by the British mal-administration" of Van Diemen's Land: "Such gross mismanagement no human mind could, with the utmost stretch of imagination, have anticipated."[91] Although this was true, money had long been a difficult issue for Montagu.

Debts

Montagu arrived in the colony in debt, and although he brought £4,000 with him, was paid between £1,000 and £1,200 per year for over twenty years, and from 1833 received "a very large annual income" as co-heir of his maternal grandfather, he never seemed to extricate himself from financial problems.[92] Montagu may have followed his father's counsel not to pay debts until the latest date allowed by law, but this was foolhardy advice for someone able to pay his creditors: his creditors often consented to a delay but charged a heavy interest on the debt for the privilege. He may also have overcapitalized in his Rosny estate. According to the *True Colonist*, Montagu incurred more debts in Van Diemen's Land.[93] This came to official attention in 1843, when the Colonial Office received two anonymous letters questioning Montagu's capacity to hold office. One letter claimed that bills of exchange worth £800 owed by Montagu had been placed in the hands of the solicitors Allport and Roberts, who were taking steps to recover the amount. The author demanded that Montagu be removed for placing himself "in the power of men" of whom he should be "entirely independent." The other letter claimed that Allport and Roberts had held the bills of exchange for two years and insinuated that they had used the threat of recovery to influence Montagu's decisions. Montagu was "in their power."[94]

Eardley-Wilmot investigated and found that the solicitors did hold bills against Montagu, but they did not suspend proceedings to influence his "judicial conduct."[95] Their legal steps to recover the amount owing were rendered futile by Montagu's claim that they could not sue a Supreme Court Judge. Secretary of State Stanley found Montagu's defence unacceptable and ordered him either to pay the debt or take leave of absence for as long as it took to try any action that the solicitors might institute. Montagu paid off his debt and remained in office.[96] But he had incurred other debts, and one of these led to his amoval.

Amoval

Montagu's financial mismanagement caught up with him in November 1847, when Anthony MacMeckan prosecuted him in the Supreme Court for the recovery of a debt for £280.[97] Montagu again asserted that he could not be sued in his own court, and Chief Justice Pedder agreed with him. On 23 November, MacMeckan petitioned Lieutenant-Governor Denison to suspend Montagu so he could institute proceedings against him. Three days later, Montagu told Denison that he had an agreement with MacMeckan that he would pay the debt once certain property was sold and that, though he had offered to settle the debts without paying the costs of the court case, his offer had been declined. Montagu argued that it would be "unjust" to suspend him as it would take twelve months "to try the case in equity," and he would lose £100 in salary a month.

While Denison was deciding what to do, on 29 November Pedder and Montagu held that the *Dog Act* was unconstitutional.[98] The ostensible aim of this statute was to impose a registration fee on dogs to stop them from roaming around and becoming public nuisances, but Montagu held that the *Dog Act* was an act of taxation as the sum raised would go into the general revenue. As section 25 of the *Australian Courts Act* stated that "if taxes are levied it shall set forth 'distinctly in the body of the Act' the local purposes for which the levies were to be appropriated," Montagu pronounced the *Dog Act* an "illegal, unconstitutional" enactment. He further angered Denison by converting Pedder to his way of thinking. Denison needed the £3,000 a year in revenue that the *Dog Act* would raise and was worried that similar statutes would also be declared illegal.[99]

On 3 December, Thomas Young, MacMeckan's solicitor, cast doubt on the veracity of Montagu's response to Denison's order for an explanation of the debt and added fresh allegations. He advanced hearsay evidence that Montagu had other debts and questioned Montagu's conduct in a case where Young was solicitor for the plaintiff and the defendants held "overdue acceptances of Mr. Justice Montagu to a large amount." In this case, Young was solicitor of the Hobart Town Branch of the Bank of Australasia and brought two actions against John Addison and Alexander Fraser for the recovery of promissory notes amounting to £7,000. The defendants ultimately paid the money, but in the earlier hearings, Montagu had decided against, and Pedder for, the bank. While the case was before the Court, Montagu was in debt to Addison, and Addison was pressing him for repayment of the debt incurred in 1840. Young had also been told that Montagu owed Fraser money too. Young asserted that Montagu should have paid those debts before adjudicating in the case. Denison thought Montagu's conduct in the case was "neither wise nor proper."[100]

After reviewing the evidence, Denison agreed with the Executive Council that Montagu's transactions were "highly discreditable" to him and that they threw "discredit upon the administration of Justice."[101] Montagu was asked to show why he should not be suspended from office "until the Queen's pleasure be known." Montagu answered the various charges made against him, pointed out that Pedder had confirmed the legality of using his position to frustrate a creditor, denounced his accusers for trying to injure him due to self-interested motives, and argued that only the Queen had the power to amove or suspend a judge.[102] As for Young's fresh allegations, Montagu claimed to be free of "bias" when hearing the case involving Addison and Fraser. After twenty years, Montagu believed that neither friends nor enemies would question "my integrity, my independence and honourable conduct," and he dismissed Young's "malicious and wicked insinuation."[103]

This defence made no impression on Denison, who found Montagu's conduct "most unbecoming to a man in his position, and most injurious to his character." In a penal colony, "men of high station" should show "a good example to the community—the injury to society consequent upon such misbehaviour is enhanced tenfold." Montagu could not remain a judge in "a state of subordination to men who might at any time exercise an influence over him." That influence need not be "positive and direct, and shewn by actual threats; it is equally or even more injurious when it acts through the medium of self-interest to warp a mind, perhaps even unconsciously to the person so influenced." It would be "impossible" to produce evidence that Montagu had been influenced in his decisions, but he had placed himself in a position of "doubt and suspicion," which "must injure his efficiency" as a Judge.[104] On 31 December 1847, as Montagu had failed to mount a convincing defence and had even shown himself in a worse light, Denison, acting on the advice of his law officers, felt justified in amoving Montagu for misbehaviour in office under the *Colonial Leave of Absence Act 1782,* known as *Burke's Act.*

In a separate dispatch, Denison hammered home his view that Montagu was "very unfit" to discharge judicial functions.[105] He now felt it expedient to draw attention to past dispatches by lieutenant-governors to assert a pattern of misbehaviour similar to that of 1847, which showed "a want of temper and discretion and uprightness of conduct." Colonial Office Permanent Undersecretary Herman Merivale, an old friend of Montagu's, doubted that "making a legal defence to an action can be statutable 'misbehaviour in office.'"[106] If a governor could remove a judge for "any moral misconduct which impaired" his efficiency on the bench, this would deprive the Secretary of State of "all power of interference." Merivale thought it best to obtain the views of the law officers, but this could not be done until Montagu's appeal to the Privy Council had been decided.[107]

Merivale realized that Montagu's hostile decision over the *Dog Act*—perhaps for "factious motives"—was a material factor in his dismissal.[108] Although the other charges against Montagu were "serious enough," they were "so nearly contemporaneous" with the *Dog Act* dispute that it would be difficult to counter the charge that Denison was "influenced in punishing Mr. Montagu by the desire of getting him out of the way." That was exactly how the press interpreted Denison's actions. No newspaper condoned Montagu for using his position to evade paying a debt, but he was transformed from villain to "martyr" by what many saw as Denison's illegal amoval.[109] The *Hobart Town Courier* condemned Denison for destroying "the independence of the Bench" and converting it into "an engine for the collection of illegal taxes."[110] That was to add "the deadliest sin, that of hypocrisy, to open outrage" because Denison had ostensibly amoved Montagu on the ground that his indebtedness had compromised his independence. The *Courier* further alleged that, when MacMeckan's complaint had first been submitted, Denison was willing to let the matter drop, but then Montagu decided against the *Dog Act,* and he revived the complaint for self-interested motives.[111]

Although the anti-transportationist *Examiner* was not inclined "to palliate the eccentricities" of Montagu or "to excuse his colonial speculations," the community was "deeply indebted to him" for exposing "the enormities" of the probation system that was "fast corroding every material and moral interest." Given Denison's interference with the independence of the Judges, the *Examiner* asked "do WE live in the nineteenth century, or have we been thrown back on the sixteenth?"[112] On 15 January 1848, a public meeting denounced, in the words of lawyer Charles Brewer, Denison's interference with the "sacred independence of the judicial seat," which was a protection against "the assumption of illegal and irresponsible power by the Local Government."[113] Public protest failed to save Montagu, who sailed for England on 30 January. His fellow colonists wished him a successful appeal to the Privy Council "against a stretch of arbitrary power unexampled in modern times."[114] Friends raised a subscription for his passage, and his major creditors did not seek their money so that Montagu "might leave the colony without molestation."[115]

Denison and the Colonial Office must have been hugely relieved when in July 1849 the Privy Council confirmed that there were "sufficient grounds" to amove Montagu under *Burke's Act.*[116] Although Their Lordships noted "some irregularity" in ordering Montagu's removal from office when he had only been asked to show cause why he should not be suspended, they felt that Montagu had not "sustained any prejudices by such irregularity." The Colonial Office sanctioned Denison's amoval of Montagu and the appointment of Attorney General Thomas Horne to replace him, even though Horne was more in debt than Montagu.[117]

Denison's intimidation of the judges was raised in the House of Commons, where William Gladstone justified the amoval. He claimed that, in the colonies, the relationship between the government and the judges differed from that in England and that "the independence of the judges did not exist in the colonies."[118] Gladstone was wrong to deny in such absolute terms that colonial judges were independent of the executive. Their role was to give independent and impartial advice, not to be subservient to lieutenant-governors or the Legislative Council. Secretary of State Grey severely reprimanded Denison on this point when he tried to force Pedder to take eighteen months' leave so he could pass the *Dog Act* in his absence.[119] It is true that judges held their office "during pleasure" and not "good behaviour," but removal was an extreme step requiring clear justification before governments or the Colonial Office dared to interfere with judicial independence.

Montagu had flaws but believed that judicial independence was a necessary barrier to the irresponsible actions of executive government, especially in a penal colony where lieutenant-governors had so much power. Although he officially forfeited the right to hold judicial office because of his indebtedness, his financial difficulties had long been known, yet he had retained his office. In reality, he was dismissed because he was *too* independent of executive authority. For not respecting his adherence to that hallowed principle of British constitutional history, both Denison and the Colonial Office deserve censure.[120] The disgrace of his amoval did not end Montagu's legal career. No doubt again through patronage, in 1850 he was appointed resident Magistrate in the Falkland Islands and in 1854 was transferred to Sierra Leone, where he was variously Registrar of Deeds, Master of the Court of Records, Clerk of the Crown, and Registrar of the Court of Chancery.[121] In 1857, overcoming a series of sexual and financial scandals, Montagu published the *Ordinances of the Colony of Sierra Leone,* which went through seven editions, and he even served at times as Chief Justice. He died in London in 1880.

CHAPTER NINE

"NOT IN KEEPING WITH THE TRADITIONS OF THE CARIBOO COURTS"

Courts and Community Identity in Northeastern British Columbia, 1920-50

*Jonathan Swainger**

At the opening of circuit, Judge William Hereward Barber begrudgingly accepted that wartime exigencies obliged him to do without the traditional blare of trumpets hailing his arrival. Duty to the larger cause required sacrifices by all, even judges such as Barber, who though accepting the strictures of the day, was quite sure that his predecessors would not have been inclined to dispense with so critical an ingredient for carrying off the Court's business. In this instance, justice would have to struggle onward supported by only a small retinue of liveried officials, some of whose attire was, sadly enough, redolent of the unmistakable tang of mothballs.[1]

That this opening to circuit is provided at the outset of Cyril Hare's 1942 legal thriller *Tragedy at Law* reinforces our sense that courtrooms have always been a theatre for playing out power relations within a community. And in being conscious of, if not obsessed with, the trappings of his office and the ceremony of assizes, Hare's fictional Judge Barber shared a great deal with many of those who actually assumed a seat on the bench. Indeed, the fact that the assizes were theatre has long since passed from debate thanks, in no small part, to Douglas Hay's keystone essay "Property, Authority, and the Criminal Law," published in 1977.[2] At the same time, even if all judges were less concerned than Judge Barber, we are left to wonder about the extent to which the judiciary remained part of the theatre of the assizes, even when not on

---

* Thanks to Hamar Foster and Benjamin Berger for their good humour, patience, and counsel in preparing this essay.

the bench. Was there an ideological cachet carried by the Court and its officials, and more specifically the Judge, when he or she was not presiding over a case? Did the community continue to take stock of the Judge's manner inside and outside of court, so as to gauge how well the Judge fulfilled the community's needs?[3] If some sort of affinity existed between a court or a particular judge and a community (or its individual members), was that community more inclined to believe that it was especially well served by the Judge? Did that sense lend itself to a perception that the Judge or the Court subscribed to the ideals that the community held dear?

In the Peace River region of northeastern British Columbia from the First World War to 1950, we find that, though British Columbian County Court Judge H.E.A. Robertson certainly subscribed to the common sense ideals underpinning life in the Peace and was believed to dispense a brand of justice in tune with the region, this latter expectation was maintained in the absence of compelling evidence from the bench. Still, although there is little evidence to suggest that Robertson catered to regional prejudices, his behaviour off the bench suggested an affinity for the Peace and its people who, in turn, reciprocated with a positive estimation of the provincial legal system. It was not that his rulings were irrelevant to community perceptions of his qualifications. Rather, it seems that the combination of his no-nonsense approach to judging with a genial manner and heartfelt enthusiasm for outdoor life silently legitimated the decision of those who had pulled up stakes in search of new beginnings and opportunities in the Peace (see Map 9.1). The popular view was that because this representative of justice, whose duty was to ascertain truth, valued *our* lifestyle and *our* choices in coming to northeastern British Columbia, his judicial method *must* reflect *our* values. Rooted as it was in their ideals, hopes, and beliefs for the future, it was an important affirmation for those who sought out a better life in the Peace. But it was an attestation that occurred with little judicial support from Robertson.

And what precisely were these values that existed at the core of a Peace country identity? Settled later than most of British Columbia and the Prairie provinces, geographically isolated from British Columbia, and representing the northern edge of the great interior plain, the Peace River region was in between — physically and demographically part of the Canadian prairies but resting politically inside the boundaries of British Columbia.[4] One of the consequences of this blurring was an

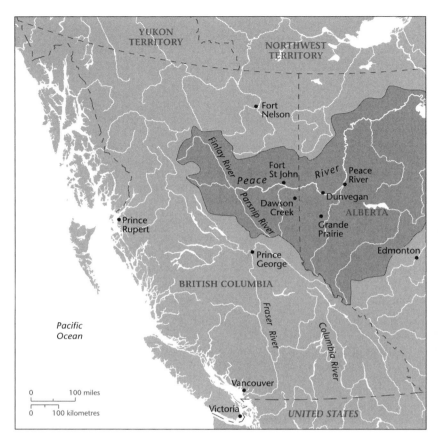

MAP 9.1 The Peace River region of British Columbia
Cartographer: Eric Leinberger

emergent exceptionalism—having arrived mainly from the Canadian prairies and the American Midwest, many of the settlers felt stronger ties to the flatlands than to the distant and often foreign environment of British Columbia. But at the same time, they were not "proper" prairie people because they lived in British Columbia. Placed as they were, they could easily see themselves as quite distinct, a people true to the spirit of the "Last, Best, West." And though other regions and local identities drew upon a self-perception of distinctiveness, the thread of exceptionalism and an imagined distinctiveness was especially prominent in the Peace, even within the context of the Prairie West and British Columbia.[5]

When drawn together, the settlement and judicial history of the Peace before 1950 provide an intriguing snapshot of how, given the necessary ingredients, a legal system could nurture ideals and notions that were removed from the business of courts and judges. Essentially, there is nothing to suggest that Mr. Justice H.E.A. Robertson set out to legitimize Peace country self-perceptions when he began his circuits to the northeast in 1916. Admittedly, the relationship between Robertson's affinity for outdoor life, the degree to which this endeared him to Peace residents, and how this combination lent itself to a localized idea that the Judge subscribed to Peace country notions of right and wrong is speculative. It is entirely possible that Robertson's actions and demeanour were nothing more than a reflection of his personality and a willingness to make the most of his duty to hold court in the Peace. But at the same time, it is difficult to discount the sense that Robertson occupied a distinct role in shaping the Peace country's sense of self, regardless of the Judge's intention.

Traditions of the Cariboo Courts

It is almost impossible to exaggerate the effects of the Second World War on the Peace region of British Columbia.[6] Yet, though emphasis has always been placed on the construction of the Alaska Highway as the key event, in truth the highway was the first in a series of events stretching well beyond the war years and into the 1950s and 1960s.[7] For, not only did the war see the construction of the highway, but that road brought the Peace fully into the broader orbit of North American culture, society, and economic development. And in time, new rail and highway connections to British Columbia, along with the establishment of the oil and natural gas industry, fundamentally transformed the region. That enormous changes had been sparked was certainly understood during the war and its aftermath, and there is no doubt that some observers were alarmed by the prospects.

In the south Peace community of Dawson Creek, which served as a primary staging area for highway construction, wartime concerns over increasingly chaotic conditions were underscored by a massive fire and explosion levelling all but one business on a downtown block in the early evening of 13 February 1943.[8] The year that followed saw little relief, as local government collapsed and the increasingly heavy court dockets signalled the level of turmoil.[9] Although newspaper reports in Fort St.

John, on the north shore of the Peace River, adopted a less sombre tone while denying that Fort St. John was troubled by crime, the columns of the *Alaska Highway News (AHN)* told a different story. After reporting on all manner of police court infractions, widespread theft along the Alaska Highway, a bloody murder on the streets of Fort St. John, the prosecutions of individuals refusing to appear for selective service, and a number of local suicides throughout 1944 and 1945, Margaret "Ma" Murray of the *AHN* claimed that "this area of the Peace River is so crimeless as to be almost stuffy."[10] And following a similar string of crimes and misdemeanours reported during 1946, Murray suggested that police in Fort St. John could dedicate their energies to community betterment.[11] If we set aside Murray's peculiar reading of events, the Dawson Creek and Fort St. John newspapers reveal an environment of increasing disorder and criminality, an impression reflected in police and court statistics.

Although the content and style of reporting in the two newspapers continued beyond the war years, revelations of a homicide at mile 101 of the Alaska Highway in September 1948 and the trial that followed drew an intriguing broadside from Murray when she learned the fate of convict Gustav Weigner. Briefly told, Weigner's manslaughter trial was the final act in a tawdry business in which John McComas, his thirteen-year-old daughter Louise, and Weigner had headed north to Alaska in search of fresh beginnings and adventures in the late summer of 1948.[12] Having stopped at a roadside turn-out near mile 101, Weigner accidentally shot the elder McComas while allegedly attempting to shoot a squirrel. Weigner fled the scene with the girl and returned to Nebraska where they lived as brother and sister until, overcome by guilt, Weigner surrendered to authorities.

After two days of testimony during his Prince George trial, Weigner was found guilty of manslaughter and sentenced to two years in the penitentiary. In reporting the verdict and despite her inclination to trivialize the disorder and crime in Fort St. John, Murray was outraged at its leniency.[13] Echoing the sense that outsiders were responsible for crime, the ex-patriot American and recent arrival Murray described Weigner as an "oily young Ohio salesman." And, notably, she claimed that the manslaughter verdict and the two-year sentence were "not in keeping with the traditions of the Cariboo courts." In support of her assertion, she referred to the October 1945 trial of American Byron Potter in Dawson Creek, where the accused had been found guilty of murdering his lover, a divorced mother of two. And in that case, Murray approvingly remarked, Potter "got hanging and had his head wrenched from his body when dropped through the scaffold at Oakalla prison farm."[14] If Murray's intimation is to be taken seriously, the accidental decapitation of Potter more closely approximated Peace country notions of law and order than did Weigner's two-year term in the penitentiary. Admittedly, given Murray's penchant for hyperbole, it is easy to dismiss the comment as little more than her usual editorial excess. Yet, at the same time, there was something in what she said, even if her claim was a rather sweeping one.

Although Murray rarely paused to explain herself or her editorial eruptions, her identification of a Cariboo tradition seemingly owed itself to a number of entwined factors. The settlement history of the Peace gave birth to and emphasized the ideal that, since farming families predominated in the region, it could claim a heightened morality. Essentially, this version of the country life ideology encouraged Peace residents to believe that those who worked the land subscribed to a higher morality than did denizens of corrupting cities.[15] Consequently, it was easy to believe or, more accurately, to imagine that the region was untroubled by crime — in effect, that they lived in the crime-free Peace. Yet, although the region was peopled with hard-working and honest country folk, it was impossible to pretend that the Peace was free of disorder and crime. In a settlement society, conditions and people could be rough. Indeed, the entire enterprise of establishing farms and communities was unforgiving and could impose demanding situations that might blur the lines of "civilized" behaviour. Still, such outbursts could fall within a category of acceptable disorder. Thus, when a trapper was believed to have been in-country too long, it was suggested that his best course was to get out and have a "good drunk."[16] In one instance, a lifelong resident remarked that, in the Peace, drinking and fighting were not a crime, they were recreation.[17] Or, as another recalled, as late as the 1950s and 1960s, parking in front of the Toronto Dominion Bank in Fort St. John provided a ringside seat for the all-but-assured impromptu brawls.[18]

However, even in a community that created and expanded its categories of what constituted acceptable levels of disorder, there remained those behaviours that invariably crossed the line. Even here, however, classifying was no simple affair since what was serious was often framed by who did what and in what circumstances. Thus, when Bert Sheffield and Henry Courvoisier robbed the Hudson's Bay Company post in Fort Nelson in 1936 and carried off $36,000 in furs, one long-time resident characterized the crime as a good deed.[19] And when the two men re-turned from having served five-year terms in the penitentiary, they were welcomed back into the community with few recriminations. On the other hand, when acquitted of murdering Morely Kier in the aftermath of a poker game, Belo Mathews was subjected to an assortment of extra-ordinary innuendo for the remainder of his life.[20]

So, when a crime did occur, local residents consciously and uncon-sciously categorized the offence and the offenders — so that it and they were "knowable." Therefore, crimes could be viewed as instances in which the "boys" were blowing off steam and things got a bit out of hand. Or the alleged offender was not suited to the Peace country — he or she did not have the "right stuff," and the crime did not reflect the region's supposed higher morality. The most common version of this explanation was to suggest that outsiders or outside influence were re-sponsible for incidents of crime. Thus, when in 1938 extensive vandalism was discovered in a local community park, the *Peace River Block News (PRBN)* suggested that "[a]nyone with a grain of manhood or sense of fair play would not for a moment countenance such a procedure [the vandalism] ... The general opinion is that the perpetrators were transients as it is hardly reasonable to presume that anyone located in the district would be guilty of such an act."[21] That local readers could rest easy in the knowledge that such unmanly behaviour did not reflect local sens-ibilities suggests a great deal about how they imagined themselves. And at the same time, the view lends credence to what was observed of the Peace in 1934: "There were those who abused frontier hospitality, and were guilty of acts which no decent community would countenance. Of them ugly and sinister tales are still told, and their narrative prevents an indiscriminating idealization of the frontier."[22]

But as much as this explains how Peace country residents imagined themselves, it casts only indirect light on Murray's thinking. Although she recognized elements of the Peace country sense of self, Murray in-explicably concluded that these notions meant that local sympathies were tough on crime. Further, when she wrote of the traditions of the Cariboo courts in 1948, Murray had lived in Fort St. John for little over four years, although she, along with her husband, George Murray, had celebrated the Peace and its potential since at least the early 1940s.[23] It seems that both Murrays had idealized the Peace region, and when "Ma" surveyed the community, she saw what she expected and believed to be true, es-pecially when her own predispositions were confirmed. When she identified the traditions of the Cariboo courts, she was reading her own views into the community fabric of her newly adopted home.

Still, the extent to which these imaginings and interpretations actually shaped the administration of criminal justice is another question. It is certain that, though the approaches to fulfilling one's duty as a policeman were as varied as the personalities of individual constables, it is equally true that discretion informed by a sense of the local environment coloured the way that the police functioned. This owed a great deal to the predominant style of policing within the British Columbia Provincial Police (BCPP)—a style that encouraged being part of the local community.[24] Here was a pragmatic "common sense" approach that would have resonated with localized notions of knowing what type of behaviour posed a genuine threat. And when recalling those who served with the BCPP, most residents were apt to remember individual officers and men in ranks because of their community work as opposed to their actual policing. Policing style mattered but so too did lifestyle; those who were active in the community and lived like ordinary citizens—riding horses, hunting, and pursuing simple and unadorned lives—enjoyed a different type of success and, at least, were fondly remembered.

Although policing behaviour may have aligned with local perceptions, there is little to suggest that members of the bench tailored their behaviour to mirror the imaginings of Peace country residents. Yet we are left with Murray's notion of a tradition in Cariboo courts. Its possible source may rest in the presence of one individual—Judge H.E.A. Robertson—who had been dead for over three years by the time of Murray's eruption in 1948. For, it was Robertson, sitting as a County Court Judge for the Cariboo district from May 1915 to March 1943, who had been "the" Judge in the Peace River region for almost twenty-eight years before his death. But, in having passed from the scene, Robertson was an ideal source for the notion of a Cariboo court tradition. He had liked the Peace and its people and approached his judicial responsibilities with a plain-spoken no-nonsense attitude. And as these perspectives coincided with Murray's, it required little effort to conclude that they—the Peace, Robertson, and Murray—*must* have shared a broader accord.

A JUDGE FOR THE NEW COUNTRY

Robertson's appointment raised him to a Court that occupied a singular place in the province's history. Examined by Hamar Foster, the creation of a County Court in 1867 triggered over a decade of acrimony highlighting the tangle of personalities, jurisdictions, and political infighting colouring the transition from colonial to provincial status.[25] Once established, the County Courts held out the promise of regular court sittings and a resident judge in communities far removed from Victoria, the Lower Mainland, and the regular Supreme Court assizes.[26] County Court judges were empowered to act in any instance that might otherwise appear before the Supreme Court, with the exception of cases concerning malicious prosecution or any libel or slander, criminal conversation, seduction, breach of promise to marry, or any complaint alleging wrongdoing by a justice of the peace.[27] Court sessions were scheduled by the Lieutenant-Governor in Council, although the Judge could set additional sittings on his own authority, typically on circuit outside of the larger communities.

In many ways, Robertson was an ideal Judge for the Cariboo district. His father, Alexander Rocke Robertson, had been a provincial Supreme Court Judge who had practised law in the gold rush community of Barkerville.[28] In fact, the elder Robertson had played a role in the drawn-out contest over the creation of the County Courts.[29] For his part, H.E.A. Robertson had been in the Yukon during that gold rush and was well acquainted with the character of "frontier" life. But, though Robertson's legal and personal pedigree suggested a good fit for the northern circuit, it was his fondness for taking to the country that suggests his role in representing the tradition to which Ma Murray referred (see Figures 9.1 and 9.2).

Indeed, Robertson's initial circuit in the autumn of 1916 was hailed as a path-breaking enterprise. According to the *Kamloops Standard Sentinel,* Robertson's trip north would probably establish "a precedent in way of the administration of justice, with rivers and lakes as the highway of travel and a paddle propelled canoe as the means of locomotion."[30] Overlooking the judicial history of British Columbia's Supreme Court judges travelling by horse, boat, and foot throughout the Interior prior to Confederation, this depiction resonated with the expectation that a special individual would be required to handle the challenges of northeastern British Columbia.[31] This idea, that not everyone could face the rigours of living and working in Peace River country, was an article of faith among those who did establish farms and homes during and after the First World War. If the Judge proved equal to the task of fording rivers, sleeping on the ground, and bringing down his supper with a shotgun

FIGURE 9.1 H.E.A. Robertson, 1915
The Exploration Place, Prince George, BC (2003.15.36)

or pulling it out of a river with a rod and reel, then Robertson was cut from the same cloth as were the residents of the Peace.[32]

Robertson's return from that first circuit was noted in the *Prince George Star* of 3 November 1916, which concluded that "very seldom does it

FIGURE 9.2 H.E.A. Robertson, 1935
The Exploration Place, Prince George, BC (2003.15.49)

fall to the lot of the present day judge to have to travel a distance of 1200 miles for the purpose of untangling the knotty problems which the ordinary mortal is prone to be mixed up with. Judge Robertson spent nearly two months in the northern part of the district, holding court in five of the settled centres of the territory. In going he utilized the canoe route, going about 400 miles by this means of travel, returning by way of Edmonton."[33] Although it doubled the actual time that Robertson spent on circuit, the report captured the challenges faced and provided an early indication of the Judge's fit for both the Cariboo district and the Peace region. Most important for Peace country ears was Robertson's praise "for the territory through which he travelled" and that it was "populated by many earnest, hard-working people, who have absolute faith in its future as an agricultural and mining possibility." Indeed, it was a land of immense possibilities and might prove to be the province's greatest region.[34]

The inaugural tour of 1916 was the first of many, and only three years after beginning the circuit, Robertson was comfortable enough with the rigours of travel to bring two of his daughters.[35] Still, although the trips to the Peace became but one piece in the duty of being a County Court Judge, the challenges of northern travel were anything but routine.[36] Indeed, the trip in autumn of 1926 almost proved to be Robertson's undoing. After fighting early snowstorms and low river levels, the boat was swamped in heavy water on the Parsnip River, where the judicial party spent three days in a vacant cabin, subsisting on coffee and wet bread. Eventually retrieving the boat but missing an outboard motor, they floated downstream to a trapper's cabin for their first meal in thirty-six hours. Outfitted anew, the party eventually arrived at Hudson's Hope below the Peace Canyon falls on 25 September, a week after their first boat had been capsized.[37] According to the *Peace River Record,* once Robertson was safely in the Peace, he presided over the Court sessions dressed "in mackinaw breeches and a flannel shirt."[38] A decade later, this time with his son Seymour, Robertson was stranded in a trapper's cabin above the Hudson's Hope portage where they waited out an autumn snowstorm. According to Anglican missionary Monica Storrs, "the Judge waited for three days with hardly any food while the son forced his way on foot to Hudson Hope and brought back a sleigh and a strong team of horses to rescue him."[39]

Once safely in the more settled portions of the Peace, Robertson lodged in police barracks or with local families and was soon drawn into the region's social circle.[40] In fact, the Judge's arrival was a high point in the social calendar, as his presence sparked a great deal of entertaining for "those of us who managed to keep out of trouble."[41] During a rare late spring circuit in June 1937, Robertson's "genial face was observed at the music festival at Rolla"—he was on hand to present the Robertson Cup to local softball champions.[42] The same trophy had previously been awarded to local curlers.[43] Socializing also included sitting down for cards, and the story is told that, in one instance, while Robertson played poker at one table, the accused in a trial for the next day was similarly occupied nearby.[44] In another instance, if the anecdote is to be believed, "the beloved old judge" Robertson was willing to enter into the spirit of a situation. The story is told that, while he presided over a case of alleged bootlegging, a loud report was heard from the adjoining quarters occupied by Constable Ray Sandy of the BCPP. Robertson did not flinch until another barrage was unleashed. An inquiring glance toward Sandy informed the Judge as to the situation and brought about a quick end to proceedings. Sandy and Robertson then adjourned to the backroom to sample some of the Constable's homebrew that had been stored too close to the stove.[45]

That the Judge was up to the challenge of travelling through the wilds of northern British Columbia and, having done so, brushed off the dust, shared a meal, and enjoyed the best that Peace country society offered, was an important ingredient in the theatre of the circuit outside of the courtroom. In recalling Robertson's career after his passing, Prince George government agent and stipendiary Magistrate George Milburn specifically noted how much Robertson had enjoyed the Peace, even if the trips were sometimes "perilous adventures."[46] Added to this, Robertson's enthusiasm may well have bolstered the region's sense of its own distinctiveness. For, in embracing a lifestyle and crediting the manner in which residents imagined themselves, Robertson legitimized that image and the choices that had brought the settlers to the Peace. In a community where doubt and disappointment were well mixed with success, any signal as to the foresight of pursuing the good life in the Peace was enthusiastically welcomed.[47]

Although the yearly judicial visits may have reinforced the legitimacy of the imagined Peace, there is little evidence that Robertson's enthusiasms for the region exerted much influence once he donned his judicial robes. At most, the glimpses of Robertson in court suggest an unaffected manner that would have resonated with many residents. An early trial involving passing bad cheques moved Robertson to note that since it was the first case of that type to come before him in the district, he would be lenient. Subsequent occurrences would not receive such generosity.[48] A year later, when a series of burglaries around Dawson Creek

ended with the arrest of three men, Robertson—the Judge and fron-
tiersman—asserted "that a man in a district like this should be able to
leave his cabin or cache and find same intact when he returned."[49] He
indicated that there were no grounds for leniency and expected that the
two- to three-year sentences would have a salutary effect on the district.
Notably, the newspaper added that the sentences made it clear that "no
wild west tactics go here."[50] To the extent that such an interpretation
was accurate, similar notions may have coloured another case in which
a horse had been shot after destroying some crops. Robertson took time
to castigate both the irresponsibility of the horse owner while also cen-
suring the accused, who had killed the animal.[51]

Viewed in isolation, Robertson's approach to the Peace country circuit
suggests his role in the so-called tradition of the Cariboo courts. But
when he is contrasted with those judges who followed—especially the
judges of the British Columbia Supreme Court—the distinctiveness of
Robertson's manner is brought into relief. When, in the spring of 1944,
preparations were underway for the first sitting of the provincial Supreme
Court in the Peace, considerable attention was given to ensuring that
the facilities at the Pouce Coupé courthouse would befit the august
occasion. Everything from ensuring that the Registrar was outfitted in
an appropriate gown to acquiring the necessary furniture was subjected
to a flurry of correspondence.[52] The contrast with Robertson, who once
concluded Court business from his hotel bed while stricken with sciatica,
could not have been sharper.[53] Even more telling was the prolonged
correspondence dedicated to securing airplane seats for various legal
officials making the trip north—a task made all the more difficult owing
to wartime demands.[54] For Robertson, who had taken great pleasure in
plying the rivers and streams of northeastern British Columbia in jour-
neying to the Peace, and for his father's generation that had travelled by
canoe and horseback and spent nights camped out under canvas, the
anxious orchestration of appropriate transportation would surely have
elicited a wry smile.

A year later, the Supreme Court sessions in the Peace were a source
of consternation. Allan Moody stood before the Court charged with
stealing an American government truck in early July 1944 at Fort St.
John.[55] According to R.R. Earle, King's Counsel, of Dawson Creek, the
case of *Rex v. Moody*, in which the evidence was very strong, was undone
by witness "[Mohammed Hosein] Slyman (who by the way the Judge
said was very aptly named)."[56] In addressing the jury, Mr. Chief Justice

Wendell B. Farris was "exceptionally clear," and, according to Earle, "everybody" expected a guilty verdict. "But to the great surprise of everybody, they brought in a verdict of acquittal. The Judge castigated them most severely and had them discharged from further attendance at this Court."[57]

The implications of these events would be played out two years later, when attempts were made to secure a regular sitting of the Supreme Court in the Peace, as opposed to the non-scheduled appearances. Despite claims that the region had experienced impressive growth and had more judicial business than that occurring in communities south of Prince George, Chief Justice Farris dismissed the notion out of hand. Farris thought a definite assize at Pouce Coupé was unnecessary and wrote that "I was not impressed with the jurors while there, although I think that my drastic action in respect to one jury will probably result in better juries in the future, but I still think that if the scales are fairly even as between Prince George and Pouce Coupé, I would favour Prince George." And though the proponents extolled the virtues of train and aircraft service, Farris remained unmoved.[58] Although admitting that "[i]t is certainly not difficult to reach Pouce Coupé and have a special sitting for civil work if there is sufficient work to warrant it," and that some members of the Supreme Court were willing to fly, the Chief Justice was uninterested in flying to the Peace.[59] Robertson's affinity for the Peace was nowhere in evidence among his brethren on the higher court only five years after the pioneer Judge had passed from the scene.[60] When Mr. Justice James A. McGeer arrived by airplane in May 1944 to assume his place as Cariboo County Court Judge, the *AHN* noted that, though he had been a BC resident for fifty-two years, "this was his first visit to the Peace River Country."[61] To the extent that Robertson had legitimized the Peace country identity, McGeer and his brethren were unable and perhaps unwilling to continue that particular tradition of the Cariboo courts.

In as much as the character of Peace country juries explained the failure to garner a regular sitting of the Supreme Court, the region was seemingly unfazed. Indeed, if the barrel-stealing case launched against the Tompkins brothers in 1949 is any indication, local juries took positive pleasure in upsetting judges who failed to appreciate the local home-grown truths. Inundated by military and civilian personnel involved in the wartime construction of the Alaska Highway, the Peace had become an enormous storehouse of construction material. And, when presented with the opportunity, few Peace residents seemed hesitant to cart off whatever they desired. Later, at the close of hostilities, local landfills were stuffed with everything from sugar to entire truck assemblies. One resident who came to the Peace answering a call to Anglican missionary service slyly admitted that the US Army heater that had warmed her home "must have come from somewhere."[62] In a region deeply marked by the hard realities of a not-too-distant settlement frontier and the imposed frugality of the 1930s, the idea of turning a blind eye to usable items in the dump was nonsense. Faced with allegations that the US Army was discarding mountains of usable items, Colonel F.S. Strong, commanding officer of the army's Northwest Service, recognized "how poor settlers at Fort St. John and other points feel when they see stoves, mattresses and other equipment being destroyed. They hate to see anything destroyed, and they probably could make use of some of it."[63]

So, when Phil Tompkins learned of a dump having been filled with countless fifty-gallon oil drums, he dispatched two of his sons to retrieve as many undamaged barrels as possible. Having rescued twenty-eight intact barrels, the Tompkins brothers drove out of the dump, only to be arrested by the police. Given local sentiments about usable material being discarded, the possibility that a local jury might find the brothers guilty was rather remote, despite it being plainly evident that they had entered the army dump and taken the barrels.[64] Indeed, neither their verdict nor the enraged harangue unleashed by Mr. Justice J.O. Wilson, who was presiding over his first assize in the region, was a surprise. Noting Wilson's poor humour at hearing the verdict, the *AHN* offered the intriguing rebuttal that evidently "the judge had not seen any of the disposal dumps on the Alcan, nor had he read much about what had been thrown on them, or cached away in strategic places."[65] Evidently, the newspaper believed that had Wilson, a former County Court Judge resident in Prince George, been more familiar with the Peace, he would have appreciated local realities and have recognized the futility of enforcing regulations against "stealing" from the dumps.

Thus, when Ma Murray decried the two-year sentence handed down in the Weigner murder trial in 1948, her outrage owed a great deal to a personal sense of the Peace country entwined with her own imaginings of how Judge Robertson fulfilled his judicial responsibilities. And though Murray overstated the connections and misinterpreted what she had heard about Robertson, it is also certain that her lament resonated as much with the passing of an era as with a Cariboo judicial tradition. In the space of a few years, the frontier Peace had been swept away by the arrival of modern North American life, and, within the next decade, the Peace would finally be linked to the rest of British Columbia as both highway and rail connections were forged. And as those routes snaked through the Rocky Mountains, a new age of economic prosperity was heralded by the confirmation of significant oil and gas reserves. In this new world, judges could no longer paddle through mountain passes in the expectation of a bit of adventure, some leisurely fishing, a few evenings of neighbourly chat, and a relatively light docket. Robertson's circuits had been crucial for ensuring that residents of the Peace had access to the justice system existing elsewhere in the province but, more importantly, Robertson's presence reaffirmed the sacrifices made in settling the Peace. Although his rulings may have echoed localized notions of pragmatic sense, his presence and his choices when not on the bench had made a more crucial contribution to the Peace country's sense of identity. His ideals, now apparently abandoned, had been those of the Peace — it was this connection, and the judicial tradition that she believed it represented, that Ma Murray eulogized in the late summer of 1948.

PART THREE

PROPERTY, POLITICS, AND PETITIONS
IN COLONIAL LAW

STARKIE'S ADVENTURES IN NORTH AMERICA

The Emergence of Libel Law

*Lyndsay M. Campbell**

In 1835, the newspaper editor and aspiring politician Joseph Howe was tried in Halifax for criminal libel for publishing a letter charging the city's magistrates with mismanaging tax revenues. In defending himself, Howe made a novel legal argument. Basing his case on the 1830 English edition of Thomas Starkie's *Law of Slander,* Howe argued that, as a newspaper editor and publisher with particular knowledge of the magistracy's doings, he had a duty to inform his audience about their civic administration. He did not try to prove the allegations were true but merely that the occasion was protected by a qualified privilege. Indeed, proving the truth of the allegations would probably have been impossible, since the magistrates' record keeping was a central problem. In response, the prosecution argued not that the allegations were untrue but, rather, that both the privilege was defeated by evidence of malice and the defence of qualified privilege was unknown to law. The judge did not put the defence to the jury. On the law as stated, a finding of guilt ought to have been inevitable, but the jury acquitted Howe anyway.

The legal meaning of the case is ambiguous, although I think it made criminal libel an unattractive strategy for controlling the press. My purpose here, however, is to examine why this particular legal argument made it to Nova Scotia but not to Massachusetts. Qualified privilege

* I am indebted to the astute listeners who heard and commented on a version of this chapter at the Canadian Law and Society Association meeting at Harrison Lake in June 2005. I would also like to thank the helpful people at the American Antiquarian Society, the Massachusetts Judicial Archives, and Nova Scotia Archives and Records Management, and most especially Janet DeWolfe.

was a new doctrine, and one might suppose that Massachusetts, with its larger, more luminous bench and bar, its constitutional rights to freedom of the press and of expression, and a certain willingness to distance itself from its colonial past, would have been the place to look for such a legal innovation. Massachusetts lawyers and judges, however, were preoccupied with establishing the extent to which the truth of an allegedly libelous statement could be a defence to a charge of criminal libel, a concern of American libel law that was already decades old. Nova Scotians conservatively rejected the possibility that truth could ever be a defence, but, nevertheless, Joseph Howe was able to articulate a defence of qualified privilege, which focused not on what had been published but on the circumstances around publication. Key to these jurisdictions' different trajectories were their differing historico-legal traditions and their legal-book publishing practices. Contrasting the handling of defences to criminal libel in these two places draws our attention to the importance of local circumstances in colonial legal practices. The story is one of overarching cultural imperatives, of the material reality of publishing, and of individuals' strategic decisions in libel cases. Neither jurisdiction had a strong, carefully enunciated black-letter constitutional tradition against which decisions were made.

In several respects, this chapter follows the kinds of research trajectories John McLaren has set. It investigates the transmission of English law into a colonial setting and one that was only recently post-colonial, a process John has examined in the context of Australia. It explores how law, enmeshed in social life, operates to regulate lives and construct reality, themes that have emerged in John's work on prostitution and pornography and on the Doukhobors.[1] It attends to the personalities and social realities that came into play on legal questions. This work aims to emulate John's close attention to material reality and to the vicissitudes of personalities. For methodology and inspiration, I am much in John's debt.

The Appearance and Uptake of Libel Texts

Between about 1790 and 1830, the body of law now known as libel law came into existence in the Anglo-American world, emerging out of a blend of old and new forms of action for civil libel and slander and the variants of criminal libel (defamatory, obscene, seditious, and blasphemous). English libel texts multiplied, but they did not all cross the Atlantic or do so at the same speed.

Before about 1790, there was no cohesive body of law called libel. There were a few very old texts on civil defamation law and the related tort of false imprisonment. General legal digests and books of pleadings discussed defamation in one part and prosecutions for different kinds of speech offences elsewhere. The mid-eighteenth century in Britain was relatively calm, but newspapers were beginning to multiply and become accessible to broad swaths of the population. John Wilkes' attacks on the government in the 1760s initiated an upsurge in prosecutions of the press that reflected the enormous political, religious, social, and economic tensions associated with the American and French Revolutions and the Napoleonic Wars. Certain material thought to threaten the moral integrity of vulnerable segments of the population, such as women, the poor, and children, also became criminalized as obscenity during this period. As England careered from one speech-related crisis to another, turn-of-the-century writers started opining on libel law.[2]

The earliest tracts tended to defend those accused of speech-related offences and to urge juries to acquit prisoners, despite judicial instructions.[3] The first fully realized texts on libel, by Sir Francis Ludlow Holt and Thomas Starkie, appeared in 1812 and 1813, respectively.[4] Both showed an intention to draw together disparate offences relating to expression to demonstrate the logic of English law and reconcile these offences with constitutional rights to freedom of speech and press. Holt adopted a Blackstonian scheme, in which the person defamed (God, morality, the Constitution, the Houses of Parliament, the Courts of Justice, the magistrates, ordinary people) was the organizing principle. Starkie paid more attention to the pleadings, describing the case for the Crown or plaintiff and for the defence. Holt's second edition appeared in 1816 and his first American edition in 1818.[5] Initially, Holt's texts had wider circulation than Starkie's, but ultimately it was Starkie's that survived and prospered. American editions of Starkie were published in 1826 and 1832, a second English edition was published in 1830, and new editions were printed through the nineteenth century.[6]

These books entered an American market that already had two centuries of legal experience with the regulation of speech but lacked domestic libel treatises. In the 1730s, in a New York case that was to acquire enormous symbolic importance, John Peter Zenger had been prosecuted and eventually acquitted by a jury after putting forward a defence of truth to charges arising from material printed in a newspaper. Later, between 1776 and 1820, a party system developed, with newspaper editors playing key roles in promoting the interests of individuals and parties.[7] In the late 1790s, concerned that the French were conspiring with Jeffersonians to undermine the republic, John Adams' government passed the 1798 *Sedition Act* and initiated federal proceedings against about twenty-five individuals for promulgating sedition, which looked a lot like Jeffersonianism. When Jefferson succeeded Adams in 1801, the Jeffersonians turned common law libel against Federalist newspapers in the state courts.[8] One legacy of this period was that it provided a collective legal experience with criminal libel.

Political life and newspapers continued to be animated and fractious in Massachusetts for the next couple of decades, both on a quotidian basis and in connection with particular controversies, such as the vehement opposition to Jefferson's 1807-09 embargo, which barred the shipping of American goods from American to foreign ports, to the great detriment of port cities such as Boston. Nova Scotia, on the other hand, was being governed reasonably peaceably. There were few newspapers. During the American Revolution, some treason and sedition proceedings did occur, but the climate of paranoia had passed by the mid-1780s.[9] The French Revolution did not bring a sense of crisis to Nova Scotia as it did to Upper and Lower Canada. Newspapers were involved in the controversy over an effort to impeach two judges of the Nova Scotia Supreme Court in the late 1780s and early 1790s, but this conflict was well in the past by the 1820s.[10]

Nova Scotia profited, through smuggling, from Jefferson's embargo and was buffered against the War of 1812 by New England's neutrality. Political prosecutions were rare, although one man was convicted of seditious libel in 1820 for lambasting every political body in the colony except the governor.[11] But in the later 1820s, newspapers multiplied in the colony, and conflicts between the Assembly and the Council became common. Twice, governmental bodies called for apologies from the press.[12] The Nova Scotian newspapers between 1820 and 1835 reveal a tremendous increase in political content and in the vehemence of their criticism on a wide range of issues, including road building, excise taxes, banking, quarantine, and higher and lower education, but they generally did not question the structure of the institutions of government. Although tensions were mounting, the boundaries around sedition were approached with great caution, and consequently there was little local legal experience with the subject.

The evidence suggests that Holt's and Starkie's libel texts were not immediately absorbed into the Massachusetts legal world. By 1820, Boston had a thriving publishing industry, and law books were a significant part of it. Domestic law reporters, digests, and the first treatises were being published and sold alongside English imports. Important law libraries had been established by notable judges and lawyers as well as at Harvard.

An examination of Massachusetts' booksellers' catalogues and the holdings of libraries reveals no sign of either Holt or Starkie before 1826.[13] It seems to have taken a few years before these texts were accepted as valuable, and this may not have happened until American editions were available. Holt was accepted first: the American edition of 1818 appears in the Harvard law library catalogue in 1826.[14] Booksellers seem to have started marketing Starkie around 1827, shortly after the first American edition was released.[15] The other references to these texts, in journals and library catalogues, suggest that these books did get drawn into the Massachusetts legal market, but their progress was somewhat slow and uneven.[16]

The evidence from case citations suggests, similarly, that Holt was accepted before Starkie and that these books had at least some circulation before they appeared in library catalogues or booksellers' lists. The case citations are almost always by counsel, not judges. The first citation I have found to either text was to Holt in an 1822 prosecution, with other references in 1823, 1824, and 1825.[17] Starkie made its first appearance in 1825.[18] It was not until the mid-1830s that citations of these texts became common, with Starkie outpacing Holt.[19]

It is often difficult to know which edition of these books was being sold or cited. Booksellers did not usually specify, and the references in case reports have generally been updated by subsequent editors, making it difficult to determine what if anything was originally cited. In the two cases that do seem reliable, both from 1834, it seems most likely that the edition of Starkie cited was an American one; the Holt texts are often too similar to distinguish, although the 1818 American edition is usually the most likely source.[20] Auctions of law books in 1827, 1828, and 1829 show a tapering off in the number of copies of "Starkie on Slander" being marketed, which suggests that the text was the 1826 American edition, for which demand gradually dissipated.[21] The admittedly thin evidence suggests that it was the 1826 edition of Starkie and probably the similar second American edition of 1832 that made the largest impression on Massachusetts during this period.[22]

Tracking these books in Nova Scotia is even more difficult, owing to the absence of legal reporting or a book trade large enough to have spawned catalogues. Nova Scotia did not get official law reporting until 1853, and the editor at that time did not include any speech-related cases in the 1834-51 volume. The publishing industry in Nova Scotia was far less developed than that in Massachusetts. Halifax's few booksellers in the 1820s probably did very little trade in law books. After all, as Philip Girard has found, in 1820, Nova Scotia had only thirty-eight lawyers; by 1830, it still had only seventy-five.[23] Even in 1837 Halifax bookseller Charles Belcher advertised only fifteen law books for sale, all of them generalist texts; Boston booksellers at the same time were advertising hundreds of titles.[24] Nevertheless, law books did make it to Nova Scotia, either through the mail, special orders with booksellers, or sent by friends and relatives abroad.[25] John Macleod has noted that an 1830 probate inventory of Attorney General Richard John Uniacke's property revealed 260 titles in 800 volumes, and Uniacke had another 500 legal titles in about 1,000 volumes in his office.[26] The Halifax Barristers' Library catalogue listed more than six hundred titles in 1835.[27] Halifax lawyer William Young had 297 titles in "some 595 volumes" in 1835, according to William Laurence.[28] These libraries were significantly smaller than the Harvard law library, which had around fourteen hundred titles in 1834, but they were still substantial.[29] Significantly, though, while the Bostonians were beginning to look first to an indigenous legal publishing and bookselling industry, Nova Scotians imported their legal texts, mainly from England.

There is too little evidence from Nova Scotia to reveal conclusively whether Holt or Starkie arrived first, or how quickly the legal culture absorbed each text, or which editions were most influential. Like Harvard, the Nova Scotia Barristers' Library acquired Holt before Starkie and listed it in its 1835 catalog, with no mention of Starkie.[30] Similarly, William Young in 1835 had a text he called "Holt on Libels," and Joseph Howe cited Holt during his 1835 trial.[31] However, and significantly for my purposes, the 1830 English edition of Starkie made it to Nova Scotia and was in use well before it appeared in any Massachusetts record.[32] It was one of the titles auctioned in Uniacke's estate in 1830, Young owned it in 1835, and Howe cited it the same year.[33] No other edition of Starkie appears in any Nova Scotian source.

The Difference It Makes

Starkie was more helpful to an accused than was Holt. The two American editions of Starkie closely tracked the conservative first English edition. By the time Thomas Starkie composed the second English edition, though, he seems to have become more concerned about the ability of newspapers to defend themselves against libel actions.[34] For my purposes, the most important difference lies in the definition of the defence of qualified privilege. The 1832 American edition identified it as attaching simply "[t]o those who act in a friendly character toward the plaintiff ... And to those, in general, who appear to act in the discharge of any duty which the convenience or exigencies of society call upon them to perform; as, where a master gives the character of a servant, or a critic that of a book, for the information and advantage of the public."[35] In the 1830 English edition, however, the privilege received more attention and was argued to cover all kinds of non-malicious publications on subjects of general concern that were of interest to both the author and the community — in short, "to extend to all publications made in the fair discharge of any public or private, legal or moral duty, of which the ordinary exigences of society, or the party's own private interests, require the performance."[36] The privilege could be rebutted by evidence of actual malice, such as evidence that the allegation was false. Joseph Howe relied heavily on this defence and extensively cited the 1830 edition of Starkie.[37] He argued that he had a duty to publish the letter about the magistrates' misdeeds because of his situation as a newspaper editor and because of what he had learned during his stint on a grand jury some time earlier. He emphasized that he was barred from proving the truth of the statements, and he elaborated on his beliefs as they had affected his actions in publishing the allegedly defamatory material. He left it to the prosecution to try to prove falsity as part of showing malice on his part. They did not even try. The structure of Starkie's qualified privilege defence held out considerable promise to the press, in that it left falsity to the Crown to prove and emphasized the importance of the occasion of publication.

Nova Scotia lacked a long tradition of litigating and publicly debating the parameters of libel law, but there was one earlier case in which an argument that presaged a privilege claim was made, by none other than S.G.W. Archibald, Howe's prosecutor, then acting for the defence. In that 1821 case, Archibald argued that a newspaper editor was entitled — and indeed had a duty—to publish material on subjects of general interest that were proper to publish.[38] The case was a civil suit, and it may have been truth or other factors that inspired the jury to side with Archibald and exculpate the defendant, but an argument that sounded like qualified privilege was made as well. There is no evidence that Howe referred to the case, but it does suggest that the climate was not hostile to a privilege argument. Howe and his legal friends could bend the 1830 edition of Starkie to their will and even overlook the fact that Starkie cited precious little authority for the broad principles he set out. However, as I outline later, though it may be possible to detect in Massachusetts a couple of efforts to inject some qualified privilege thinking into the law of libel, the defence was basically ignored in practice. The battle over the rights of the press was fought around the truth defence.

The idea that truth ought to be a full defence to a charge of criminal libel—as it was to civil defamation—had a long pedigree in the United States. It retained its symbolic currency among those who crusaded for a free press despite its failure to be of much help to those prosecuted under the 1798 *Sedition Act,* which did make truth a defence. In 1803-04, as Jeffersonians avenged themselves on Federalist newspapers, Alexander Hamilton defended Harry Croswell, the editor of a Federalist newspaper in New York, against criminal libel charges. Hamilton drew on the legacy of the near-legendary defence of John Peter Zenger in 1735 in which the argument had been made that, contrary to English law, truth ought to be a defence.[39] The common law held that a truthful libel might be even more likely than a false one to disturb the peace. When Hamilton defended Croswell, he did not argue that truth ought to be a complete defence but that it should be admissible to prove an accused's innocent motives. At English common law, bad intent was generally inferred from the face of the matter published, so that the accused's good motives were usually legally irrelevant. In Hamilton's assessment, the intention to do harm simply had to be relevant to this crime, as with any other. The burden of proving good intention though, fell to the defence.[40]

In *Comm. v. Clap* in 1808, the Massachusetts Supreme Judicial Court incorporated the *People v. Croswell* reasoning but limited it to cases in which the alleged libel was a complaint to the legislature to remove an unworthy officer, or concerned someone who was standing for election or was currently sitting and would presumably stand again.[41] *Clap* contemplated that having a justifiable purpose and good intentions might excuse a libel on such a person. In these cases, once a justifiable purpose was shown, truth might be admissible to prove this lack of malice and intent to defame.[42] *Clap* brought a limited version of the truth defence to Massachusetts.

The history of the truth defence in the 1820s and 1830s shows judges in criminal libel cases wrestling with how best to handle such evidence in prosecutions that involved a new breed of public figures, those bent on drawing the faithful away from orthodox Calvinist Christianity or bringing changes in public morals. Judges saw value in allowing a thorough public investigation of such figures' characters but did not want to encourage them to invade the private lives and damage the reputations of others in their efforts to bring about reform. Since truth was useful in one set of circumstances and highly problematic in the other, the law took some ungainly twists. The prosecutor permitted evidence of truth to be adduced in an 1822 case, *Buckingham,* which concerned an allegation that an itinerant Methodist revivalist had lied about his humble origins, made inappropriate advances to young women, and did not really believe what he preached but liked the access to the ladies that his position gave him.[43] Controversy within the legal community followed when the Judge, Josiah Quincy, formally ruled that such evidence was admissible, despite the fact that the minister was not a *Clap* type of figure.[44] Commentators worried that truth would be used to excuse all kinds of invasive expression, but this eventuality did not come to pass during this period.

In 1824 a different Municipal Court Judge excluded evidence of truth in a defence against a charge of libelling Boston's Russian consul. The consul, though a representative of a foreign government, was held not to be a *Clap* sort of person — an unworthy officer or an electoral candidate — and his brawling at a ball was a private matter. In 1825 more controversy followed a decision to exclude, as inadmissible evidence of truth, evidence of a coroner's inquiry in a case concerning an allegation that an innholder had, by serving alcohol, caused a patron's death.[45] In that case, *Comm. v. Blanding,* the Judge emphasized that complaints about a person's conduct pursuant to a liquor licence were to be addressed through testimony before the Court of Sessions when the licence was to be renewed, not by writing to a newspaper. Newspapers, he feared, would divulge not just crimes but also minor foibles; accusations would not be made to the proper body; reform-minded "intermeddlers" (such as Blanding, presumably) would expose errors and faults in private lives that had been overlooked or pardoned by those most concerned; and duels and assassinations would become common.[46] To this Massachusetts Judge and most others, truth could be dangerous, at least if wielded by a certain class of person. The innholder, like the Russian consul, would be shielded: evidence of the truth of allegations against them would be inadmissible.

In 1826 the state legislature made evidence of truth not only admissible in all libel cases but also, in fact, potentially a sufficient defence, if it was also shown "that the matter charged to be libelous was published with good motives and for justifiable ends."[47] The truth defence was frequently pleaded in subsequent criminal libel cases.[48] Judges, however, continued to be wary and to grapple with how truth evidence should be used when certain kinds of people had been libelled or had libelled others. Judges repeatedly expressed concerns about a licentious press exposing a person's long-past, now irrelevant misdeeds or provoking violence. Now evidence of truth was admissible in all cases, but it continued to be treated carefully, so that its impact would be controlled. In a case called *Comm. v. Snelling,* judges required a defendant to particularize his truth defence to help the Commonwealth refute it. Snelling, an anti-gambling crusader, had alleged in a newspaper that one of the magistrates of the police court had appeared on the bench drunk and otherwise misconducted himself. Prosecuted for libel, Snelling said he would prove the allegations were true. The Commonwealth succeeded in restricting Snelling's defence to those incidents that he outlined in his pleadings, on the theory that it was really the defamed magistrate who was on trial and needed to defend himself.[49]

Judges much more readily permitted evidence of truth to be used when it was reformers or religious figures whose pasts had been dug up and whose reputations had been damaged. In one case, a judge observed that a person who set himself up as "a teacher, a guide and instructor of mankind, in religion, morals, or government" had to expect that his character would be publicly scrutinized.[50] If such a person found himself libelled, he should expect truth to be mounted as a defence against any prosecution he might instigate.

Amidst all of these struggles over the truth defence, a couple of efforts were made to introduce the qualified privilege defence, or elements of it, into the law of Massachusetts. David Lee Child was prosecuted in 1828 for alleging in a newspaper that a Jacksonian Massachusetts senator had inappropriately favoured a Jacksonian printer for government contracts, over another, cheaper, Federalist one. Defects in the pleadings ultimately cleared Child, but during the course of the trial, his counsel argued for modifications to the truth defence in language that suggests he was thinking along the lines of privilege. Child's defence had two prongs: first, that the matter was true and, second, that Child lacked what ought to be the requisite criminal intent: "That if the matter alleged was not true, it was published without malice, from good motives and justifiable ends, the Defendant having good grounds to believe, and conscientiously believing it to be true."[51] This argument had elements in common with a defence of qualified privilege, as evident in counsel's assertion that "whenever a man publishes, with an honest intent, that which he believes to be true, to those only who have an interest to know the fact, or to be put upon inquiry, this is no criminal libel, although the information communicated should turn out to be untrue."[52]

Asserting privilege involves arguing that the occasion and circumstances in which a statement was made are such that the speaker or writer ought to be protected. Child's argument shows this kind of thinking, but clearly the truth defence was the mainstay of the structure, and other arguments had to support it. In a second prosecution of William Snelling a few years later, Child, now a lawyer himself, likewise argued that Snelling ought to be excused because he had reasonably believed, on the best authority, that the libellous information was true, even if it was not. This argument again went nowhere with either the Boston Municipal Court or Chief Justice Shaw.[53] Shaw observed that the law would be ineffectual "to guard against the abuses of the press and the freedom of publication, if information and belief would amount to a justification."[54] Wary as the judges were of truth, they were even more sensitive to the possibility of excusing accidental falsehoods, regardless of good intentions or particular circumstances.[55]

The only explicit effort I have found to introduce qualified privilege into Massachusetts occurred in 1835. Reverend George Cheever was prosecuted for an obviously fictitious pamphlet that described demons distilling alcohol in a distillery owned by a deacon who peddled bibles out of the same room. The jury believed that it aimed at the complainant, an Essex deacon who ran a distillery, and Cheever was convicted. On appeal to the Supreme Judicial Court, Cheever pleaded no contest. However, he also made a speech in which he argued that he had an obligation to publish the tract to promote temperance in the face of alcohol's detrimental effects on society. He cited not "Starkie on Slander" but instead the 1824 London edition of Starkie's evidence treatise, which included a section on proving the defences to libel.[56] For his efforts, Cheever was harshly sentenced: thirty days in jail, a $1,000 fine, and bonds to keep the peace for two years. As far as I can tell, no subsequent cases picked up on Cheever's argument.

The Massachusetts judiciary had to accept the truth defence after it was legislated, but they wrestled with its implications. So absorbing was their preoccupation with truth and its effect on privacy that they refused to countenance the emergence of any defences, such as qualified privilege, that might have allowed falsity to be explained and excused as owing to good intentions. As long as the accused really had published defamatory material about the complainant, truth was the only significant defence available, and its possibilities were carefully circumscribed.

CONCLUSION

In Massachusetts, the battles over criminal libel and free expression were fought around the truth defence, whereas in Nova Scotia, it was possible for another defence, that of qualified privilege, at least to get a hearing in court. By the time Thomas Starkie had articulated a broad view of the qualified privilege defence, Massachusetts was already firmly set on a legal and cultural trajectory centred on the argument that one should not be convicted of criminal libel for publishing the truth. Looking back to Andrew Hamilton's defence of Zenger and the political prosecutions that flowed in the wake of the 1798 *Sedition Act,* defence lawyers reasoned that in a republic it had to be permissible to criticize the government and individuals involved in public life. The Massachusetts cases, from *Clap* on, hammered away at the reach of the truth defence. On the other hand, judges, mainly old Federalists surveying the fractious, disorderly party presses and the rise of meddlesome moral reform movements, were seldom keen to limit exposure to criminal libel. They managed the operation of the truth defence so as to prevent any protection of falsity, regardless of good intentions, and to protect certain people's reputations and expose those of others.

Into this milieu, the 1830 English edition of Starkie eventually came, but it had little impact. Massachusetts lawyers generally referred to American editions, but these editions contained only the unpromising qualified privilege defence that Starkie articulated in his first English edition. The strong version of the qualified privilege defence went unread and unconsidered. In effect, through a combination of publishing practices and social, political, and legal preoccupations, Massachusetts jurists continued to struggle over the truth defence, rather than looking for another solution that would simultaneously protect the press and reputations.

Nova Scotia, on other hand, was a colonial setting with barely any domestic legal publishing, with little experience of an unruly press, fractious politics, or politicized libel trials. The temperance movement was afoot, but as yet, reformers had not tried to reform middle- or upper-class habits by exposing them to public view in the press. The law of criminal libel was taken to be what English judges and commentators said it was. There was no history of arguing about the importance of truth in political life, as, indeed, the view that government should be responsive and responsible to the will of the public did not start to be evident in Nova Scotia newspapers until the late 1820s, and, even then, there was considerable caution about appearing to espouse republican sentiments. These absences of legal and intellectual history and of particular social conditions, combined with the lawyers' and judges' habits of acquiring and relying on English law books, meant that a nearly novel argument could be understood by Howe and his legal friends and articulated in court, even if the judge told the jury to disregard it. The legal impact of *R. v. Howe* is enigmatic, but the qualified privilege defence does survive in Canadian law, and the case does seem to have relieved the press of anxiety about prosecutions for publishing political criticism.[57]

This chapter has emphasized elements of the colonial project that John McLaren has frequently highlighted: the importance of attending to a culture's socio-legal preoccupations, its pre-existing legal trajectories, and the material dimensions of the flow of information to and within that culture when assessing the migration of English law to its colonies and ex-colonies. As ever, the lawyers and judges of Nova Scotia and Massachusetts bought and read what they could get, and they made arguments that reflected their sense of the perils of their place and time. Different historico-legal lenses and reading different editions of the same text led them to different approaches for balancing freedom of the press and the protection of private reputation.

CHAPTER ELEVEN

THE LAW OF DOWER IN NEW SOUTH WALES AND THE UNITED STATES

A STUDY IN COMPARATIVE LEGAL HISTORY

A.R. Buck and Nancy E. Wright

DURING THE late Antipodean winter of 1850, the Legislative Council of New South Wales established the Select Committee on the Real Property and Dower Bills to investigate the operation of the law of dower in the colony. Dower was a common law property right providing a widow with a life estate in one-third of all the freehold lands that her husband had owned during their marriage. The Select Committee was established in response to a Bill that proposed changes to statute law governing dower in New South Wales. The Bill was designed to prevent dower from attaching to lands owned by a husband in the colony if his wife had not also resided in the colony when the land was acquired. One Councillor, G.K. Holden, was quite adamant that the widow should have no claim, arguing: "[W]hen she married in England she never could have considered it part of her matrimonial contract that she could have dower out of land that her husband might purchase in New South Wales, any more than out of land which might be purchased by him in South America, where she would not be entitled to Dower."[1]

This was a curious argument because the existing law allowed for precisely that eventuality. Moreover, not all agreed with Holden's assessment. In evidence to the Committee, another Legislative Councillor, Robert Johnson, argued: "[T]he law of Dower is a legal right, and that it would be unjust to deprive a widow of her legal right because she might be absent or unknown."[2] Holden's concern was not with the legal rights of widows but instead with facilitating a market environment that rendered titles to land "clean" and unencumbered with them. Holden argued: "The law of Dower is here a mere accident, and I think clean titles with regard to third parties, much more important."[3] Johnson's voice, it turned out, was a minority one, with the resulting Act limiting widows' access to dower. Clean titles took precedence over widows' legal rights. Ultimately, in New South Wales, it was Holden's argument about "clean titles" rather than Johnson's concern with "legal rights" that shaped the statutory development of dower in colonial Australia.[4] What insights might accrue from comparing the Australian experience with that of another jurisdiction? In this chapter, we will compare the debate over, and fate of, the law of dower in colonial Australia and the United States in the nineteenth century. We will argue that there are distinct advantages in adopting a historical approach that is both comparative and contextual. This discussion is not intended to be an intervention into the rich tradition of American legal history. Rather, in it, we pose a question: what might a comparative approach reveal about the legal history of dower in particular, and about property in general, in Australia?

AUSTRALIA AND AMERICA IN COMPARATIVE PERSPECTIVE: HISTORY AND HISTORIOGRAPHY

Why compare the United States and Australia? In many respects, they are ripe for comparison, and it is surprising that more comparative work has not been done.[5] Both are settler societies founded during a period of British imperial expansion. Both saw the transplantation of English common law and English constitutional principles. The Australian Constitution owes at least as much to its American counterpart as it does to the Westminster tradition. Both countries possess, for example, bicameral legislative chambers in which constitutional politics has historically been preoccupied with the question of state's rights. The constitutional and legal history of both jurisdictions, particularly, although not exclusively, has been integrally tied to the dispossession of indigenous populations. Reference to politics alerts us to another significant point of comparison — the slippery notion of democracy. Here, at last, we arrive at the point to which contemporaries in colonial Australia made explicit reference (not altogether of a complimentary nature). The Janus face of emergent democracy was established conservatism. And at the interface of democracy and conservatism was a rich tradition of political rhetoric. As the conservative Australian newspaper the *Southern Courier* stated in August 1861, "[o]f all the communities in the world, next to the Americans, the British Australians are more given to a kind of gregarious to[a]dyism than any other. If a man be successful in his worldly ventures, and build up a fortune, no matter with what materials, he is at once 'great' in the eyes of the sycophant mob."[6] Democracy was a fiercely contested idea and the subject of much anxiety in the nineteenth century.[7] Of perhaps greater importance for our purposes is the relationship of the question of democracy to the "land question": Who should occupy the land? Was it to be the rich man or the poor man, the farmer or the investor, the pastoralist or the agriculturalist? Needless to say, it was not to be the indigenous population, for the land question in nineteenth-century politics was restricted to competing levels of white settler society.[8]

Both jurisdictions, then, adapted and adopted English law, with respect to property. The political cultures of both jurisdictions were informed (or perhaps it would be more accurate to say "misinformed") by the notion of an abundance of uncultivated land. In both societies Lockean notions of "improvement" informed debates.[9] In the case of New South Wales (which is the colonial Australian jurisdiction we draw upon), land legislation, known as the *Robertson Land Acts,* was passed by a reformist government in 1861. The stated purpose of that legislation was to put the poor man on the land. As a result of pre-emptive rights of purchase given to pastoral lessees by imperial legislation in 1846, many contemporaries argued that the land had been "locked up" on behalf of the pastoral interest.[10] After the establishment of manhood suffrage in 1858, and in a context of rapid urban growth and urban unemployment, a popular demand arose to "unlock the lands" on behalf of "the poor man," a ubiquitous figure of the political rhetoric in the years following the introduction of manhood suffrage.[11] In essence, the campaign to "unlock the lands" on behalf of "the poor man" involved legislation enabling any person to enter the Crown leaseholds of a pastoralist (or "squatter" as they were known colloquially) and "select" an area prior to a government survey, which he or she could then buy in freehold from the Crown.[12]

Compare this to the United States. On first glance, the similarities are striking. Abraham Lincoln, shortly after his election, referred to proposed land legislation when he stated: "I am in favour of settling the wild lands into small parcels so that every poor man may have a home."[13] The *Homestead Act* of 1862 opened all federal lands under Union control to settlement. The legislation allowed a qualified person to settle 160 acres of land upon payment of a ten-dollar registration fee. The conditions required settlement for five years and visible improvement to the land.[14]

But there were differences as well as similarities. The provisions of the American legislation included an oath of future loyalty and an exclusion of all who had borne arms against the Union. From a source of revenue, the public lands had been transformed into the mechanism for achieving rapid settlement. It has been argued that the *Homestead Act* "represented the apotheosis of free soil, free labor Republican ideology."[15] Consequently, though the two jurisdictions seem to bear striking similarities, there were subtle but important differences between them. Sometimes those differences are hidden by the sweeping generalizations of historians, politicians, and popular commentators. Let us briefly examine them.

National histories are replete with historical shibboleths. Two of the most abiding with reference to the history of the United States and Australia are that, whereas the former expressed values of frontier individualism, the development of the latter was informed by a type of "colonial socialism." Like many shibboleths, these notions continue in the popular psyche long after they have been dissected and critiqued by academic historians and other scholars. The American variant is the idea that the legal history of property law and the historical development of property rights in the United States were marked by commitment to "rugged individualism." Individual initiative on the frontier, rather than the role of government, shaped the law of property and the culture of property rights. In two recent articles that analyze land use law before and after the revolution and its implications for contemporary judicial decisions, John F. Hart demonstrates that such a notion continues to inform public and judicial opinion.[16]

The Australian shibboleth is the notion of "colonial socialism" used to explain the historical development of Australia. It runs something like this: when the first fleet arrived at Botany Bay in 1788, Governor Phillip claimed the entire eastern half of the continent for the British Crown. When settlement took place at Swan River on the western coast adjacent to the Indian Ocean in 1829, the Crown claimed sovereignty over the entire continent. Most importantly, the lands of the whole continent became vested in the British Crown. The development of the principle of *terra nullius,* through legal decisions in the first half of the nineteenth century, meant that the state, from the formative years of development in Australia, was in a position of enormous economic importance.[17] All decisions about how the land should be owned, occupied, and utilized were refracted through the apparatus of the state. All access to land had to be negotiated with the government. The size of the continent, combined with the lack of water, effectively inhibited small-scale agriculture in favour of large-scale pastoral development. There was, in other words, little opportunity for a massive westward migration to find land for settlement. The pastoral development of the nation, begun in the early years of the nineteenth century, resulted in Australia's population becoming one of the most urbanized on the planet. Colonial contemporaries were only too aware of the extent to which the country had been turned into a vast sheep run. The economies of scale arising from westward migration in the United States were absent in Australia. As a result, the railways in Australia were simply uneconomic from the perspective of the private sector; therefore, they were owned and developed by the state. One consequence of the *Robertson Land Acts* in New South Wales was the piecemeal transfer of public lands from Crown leasehold to private freehold. But it was the wealthy corporate pastoral sector that accounted for this, not the "poor" selectors for whom the legislation was purportedly intended. By the end of the 1880s, the corporate pastoral sector was more entrenched than it had been prior to the land legislation of the 1860s. The effect of this change to land tenure was to see colonial Australian governments become extremely wealthy from land sales. This provided the government with the revenue necessary to fund the expansion of infrastructure such as railways. Consequently, when Australian scholars accounted for Australia's peculiar economic development throughout the nineteenth century, they coined the term "colonial socialism" in preference to the "rugged individualism" of Frederick Jackson Turner's "frontier" in the United States.[18]

On the other hand, if we focus not on the setting, but on the subject — and, in particular, the subject of property — could we see conformity rather than exceptionalism in the experience of these two countries? In his recent entertaining history of land surveying in America, Andro Linklater makes an explicit claim about the underlying similarities between Australia and America in relation to property in land. Australia, Canada, New Zealand, South Africa, the United Kingdom, and the United States, he argues, shared not only a common language and form of government but also a third "and perhaps more fundamental" tie: "To protect what they claimed as theirs against overly greedy rulers, landowners had struggled to establish a system of individual rights and a form of government in which their interests were represented. Thus for all six nations property and democracy became intertwined at the same point, the enclosures in Tudor England."[19] Linklater's template is the notion of "modern, liberal property relations." Well, is it as simple as that? In order to see what insights we might gain into the broader comparative history of property, let us now turn to a law that has not yet been the subject of comparative analysis between American and Australian jurisdictions — the law of dower.

In 1833 a *Dower Act* was passed in England, which simplified the means by which a husband could will his lands without the right of dower being attached.[20] This legislation was adopted in New South Wales in 1836.[21] It meant that, from 1 January 1837, dower did not apply to any lands that a husband had disposed of absolutely by means of sale or by his will. It also provided that a husband could wholly deprive his wife of her right to dower by making a declaration to that effect in his will or by any deed. This provision was later applied to any transfer under the *Real Property Act* of 1862, which introduced Torrens Title.[22] A husband could, moreover, exclude his wife from enjoyment of dower even if he died intestate, by executing a declaration to that end. After 1837, in other words, the widow's right to dower was weak. But that did not satisfy its critics. In 1850 the amending legislation further restricted a widow's access to dower.[23] The few residual rights to dower were further attacked in parliamentary debate in 1879 and 1881. Finally, they were abolished in 1890 when the *Probate Act* was passed in order to consolidate and rationalize the entire law of inheritance.[24] Dower was one of its victims. Importantly, the 1890 abolition of married women's common law right to dower preceded the passing of the 1893 *Married Women's Property Act*.

DOWER IN THE UNITED STATES

How does this compare to the American story? Tracing the development of English common law in US laws regulating the ownership of property in and beyond the life of a marriage is inevitably complicated by the fact that, by the end of the nineteenth century, eight jurisdictions — Arizona, California, Idaho, Louisiana, Nevada, New Mexico, Texas, and Washington — had adopted a system of community property, whereas the other states retained the common law system of property law.[25] For the purpose of comparison, however, we will restrict ourselves to the common law states.

In their study of inheritance law in the United States, Carol Shammas, Marylynn Salmon, and Michel Dahlin examine the transformation of the laws of property affecting married women — including the law of dower—from the point when nineteen territories entered the Union from 1850 on, up to 1890, a date for which they present detailed data on the state of inheritance laws. Of this period they note:

> From about 1850 on, most states passed legislation allowing married women, rather than their husbands, the ownership and control over all the personal and real property they had inherited or been given. These acts automatically endowed women of the capitalist class with rights only obtainable previously through the complicated marriage settlement process. Married women's inheritances became separate property that they could will to whom they chose and daughters could finally benefit from the intestacy laws that gave them an equal share to that of the eldest brother. The nineteenth-century reforms substantially increased the number of testators who were women and the amount of wealth they bequeathed.[26]

It is in light of that conclusion that we can examine the fate of the law of dower in the American jurisdictions in the nineteenth century.

As Shammas, Salmon, and Dahlin point out, over two-thirds of those territories entering the Union from 1850 onward abolished dower, but in its place most post-1850 jurisdictions embraced homestead protections. The importance of the homestead legislation was that it exempted the homestead from creditors and other claimants so as to protect widows and children from destitution. The homestead provisions were first instituted in Texas in 1839 and were copied in practically every other post-1850 territory. The pre-1850s states, although more reluctant to implement homestead provisions, were also less reluctant to abolish dower.[27]

To understand the significance of the legislative history of dower in the United States in the nineteenth century, moreover, it is important to situate it in the context of the history of married women's property legislation. Beginning with the New York legislation of 1848, married women's property legislation preceded, rather than followed, changes to the laws of dower.[28] What this meant was the *Married Women's Property Acts,* which, by removing a husband's interest in his wife's property, also removed a condition that in many respects had been used to justify the existence of dower.[29] Consequently, in a survey of the legislative history of dower in the United States during the mid- to late nineteenth century, it is the context within which abolition took place that is of crucial importance. As George Haskins concludes in his treatise on the history of dower in the United States, "[p]erhaps the most notable feature of nineteenth century legislation was the increased protection afforded the widow by extending the kinds of property subject to dower and by supplementing protection in the form of homestead and other protections."[30] In other words, the context reveals a complicated articulation of the abolition of dower with provisions that gave legal protection to widows by other means.

DOWER IN NEW SOUTH WALES

How does the situation in colonial Australia compare? Between 1850 and 1890 (the same years examined by Shammas, Salmon, and Dahlin in the United States), the legal right of dower was substantially weakened and finally abolished in New South Wales.[31] But the context of that abolition was entirely different. One effect of the 1850 *Act to Amend the Law of Dower in Certain Respects* was to eliminate "the remaining old cases" of dower that involved only women married prior to 1 January 1837.[32] According to the provisions of the statute, no widow was entitled to dower unless it should be proved that, first, she resided in the colony as the wife of the deceased while he still owned the land and that, second, the purchaser had notice before, or at the time of the sale, of the deceased owner having been married to her. In cases where the defendant derived title through a purchaser other than the widow's deceased husband, in order for her to claim dower, she must show that, first, the defendant had been informed of the marriage before he made the purchase and that, second, she had resided in the colony. The 1850 statute also enacted that, when land had been alienated, the claim to dower was to be limited to one-third of the estimated rent of the land, based on its state of improvement at the date of its alienation by her husband. As a result of these provisions, dower was reduced from a life estate in one-third of a husband's lands to only one-third of the estimated rents of the land.

If we examine the debate over dower in light of adjacent legal reforms, we discover similar concerns regarding the role of property in the colonial economy. In 1849 there was an attempt to pass a bill shortening the period of limitations, then twenty years, covering a mortgagor's right of redemption. Under the existing law of real property, the mere possession of land did not conclusively prove ownership. On the contrary, the ownership of landed property differed from the ownership of other property in

English law because title to land could be modified by deeds into a number of degrees of ownership. In order to transfer title to land, it was necessary to draw together the lesser ownerships so as to confer the complete title. Under the existing law, moreover, there was no record of the derivation of title, except through the title deeds. As a result, it was quite feasible for any of those deeds to be suppressed. Consequently, to ensure against fraud, all transactions required a complete and expensive retrospective investigation of the title. Those problems were exacerbated in New South Wales because a large proportion of the population had interests in land. "Property changes owners here more frequently than at home," noted Robert Johnson in evidence to the Select Committee on the Real Property Law Bill on 24 July 1849. Johnson accurately asserted: "Such changes would not occur in England in a hundred years as occur here in twenty." It was for this reason that Johnson argued for a shortened period of limitations. Such a move was necessary, he felt, because of "the rapidity with which property changes hands here."[33] However, to shorten the period of limitations could unfairly bar the claim of a genuine owner. That was why the period was so lengthy. For some witnesses, such as G.K. Holden, who gave evidence to the same committee, "the general advantage gained in security, simplicity and economy in all transactions in land, far outweighs the occasional hardship of a claim prematurely barred."[34] His market rhetoric explained the financial benefits that would accrue from legal change that subordinated the legal rights of owners with genuine titles to land and of married women with genuine entitlement to dower to the interests of third parties who had the legal and economic agency to buy land.

The juxtaposition of political democracy and a vigorous market in land would have profound consequences for the widow's right to dower in the second half of the nineteenth century. Perhaps the most important exponent of law reform in the Australian colonies in the years following the introduction of responsible government in 1856 and manhood suffrage in 1858 was Robert Richard Torrens, who developed the system of registration of title, or, as it is commonly known, Torrens Title.[35] "In Australia," as Torrens said, "the great mass of the people are, or confidently look to become, landed proprietors. In Australia, therefore, 'thorough law reform' is essentially 'the people's question.'"[36] His view was widely shared. "The land," noted the *Sydney Morning Herald* on 23 June 1859, "is not all in possession of a limited number of families from generation to generation. It is greatly subdivided; it is held to a great extent by small capitalists; it is the working man's savings bank; and it is constantly being mortgaged and transferred."[37] Law reform advocated by Torrens was justified with market rhetoric that emphasized how the system of Torrens Title would enhance the opportunities of "small capitalists" to own and sell land. This objective coincided with the concerns of another great law reformer of the nineteenth century, John Stuart Mill, who argued: "It is not the subversion of the system of individual property which should be aimed at; but the improvement of it and the participation of every member of the community in its benefits."[38] Torrens was one of many colonial reformers fond of quoting John Stuart Mill's line that "[t]o make land as easily transferable as stock would be one of the greatest economical improvements which could be bestowed on a country."[39] By this, Torrens and others implied that a simplified and accurate system of registering title would increase the marketability of land. This objective of facilitating ease and cheapness in dealings with land was central to the market justification used by those intent on reforming the law of property in the second half of the nineteenth century.

Dower was criticized as an impediment to efficient registration of land transactions during the Real Property Commission of 1879. The purpose of the *Real Property Act* of 1862 was to make land more attractive commercially and more saleable. According to evidence given to the Real Property Commission of 1879, "the practice of noting dower" was a "troublesome matter" if an applicant desired to convert land from old title to the more saleable Torrens Title.[40] When introduced in New South Wales in 1863, Torrens Title required an application to state whether the owner was married.[41] If the owner had married before or on 1 January 1837, he was required not only to state whether his wife was entitled to dower but also to negate dower by statutory declaration. As these provisions indicate, since 1863 a married woman's right to dower, without her consent, could easily be invalidated by a statutory declaration to that effect by her husband. Despite this simple procedure to invalidate dower, evidence given to the Real Property Commission of 1879 criticized dower as a vestige from the past that posed an impediment to transactions in land: "There are very many certificates issued in which dower is noted as an encumbrance, and the chances are ten to one, owing to the lapse of time since the Dower Act, there is no dower at all, and yet it is a blot on the certificate."[42] This assertion (for which no proof was offered) evaluated dower from the perspective of buyers and sellers whose opinion guided legislators toward the absolute abolition of dower. The consequences of abolishing dower for women who had married before 1837 were dismissed as irrelevant by Edward Ward, who suggested in "ninety-nine cases out of a hundred who were married before 1837 have not the slightest idea of having any interest in the land of their husbands."[43] His rhetoric reduced dower from the concept of a legal right and status-based entitlement of married women to a mere economic interest. As a result of such evidence, the 1879 Commission recommended that the law be revised in order to benefit the market in property by applying the *Dower Act* of 1836 retrospectively so that women married before 1837 would be on the same footing as women married in or after that year. The only means for women married before 1837 to retain their right to dower would be by lodging a notice in the Registrar General's office within a limited period of time. These recommendations would further limit a wife's ability to claim dower.

How was dower treated in the courts? Was it treated more favourably by judges than by legislators? Not all of the widow's rights had been eroded by the English *Dower Act* of 1833. In adopting the colonial legislation of 1836, if a husband died beneficially entitled to land, the widow would be entitled to dower in equity. Moreover, a husband could enter into a covenant or agreement not to bar dower, which the court of equity was bound to enforce.[44] The question then arose as to what the position was with regard to rights to dower before the passage of the *Dower Act*.[45] In *Carr v. Harrison* (1871) it was held that dower of the purchaser's widow was barred, notwithstanding that her marriage had taken place before the Act. In the same case, "it appeared that the Court would be prepared to regard dower as being barred *in equity* after a lapse of twenty years by analogy to the Statute of Limitations."[46] This was one of many decisions that weakened widows' claim to dower.

In 1862 the *Real Estate of Intestates Distribution Act* (which abolished primogeniture) also provided on the death of the husband intestate that, should the intestate's realty be sold, a payment equivalent to the widow's dower was to be made to her. When the Court was asked to consider what that payment might be, as it was asked in *Ex parte Murphy* (1867), it held that the widow was entitled to dower only out of the proceeds of sale reckoned as if invested in government debentures at 6 percent.[47] It was hard luck for the widow if the sale were a profitable one, especially if it greatly exceeded the 6 percent sum. Or consider *Merriman v. The Perpetual Trustee Co. Ltd.* (1896).[48] The Full Court held through the partial failure of a trust for the conversion of realty, a testator had died intestate.

As a result, the proceeds of conversion passed to the executors as personalty to which dower did not apply. Accordingly, by the terms of the *Real Estate of Intestates Distribution Act* of 1862, the widow took nothing. Clearly, a pattern was emerging that was hostile to the legal rights of widows.

What was important about the Australian story was the context within which all this was happening. As Chief Justice Sir Alfred Stephen remarked in despair, "[t]he tendency of the community is, it seems to me, for each man to think himself perfectly equal to any other."[49] Indeed, in New South Wales, the nature of the polity reflected a quite assertive "democracy." Economic relations took the form of a remarkably "egalitarian" market economy, where as few barriers as possible were placed in the way of the greatest possible number becoming participants in the system of buying and selling—particularly in the case of land. Finally, the community evidenced no "feudal attachments" but instead was marked by a tendency, as Stephen C.J. put it, for each man to think himself perfectly equal to any other. The nature of the community itself, in other words, was "democratic" but within the context of an "egalitarian" market economy.

The political culture of mid- to late nineteenth-century New South Wales was a type of "distributive democracy" that informed a relationship between property, law, and society that we term "possessive egalitarianism."[50] Statutory reforms, including the introduction of Torrens Title, the abolition of primogeniture, and the erosion of dower, were all indicative of a widely shared set of values that valorized the market over ancient rights.[51] In such a society as that of late nineteenth-century New South Wales, the widow's right of dower was not protected or extended because dower was not articulated as a right; rather, it was overwhelmingly articulated, as Hargrave J. decided in *Underwood v. Underwood* (1879), as a "burden of a feudal nature."[52]

CONCLUSION

What conclusions, then, might we draw about the history of the law of dower (and, by implication, about the history of property rights) in colonial Australia by adopting a comparative approach as we have undertaken here? In the United States and colonial Australia in the nineteenth century, the stories of dower are broadly similar, yet the nuances of the similarities are of most interest. It is clear that, in both jurisdictions, women's dower rights were eroded in the course of the nineteenth century. Because of its longer settler history, it is also clear that this had occurred in the later years of the eighteenth century in America. This has been established in a detailed analysis of case law before and after the revolution by Joan Hoff.[53] Nor should we assume that an examination of United States case law in the second half of the nineteenth century would reveal substantial differences in the attitudes toward dower. Courts in the United States saw dower, as did the Australian courts, as an encumbrance upon a title. As Lathrop J. stated in *Flynn v. Flynn* (1898), "[t]here is no doubt that the inchoate right of dower is an encumbrance upon land."[54] But the comparison of the trend toward abolition in the nineteenth century indicates the erosion and abolition of dower in colonial Australia constituted more of a loss for married women there than in the United States. As we have seen, this was partly the result of the implementation of homestead provisions and partly due to the fact that those states that abolished dower did so subsequent to the implementation of *Married Women's Property Acts,* not prior to them as was the case in Australia. What seem, at the outset, to be broad similarities, explained by reference to "modern, liberal property relations," are more nuanced. Only through an approach that is both comparative and contextual are these nuances revealed.

To draw our focus back from dower to the larger subject of property law and property rights generally, we might also posit that, in an examination of this broader question of the legal history of property, the issue of exceptionalism is of less use than those models of historical change that emphasize the development of modern, liberal property relations. But a method that includes many different jurisdictions — each with its own peculiar social context, political culture, and constellation of legal and political rhetoric — under a broad rubric such as Linklater's "modern, liberal property relations" may be too blunt an instrument. Adopting a comparative and contextual approach, as suggested in this chapter, may provide a method of understanding the broad contours of historical change, while allowing us to appreciate the nuances and subtle variations of those contours.

CHAPTER TWELVE

CONTESTING PROHIBITION AND THE CONSTITUTION IN 1850s NEW BRUNSWICK

*Greg Marquis**

IN THE 1850s prohibition was debated in a number of the legislatures of British North America, but only in New Brunswick did lawmakers attempt to ban the sale of beverage alcohol. The partial prohibition measure of 1852 and the more comprehensive enactment of 1855 were important antecedents to the provincial prohibition statutes of the 1901-17 period. Although the temperance movement has been studied, the colony's experiment with prohibition has not been examined in detail since the classic 1954 article by James Chapman. The following chapter discusses the legal and constitutional aspects of the 1852 and 1855 laws, specifically their origin and enforcement, and the constitutionality of the actions of Lieutenant-Governor Manners-Sutton in 1856 in relation to colonial responsible government.[1] It is inspired by the approach taken by John McLaren and John Lowman in their essay on the legal responses to prostitution in early twentieth-century Canada. That study indicates the complex and contested social, legal, and professional factors that shaped the response to prostitution in the period 1890 to 1920.[2]

Created as a Loyalist haven in 1784, New Brunswick was governed by a governor appointed by Britain, his appointed council, and a bicameral legislature consisting of an appointed Legislative Council and an elected Assembly. The suffrage, although limited to males, was fairly liberal. Unlike in Nova Scotia and the United Canadas, where responsible government was "granted" in 1848, in New Brunswick the situation was more

* The author acknowledges the support of the Social Sciences and Humanities Research Council of Canada.

complex. Responsible government, meaning government responsible not to the monarch or the governor, but to the colonial Parliament, developed in stages. One structural factor that delayed fully responsible ministries in the colony was the decentralized nature of administering public finance.[3]

New Brunswick was typical of British North America in that consumption of spirits peaked in the early 1800s. The liquor trade was an important sector of the colonial economy, and customs and excise duties formed a major stream of public revenue. Beyond the port city of Saint John, the towns of Moncton, Fredericton, and Woodstock, and a number of smaller centres, the colony's population was scattered along the valleys of the Saint John, Petticodiac, and Miramichi Rivers and their tributaries and the shores of the Bay of Fundy, the Gulf of St. Lawrence, and the Bay of Chaleur. A majority of the colonists were English-speaking Protestants, but there were also Irish Catholic and Acadian minorities. Inns were frequented by both sexes and all classes, and liquor was a staple in rural general stores. Apprentices, servants, and children under sixteen were excluded from taverns by mid-century. Although consumption rates began to decline, the incorporation of rum into work, family, and community life, combined with a growth in evangelical religion, sparked a backlash against liquor abuse in the 1820s and 1830s. James Chapman highlighted the spread of an American organization, the Sons of Temperance, into the colony in the late 1840s, but temperance as a social movement was well established in both urban and rural New Brunswick a decade earlier.[4]

TEMPERANCE TO PROHIBITION

Early temperance, rooted in Protestant evangelical churches, was based on the individual cutting back on, or abstaining from, "ardent spirits" such as rum. Such was the goal of the Saint John Temperance Society, organized in 1830. During the 1830s local organizations began to promote total voluntary abstinence, based on signing a pledge. Temperance cut across class lines, which in the nineteenth century were often blurred by religion and ethnicity. Methodists, Baptists, Presbyterians, and Low Church Anglicans were the most active in "saving" not only themselves, but also others. By 1834 20 percent of the adult population of Saint John were signed-up members of various temperance groups.[5]

Temperance activism was a way for individuals outside the political mainstream, such as artisans, to assert themselves. Women, who could not vote, attended temperance meetings, organized groups, and signed mass petitions against the liquor traffic. By 1840 30 percent of the members of the largely Protestant Saint John Total Abstinence Society were women. Many pledge takers were children and youth.[6] Women from Saint John, Woodstock, and Fredericton signed anti-liquor petitions prior to the 1850s; during that decade, their rural counterparts became more active. This activity was an early articulation of maternal feminism, the need for women to influence public policy or law in the name of the family.[7]

By the early 1850s temperance, a multi-faceted movement, was a key social force in English New Brunswick. The movement reached beyond Protestant faiths to include the Roman Catholic Church, whose parishes in New Brunswick, Nova Scotia, and Newfoundland were organized in the early 1840s. As of 1841, there were twenty-five hundred Catholic drys in the Miramichi region. The Saint John Roman Catholic Total Abstinence Relief Association included children, who pledged not to drink until they were adults. In the 1850s the Acadians were only 15 percent of the population and had not yet begun to form temperance and other self-help organizations. Although Catholic groups, supervised by clerics, were cool to prohibition, they were hostile toward the liquor trade. In 1853 the two major societies in the Saint John area enrolled fifty-six hundred members. Drys, although lacking a political party, exerted influence through the Saint John Common Council and the county sessions.[8]

Temperance widened its scope from religious and moral issues to develop a series of secular justifications, including individual and public health, middle-class self-improvement, an interest in improving worker productivity and combating absenteeism, and a move away from the truck system in favour of paying labourers in cash. In Saint John the important artisan class was the vanguard of temperance prior to 1850. Temperance and prohibition fit into the Victorian interest for social betterment. In the 1840s and 1850s much was made of liquor's contributions to poverty, family violence, crime, and related social problems.[9] The medical superintendent of the New Brunswick Lunatic Asylum blamed intemperance for the bulk of "mental disease" in the colony. A prominent prohibitionist claimed that only two of thirteen hundred Sons of Temperance members in Saint John had died in the 1854 cholera epidemic. Saint John police court convictions in the period 1849-52 were dominated by offences such as public drunkenness and being drunk and disorderly, and the bulk of offenders in the records of the magistrate in neighbouring Portland parish were intemperate.[10]

Although later generations regarded prohibitionists as old-fashioned, conservative, and intolerant, a number of historians view them, in the context of the nineteenth century, as "modern." Far from wanting to conserve the present or hearken back to a past golden age, prohibitionists were idealists who strove to free their sisters and brothers from the "slavery" of the liquor traffic. As a form of "identity politics," temperance in mid-nineteenth-century North America encouraged legislators to limit the number of liquor licences, devote more attention to enforcement, and introduce local option plebiscites to dry up towns and counties. The next logical step was prohibition.[11]

The increasing influence of the Sons of Temperance as an extra-parliamentary force is a key part of the politics of prohibition in the 1850s. W. Stewart MacNutt described the Sons, with their auxiliary organizations for women and children (Daughters and Cadets of Temperance), as "a state within a state."[12] A fraternal self-help organization that flourished in Protestant areas, the Sons countered drinking culture with a range of dry activities that appealed to socially ambitious farmers, artisans, shopkeepers, and skilled workers and their families. The temperance hall was a healthy alternative to the dram shop. Although most members were no doubt Protestant evangelicals, the organization thrived as a network of community-rooted lodges. The first division opened in the border town of St. Stephen in 1847. The Sons of Temperance maintained seventy divisions in New Brunswick by 1852, the year of the first prohibition law. Its newspaper, the *Temperance Telegraph,* was subsidized by the colonial legislature.[13]

Liquor control began to move from voluntary abstinence for the minority to legal compulsion with the advent of the "Maine Law" of 1851. Similar prohibition laws were adopted by ten additional states in the 1850s. In his pioneering article of 1954, Chapman saw prohibition as a movement that spilled over from Maine, with New Brunswick as a northern extension of New England's cultural and social frontier, a natural result of geography and trade. Religious revivals had followed similar patterns. The economic manifestations of increasing north-south ties were railway projects and the 1854 Reciprocity Treaty.[14]

In the late 1840s and early 1850s, politicians in the United Canadas, Nova Scotia, and New Brunswick devoted considerable attention to alcohol and its control.[15] In Canada East Father Chiniquy's temperance movement had inspired 400,000 Catholics to take the pledge between 1848 and 1851, dozens of parishes to go dry, and distilleries to cut back on production.[16] In the absence of statutory prohibition or local option plebiscites, local authorities implemented administrative prohibition. In 1849, for example, the magistrates in the Saint John county sessions voted not to issue liquor licences, a policy also practised in many areas of rural Nova Scotia.[17] In the early 1850s Saint John's first Mayor to be elected by the Common Council, Thomas Harding, favoured a no-licence policy for areas of the city where temperance was strong.[18] Legislative committees in Nova Scotia and Canada East in the late 1840s reported on the need to restrict liquor sales. Prohibition measures were debated for Canada West and Nova Scotia, but legislative approval was blocked in the upper chambers of the respective Assemblies.[19]

The immediate inspiration for the New Brunswick law was the Maine Law, passed by the state's Democratic legislature at the urging of temperance leader Neal Dow, Mayor of Portland. Although often evaded, a law of 1846 had banned the sale of alcohol in quantities of less than twenty-eight US gallons. The 1851 statute outlawed the manufacture and sale of intoxicating alcohol, gave the authorities the right of search and seizure if three citizens complained, and permitted confiscation of illicit stocks. Third offences were to result in a prison sentence. The law allowed sale for medicinal, industrial, and sacramental purposes, as well as importation from other states for personal use.[20]

PROHIBITION LEGISLATED

A partial Prohibition Bill was introduced in the New Brunswick Assembly, then controlled by a hybrid coalition, in 1852. The Bill was a modified version of a measure attempted in 1851. Prohibition was not a party measure, partly because disciplined political parties were still emerging in the 1850s. Gail Campbell's case study of Charlotte County from 1846 to 1857 explains how temperance helped transform elections from a focus on individual candidates to party slates. In the era before party platforms existed, individual candidates sounded very much alike. Temperance provided a divisive issue for both candidates and the electorate.[21]

Prohibitionists presented the legislature with a petition bearing nine thousand names (26 percent of them female) asking for an end to the importation of beverage alcohol. The resulting *Act to Prevent the Traffic in Intoxicating Liquors,* a modification of a Sons of Temperance Bill, did not cover cider, ale, beer, and porter (an important exemption added by the Assembly), and it permitted importation and manufacture for medicinal, chemical, and religious purposes. The conditions governing warrants for searching private premises were stringent—a witness had to swear an oath that an illegal sale had taken place. The law's preamble explained that liquor was "the cause of a very large proportion of the ills that affect communities in producing crime, poverty, disease and demoralization," and that it was the duty of government "to legislate for the happiness, comfort and prosperity of the people."[22]

The limitations of the law, which went into effect in June of 1853, were immediately apparent. Powerful economic interests were at stake in Saint John, the chief seaport and commercial centre, traditionally responsible for most of the colony's import revenues. In 1854, the year that the first prohibition law was repealed, more than 660,000 gallons of spirits (3.4 for each colonist), 280,000 gallons of wine, and more than 1 million gallons of molasses, used in making rum, were imported into the province. Prominent merchants and police Magistrate John Johnson opposed the law. Enforcement was complicated by the fact that the provincially appointed Magistrate, by virtue of the police reform law of 1849, controlled the municipal police.[23] The Act made special mention of liquor sold in tents, shanties, huts, and other facilities providing refreshments at cattle shows, agricultural exhibitions, militia musters, and other public occasions. Magistrates, aldermen, and constables were required to pay extra attention to such venues. Enforcement and the supervision of manufacturing for permitted purposes were local responsibilities, yet county sessions and town councils had been denied licensing revenues. The Sons of Temperance, although dissatisfied by the legislature's intervention with its Bill, felt obliged to support the 1852 law, however flawed.[24]

As the sale of spirits and wine was outlawed, liquor dealers laid in large stocks of spirits in advance of the law. Six thousand gallons of brandy were reported entering the port of Saint John in early March of 1852. With at least two hundred taverns in the Saint John and Portland area, the liquor trade was an important economic sector, not to mention a source of municipal revenue. Saint John Mayor William O. Smith, an anti-prohibitionist wholesale druggist, claiming authority from the city's 1785 Charter, continued to issue tavern and shop licences. Smith's actions suggest that local officials, as they had since the founding of the Loyalist colony, regarded liquor control as a local, not a provincial, government matter. The Common Council during this period was embroiled in a larger struggle with the appointed police magistrate over control of the police force. Licences were also granted, in defiance of the law, in King's, Charlotte, Restigouche, and Westmoreland Counties. The justices of the peace in Queen's refused. Critics argued that similar restrictions in American states had spawned smuggling and a black market retail network. In areas of the province where magistrates ceased to issue licences, illegal rum dens opened.[25]

Lieutenant-Governor Edmund Walker Head disliked the law and contacted the Colonial Office on the question of disallowance.[26] The Executive Council continued to support it—an assertion of the very political responsibility Head claimed did not exist in the colony.[27] Another critic was Judge L.A. Wilmot, a former member of the coalition that had ruled since 1848, who denounced the law as one that was "conceived in tyranny and ended in fanaticism and violence."[28] He may have been reacting to the Act's restrictions on appeals from the judgments of justices of the peace and police magistrates. Head, whose term as Governor was about to end, appealed to the Colonial Office for intervention, but without success. The Governor had interpreted previous instructions from the Colonial Office on responsible government in a way that avoided recognizing a majority party in the Assembly. As a recent dispute revealed, he "continued to act as his own prime minister," by appointing a judge over the advice of his council.[29]

The contentious statute was repealed by the legislature in 1854 and replaced by an *Act to Regulate the Sale of Spiritous Liquors,* a measure to control wholesale and tavern licences. This returned the granting of wholesale and tavern licences to county sessions and town and city councils. Taverns or inns had to be run by persons of good character and had to provide for travellers. Tavern keepers were not allowed to extend credit and were legally prevented from collecting debts from customers. Wholesalers were required to sell in amounts of at least one pint and not permit drinking on their premises. The key officials charged with supervising licensed establishments were not peace officers but town clerks.[30]

Because the Governor was reluctant to introduce the full principle of responsible government, the election of 1854, which brought sixteen new assemblymen to Fredericton, did not result in any change to the Conservative-dominated Executive Council. In November the ministry headed by G. Street was defeated on a confidence vote, and the Reformers came into power, an act that established a new precedent for responsibility. The new ministry was led by Charles Fisher, a Fredericton lawyer who recently had served on a commission to consolidate and codify New Brunswick's statutes.[31] The new Executive Council included no Catholics. Head's replacement, feared by Reformers as an opponent of responsible government, arrived in the fall of 1854 as support for prohibition was reviving. John Henry Thomas Manners-Sutton was an English Tory aristocrat and son of a speaker of the House of Commons. Manners-Sutton's initial concern was implementation of the new Reciprocity Treaty with the United States. He personally opposed prohibition and blamed the New Brunswick movement on the dangerous influence of the Baptists.[32]

The Liberal-dominated legislature of 1855 was concerned about its powers vis-à-vis the Governor, economic affairs, and the privately owned European and North American Railway (ENAR), which was being constructed from Saint John to near Shediac. The most publicized measure of the session was a private member's Bill, introduced by Liberal Samuel L. Tilley, to impose a Maine Law on New Brunswick. Tilley, an Anglican born at Gagetown in the lower Saint John Valley, had experienced a religious conversion in 1839 and became involved with the Portland Total Abstinence Society in the 1840s. A prosperous Saint John druggist and leading figure in the Sons of Temperance, he was an Assembly representative for Saint John. He had campaigned on a liberal franchise, the secret ballot, government initiation of money grants in the legislature, and the right of the people to decide on the liquor question.[33] In the summer of 1854 Tilley was elected Most Worthy Patriarch of the Sons of Temperance for North America. The temperance movement had responded to the new licence law with a "monster" prohibition petition bearing twenty thousand names, equivalent to 10 percent of the population.[34] A Tory publication encouraged enemies of the Liberals to attend the fall provincial temperance convention in order to safeguard the interests of the party. The *Morning News,* which initially had opposed prohibition, now chose to support it for partisan reasons and complimented the Sons of Temperance for its work in raising funds for the wives and children of British troops killed in the war then raging in the Crimea.[35]

Tilley was Provincial Secretary in the Fisher government, but he explained that the Bill was not a party measure. Yet it was endorsed by most Reformers, many of whom had promised their constituents to support prohibition. One exception was radical Liberal Albert J. Smith of Westmoreland, a member of Fisher's cabinet, who opposed the Bill as arbitrary, coercive, and "cruel." The debate in the Assembly was witnessed by the "fair occupants" of the "ladies" gallery, as well as by many male spectators.[36] Although it did not propose to ban personal possession, the Bill outlawed the manufacture, importation, and sale not only of spirits but also all intoxicating liquors. Saint John at this time had several breweries, and all were threatened. The Bill passed in the Assembly in March by three votes. James Hannay, a Whiggish biographer of Tilley, deemed the measure "a bold experiment ... more bold than wise."[37] According to Hannay, a number of assemblymen supported the law, assuming that it would be defeated by the appointed Legislative Council; to their shock it passed by a vote of ten to seven. The Executive Council, exercising its autonomy from the Governor, also approved of the Bill, despite the fact that prominent Liberals such as W.J. Ritchie and Albert Smith opposed prohibition.[38]

Despite the evolving practice of responsible government, which many thought had arrived in New Brunswick by mid-century, the British government retained the authority to disallow colonial legislation that was repugnant to imperial interests. Manners-Sutton appealed to the Colonial Office to intervene, citing a number of objections to New Brunswick's innovation, which he described as "impolitic, anti-commercial and unjust."[39] The Colonial Office also received petitions bearing the names of prominent merchants and magistrates. In his correspondence to London, the Governor was critical of, and condescending toward, the political integrity of the colony's elected representatives, whom he accused of "moral cowardice." He explained that he had assented to the law because he did not want to force the resignation of the Executive Council and feared that he would be unable to find a suitable replacement council.[40]

A key critique was the new law's potential impact on colonial revenues: up to £25,000 yearly was at stake. Like those of other North American colonies, New Brunswick's public finances in the 1850s were linked to railway projects: both the existing ENAR and the potential Inter-Colonial. It was feared that the ENAR, completed from Saint John to Moncton in 1860, would be a heavy burden on the provincial treasury.

For this reason, the Executive Council discussed raising general import duties in order to counter any losses and prepared a budget statement that projected a surplus for 1856.[41] Similar issues had been at stake in Saint John where James Olive, the first Mayor elected by popular vote, had followed the advice of a majority of the Common Council and refused to issue any liquor licences for the 1854-55 term. This denied the corporation £2,000 in revenue.[42]

The prohibition law took effect on 1 January 1856. The penalty for manufacturing, importing, or keeping liquor for sale was a £10 fine, double for a second offence, with the possibility of up to three months in jail. The statute defined liquor as brandy, gin, whiskey, rum, wine, ale, porter, "or any other alcoholic, spirituous or intoxicating liquor," but offered no scientific definition. The possession of private stocks ordered prior to 1856 was legal. In the 1850s even temperance supporters questioned whether beer was intoxicating, but the law did not require proof of alcoholic content. Following the approach of the 1852 law, sale of alcohol for permitted purposes was to be through agents appointed by county sessions (benches of magistrates) or county councils where they existed. The agents were early versions of what later prohibition laws would term vendors. Revenue officers were empowered, on suspicion, to search any vessel or vehicle entering the province for contraband. In keeping with customs law, vessels employed in smuggling that did not exceed fifteen tons' burthen could be confiscated. Allowance was made for "a reasonable quantity of liquors as required for ship stores" and for distilled liquor for use by chemists, manufacturers, and artists. A magistrate could issue a search warrant for any building that was not a dwelling house on the sworn testimony of one "reputable person." The testimony of three persons was necessary in order to search a private dwelling—a clause borrowed from the Maine Law. Section 15 contained a stiff penalty for perjury—two years in prison. Section 18 compelled persons arrested for public drunkenness to name the source of the alcohol or suffer a fine or a short jail term.[43]

PROHIBITION CONTESTED

In June of 1855 the Attorney General reported on the new law for the Governor and Colonial Secretary in London. Manners-Sutton provided a gloss on the report. He objected to the law on several grounds, such as the fact that it penalized both the temperate and intemperate and that it was not accompanied by sufficient enforcement resources. The Act's procedure was "inquisitorial and highly penal." New Brunswickers, he added, were no more abusive of alcohol than were residents of other colonies. Yet "the maintenance of the authority of the law" required that the authorities attempt to enforce the statute, despite its unpopularity and flawed machinery. Arguments in favour of disallowance included the allegation that the prohibition law violated trade law and the rights of shipping, issues that London officials discounted.[44]

The matter was considered by Lord Palmerston and the imperial Board of Trade in October and by Colonial Office officials a month later. It was also raised in the House of Lords. Increasingly, the trend was for the imperial government to let colonial legislation stand.[45] Despite petitions from the city and county of Saint John and the counties of Charlotte and Restigouche as to the law's arbitrary and tyrannical nature, the imperial officials did not intervene. One gathering in Fredericton regarded the law as "insulting" but grudgingly decided to give it a fair trial. The Restigouche document regretted that it was illegal to import wine from Britain's "valiant ally, France" and appealed to bourgeois rights: prohibition invaded "the sacred privacy and privileges of domestic life" and was "diametrically opposed to the spirit of the age." A protest meeting in Salisbury urged provincial parliamentarians to "read Blackstone on the British rights of man" and to consult other authors on "the invalidity of colonial statutes having inconsistency and a lack of uniformity to common law." The anti-prohibition meeting at Baie Verte, Westmoreland County, was held in a temperance hall. In these gatherings, a number of speakers, prominent Conservatives, were motivated in whole or in part by partisan considerations. The response in the Colonial Office was to let an internal matter such as liquor control rest with the representatives of the New Brunswick voters.[46]

The law encountered resistance and evasion, and within weeks there were reports of widespread open sale. In 1855 in defiance of the incoming law, a number of municipalities had issued liquor licences. The county sessions of Charlotte, for example, had authorized, with the exception of four parishes, licences to extend from April 1855 to April 1856. Individuals charged with illegal sale or keeping for illegal sale employed lawyers (some of them leading Conservative politicians such as John Ambrose Street, leader of the government that had resigned in 1854) to fight prosecution. A number of commentators feared that the legal system would be discredited.[47] One criticism was that the 1855 law gave too much power to individual justices of the peace. The 1852 partial prohibition statute, and the licensing law of 1854, had empowered pairs of magistrates to hear evidence. Governor Head had worried that the first law was an unwarranted expansion of summary justice that undermined trial by jury. The 1855 statute created no special inspectors or prosecutors to aid in enforcement. In the rural areas criminal justice depended on appointed part-time magistrates and constables who were well connected to their communities. There were only two police forces (Saint John and the parish of Portland) and a handful of police magistrates in the entire colony.[48]

Public opinion and legal setbacks, paralleling the reaction to early prohibition in most of New England, proved difficult obstacles.[49] Ethnic and religious reactions are difficult to measure, although Catholics and Anglicans were known to be suspicious of prohibition, and evangelicals were more likely to support the Liberals in 1854. In 1851 Irish immigrants constituted one-third of the population of Saint John and nearly 40 percent of adjacent Portland parish. According to the 1861 census, 39 percent of the population of the city and county were Catholics. Following a decade of sectarian violence between Irish Catholic immigrants and Protestant Orangemen (Irish and native born) that had peaked with the bloody York Point Riot in 1849, the two communities had been relatively free of social violence. Although Orange lodges often held temperance events, there is no evidence that the Orangemen as a group supported prohibition or even temperance. Many may have suspected both as radical Yankee innovations.[50]

Magistrates delayed decisions and employed considerable discretion in interpreting the law. In the case of Mrs. Finnigan, a widow who operated a grocery store near Marsh Creek, Portland parish, the magistrate ruled that several gallons of spirits on the premises were illegally being kept for sale. The constable brought along two assistants because he had been threatened with violence. A witness had testified that he had purchased liquor from the shop for his shipyard crew. All the same, the magistrate demanded no fine or jail term, only that the stock be destroyed. In another case, the defendant was acquitted because the two witnesses whose testimony had instigated the charge—members of the Sons of Temperance—had been unable to prove satisfactorily the identity of the seller.[51] The Mayor of Fredericton, W.A. Needham, issued written judgments in his role as Magistrate in two York County cases. Written decisions were quite rare in the inferior courts of New Brunswick in the nineteenth century. Prepared by an experienced lawyer and recent secretary of the provincial law reform commission, the judgments were backed up by case law references. Needham dismissed the first case. In the second, he overruled several objections raised by defence counsel, including the issue of the burden of proof, stating that the Supreme Court of New Brunswick would decide the matter.[52] In Moncton the mayor convicted an offender, only to have the case dismissed on appeal. The Westmoreland County magistrate convicted and fined a former tavern keeper £10 in early 1856, despite the presence of defence counsel Bliss Botsford, a Conservative politician.[53]

When members of the Sons of Temperance helped to enforce the law, public opinion grew more hostile. The press reported that a crowd had intimidated three Saint John magistrates during the first major prosecution in 1856, that of Robert Stewart. Witnesses for the prosecution included the editor of the *Temperance Telegraph* and a high-ranking official of the Grand Division of the Sons of Temperance. Moderate anti-prohibitionists were disturbed that "British justice" could be overawed by a crowd. Later, Tilley was burned in effigy, and police charged with sabres to break up a rowdy group of protesters, complete with a band, suspected of planning to break a prisoner out of the watch house.[54] Violence also ensued in Woodstock—site of sectarian rioting in the 1840s —when a group of men obstructed a part-time constable during a search of a dwelling. The constable, who fired a pistol, was arrested by the county sheriff for his own protection and charged with use of an "unlawful weapon."[55]

As the Assembly debated an unsuccessful Bill in March and April of 1856 to repeal the prohibition law, waning Liberal support was apparent. The government barely managed to defeat a motion calling for a new election, and the decision to give the repeal Bill a "three month hoist" passed by a slim majority.[56] During debate on a Bill to incorporate the Sons of Temperance, which had amassed considerable property, the impact of the organization on public policy was both attacked and defended. Tilley denied that he headed a political entity but explained that the Sons exerted legitimate influence by rewarding political friends at the polls and punishing enemies. Critics insinuated that temperance activists had attempted to influence magistrates and other public officials. William End, an Irish lawyer who represented largely Acadian Gloucester County, described the Sons of Temperance as being "against British liberty." As for the practice of women petitioning for social reform, he abhorred "that animal called a strong-minded woman." The attorney general supported the Sons of Temperance but was not in favour of prohibition. The Sons of Temperance were granted a charter until 1863.[57] Between 1854 and 1856, the Sons experienced a significant fall in membership: it declined by more than a quarter in Saint John and by more than half in Portland.[58]

THE 1856 ELECTION: RUMMIES VERSUS SMASHERS

Manners-Sutton, far from acting as a neutral arbiter, put pressure on Fisher's cabinet to enforce the law or repeal it. The council's advice, which, according to the emerging principles of responsible government, the Governor should have accepted, was that the law should be given more time and that it was too soon to call a new election. It refused Manners-Sutton's suggestion that it should resign. On 21 May, the Governor, believing that the people should decide on the issue, responded by dissolving the legislature, without seeking the advice of the ministry. The Liberals resigned, and the Governor, who was puzzled by constitutional objections to his decisions, assembled a new ministry, which agreed with his call for a general election.[59] Back in London, Colonial Secretary Henry Labouchere noted this decision to be "ill advised" and speculated that the Governor's "influence for any useful purpose would be utterly destroyed."[60]

The Liberals, or "Smashers," had their issue. It was not prohibition, but the larger question of the abuse of the Governor's prerogative. The Conservatives, or "Rummies," were criticized not simply as opponents of responsible government but also as supporters of the liquor traffic.[61] Supporters of the Governor included Irish Catholic leader T. W. Anglin, influential editor of the *Freeman*. Anglin, previously a Reformer, interpreted prohibition in part as a cultural assault on Roman Catholics, akin to the nativist response of 1850s America toward Irish immigrants. It was both a dangerous imposition of the will of the minority and a passing fad, like Mormonism or spirit rapping. A former leader of the large provincial Catholic temperance society that claimed several thousand members, Anglin also cited personal liberty and loss of government revenues as objections.[62] The *Freeman* denounced the law as giving justices of the peace, "ignorant, fanatical or unprincipled as they may be," legal powers unprecedented "in any part of the British empire, not under martial law."[63]

The 1856 election, which pitted the Smashers versus the Rummies, was a hotly contested fight. This was especially true in Saint John city and county, which voted solidly wet. As if to emphasize the fluidity of political opinion, novice assemblyman J.W. Lawrence, who would help defeat prohibition, had spoken in defence of Tilley's Act months earlier. Robert Duncan Wilmot, who had voted for Tilley's Bill in 1855 and against its repeal in 1856, joined the Rummie cabinet as Provincial Secretary. Tilley went down to personal defeat, although he would be re-elected as a Reformer in 1857. The constitutional issue took second seat to the unpopularity of the prohibition law. The Rummies won a slim majority. As the legislative vote would reveal, the Assembly included fourteen or fifteen anti-prohibition Liberals.[64]

The electorate had rejected prohibition. The new Gray-Wilmot ministry repealed the prohibition law in July 1856, with only two members dissenting.[65] The "rum session" restored the licence law of 1854. A resolution backing the actions of Manners-Sutton passed by a more narrow margin.[66] The Governor explained that repeal would "have a material effect in improving the financial condition of the Province."[67] In his speech to the new session of the Assembly, he referred to the beneficial exercise of power "entrusted to me by the Constitution." To the Colonial Office, he explained that the ease of repeal was proof that "the late House of Assembly did not represent the feelings or wishes of the constituencies."[68] The Liberal press in neighbouring colonies joined publications in New Brunswick, such as the *Westmoreland Times* and the *Woodstock Journal,* in condemning the Governor's actions as despotic, illiberal, and worse than the excesses of enemies of responsible government in the Canadas such as Sir Francis Bond Head and Charles Metcalfe. They interpreted the outcome not as a triumph of popular will, but of the Governor or the clique that had ruled the colony until 1854.[69]

On topics other than its opposition to prohibition, the Conservative government enjoyed little cohesion. Once the prohibition law had been repealed, a political deadlock developed. In 1857 the Rummie government fell, and a yet another election ensued. That year the franchise was expanded and the secret ballot introduced. The 1857 contest resulted in the victory of the famous Smasher government, the Liberal regime that would rule New Brunswick for the next several years. As they had been in 1854, the new political leaders were middle class and commercial in orientation; they opposed privilege and supported electoral and other reforms. With Tilley as their emerging leader, the Liberals preferred to leave the liquor issue to moral suasion and local licensing decisions.[70]

In 1857 Manners-Sutton, who was chastised by the Colonial Secretary for not forwarding the views of his advisers, feared that the Liberals, if they returned to power (as they did) would attempt to hold a provincial plebiscite on the prohibition issue, an approach he deemed to be highly unconstitutional. The Colonial Office, equally concerned, reminded Manners-Sutton of the principle of responsibility, but offered advice on how to nullify any bill emanating from a plebiscite.[71] Although they continued to benefit from temperance and evangelical Protestant support, the Smashers avoided divisive cultural issues such as prohibition and focused on railroad and economic development. For the duration of his governorship, Manners-Sutton was more cooperative with the Liberals, who shared his apprehensions about a larger British North American union. In 1861 he departed to govern Trinidad. He later served as a popular Governor of Victoria, Australia, before taking up his seat in the House of Lords.[72]

CONCLUSION

The constitutional aspects of New Brunswick's 1855 prohibition law are not well known outside of regional historiography, but they are worthy of comparison to the "double shuffle" affair in the United Canadas and the famous King-Byng dispute of 1926. Like the better-known Canadian examples, the use of the prerogative benefited the Conservatives and hurt the Liberals. As noted earlier, Whig historians such as Hannay and Liberal partisans found much to condemn in the actions of Manners-Sutton. Alpheus Todd, the Victorian chronicler of Canadian constitutional development, described the Governor's actions as "prompt and decisive," and argued that both Houses in the legislature endorsed "the constitutionality and expediency of the governor's actions."[73]

In 1858 the Macdonald-Cartier ministry was close to being defeated in the legislature of the United Canadas. John A. Macdonald resigned, hoping that the opposition Liberals and the Parti rouge would be unable to command a majority, paving the way for a Conservative return. Governor General Edmund Head, who had questioned New Brunswick's 1852 prohibition law, asked Canada West Liberal leader George Brown to attempt to form a ministry. Brown formed a government with rouge leader A.A. Dorion. Head made no promise to call an election if the

Brown-Dorion ministry were defeated in the Assembly. A general election had taken place fewer than eight months previously. The Liberal government, voted down in the Assembly, lasted less than two days. Brown requested the Governor to dissolve the House but was refused. Following the resignation of the Brown-Dorion government, Head approached Macdonald to attempt to forge a new ministry. The result was the Cartier-Macdonald government, which overcame its precarious position through the "double shuffle." Precedent dictated that newly appointed cabinet ministers had to temporarily resign and seek electoral approval in by-elections. Guided by a recent British statute, the Conservative ministers assumed office, resigned their portfolios, and then were sworn back into their original offices. The Governor General did not object. This and his refusal to dissolve the Assembly upon Brown's request drew criticism from contemporaries and later historians that Head was anti-Liberal. J.M.S. Careless, Brown's biographer, concluded that although the Governor may have been influenced by "personal leanings," he was within his rights to refuse a dissolution.[74]

The Whig interpretation of responsible government insisted that governors "take the advice" of their ministers. Head's use of the prerogative in the 1850s was more consistent than Baron Julian Byng's in 1926. In the summer of that year, William Lyon Mackenzie King, under pressure from a customs scandal, feared being voted down in the House of Commons. The Liberal leader asked Governor General Byng for a dissolution, which was denied. Byng, a popular British general in the First World War, believed that the Conservative opposition, under Arthur Meighen, could form a workable coalition government. The Prime Minister advised that the Governor seek advice from London, which he did not. King immediately resigned, before Byng could ensure a smooth transition. Meighen's minority government collapsed after three days in Parliament, and this time the Governor granted a dissolution. Although Byng's actions were not a major factor in the ensuing election, which the Liberals won, King and his sympathizers made much of the Governor General's alleged favouritism and lack of regard for Canada's autonomy. Most analysts concluded that Byng's actions were constitutionally sound.[75]

The New Brunswick case was a more questionable exercise of the Crown's prerogative than the 1858 and 1926 affairs. Even today, the governor general and provincial lieutenant-governors have the constitutional authority to dismiss minority governments, ask opposition leaders to attempt to form new governments, or to dissolve Parliament or legisla-tures.[76] In 1856 the New Brunswick Liberals were not in a minority position and had passed substantial legislation during the term. They had defeated a prohibition repeal bill, incorporated the Sons of Temper-ance, and were making progress on railway policy when Manners-Sutton presented his ultimatum. The fact that the Conservatives later approved of the Governor's actions, and that most of the legislators in the new Assembly opposed prohibition, does not detract from the fact that the Queen's representative, in the new era of responsible government, dis-solved the Assembly and called an election on a policy disagreement with his elected advisers.

The experimental prohibition law effective in 1856 represented the peak of pre-Confederation temperance sentiment in New Brunswick. In a parallel to the reactions to prostitution examined by McLaren and Lowman for the period 1892-1920, the political and legislative genesis of prohibition and its enforcement revealed the contested nature of morality control. Although statutory prohibition was defeated, the con-stitutional controversy helped pave the way for full responsible govern-ment in the colony. Manners-Sutton had attempted to interpret public opinion and dictate the terms of public policy. Many Liberals had sup-ported prohibition not out of ideology but simply because the Governor and the opposition did not. In this sense, prohibition as an issue had helped to create the "responsible executive" that was the heart of colonial self-government by the late 1850s.[77]

Temperance, as determined by the social habits of the population, was successful in New Brunswick during the second half of the nineteenth century. Despite the bourgeois rhetoric of self-control and social bet-terment, support for, and opposition to, the laws of 1852 and 1855 cut across class lines. Although pre-Confederation statistics are somewhat uncertain, the consumption of spirits fell noticeably, starting in the 1840s. Between 1871 and 1894, per capita consumption of spirits fell by almost 50 percent. Employers stopped paying workers with drink, and social drinking became more of a segregated, male activity. At least part of this cultural change was the result of political will and legal change. In Saint John, for example, there was a dramatic 80 percent reduction in the number of saloon licences between 1860 and 1890.[78] Local authorities gradually lost their discretion over licensed premises. The law governing licensed sales also was gradually tightened up; music and dancing were banned from saloons, hours were curtailed, and in 1871 Sunday sales were outlawed.[79]

The 1856 law had not settled the issue of liquor regulation. During the 1860s and '70s, the Sons of Temperance agitated for local option laws. This principle was enshrined in the federal *Canada Temperance Act (CTA)* of 1878, which permitted towns, cities, and counties to vote out licensed premises. Breweries, distilleries, and wholesale liquor dealers were allowed to operate in *CTA* municipalities, residents could import for personal use, and doctors and druggists were permitted to distribute alcohol prescriptions. Between 1879 and 1884, nine of the province's counties and the city of Fredericton voted out saloons and liquor dealers. This area contained the bulk of the province's English-speaking Protestant population. Local prohibition in Saint John County existed from 1886 but was voted out in 1892. The city of Saint John said no to local prohibition in 1882 and 1884. *CTA* prohibition applied to the neighbouring town of Portland between 1886 and 1890.[80]

Although judged a failure and for decades cited by opponents of prohibition as examples of the dangers of sumptuary legislation, the laws of 1852 and 1855 were important manifestations of an international social reform movement. Their "non-partisan" aspects and their origins in lobbying by extra-parliamentary organizations were forerunners of how alcohol control would be handled in most parts of Canada, starting with the *Dunkin Act* of the United Canadas (1864), continuing with the *CTA* and provincial prohibition laws in place between 1902 and 1930. Neither New Brunswick's prohibitory *Intoxicating Liquor Act* (1917-27) nor the succeeding liquor control statute were identified as party measures. The use of plebiscites to determine alcohol control policy—a prospect dreaded by governors and Colonial Office officials in the 1850s as "un-British"—would be a preferred political management tactic in most parts of Canada from the 1870s to the 1920s.[81]

CHAPTER THIRTEEN

FROM HUMBLE PRAYERS
TO LEGAL DEMANDS

The Cowichan Petition of 1909 and the
British Columbia Indian Land Question

Hamar Foster and Benjamin L. Berger

CANADIANS IN the twenty-first century are faced with the challenge of reconciling the Aboriginal rights of Canada's Aboriginal peoples with the sovereignty of the Crown, and to date this process — whether it involves treaty making or other forms of negotiated accommodation — has largely been driven by judicial decisions.[1] It was not always so.

In British Columbia, for example, only a few land cession treaties were made in the colonial period (1849-71), and from the 1860s on, successive colonial and provincial administrations adamantly opposed the making of any more.[2] This left most of the province subject to unextinguished Aboriginal title claims that these same governments refused to allow the courts to adjudicate.[3] And although all but one of the legal barriers to litigating title claims fell away in the 1950s, a century after the "Indian land question" first arose, it took another four decades for the province to drop its opposition to treaty making.[4]

The conventional starting point for any account of how British Columbia moved from the policies it pursued between the 1860s and the 1980s to the modern era of negotiating treaties is *Calder v. British Columbia (Attorney-General).*[5] This landmark decision of the Supreme Court of Canada in 1973 persuaded the federal government that the matter of unextinguished Aboriginal title had to be addressed. Although the BC government resisted the implications of *Calder* until the courts unequivocally rejected the province's position in the late 1980s, it cannot be denied that *Calder* was the turning point.[6] But when Frank Calder and the other Nisga'a leaders restarted the campaign to secure a judicial decision on title in the 1950s, they looked back as well as forward. In fact, they deliberately adopted many of the strategies of their early twentieth-century predecessors who, in the Nisga'a Petition of 1913 and the campaign they waged until 1927 to get Aboriginal title into the courts, had articulated the bases for the legal battle that would continue in the latter half of the twentieth century and into the present.[7] What is not generally acknowledged, however, is that the path followed by the drafters of the Nisga'a Petition, an undeniably critical step in the pursuit of Aboriginal justice in modern Canada, had been cleared by another remarkable document, the Cowichan Petition of 1909.

It is not our intention to in any way devalue or underestimate the importance of the *Calder* case or the Nisga'a Petition of 1913. The historical pre-eminence of both is secure, and nothing we have to say can or should change this. But we do want to draw attention to the historical circumstances that made petitions a logical and, in fact, the only possible way—short of civil disobedience or violence—for Aboriginal people to protest their situation. Even more importantly, we want to describe, analyze, and situate an important but neglected event in the history of the land question: the drafting and submission of the Cowichan Petition of 1909. In our view the Nisga'a Petition cannot be properly understood outside of this context.[8]

Neither petition, moreover, can be understood without appreciating what, in Chapter 1 of this volume, Barry Wright has called the "incomplete implementation of the British Constitution" (p. 21) in colonies such as British Columbia. As John McLaren has shown so effectively in his work on colonial judges and on the application of law to minorities such as the Chinese, the extent to which settler legislatures were willing to apply the law equally to all was highly problematic, and sometimes they set those legislatures on a collision course with the local judiciary.[9] The rallying cry of the disaffected tended to be framed as demands for British justice, and so it was with the Indian land question in the early years of the twentieth century. Haida Chief Peter Kelly rather floridly took this course in 1911 when he told Premier Richard McBride that their delegation of nearly a hundred chiefs had come to Victoria "because of our great faith in British justice, and our confidence that, wherever the Union Jack floats, there reigns justice of the highest order, unmolested, not only to white men, but unto every British subject, which we lay claim to be in the fullest sense."[10] But McBride was adamant: no court should ever pronounce on a question so fraught with economic implications as unextinguished Indian title.[11] And until the *Calder* case, no court did.

In what follows we propose to defend the view that the Cowichan Petition was not only the key document in the early history of the campaign for Aboriginal title in BC but that the Nisga'a Petition was very much its "child." More specifically, in our opinion the Cowichan Petition represents a transition in which Aboriginal people increasingly relied on lawyers rather than missionaries to assist in conveying their message to government, and it was the first time that a legally sophisticated argument for title was made, an argument that has since been adopted by the courts and become legal orthodoxy. In fact, the Cowichan Petition was the high-water mark of the campaign for Aboriginal title in the first half of the twentieth century. At no time before the 1960s did Aboriginal people come closer to having the land question adjudicated by the courts than they did in the two years between the presentation of the Cowichan Petition in the spring of 1909 and the Dominion election in the fall of 1911.

To make our case, we will first look very briefly at the phenomenon of petitions to the Crown. We will then consider missionaries and their role in the early BC petitions, look to some of these petitions themselves, and address the economic and other changes that took place after 1900 that precipitated a new sort of campaign for title—an overtly legal campaign. Then we will focus on the specific background of the Cowichan Petition, the critical importance of the Royal Proclamation of 1763, and, finally, the text of the petition itself and its fate after 1909. (For a verbatim reproduction of the BC Archives copy of the petition, see Appendix 13.1.)

Petitions in British Columbia before 1900

In the nineteenth century, indigenous peoples across the British Empire were subject to severe limitations on their right to vote, their eligibility for elected office, and their access to the courts.[12] Furthermore, the doctrine of sovereign immunity, which permitted title lawsuits against the Crown only if the Crown consented, further restricted indigenous peoples' capacity to seek justice through conventional democratic and juridical means.[13] Nor were these disabilities confined to the nineteenth century. The Indians of British Columbia, for example, did not enjoy the right to vote in provincial elections until 1949, and the federal franchise was not extended to Indians until 1960.[14] Of equal significance is the fact that as late as 1927 Parliament amended the federal *Indian Act* in a way that effectively prohibited Indians from hiring lawyers to pursue land claims. This law was not dropped from the statute books until 1951.[15]

Given such strictures, it is hardly surprising that indigenous peoples resorted to petitions — that is, written prayers for relief addressed usually to the monarch, calling for attention to their grievances and requesting remedies.[16] In British Columbia from the 1860s on, various groups, denied any other mode of redress short of making war, wrote petitions and sent delegations to local, provincial, federal, and imperial officials and, significantly, to the King himself. Although signatories to petitions did not necessarily appreciate the subtle legal differences between a legislature and a court, or between an elected and an appointed official, they definitely made a distinction between the Crown and the local authorities, and between those who represented the Crown and those who did not. This was largely because it was clear to them that colonial legislatures and, later, provincial premiers did not have their best interests at heart. "The Queen," on the other hand, had always been represented to them as the guarantor of their rights. As a result, by 1909 it was not very much of an exaggeration for a lawyer retained by the Dominion government to state that "[n]o Indian in Canada has ever recognized the sovereignty of any Colonial, Provincial or Dominion Government — whenever his primitive rights to his lands are threatened, he appeals directly to the King, or to the Governor or other officer whom he understands to be the King's personal representative."[17] Despite these direct appeals, as the Aboriginal proportion of the population continued to decline, and so long as non-Aboriginal immigration was largely confined to the already settled parts of the province, matters did not come to a head.[18] After 1900, this would change; and the Cowichan Petition of 1909 is a profound symbol of that change.

MISSIONARIES, LANGUAGE, AND THE RHETORIC OF APPEALS

Even a cursory visit to the archives will reveal that the "meddlesome priest" is as familiar a figure in nineteenth- and early twentieth-century British Columbia as in the England of Henry II. Yet the confident assertion of so many settlers and their governments, not only in BC but also throughout the British Empire, that land claims would not exist were it not for the missionaries was more than a false belief — it contributed significantly to the government's inability to understand the nature of Aboriginal discontent.[19] Of course, missionaries had their own axes to grind and usually enjoyed a significant degree of administrative and judicial power.[20] Often, therefore, they were not keen to see this eroded by Dominion and provincial government policies, much less supplanted by "the arrival of ordinary civil authority in the form of Indian agents."[21] But even if their advocacy of land claims was not always disinterested, the claims were not a missionary invention.[22] From Captain Cook onward, explorers, traders, and government officials noted the intense proprietary sentiments that existed in BC and, in particular, among the coastal tribes.[23]

What is true, however, is that some missionaries not only sympathized with Aboriginal land claims but were willing to help their parishioners by putting their concerns into words that these officials could at least understand.[24] As one scholar has put it, describing the Tsimshian of Metlakatla, "they were well versed in those mechanics of petitioning and letter-writing that characterized the relations of dissatisfied citizens with their government."[25] Given the small number of people who could read and write English within Aboriginal communities at the time, missionaries were essential allies if oral grievances were to be transformed into written complaints.

The characteristic feature of the early missionary-influenced petitions and delegations is that they usually begged for, rather than demanded, recognition of their social and economic plight, their land title, and their hunting and fishing rights. They did not make sophisticated legal arguments or claim specific legal rights. Indeed, in 1906 a predecessor of the Cowichan Petition that displays a strong missionary influence claimed, perhaps a little disingenuously, that "[w]e are but poor ignorant Indians, and know nothing of the white man's law."[26] Instead, appeals to colonial justice were made in the religious, philosophical, and moral sense of that term. The petitioners' ancient occupation of their lands and traditional activities were stressed, the facts of their grievances were recited, and those in authority over them were implored to do what was right. Sometimes legal arguments were made, but they invoked the law of nature or of God rather than the law of the land.[27] Even missionaries who had been well educated were unlikely to know much about the status of Indian title at common law. How could they? At that time, lawyers themselves knew nothing about it.[28]

Things shifted dramatically in the early twentieth century, however, and one can see both the vestiges of the older missionary influence and the impact of the events of the early 1900s in an exchange between a *Victoria Daily Colonist* reporter and the Nisga'a Land Committee. When the reporter asked the Committee members why they thought their case was strong, they initially quoted scripture—"Cursed is he that removeth his neighbour's landmark"—and added that their suit would prosper because "God hates injustice." The reporter commented that, if that was all they had by way of argument, their case would not be considered very strong in court. He asked if they had anything better. Yes, they said: the Royal Proclamation of 1763, which had the "effect and operation" of an imperial statute. They continued in this vein until the reporter, clearly impressed, asked them how they knew all this, given that "I'm a white man and yet I had no idea of what you are telling me—how do you know?"[29] The Land Committee members ignored this patronizing inquiry, but the exchange is a telling one: it is an unfortunate lesson of history that, if you want those in power to listen, you have to speak their language.[30] At first gradually, and then very quickly, the Aboriginal peoples of British Columbia came to realize that the language of power in the province was not that spoken by missionaries.[31] This realization, combined with the social and economic changes of the early nineteenth century, pointed the way to new forms of Aboriginal title advocacy.

SOCIAL AND ECONOMIC CHANGES — AND THE COMING OF THE LAWYERS

Certain factors that came together in British Columbia at the beginning of the twentieth century created social and economic conditions conducive to a break from the unpromising earlier forms of appeal and to the emergence of more effective Aboriginal advocacy. In the first place, in the early 1900s the individuals who would later lead the campaign for title were being educated in residential schools. Although the impact of these schools on Aboriginal culture and community life has been rightly condemned, they were nevertheless a setting in which future leaders not only improved their English, but made contacts and became increasingly aware of the nature of non-Aboriginal society. Some carried this education and experience further. Haida Chief Peter Kelly, for example, went on to theological college, and Squamish leader Andy Paull apprenticed to a lawyer—although he was not called to the bar because, as an Indian, he could not vote.[32] Both men would soon focus their education and attention on learning about Aboriginal land rights under British law. By 1916, Kelly would be Chairman and Paull would be Secretary of the Allied Indian Tribes of British Columbia.

Second, the new century saw the start of a decade-long economic boom in British Columbia. The lesson of this boom was soon all too clear to Aboriginal people: it was that, although some of them would benefit from it, many would not. In fact, it became apparent that without clearly articulated land rights much of their traditional territories would be expropriated or despoiled.[33] These incursions into their lands produced intensifying protests. Indeed, by the time the Cowichan Petition was filed in the spring of 1909, it was simply the latest in a series of early twentieth-century petitions and other, less genteel, messages that the Aboriginal peoples of British Columbia addressed to authority. Although details about many of these appeals are sketchy, they nonetheless represent a clear reaction to the pressure being brought to bear on Aboriginal lands and resources, both in the southern, more developed parts of the province and, increasingly, in regions hitherto relatively unaffected by non-Aboriginal settlement. The movement began, however, in the south (see Map 13.1).

As early as 1901, missionary Charles M. Tate drafted a petition to King Edward VII for the Cowichan, whose traditional territory had been drastically affected by the massive Esquimalt and Nanaimo Railway grant in the nineteenth century; and in 1904 two chiefs from the Interior journeyed with Oblate priest J.-M. LeJeune to England for an audience with King Edward and then on to Rome to see Pope Leo XIII.[34] Not much is known about the particulars of their appeal, but the effects of white settlement and growing restrictions on Aboriginal hunting and fishing were the main reasons for the trip. This was especially so on the south coast and in the Interior, where the burgeoning non-Aboriginal population was demanding—and taking—a larger and larger share of the available resources. These people wanted more and were pushing hard against reserve boundaries they saw as too generous to the Indians. But the Aboriginal leadership was pushing back.

In 1906 another delegation went to England, this time with a petition that specifically raised the matter of Indian title and stated the case most succinctly. "In other parts of Canada," it read in part, "the Indian title has been extinguished reserving sufficient land for the use of the Indians, but in British Columbia the Indian title has never been extinguished, nor has sufficient land been allotted to our people for their maintenance."[35] That was it in a nutshell, and at this stage the campaign

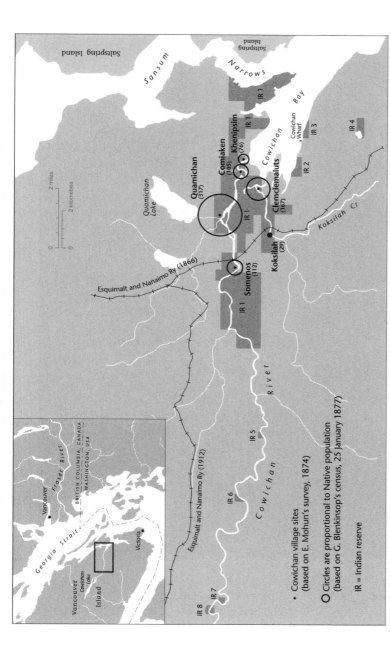

MAP 13.1 Cowichan reserves and villages. Traditional fishing sites included the mouth of the Fraser River (inset map), across the Strait of Georgia.

Cartographer: Eric Leinberger

FIGURE 13.1 Squamish Chief Joe Capilano, a leader of the land claims movement and a member of the delegation that went to see King Edward VII in 1906.
Photograph by G.G. Nye, courtesy of the North Shore Museum and Archives, Vancouver, BC (NVMA 2849)

was very much a Salish project. The three Chiefs who led the delegation were Joe Capilano (Kayapálanexw) of the Squamish (Figure 13.1), Charlie Tsulpi'multw from the Cowichan (Figure 13.2), and Basil David of the Bonaparte tribe near Ashcroft. The decision to go had been preceded by meetings in Nanaimo, Quamichan, and Vancouver, and in the spring the Cowichan had presented an address to King Edward's nephew, the Duke of Connaught, who had come to BC to fish the Cowichan River. This was followed by a series of potlatches at which the idea to go to England again was vetted, and the delegation also visited Kamloops and North Vancouver for tribal gatherings before it departed.[36]

What occurred after this delegation came home is critical to understanding why the Cowichan Petition of 1909 was so timely and why it was, for a while, so successful. The Chiefs had interpreted their meeting

FIGURE 13.2 Cowichan Chief Charlie Tsulpi'multw, who was also a member of the 1906 delegation, addressing the Royal Commission on Indian Affairs for the Province of British Columbia in 1913.
Courtesy of Royal BC Museum, BC Archives, Victoria, BC (H-07047)

with the King and with Lord Strathcona, the Canadian High Commissioner to Great Britain, as supporting their cause. As a consequence, more petitions followed—there were two in 1907 alone, signed by Fraser River chiefs and chiefs from the north as well as Vancouver Island, the Squamish, and the southern Interior—and the newspapers reported a more aggressive and militant mood to the campaign. Squamish Chief Capilano, in particular, kept up the pressure and thoroughly annoyed the authorities by travelling around the province, spreading the word.[37] Events then began to move very quickly. The Nisga'a Land Committee was formed at this time, protests and even violence began to characterize resistance to land sales in the Nass and Skeena regions, and the province abruptly put an end to the Indian reserve allotment process that had been in place since 1876.[38] In 1908 a large delegation of chiefs from all over BC travelled to Ottawa to protest, and in our view, at about this point something else very important happened: lawyers became involved. This is really the third piece in the puzzle that led to the Cowichan Petition of 1909 and to the particularly pivotal role that we argue it would play in the history of Aboriginal title in Canada.

Although it is difficult to be sure, it appears that what triggered this involvement was the local government's attempt in 1908 to have the BC Supreme Court rule on whether the Dominion had any proprietary interest in the province's Indian reserves. Ottawa would not take part, and the Court declined to decide the issue.[39] But the case seems to have had at least two important effects. It contributed to the continuing unrest among Aboriginal people in BC, particularly on the northwest coast, and it prompted a small number of lawyers to offer, and some Aboriginal groups to seek, legal advice.

By the end of 1908, Arthur Eugene O'Meara, who was both a lawyer and an Anglican priest, was turning his attention from the Yukon to British Columbia, where he soon took up residence.[40] O'Meara acted as legal adviser to the Nisga'a from 1910, and when the Allied Indian Tribes of British Columbia was formed in 1916, he became their representative as well. O'Meara was also instrumental in establishing the Conference of Friends of the Indians of British Columbia, a non-Aboriginal support group that included at least one other lawyer, F.C. Wade, King's Counsel Wade was a Vancouver lawyer and businessman who had been one of the counsel for Great Britain before the Alaska Boundary Tribunal. A lifelong Liberal, he was President of the Sun Publishing Company and had a definite interest in opposing the policies of the

Conservative McBride government in BC.[41] Also extremely important at this time was John Murray McShane Clark, King's Counsel, of Toronto. As we shall see, Clark and O'Meara were the lawyers behind the Cowichan Petition, and Clark—one of the most prominent barristers in the country—became counsel for the BC Indian Rights Association, which was also established at about this time.[42]

The sudden involvement of lawyers on the Indian side of the issue prompted a parallel response on the part of the Dominion government. Until 1909 the Department of Justice had dealt with legal matters affecting the Aboriginal peoples living in the province, then referred to as "B.C.'s Indians." But in April of that year, prompted by the disturbances in the Nass and the Skeena, and by the Colonial Office's referral of the Cowichan Petition to Ottawa for an explanation, the Minister of the Interior decided to retain outside counsel to provide the Dominion government with a legal opinion on Indian title. The lawyer they hired was T.R.E. McInnes and, no doubt to the surprise of many, he concluded that there was unextinguished Indian title in BC, that the province had behaved badly since at least the 1860s, and that Ottawa, as trustee for the Indians, was honour-bound to force BC into court over the issue.[43]

As we will show, the involvement of lawyers in the petition process changed the style and terms of the campaign for title in a way that forced the issue more powerfully and successfully than had heretofore been the case. In our view, one of their most critical contributions involved a legal document that would eventually become fundamental to the law of Aboriginal title.

The (Re)Discovery of the Royal Proclamation of 1763

By the time the Cowichan Petition was drafted, the Royal Proclamation of 1763 had been an important document in Aboriginal litigation in Ontario for some time, notably in the leading case of *St. Catherine's Lumber and Milling Company v. The Queen,* decided by the Judicial Committee of the Privy Council in 1888.[44] In BC, however, the situation was rather different. In 1875 the Dominion Minister of Justice had relied strongly on the Proclamation when he recommended disallowing British Columbia's Crown lands legislation because of its failure to accommodate Aboriginal title.[45] However, insofar as the documentary evidence is concerned, the Proclamation then slips below the event horizon of the land question until it re-emerges in the Cowichan Petition in 1909. How, then, did the early twentieth-century campaigners for title learn of the Proclamation and its guarantees?

One writer, Dara Culhane, has suggested that BC Indians became aware of the Proclamation when they read newspaper accounts of the *St. Catherine's* case, presumably in the late 1880s.[46] This is quite possible. However, Culhane cites no source, documentary or oral, in support of her thesis, and we know of none.[47] Paul Tennant, after noting the political action taken by the northwest coast Chiefs in 1887, as described earlier, states that "subsequently" the Royal Proclamation became critical in Indian political thinking.[48] He does not elaborate, although later in his book he seems to imply that the Proclamation did not become known on the coast until the Nisga'a Petition was drafted in 1913.[49]

The better view, we think, is that the Proclamation became known to the Aboriginal leadership some time between 1906, when the three Salish Chiefs petitioned King Edward VII without referring to it, and 1909, when it appears in the Cowichan Petition. One possibility is that one of the Nisga'a Chiefs, Charles Barton of Kincolith, learned about it. As Tennant points out (citing a conversation with Frank Calder), Barton was fluent in English and had travelled extensively. It was his idea to establish the Land Committee: "He brought the idea of the committee from Ontario, where he had encountered associations formed of the neighbouring Indian communities."[50] If Barton spent enough time in Ontario to be inspired in this fashion, it seems likely that he would have heard about the Royal Proclamation and brought news of it back, as well.[51] Another possibility is that because the three Chiefs who went to England in 1906 stopped in Ottawa en route and apparently stayed on a local Indian reserve, they could well have learned of the Proclamation on that occasion. If so, they may have learned of Clark's expertise, as well.[52]

A third possibility — and these are not mutually exclusive — is that the Proclamation entered the discourse about Aboriginal title in BC via the lawyers Clark and O'Meara. And even if the Nisga'a and the Cowichan did know about the Proclamation before this, it was Clark, O'Meara, and Tate who introduced it into the written discourse. In December 1908 O'Meara wrote to his bishop, telling him that he had recently obtained information about the rights of BC's Indians — either from Clark and some of the missionaries or directly from the Cowichan — and referring to the Royal Proclamation as key.[53] So far as we can tell, this is the first documentary reference to it in BC since 1875. By February 1909 O'Meara was meeting with Tate to plan strategy.[54] By March he was in Toronto consulting Clark, who had "an expert knowledge of the matter of Indian title" and with whom he had already corresponded.[55] Because O'Meara then took the Cowichan Petition to England and was back in North America by the end of April, it seems reasonable to conclude that Clark and O'Meara drafted the final version when O'Meara was in Toronto.

So, at least insofar as the documentary use of the Royal Proclamation is concerned, it came to British Columbia via the lawyers. Perhaps O'Meara's research uncovered the Order-in-Council relating to the disallowance of BC's *Crown Land Act* in 1875. Perhaps Clark, who had already litigated at least one Indian title case in the Judicial Committee of the Privy Council, brought it to O'Meara's attention.[56] Or perhaps the Proclamation was known to the Cowichan already. Whatever the case, news of its legal importance was spreading, and within a year of the Cowichan Petition, many other tribal groups were citing it in support of their claims.[57]

THE PETITION ITSELF

Basing its arguments upon general principles of justice and equity, the Cowichan Petition is an eleven-page legal argument dated 15 March 1909 and addressed to "[t]he King's Most Excellent Majesty." It enlists both history and law in support of its prayer for relief, which is that "steps be taken to protect the usufructory right of your petitioners in [the land of British Columbia], or, that in the alternative the whole question of the rights of the [Cowichan] Tribe be submitted to the Judicial Committee of the Privy Council for decision and determination."[58] It was followed in September 1909 by a resolution from the Cowichan petitioners and representatives of other tribes urging the Dominion government to act on the petition, and a concise "Statement of Facts and Claims on Behalf of the Indians of British Columbia" written by Clark in January 1910.[59] The resolution was drawn up at a Vancouver meeting described by one newspaper as announcing that the Indians were "on the warpath." Not the warpath of violence, "but the belligerent highway of legality and constitutionality which more befits the enlightened though still the original son of the wilds." The editors also noted that the Indians had put down on paper their determination "to maintain with moderation and firmness the independent stand [that] has been taken in defence of these rights."[60]

As noted, we have reproduced the text of the petition in Appendix 13.1. Its historical significance, in our view, lies in the particular legal submissions that were introduced in its pages. These submissions had an immediate impact on the law and politics of Aboriginal title in British Columbia and produced unprecedented promise for the successful resolution of the issues — a promise, as we will explain later, that was short-lived owing largely to the Dominion election of 1911. The submissions contained in the Cowichan Petition also established the template for the Nisga'a Petition and, ultimately, would form the basis of the arguments accepted by Canadian courts in fleshing out the modern law of Aboriginal title.

The first point that makes the petition worthy of note has been discussed earlier: it marks the reappearance, after an absence of some thirty-five years, of the Royal Proclamation of 1763 in the discourse of the Indian land question. In other words, the petitioners were not simply asking for grace or even relying solely on their own laws to assert their rights. They were arguing that these rights were also recognized and protected by British law. It is therefore noteworthy that, in 1875, the Dominion Minister of Justice did not appear to doubt the Proclamation's relevance to the land question in BC, and that Clark was also confident of its importance.[61] It was only when the campaign for title was revived in the latter half of the twentieth century that BC advanced the argument, which was accepted by the Court of Appeal in *Calder,* that the Proclamation did not apply to BC because in 1763 the province was *terra incognita.*[62]

The second important feature is the petitioners' reliance on the *St. Catherine's* case. Decided by the Judicial Committee of the Privy Council in 1888, *St. Catherine's* established that the Indians' "usufructary" rights were a legal interest in land that was protected by section 109 of the *British North America Act.* In other words, provincial title was subject to the Indian title until the latter had been lawfully extinguished — which of course had not been done in most of BC.[63] As the petitioners put it, the lands of the Cowichan had never been "ceded to or purchased by the Crown nor was the Indian title otherwise extinguished" (para. 3), and were therefore reserved lands within the terms of the Proclamation (para. 4). This is a classic use of a judicial precedent, and it was a critical legal point. In the abortive 1908 reference, counsel for BC had glossed over the fact that Indian title to the land claimed in *St. Catherine's* had been extinguished, asserting instead that the case was a powerful authority for the province.

The third main argument, less important today but critical at the time, involved Article 13 of the Terms of Union. Article 13 provided that "tracts of land of such extent as it has hitherto been the practice of [BC] to appropriate for [Indian reserves] shall from time to time be conveyed by [BC] to the Dominion Government for the use and benefit of the Indians, on the application of the Dominion Government."[64] Simple enough. BC, however, was in violation of this Article: by 1909, nearly forty years after the Terms of Union were signed, not a single reserve had been conveyed to the Dominion. Instead, relying on an agreement between the two governments in 1876, the province maintained that it, and not the Dominion, held the underlying title to the reserves. The point here is not simply that the BC government relied on the Article's requirement that it allot only as much land for reserves as the colony had in the past — which was precious little. It was rather that even this small amount had not been conveyed in trust to the Dominion and that the province regarded the 1876 agreement as trumping the Constitution. The dispute led to the suspension of the reserve allocation process in 1907 and was yet another reason that the pressure to do something about the land question escalated in these years.

Even more significant for the petitioners, however, is another provision in Article 13. It provided that, if BC and Ottawa could not agree on the conveyance of lands, the matter "shall be referred for the decision of the Secretary of State for the Colonies." In other words, it was Dominion-provincial disagreement about reserves that opened the door for the Indians and their supporters to demand imperial intervention. Yet there would be no imperial intervention, even though BC did not formally convey the reserves to the Dominion until 1938.[65]

Finally, the petition — and Clark's "Statement," submitted in 1910 as a sort of clarification — refers to a number of legal and historical facts and authorities that came to dominate the debate for the next eighteen years, many of which reappeared when the campaign for title was taken up again in the 1950s and '60s. In particular, the case of *Campbell v. Hall*, the reference to BC as part of the "Indian Territories" before the establishment of the colonies, the petition by the Vancouver Island Legislative Assembly in 1861, and Lord Dufferin's address to the Provincial

Legislative Assembly in 1876 all became part of an argument that would batter repeatedly against the office doors of politicians until finally, in 1927, even Ottawa had had enough.[66]

The petition closes by stating that the petitioners have "waited patiently" for justice but "have at length exhausted all other constitutional means known to them." The Judicial Committee was their "last resort." In fact, their long wait was only just beginning. But recall that just three years before this complex legal document was written, the Aboriginal petitioners of 1906 had protested that they were "but poor ignorant Indians [who] know nothing of the white man's law."[67] Better evidence of what had changed in those three short years is difficult to imagine. After 1909 critics of the campaign for title would have to change tack and blame lawyers instead of missionaries for the "agitation" they claimed would otherwise not have existed. And, of course, they did.[68]

That the Cowichan Petition set the terms for the long legal debate that would follow is made clear by comparing it to the Nisga'a Petition. Although there are a number of textual differences, this petition, submitted only four years later, is strikingly similar in the logic, organization, and legal authorities invoked in its core arguments.[69] It asserts possession since time immemorial; it refers to the same legal authorities — pre-Confederation imperial statutes, the Terms of Union and, most notably, the provisions of the Royal Proclamation of 1763 — cited in the Cowichan Petition; and it makes it clear that the Nisga'a (like the Cowichan) had never ceded any of their territory to the Crown. It differs from the earlier document in two main respects. First, the Nisga'a Petition contains a "metes and bounds" description of the claimed territory and two blueprint maps, an indication that the drafters realized that more precision was required than had been supplied in the 1909 document.[70] The second difference is that it brings the narrative up to date by citing recent developments. These include intrusions on Nisga'a territory pursuant to provincial statutes that are said to be violations of the Royal Proclamation, notices protesting such intrusions that the Nisga'a had delivered to surveyors and pre-emptors, Nisga'a participation in the mass meeting with the provincial government in March 1911, discussed later, and a strong statement that nothing in the Terms of Union or the McKenna-McBride Agreement of 1912, also discussed later in the chapter, extinguished or could extinguish their claimed rights and title. In short, the two documents are clearly parent and child.

CONCLUSION: DASHED HOPES — THE FATE OF THE PETITION

As we have seen, the British government referred the Cowichan Petition to Ottawa for a report, and although the province was unmoved, this had several immediate effects on the other actors. On the Dominion side, the Ministry of the Interior retained McInnes to provide a legal opinion on Indian title, and, because it was apparent that BC would not change its land policy, he concluded in August 1909 that Ottawa was bound as trustee for the Indians to have the question litigated.[71] On the ground in British Columbia, protests—some rhetorical, some more emphatic—continued. In September 1909 many tribes formally asked Britain to submit their claims to the Judicial Committee of the Privy Council, in accordance with the Cowichan Petition, and asked Ottawa to facilitate that submission. In January 1910 the tribes sent a "Statement of Facts and Claims" drafted by Clark to the Dominion Department of Justice, and that Department advised the government that a judicial decision should be secured. The preference, as it had been in 1908, was for a reference to the Supreme Court of Canada, and, at first, the situation looked promising.

As early as April of 1909, BC's Attorney General had told his deputy that he thought that settling the form of the questions for the Court would not be very difficult. He even thought that the case might be heard in the fall.[72] Nonetheless, it was not until May 1910 that the Deputy Attorney General and the Dominion Deputy Minister of Justice met in Ottawa and agreed on ten questions, seven of which concerned matters involving Indian reserves. The remaining three related to Indian title.[73] The list was then submitted to Clark and O'Meara, who approved them on behalf of the tribes, and to the BC government. However, it seems that when Premier McBride was consulted, he refused to proceed with the reference unless the three questions respecting Indian title were removed.

In August 1910 the Friends of the Indians of British Columbia made written submissions to Prime Minister Laurier. In September the Moral and Social Reform Council of Canada passed a resolution at the annual meeting in Toronto in support of the Friends, and in October these two organizations met with Laurier.[74] He advised them to try once more to persuade McBride to cooperate, so they did. In December they met with the Premier, but he bluntly told them that under no circumstances would

BC agree to have the matter adjudicated by the courts.[75] Then, in March 1911, ninety-six Indian delegates from tribes from most regions of the province came to the BC legislature to press their demands upon the government, which remained obdurate.[76] In April the Friends and the Moral and Social Reform Council went to Ottawa and met once again with Laurier.

It was at this meeting that the Prime Minister told the delegates that his government believed that "it is our duty to have the matter inquired into. The Government of British Columbia may be right or wrong in their assertion that the Indians have no claim whatever. Courts of Law are for just that purpose — where a man asserts a claim and it is denied by another. But we do not know if we can force a Government into Court. If we can find a way I may say we may surely do so."[77] But, in fact, they had already found a way. McInnes had recommended it in 1909: sue randomly selected homesteaders in the Skeena, claiming that they were on Indian title land held in trust by the Dominion. The homesteaders would plead their provincial Crown grants in defence, and the province would then have to intervene in the case to defend its grants. In 1909 the Laurier administration was reluctant to go this route without trying one more time to persuade BC to agree to a court reference. In 1910 the two deputy ministers did try but, as we have seen, McBride squelched the resulting arrangement.[78] All that now remained was the "McInnes gambit." The Dominion government therefore had Parliament amend the *Indian Act* to facilitate such a lawsuit in a Dominion court, allowing the Indian title issue to be litigated even though BC would not consent to a reference.[79]

Then, on 17 May 1911, the Governor-General-in-Council passed Order-in-Council 1081, which noted that because all attempts to secure BC's cooperation had failed, the Dominion government proposed to institute proceedings in the Exchequer Court to secure a judicial determination of the BC Indian land question.[80] Never before, and not again until *Calder,* were the Indians so close to having their claims considered in the courts. This momentum came to a screeching halt in the fall of 1911 when the Laurier government, which was now legally committed to a judicial resolution of the Indian land question, was defeated in the Dominion election and replaced by a Conservative government decidedly unenthusiastic about the claims of the BC Indians.

The new Conservative government appeared at first to be willing to proceed with some sort of litigation, but by the spring of 1912, just as the various Aboriginal groups and their supporters were engaged in a vigorous effort to salvage the promise of the previous year, Ottawa and BC were moving toward making a deal that would change everything. On 29 July 1912, J.A.J. McKenna, whom the Dominion government had appointed to negotiate with British Columbia, wrote to Premier Mc-Bride. He told him that if, in order to get an agreement between the two governments on the land question, Ottawa had to drop the previous Dominion government's plan either to refer the matter to the courts or to secure a judicial determination by other means, Ottawa would do so.[81] With this concession in place, on 24 September the two men signed what has come to be known as the McKenna-McBride Agreement.[82] The two governments agreed that, in return for BC giving up its claim to a reversionary interest in provincial Indian reserves, Ottawa would take the Indian title issue off the table, and a new reserve commission would be established to recommend adding or reducing reserve land (see Figure 13.3). After that, BC would convey title to all the reserves to Ottawa, as required by the Terms of Union. All this is well known. But what perhaps has not been appreciated is that the province and the Dominion regarded this agreement as ousting the jurisdiction of the Colonial Office, a result that was extremely pleasing to them and to Great Britain, but not to the Indians. Opposition to the McKenna-McBride Agreement began as soon as its ink was dry and culminated in the formation of the Allied Indian Tribes of British Columbia in 1916. However, because the two governments no longer disagreed about Indian lands, an appeal pursuant to Article 13 was now highly problematic.[83] Denied imperial arbitration under the Terms of Union, the Nisga'a accordingly sought a hearing before the Judicial Committee of the Privy Council.[84]

After 1913 the Cowichan Petition faded from the scene, and the Nisga'a Petition took its place as the rallying point for most of the tribes. However, because the McKenna-McBride Agreement on its face stated that it would be "a final adjustment of all matters relating to Indian affairs" in BC, there was no longer any real pressure on the Dominion to deal with Indian title, particularly after both governments ratified the Royal Commission's report in the 1920s. The British government was increasingly sensitive to the Dominion's concerns about interference with Canadian sovereignty, and the province had been assured that McKenna-McBride absolved it of any further responsibility. So the latter washed its hands of the Indian title question and the former, although it kept the Nisga'a file open for years, was quick to accept the Dominion's

FIGURE 13.3 This photograph was taken when the Royal Commission on Indian Affairs, also referred to as the McKenna-McBride Commission, visited the Cowichan in 1913. The man holding the portrait of King Edward VII, with whom a Salish delegation had met in London in 1906, was retained for this purpose by Cowichan Chief Charlie Tsulpi'multw.
Courtesy of Royal BC Museum, BC Archives, Victoria, BC (H-07048)

rather misleading assurances that everything required was being done.[85] And although Ottawa continued to discuss a possible treaty or court reference with the Allied Tribes, the politicians and officials concerned gradually grew weary of the seemingly interminable talks and shut everything down in 1927. It would take another forty years before a court would come to hear legal argument concerning the BC Indian land question, and it would be the Nisga'a who would make this happen. But their argument stood on the shoulders of a document that, shaped by a small group of dedicated lawyers and backed by the tireless work of Aboriginal leaders, set the terms of debate for the century to come—the Cowichan Petition of 1909.

Appendix 13.1: The Cowichan Petition, 1909

To

THE KING'S MOST EXCELLENT MAJESTY

The Humble Petition of the Cowichan Tribe of Indians in the Province of British Columbia in the Dominion of Canada one of your Majesty's Dominions Beyond the Seas.

SHEWETH:

1. *THAT* from time immemorial the Cowichan Tribe of Indians have been the possessors and occupants of the territory including Cowichan Valley containing a large area and situate within the territorial limits of the said Province of British Columbia.

2. The Indian title to the said territory was always recognized by your Majesty's predecessors. This Indian title was expressly recognized and affirmed by the proclamation issued by Your Majesty's predecessor King George III on the 7th of October 1763. This proclamation ordained among other things as follows:-
"And whereas it is just and reasonable and essential to our interests and the security of our Colonies that the several nations or tribes of Indians with whom we are connected and who live under our protection should not be molested or disturbed in the possession of such parts of our Dominions and territories as, not having been ceded to or purchased by us, are reserved to them or any of them as their hunting grounds; We do therefore, with the advice of our Privy Council, declare it to be our royal will and pleasure that no Governor or Commander in Chief in any of our Colonies of Quebec, East Florida or West Florida, do presume, upon any pretence whatever, to grant warrants of survey or pass any patents for lands, beyond the bounds of their respective Governments as described in their commissions; as also, that no Governor or Commander-in-Chief of any of our other Colonies or plantations in America do presume for the present and until our further pleasure be known, to grant warrants of survey or pass patents for any lands beyond the heads or sources of any of the rivers which fall into the Atlantic Ocean from the West or Northwest, or upon any lands whatever which not having been ceded to or purchased by us as aforesaid, are reserved to the said Indians or any of them."
"And we do further declare it to be our royal will and pleasure, for the present, as aforesaid, to reserve under our sovereignty, protection and dominion for the use of the said Indians all the land and territories not included within

the limits of our said three new Governments or within the limits of the territory granted to the Hudson's Bay Company as also all the lands and territories lying to the westward of the sources of the rivers which fall into the sea from the West and Northwest as aforesaid; and we do hereby strictly forbid, on pain of our displeasure, all our loving subjects from making any purchase or settlements whatever, or taking possession of any of the lands above reserved, without our special leave and license for that purpose first obtained."

"And we do further strictly enjoin and require all persons whatever, who have either wilfully or inadvertently seated themselves upon any lands within the countries above described or upon any other lands which, not having been ceded to or purchased by us, are still reserved to the said Indians as aforesaid forthwith to remove themselves from such settlements."

"And whereas great frauds and abuses have been committed in purchasing lands of the Indians to the great prejudice of our interests and to the great dissatisfaction of the said Indians."

"In order therefore to prevent such irregularities for the future and to the end that the Indians may be convinced of our justice and determined resolution to reserve all reasonable cause of discontent we do with the advice of our Privy Council strictly enjoin and require that no private person do presume to make any purchase from the said Indians of any lands reserved to the said Indians within these parts of our Colonies where we have thought proper to allow settlement but that if at any time any of the said Indians should be inclined to dispose of the said lands the same shall be purchased only for us in our name at some public meeting or assembly of the said Indians to be held for that purpose by the Governor or Commander-in-Chief of our Colony respectively within which they shall lie."

3. The lands belonging to and claimed by the said Cowichan Tribe as aforesaid were never ceded to or purchased by the Crown nor was the Indian title otherwise extinguished. These lands were not within the limits of the territory at the date of the said proclamation, namely, 7th October 1763 to the Hudsons Bay Company.

4. The said lands were, therefore, within the terms of the said proclamation lands reserved for the said Indians.

5. The said Cowichan Tribe as well as all Indians in North America have always regarded the said Proclamation of their great Father King George III as the Charter of their rights.

6. This Proclamation was declared in the case of Campbell v. Hall, 1 Cowper 204, by Lord Mansfield, Chief Justice of England, to have the effect and operation of a Statute of the Imperial Parliament.

7. Ever since the date of the said proclamation the Indians have continued to be the firm and faithful allies of the Crown and have rendered important military service especially in two wars, the war of the Revolution and that of 1812 and these services were expressly referred to in the judgment of Mr. Justice Strong in the St. Catharines Milling & Lumber Company v. the Queen, 4 Cartwright page 137.

8. The title of the Indians is recognized in various Imperial Statutes relating to British Columbia before the Confederation of 1867 in which the lands in question are referred to as "Indian Territories." This is also recognized by the fourteen Indian treaties made by Sir James Douglas as agent for the Hudson Bay Company which Treaties are set in the Sessional Papers of British Columbia for 1876 at page 165 et seq. The same state of affairs is recognized in the correspondence between the Secretary of State of the Colonies and Sir James Douglas during the years 1858 to 1861. These are set forth in the said Sessional papers at page 172 and following.

9. In a report made by the Indian Commissioners appointed by the Government of Canada dated 22nd January 1844 and made while the Indian Affairs of Canada were still under the direction of the Imperial Government the Indian Commissioners say "The subsequent proclamation of His Majesty George III issued in 1763 furnished them (the Indians) with a fresh guarantee for the possession of their hunting grounds and the protection of the Crown. This document the Indians look upon as their Charter. They have preserved a copy of it to the present time and have referred to it on several occasions in their representations to the Government."

"Since 1763 the Government adhering to the Royal Proclamation of that year have not considered themselves entitled to dispossess the Indians of their lands without entering into an agreement with them and rendering them some compensation. For a considerable time after the conquest of Canada the whole of the Western part of the upper province with the exception of a few military posts on the frontier and a great extent of the eastern part was in their occupation. As the settlement of the Country advanced and the land was required for new occupants rendered their removal desirable the British Government made successive agreements with them for the surrender of portions of their lands."

10. The Indian title and rights were also fully recognized by the Legislature of Vancouver Island as shown by the petition of the House of Assembly of Vancouver Island referred to in the Sessional Papers of British Columbia 1876 page 179 et seq. And in reply to the said petition the Right Honourable Secretary of State for the Colonies in his dispatch from Downing Street dated 19th October 1861 says "I am fully sensible of the great importance of purchasing without loss of time the native title to the soil of Vancouver Island."

11. In his judgment in the St. Catharines Milling Case 4 Cart. 181 Mr. Justice Gwynne quotes from a report made in 1856 by Royal Commissioners appointed to investigate the Indian land question as follows:– "By the proclamation of 1763 territorial rights akin to those asserted by Sovereign Princes are recognized as belonging to the Indians, that is to say, that none of their land can be alienated save by Treaty made publicly between the Crown and them."

12. At the time of the union of British Columbia with the Dominion of Canada section 109 of the British North America Act 1867 was incorporated in the terms of the union and expressly reserved and protects the Indian title to the said lands.

13. The rights of your Petitioners in respect of said lands therefore at Confederation remained and still continue to be under the "sovereignty, protection and dominion" of your Majesty by virtue of the said Proclamation of 7th October 1763.

14. In the St. Catharines Milling & Lumber Company v. The Queen, 14 Appeal Cases pages 58 and 59 Lord Watson refers to the interest of the Indians in the land as a burden upon the estate of the Crown and an interest other than that of the Province in the same within the meaning of section 109 of the British North America Act. It is contended, therefore, that the Indian title to the said lands remains in full force and effect.

15. This Indian title was referred to in the address of Lord Dufferin, Governor-General of Canada to the Legislative Assembly of British Columbia made on the 20th day of September 1876—

"From my first arrival in Canada I have been very much pre-occupied with the condition of the Indian population in this Province. You must remember that the Indian population are not represented in Parliament and consequently that the Governor-General is bound to watch over their welfare with especial solicitude. Now we must all admit that the condition of the Indian question in British Columbia is not satisfactory. Most unfortunately as I think there has been an initial error, ever since Sir James Douglas quitted office in the Government of British Columbia neglecting to recognize what is known as the Indian title. In Canada this has always been done; no Government whether Provincial or central has failed to acknowledge that the original title to the land existed in the Indian Tribes and communities that hunted or wandered over them. Before we touch an acre we make a treaty with the Chiefs representing the bands we are dealing with, and having agreed upon and paid our stipulated price often times agreed at after a great deal of haggling and difficulty we enter late possession but not until then do we consider that we are entitled to deal with an acre. The result has been that in Canada our Indians are contented well affected to the white men and amenable to the laws and Government."

16. The title of your Petitioners has been of the wrongfully repudiated and ignored by the Government of the Province of British Columbia.

17. By the Thirteenth Article of the terms of admission of British Columbia into Confederation it is provided "that the charge of the Indians and the Trusteeship and management of the lands reserved for their use and benefit shall be assumed by the Dominion Government and a policy as liberal as that hitherto pursued by the British Columbia Government should be continued by the Dominion Government after the Union" and it was further provided "to carry out such policy tracts of land of such extent as it has hitherto been the practice of the British Columbia Government to appropriate for that purpose shall from time to time be conveyed from the local to the Dominion Government in trust for the use and benefit of the Indians on application of the Dominion Government; and in case of disagreement between the two Governments respecting the quantity of such tracts of land to be so granted the matter shall be referred for the decision of the Secretary of State for the Colonies."

18. The Dominion Government endeavored to have such reserves set aside but did not succeed in so doing and such reserves have not up to the present time been conveyed by the Provincial Government to the Dominion Government.

19. In a Memorandu [sic], dated the 2nd day of November 1874 and approved by His Excellency the Governor-General on the 4th of November 1874 the Minister of the Interior says— "The undersigned would respectfully recommend

that the Government of the Dominion should make an earnest appeal to the Government of British Columbia if they value the peace and prosperity of their Province — if they desire that Canada as a whole should retain the high character she has earned for herself by her just and honourable treatment of the red men of the forest to reconsider in a spirit of wisdom and patriotism the land grievances of which the Indians of that Province complain, apparently with good reason, and take such measures as may be necessary promptly and effectually to redress them."

Up to the present time this appeal has been unsuccessful.

20. In the report of the Deputy Superintendent of Indian Affairs 31st December 1877, referring to British Columbia he says "The non-recognition in some instances by the Provincial Government of the title of the Indians to land occupied by them has for some time agitated the minds of the Indians of this Province. Some of these lands have already been and others are being sold without reference to the Indian title thereto. Unless the equitable claims of the Indians in respect to the lands in question are recognized and met in a liberal spirit, serious trouble may be the result."

21. The memorandum of the Attorney-General of the Province of British Columbia dated the 26th day of February 1907 and approved by the Executive Council on the 28th day of February 1907 (included in the papers and correspondence between the Government of Canada and the Government of British Columbia) comprised in a return called for by the House of Commons on January 28th 1908, the British Columbia Government says that the Dominion Government holds no proprietory rights in the Reserves and denies the power of the Dominion to deal even with the Reserves. These propositions of the Provincial Government were controverted by a report of the Committee of the Privy Council approved on the 19th day of December 1907 and the Dominion Government stating that it was ready to facilitate the Government of the Province of British Columbia in any steps it might be advised to test the question involved before the Courts. Subsequently by Order-in-Council dated the 8th day of August 1908 certain questions were submitted to the Supreme Court of British Columbia for hearing and consideration. These questions do not include the question of the Indian title but the frame of the question submitted substantially amounts to a repudiation of your petitioners title and rights.

22. On the argument of the said questions before the Supreme Court of British Columbia the Dominion Government took no part. Your petitioners are informed

that counsel for the Attorney-General on the said argument repudiated your petitioners title and stated that the St. Catharines case leaves little room for argument. In your petitioners view the judgment in that case is not applicable because the territory there in dispute was acquired by Great Britain from France and in the second place because there the Indian title to lands in question had been surrendered to the Dominion by treaty and in consideration of substantial money payments and other advantages satisfactory to the Indians.

23. Your petitioners have waited patiently for long years in the hope and expectation that their rights would be recognized and justice done to them by the Government of British Columbia but have at length exhausted all other constitutional means known to them.

24. Your petitioners as a last resort appeal across the seas to Your Majesty the fountain of justice fully assured that Your Majesty in exercise of your Sovereignty and Dominion will protect your petitioners in their extremity.

YOUR PETITIONERS THEREFORE HUMBLY PRAY that steps be taken to protect the usufructory right of your petitioners in all of the said land, or, that in the alternative the whole question of the rights of the said Tribe be submitted to the Judicial Committee of the Privy Council for decision and determination.

AND YOUR PETITIONERS WILL EVER PRAY:

Of Counsel for the Petitioners.

Dated 15th March 1909.

AFTERWORD
Looking from the Past into the Future

John McLaren

Looking forward, it is becoming apparent that enough groundwork
has been covered in the history of modern legal systems, especially
those that share the same roots, ... heritage, [and colonial experience],
to make possible comparisons and contrasts of legal cultures, as there
were in the past with ancient, medieval and early modern legal
systems. This reality opens up a rich new area of ... historiography.

— K.J.M. Smith and John McLaren,
"History's Living Legacy"[1]

Both the introduction to this book and the chapters themselves bear
clear and eloquent testimony to the truth of the quotation above, penned
at the beginning of this decade. We have moved decisively out of the era
colourfully described by the late Graham Parker as that of "cultural
cringe" (that the legal culture of mother England was the only worthwhile
focus in legal historical research and teaching) to an increasingly rich
and expansive historiography of the legal cultures of British colonies and
the modern states that have succeeded them.[2] The records of imperial
and colonial legal history, which lay for so long undisturbed, are now
being accessed by scholars who recognize that colonial legal histories
need to be exposed and excavated. The range of topics addressed herein,
the depth and diversity of analysis and interpretation employed, and the
comparative implications of what has been written demonstrate that the
writing of the legal history of former British colonies, especially the "settler" colonies, has reached or is reaching a critical mass in terms of subject
matter and detail. As a consequence, it is possible and vitally important

to locate these developments firmly in the broader context of imperial and colonial cultures of, first, England and then Great Britain, and of the temporal, geographic, political, institutional, economic, social, cultural, and strategic variables that affected imperial and colonial policy and law, and influenced how they played out in practice. Both collectively and individually, these essays add important elements of detail to that canvas.

In this afterword, my purpose is not to rehearse the work of the editors or the individual contributors. It is rather to suggest several further directions that research and teaching on colonial legal history are taking, and what we might expect as further areas of development for the future.

I am currently researching the trials and tribulations of colonial judges who, for reasons of principle, personality, or a combination of both, fell out with the governments or powerful elites in the colonies in which they served and were either disciplined or threatened with discipline for their "sins." Although, after reading these histories, one is tempted to make comparisons with *opéra bouffe* or to mutter, "A funny way to run an empire," there is within them some evidence of a guiding hand. By the nineteenth century, in the wake of an earlier, looser system of imperial administration and the seismic disturbances caused by the American War of Independence, the Colonial Office emerged as the arm of the imperial government responsible for colonial policy, its application, and the superintendence of the diverse group of territories under British rule.[3] The recent publications of Cole Harris on imperial and colonial policy regarding Aboriginal peoples, and of Russell Smandych on the law relating to slavery in the British Caribbean colonies and on the fate of Aboriginal evidence legislation in Australia, point to the importance of this remarkable government department.[4] There is room for much more work by legal historians on the Colonial Office and its influence on imperial policy and law. More attention also needs to be directed to the Office's waning role in the case of settler colonies as local desires and ambitions increasingly took centre stage and imperial officials bought into the reality of self-determination for these territories.[5]

On the same plane as the Colonial Office and its influence on imperial law and policy is the Judicial Committee of the Privy Council. Until the establishment of the Colonial Office, the Privy Council in various guises guided imperial policy and practice on colonial rule and at the same time acted as the final court of appeal from colonial suits.[6] Although, with the creation of the Colonial Office, the Privy Council was divested of a large amount of its former colonial oversight, its appellate role increased in importance. This was a result of the geographic spread of empire, the growth of colonial economies and legal infrastructures, and, as the nineteenth century wore on, the greater ease of taking appeals to London. The judicialization of the Privy Council's function in relation to the colonies and its political and constitutional significance have been well charted by colonial historians, most notably Peter Howell and David Swinfen.[7] Much less clear is the impact of the Judicial Committee on the configuration of colonial law and the extent to which it was able to encourage substantive and procedural consistency within the empire, not to mention its handling of legal pluralism in some colonial possessions. Bruce Kercher, as with so much of his work, has taken the initiative here in his study of unreported appeals from Australia to the Privy Council before 1850.[8] Clearly, there is more to be done in charting the experience of other colonies and the pan-imperial picture.

As David Williams and the editors have reminded us in this volume, institutional colonialism did not end in settler territories with the grant of responsible government, Dominion status, or the *Statute of Westminster.* The institutional dimensions of colonialist rule in Australia, Canada, and New Zealand, through various departments of government—Justice, the Interior, Aboriginal Affairs, Immigration, and so on—are also worthy of further exploration. The chapters in this volume by Hamar Foster and Benjamin L. Berger, Janna Promislow, and David Williams reflect an increasingly rich set of insights by both non-Aboriginal and Aboriginal scholars into the institutional, legal construction of the dependency and marginalization of indigenous peoples, as well as their resistance to these stratagems, in former settler colonies.[9] There is similar depth in some jurisdictions in the area of the law and policy designed to control and limit migration to these territories by, and to regulate certain categories of, non-white immigrants.[10] Paul Romney and Jonathan Swainger have introduced us to the more general rescript of the institutional colonial and post-colonial construction of law and justice in their studies of the office of the Attorney General of Upper Canada and Ontario and the Canadian Department of Justice, respectively.[11] All of this activity points to the importance of more work on institutional histories, not only of courts and the legal profession in the colonies and their successors but also of the state's multi-faceted involvement in the construction of law and justice through its departments of government and other public institutions.

The editors have drawn our attention to the law as reflective of broader political, social, economic, and cultural forces and trends, and as itself constitutive of a particular type of culture and ideology that has been influential on how issues in colonial territories and their successors have been understood and handled. The legalization or judicialization of political, social, economic, and cultural issues is one area that has not been investigated to any great extent in imperial or colonial legal history until lately. Rande Kostal's prodigious study of the Governor Eyre controversy in the mid-1860s, a controversy that arose out of that imperial official's invocation of martial law in certain parishes on the island of Jamaica, serves as an inspired guide to the potential in this sort of analysis.[12] In this story we develop a clear sense of how issues that were essentially political in character, and that demanded political solutions, related to the imperial, geographic, and cultural context from which they sprang, and were converted into what were primarily, if not exclusively, domestic legal issues and anxieties in Britain itself. The extent to which this phenomenon of transference was a factor in the invocation of law and justice or in the resistance to it in British colonial territories and their successors, and whether the balance between purely legal and political solutions changed over time, invites much more thought and comment. In this volume, Chapter 4, by Ian Holloway, Simon Bronitt, and John Williams, in decentring legal notions of the rule of law in the early history of New South Wales as a colony, and locating rule of law ideology later in its history, is suggestive in this regard.

Although it is important to be alert to the constitutive effect of an ideology of law and justice at a formal and institutional level, it is equally necessary to recognize its limitations in practice. Colonial territories often differed from England and Britain in the sparseness of the population, difficulties in travel, and the absence of an institutional adjudicative or professional legal presence in the neighbourhood. Although, as John Philip Reid has noted regarding the pioneers on the Overland Trail in the United States, those folk did have knowledge about the legal systems they had left behind as well as understandings about the rights and obligations within them, it was often not possible to apply the law in any formal way.[13] Peter Karsten has provided us with an important set of insights into the key role played by informal law and ordering in comparative colonial legal culture and how informal solutions sometimes clashed with the demands of formal law. This he has done in an exhaustive discussion of how disputes that we would characterize as contractual, tortious, commercial, or proprietary were often negotiated or mediated outside the bounds of the formal law on the "frontiers" of the British settler world, in Australia, Canada, New Zealand, and the United States.[14] The message here is clear. If we are to understand colonial law in its fullness, we need to be mindful of the significance and impact of informal law and process in its history. Moreover, as Jerry Bannister has reminded us in his fascinating study of law and custom in Newfoundland, it is entirely possible to have a working and viable legal system that is based on evolving customs and informal institutions of justice.[15] In Chapter 2 of this volume, Bruce Kercher's discussion is an intriguing reflection of this reality and of how informal practice hardened into accepted rules and principles on another frontier — the high seas and the ordering of master and servant relations in that domain in colonial law and practice.

The focus of Peter Karsten's work on aspects of private law also raises a further issue about the historiography of imperial and colonial legal history. The coverage of discrete areas of both common and statutory law, within and across colonies, is very spotty. Criminal law and justice have probably sparked most interest, although not necessarily with any consistency.[16] That is why the comparative studies by Barry Wright (Chapter 1) and Lyndsay Campbell (Chapter 10) on the invocation of libel law and that of Greg Marquis (Chapter 12) on the early construction of liquor prohibition in New Brunswick are so welcome in guiding us through relatively uncharted waters. Within civil law and liability, property law, perhaps not surprisingly, given the centrality of issues of land and place in the imperial project, has excited increasing interest, as is illustrated by Chapter 11, the work of Andrew Buck and Nancy Wright. This scholarship has benefited and will continue to benefit from the essays edited by these authors and from the impressive monographs written by John Weaver, Stuart Banner, and Lindsay Robertson on the philosophy of improvement and its dramatic effect as a guiding principle in colonization.[17] Less well served are the topics of contract, tort, and commercial law, not to mention corporate, insurance, bankruptcy, and insolvency law. The promise in R.C.B. Risk's inspired 1970s work on private law in its economic and social context in Upper Canada has yet to be realized more widely, so also has the important pioneer work of Bruce Kercher on the legal implications of indebtedness in colonial New South Wales.[18] There is a great deal of fertile soil here, waiting for eager, accomplished scholarly tillers. Peter Karsten's analysis of frontier law and custom points the way.[19]

In traditional understandings of how English law filled up the colonial spaces (with the exception of territories where a pre-existing legal system, whether European or indigenous, existed), the picture is one of wisdom radiating out from the mother country to the colonial children. Although the importance of English law in the colonies should be in no way underplayed, it is also essential, as Jeremy Finn has demonstrated, to recognize that borrowing between British colonies, and between those colonies and the United States, is a significant feature of colonial legal culture.[20] This is true, both within the confines of the common law and even more so of areas of activity governed by statutory or regulatory law in which English precedents were lacking or unsatisfactory. Corporate law, resources law, restrictive immigration law, homesteading law, and land registration law are among some of the areas that fall within this story of horizontal borrowing across empire. The further articulation of this phenomenon and the lines of communication, formal and otherwise, that were involved in this process merit more exposure. In Chapter 5 of this volume, Jeremy Finn has taken the story a further step by showing the extent to which courts in mother England have borrowed from the courts of her colonial children and their successor states.

The identity of the dramatis personae who implanted colonial law and justice across empire is, as several of the essays in this book illustrate, an important dimension of how these territories were transformed in a jural sense. The discussions of Jim Phillips and Philip Girard (Chapter 6) on judicial circuits in Nova Scotia, David Williams' (Chapter 7) comparison of the respective roles of a judge and academic bureaucrat in influencing law and policy toward the Maori, Stefan Petrow's (Chapter 8) examination of the judicial career of Algernon Montagu in Van Diemen's Land, Jonathan Swainger's (Chapter 9) insight into the impact of H.E.A. Robertson on conceptions of justice in northeastern British Columbia, and what Ian Holloway, Simon Bronitt, and John Williams (Chapter 4) have to say about Sir Francis Forbes, the first Chief Justice of New South Wales, and his role all add to our appreciation of how English law operated at an institutional, professional, and personal level. We are also sensitized to the contingencies and "accidents" of judicial selection and personality that played a part in how the law and procedures of the imperium operated in practice. As the magisterial series Lives of the Australian Chief Justices by Australian legal historian John Bennett shows, a wealth of material remains to be tapped across the former British Empire.[21]

How the agents of the spread of English law and British justice rationalized the process of transference of the ideology and traditions of these imported or imposed systems and their value to their new home is another area of scholarly research that invites much more attention. The claim that Britain's great gift to notions of law and governance at an international, as well as an imperial, level has been the implanting of the rule of law is, as both the editors and Holloway, Bronitt, and Williams have suggested, ripe for interrogation. What do we mean by the use of this term? What is its relationship to both notions of liberty in Anglo-American history and culture? To what extent were there different interpretations of this notion in colonial and post-colonial territories, and how far were they dependent on time, place, the ebb and flow of imperial policy, strategic considerations, and so on? Is the rule of law at all helpful in describing a plurality of systems of law that existed in the territories of the British Empire (can we talk of competing rules of law)? The studies of David Neal, Paul Romney, Murray Greenwood, and Diane Kirkby and Catharine Coleborne, and, in this book, by the editors and Holloway, Bronitt, and Williams among others, have helped expose some of these questions and provided partial answers.[22] There is a need to relate legal historical research on the invocation of this slippery term to a broader history of the growth of notions of liberty, liberal and libertarian ideology, and sentiment on the one hand, and on the other, attempts at countervailing movement in the opposite direction. How did it fare in the hands of Court Whigs, the Country Whig advocates of civic republicanism, Wilkites, and Bolingbroke Tories in eighteenth-century Britain? What happened to rule of law thinking when it was translated to the American colonies (especially in the lead up to the War of Independence), to Ireland, and to newer colonial territories in the late eighteenth century?[23] What about the concept's later handling in the metropolitan power by government Tories, reformist Whigs, humanitarians, radicals, Chartists, and socialists during the nineteenth century and its resonance in the colonies? Moreover, what was the fate of the notion and rhetoric of the rule of law in the light of, first, the solidification of parliamentary sovereignty and, later, the advent of written Constitutions for former British colonies, such as Australia, Canada, and New Zealand? The answers to these questions need to be considered in the context of both the rich historiography of political thought and the theoretical studies of legal and imperial historians. Scholarship in this area can also benefit from comparative cultural analysis as the path-breaking work of Lauren

Benton demonstrates.[24] Drawing on both European and non-European (Islamic) experience, she stresses the importance of cultural practices and institutions, alongside economic motivations, in shaping colonialism. Moreover, she suggests a discernible movement in imperial policy and colonial law from "multi-centric" contours in the early modern period to a more state-centred and thus rigid pattern in later periods of high colonialism.

One other important matter in terms of laying the basis for further investigation of the legal history of former colonial territories is the exposure and rationalization of archival holdings that are there, ready to be mined and used. As the late eminent Australian legal historian Alex Castles believed, a prerequisite for effective study in the archives, libraries, and other records that contain legal historical information is broad-ranging bibliographical material. Castles' own bibliographic collection of printed works on Australian law is an exemplar here.[25] For anyone who wishes to use early (and even not so early) colonial court records, the searching for, and collating and organizing of, case reports and commentary on court decisions is vital. In the Commonwealth, Bruce Kercher has been both leader and inspiration in that regard, with his excavation of, and digitalizing for public access to, the records of the Supreme Court of New South Wales in its early decades (now extended to other states, including Tasmania, under the joint supervision of Kercher and Stefan Petrow).[26] The initiative has justifiably earned Bruce Kercher the title of "a one-man Selden Society."[27] Scholars in other jurisdictions would do well to take note of the enormous value of this sort of project in providing us with a richer sense of the contours of legal cultures and systems, and insight into the mindsets of the judges and lawyers who operated within the various colonial courts. The work can also correct misconceptions among later generations of judges and lawyers about what the state of the law had been during earlier colonial eras.

The writing and tracing of imperial and colonial legal histories depends, as in the case of historical study more generally, on the arduous labour of both those tackling very specific issues and dealing with the contingencies of time, place, culture, and ideology and those who are ready to engage with the particular scholarship of themselves and others to describe the broader contours of legal development. The focus of scholarly activity at any particular time will depend on the balance between the particular and the general (the micro and macro study), and will reflect the length and complexity of the colonial experience in the territories being studied. To date, it has proven easier to produce general legal histories of Australia and New Zealand than it has of Canada, because of the different time spans represented in these territories in terms of European colonization.[28] However, whatever the legal historical context, it is important to recognize the value of focusing on particular issues and particular regions or communities. All of the scholarship in this book demonstrates commitment to that important objective. The scholars represented here are contributing to the important work of increasing our knowledge of the detail of the legal imperial and colonial historical record, developing the comparative dimensions of those histories, and laying the foundations of more general histories of the colonial legal experience and of the complexity of imperial and colonial legal culture in the world of British settlement.

NOTES

INTRODUCTION: DOES LAW MATTER?

1 E.P. Thompson, *Whigs and Hunters: The Origin of the Black Act* (Harmondsworth: Penguin, 1977) at 266, 267-68 [emphasis in original]. See also c. 4 in this volume.

2 A.V. Dicey, *Introduction to the Study of the Law of the Constitution* (Indianapolis: Liberty Classics, 1982; first published 1915) at 110-15. For a more recent formulation, see *British Columbia (Attorney General) v. Christie,* [2007] 1 S.C.R. 873 at para. 20, citing some of the Supreme Court of Canada's earlier decisions on this issue.

3 Administrative law, said to substitute bureaucratic discretion for the rule of law, was one of the first battlegrounds: see Lord Hewart, *The New Despotism* (London: Ernest Bean, 1929).

4 David Beatty has recently argued that the rule of law demands "proportionality." See Beatty, *The Ultimate Rule of Law* (Oxford and New York: Oxford University Press, 2004). Even more substantively, T.R.S. Allan argues that the rule of law requires respect for equality and human dignity and that any law that is inconsistent with either of these principles offends the rule of law. See Allan, *Constitutional Justice: A Liberal Theory of the Rule of Law* (Oxford and New York: Oxford University Press, 2001).

5 See *Reference re Remuneration of Judges of the Provincial Court (P.E.I.),* [1997] 3 S.C.R. 3; and *Christie v. British Columbia (Attorney General)* (2005), 262 D.L.R. (4th) 51 (B.C.C.A.), rev'd 2007 SCC 21.

6 See Paul W. Kahn, *The Cultural Study of Law: Reconstructing Legal Scholarship* (Chicago and London: University of Chicago Press, 1999).

7 For the rule of law and religious cultures, see *e.g.* John McLaren, "The Doukhobor Belief in Individual Faith and Conscience and the Demands of the Secular State" in H. Coward and J. McLaren, eds., *Religious Conscience, the State and the Law: Historical Contexts and Contemporary Significance* (Albany: SUNY Press, 1998) 117-35; and "The State, Child Snatching and the Law: The Seizure and Indoctrination of Sons of Freedom Children in British Columbia" in John McLaren, Robert Menzies, and Dorothy E. Chunn, eds., *Regulating Lives: Historical Essays on the State, Society, the Individual, and the Law* (Vancouver: UBC Press, 2002) 259. On historical injustices,

see *e.g.* John McLaren, "The Early British Columbia Supreme Court and the 'Chinese Question': Echoes of the Rule of Law" (1991) 20 Man. L.J. 107; and "The Early British Columbia Judges, the Rule of Law and the 'Chinese Question': The California and Oregon Connection" in John McLaren, Hamar Foster, and Chet Orloff, eds., *Law for the Elephant, Law for the Beaver: Essays in the Legal History of the North American West* (Regina and Pasadena: Canadian Plains Research Center/Ninth Judicial Circuit Historical Society, 1992) 233. On the administration of colonial law, see *e.g.* John McLaren, "'The Judicial Office ... Bowing to No Power but the Supremacy of the Law': Judges and the Rule of Law in Colonial Australia and Canada, 1788-1840" (2003) 7:2 Austl. J. Legal Hist. 177; and "The King, the People, the Law ... and the Constitution: Justice Robert Thorpe and the Roots of Irish Whig Ideology in Early Upper Canada" in Jonathan Swainger and Constance Backhouse, eds., *People and Place: Historical Influences on Legal Culture* (Vancouver: UBC Press, 2003) 11. Also useful is John McLaren, "Reflections on the Rule of Law: The Georgian Colonies of New South Wales and Upper Canada, 1788-1837" in Diane Kirkby and Catharine Coleborne, eds., *Law, History, Colonialism: The Reach of Empire* (Manchester: Manchester University Press, 2001) 46.

8   See K.J.M. Smith and John McLaren, "History's Living Legacy: An Outline of 'Modern' Historiography of the Common Law" (2001) 21 L.S. 251 at 303-10 and 315-17, describing the role of legal history in modern legal education and this collaborative project, in particular.

9   John McLaren, A.R. Buck, and Nancy E. Wright, eds., *Despotic Dominion: Property Rights in British Settler Societies* (Vancouver: UBC Press, 2005). Douglas Hay and Paul Craven, eds., *Masters, Servants, and Magistrates in Britain and the Empire, 1562-1955* (Chapel Hill: University of North Carolina Press, 2004). Diane Kirkby and Catharine Coleborne, eds., *Law, History, Colonialism: The Reach of Empire* (Manchester: Manchester University Press, 2001). In the United States, this book is distributed exclusively by Palgrave, New York.

10   Smith and McLaren, *supra* note 8 at 294.

11   John McLaren and Hamar Foster, "Hard Choices and Sharp Edges: The Legal History of British Columbia and the Yukon" in Hamar Foster and John McLaren, eds., *Essays in the History of Canadian Law*, vol. 6: *British Columbia and the Yukon* (Toronto: Osgoode Society for Canadian Legal History and University of Toronto Press, 1995) 3 at 5. McLaren, Buck, and Wright return to this point in "Property Rights in the Colonial Imagination and Experience" in John McLaren, A.R. Buck, and Nancy E. Wright, eds., *Despotic Dominion: Property Rights in British Settler Societies* (Vancouver: UBC Press, 2005) at 1-2.

12   George Orwell, "Shooting an Elephant" in *Shooting an Elephant and Other Essays* (London: Secker and Warburg, 1950) 1 at 1-2.

13   Niall Ferguson, *Empire: The Rise and Demise of the British World Order and the Lessons for Global Power* (New York: Basic Books, 2004) at 306, 317.

14   As Arthur S. Morton put it, "the Anglo-Saxon, upholder of the law though he be, has never been its victim. When law fails him, and the public interest requires it, he feels free to act as the situation demands." Morton, *A History of the Canadian West,*

2d ed. (Toronto: University of Toronto Press, 1973) at 759. See also Hamar Foster, "Shooting the Elephant: Historians and the Problem of Frontier Lawlessness" in Richard Eales and David Sullivan, eds., *The Political Context of Law* (London: Hambledon Press, 1987) at 135-44.

15 William Faulkner, *Requiem for a Nun* (New York: Random House, 1951) at 92. Frederic William Maitland, "Why the History of English Law Is Not Written" in H.A.L. Fisher, ed., *The Collected Papers of Frederic William Maitland,* vol. 1 (Cambridge: Cambridge University Press, 1911) 480 at 488-89. The original lecture was delivered in 1888.

16 For an excellent example of how this worked in one former colony, see Bruce Ziff, "Warm Reception in a Cold Climate: English Property Law and the Suppression of Canadian Legal Identity" in McLaren, Buck, and Wright, eds., *supra* note 11, 103.

17 Graham Parker, "Canadian Legal Culture" in Louis A. Knafla, ed., *Law and Justice in a New Land: Essays in Western Canadian Legal History* (Calgary: Carswell, 1986) 3.

18 Tina Loo, *Making Law, Order, and Authority in British Columbia, 1821-1871* (Toronto: University of Toronto Press, 1994), especially c. 6, citing Geertz's *Local Knowledge: Further Essays in Interpretative Anthropology* (New York: Basic Books, 1983).

19 See *e.g.* McLaren's "Maternal Feminism in Action—Emily Murphy P.M." (1989) 8 Windsor Y.B. Access Just. 234; "The Early British Columbia Supreme Court," *supra* note 7; "The Early British Columbia Judges," *supra* note 7, 233; "The Judicial Office," *supra* note 7; and "The King, the People, the Law," *supra* note 7, 11.

20 A twentieth-century example might be the transcendent reputation of Justice Dixon of the High Court of Australia, referred to in c. 5 of this volume.

21 For a more geographically restricted look at a variety of this phenomenon, see Hamar Foster, "Mutiny on the Beaver: Law and Authority in the Fur Trade 'Navy' on the Northwest Coast, 1836-1839" (1991) 20 Man. L.J. 15. This essay is also in Dale Gibson and W. Wesley Pue, eds., *Glimpses of Canadian Legal History* (Winnipeg: Legal Research Institute, University of Manitoba, 1991) at 15-46.

22 For a thoughtful recent analysis of this almost inevitable challenge of colonialism, see Jonathan Lear, *Radical Hope: Ethics in the Face of Cultural Devastation* (Cambridge, MA: Harvard University Press, 2006).

23 In British Columbia, for example, the Chairman of the Allied Indian Tribes of British Columbia, which led the fight for Indian title between 1916 and 1928, was a Methodist who supported the law banning the potlatch.

24 Karl Llewellyn, "The Constitution as Institution" (1934) 34 Colum. L. Rev. 1 at 26.

25 Sir Frederick Pollock and Frederic William Maitland, *The History of English Law before the Time of Edward I,* 2 vols. (Birmingham: Legal Classics Library, 1982; 2d ed. first published 1899) vol. 2 at 674.

26 In the recent confrontation between General Pervez Musharraf and Pakistan Chief Justice Iftikhar Mohammmed Chaudhry, the Chief Justice declared that the superior courts of his country had to "do justice even though heavens may fall." *Globe and Mail* (14 September 2007) at A22. He was of course paraphrasing the words of Lord Mansfield, an eighteenth-century Chief Justice of the Court of King's Bench, in *Somerset's Case* (1772), 27 State Tr. 1, 98 E.R. 499.

Chapter 1: Libel and the Colonial Administration of Justice

1 Bruce Kercher, *An Unruly Child: A History of Law in Australia* (Sydney: Allen and Unwin, 1995) at 204-5.

2 John McLaren, "'The Judicial Office ... Bowing to No Power but the Supremacy of the Law': Judges and the Rule of Law in Colonial Australia and Canada, 1788-1840" (2003) 7:2 Austl. J. Legal Hist. 177.

3 See Jürgen Habermas, *The Structural Transformation of the Public Sphere: An Inquiry into a Category of Bourgeois Society,* trans. by Thomas Burger (Cambridge, MA: MIT Press, 1992). For an application of these ideas in a colonial setting, see Brendan Edgeworth, "Defamation Law and the Emergence of a Critical Press in Colonial New South Wales, 1824-1831" (1990) 6 Austl. J. L. & Soc'y. 50. The recent work of British literary scholars on the history of the republic of letters includes studies of legal responses, such as John Barrell, *Imagining the King's Death: Figurative Treason, Fantasies of Regicide, 1793-1796* (Oxford: Oxford University Press, 2000); and Kevin Gilmartin, *Print Politics: The Press and Radical Opposition in Early Nineteenth Century England* (Cambridge: Cambridge University Press, 1996).

4 See generally James Fitzjames Stephen, *A History of Criminal Law* (London, 1883) vol. 2 at 298-300; Thomas Andrew Green, *Verdict According to Conscience: Perspectives on the English Criminal Trial Jury 1200-1800* (Chicago: University of Chicago Press, 1985) at 319-21; P. Hamburger, "The Development of the Law of Seditious Libel and Control of the Press" (1985) 37 Stan. L. Rev. 727 at 727-31, 738, 742, 761. Defamation, directed at an individual allegedly held up to contempt or ridicule, was pursued by way of a civil action or private prosecution. Sedition, directed at the state, where the authority of its policies or representatives is allegedly undermined, was prosecuted by law officers of the Crown or other lawyers retained by the state. Sedition is also conceptually related to the offence of contempt against the privileges of Parliament, an offence punishable by expulsion, imprisonment, and reprimand of non-members. Although privilege protects members' freedom of speech in the House, it also reflects Parliament's residual function as a court, as demonstrated by the expulsions of John Wilkes, 1769-74, and the imprisonment of Francis Burdett in 1810. Canadian cases are examined in F. Murray Greenwood and Barry Wright, "Parliamentary Privilege and the Repression of Dissent in the Canadas" in F. Murray Greenwood and Barry Wright, eds., *Canadian State Trials,* vol. 1: *Law, Politics, and Security Measures, 1608-1837* (Toronto: Osgoode Society for Canadian Legal History and University of Toronto Press, 1996) 409.

5 See *e.g.* Dean of St. Asaph (1783-84), 17 Howell's State Trials 847 at 950, 1033-40. The jury was urged to find a verdict on the fact of publication only, and the Chief Justice, on application for a new trial, condemned general verdicts that intruded on questions of law.

6 Geo. III., c. 60. See Barrell, *supra* note 3; C. Emsley, "An Aspect of Pitt's 'Terror': Prosecutions for Sedition during the 1790's" (1981) 6 Social History 155; F.K. Prochaska, "English State Trials in the 1790s: A Case Study" (1973) 17 J. Brit. Stud. 63; Michael Lobban, "From Seditious Libel to Unlawful Assembly: Peterloo and the Changing Face of Political Crime c. 1770-1820" (1990) 10 Oxford J. Legal Stud.

307. The shift from seditious libel to unlawful assembly offences was facilitated by the development of professional policing.

7 6 & 7 Vict., c. 96.

8 Habermas' concept of the "public sphere" is based on his analysis of developing political opinion in eighteenth-century Europe. In Britain, this expands from privileged men of letters to new discursive spaces (such as the coffee house, unauthorized publications of parliamentary proceedings, and an independent press, which flourished with the demise of licensing after 1695). It gains formal legitimacy with the *Reform Act 1832* and the acceptance of independent parliamentary reporting. See Habermas, *supra* note 3; Craig Calhoun, ed., *Habermas and the Public Sphere* (Cambridge, MA: MIT Press, 1992).

9 Stephen, *supra* note 4 at 299.

10 For further comparative exploration of continental differences and similarities derived from the experiences of revolution, migration, and imperial retrenchment, see Barry Wright, "Migration, Radicalism and State Security: Legislative Initiatives in the Canadas and the United States c. 1794-1804" (2002) 16 Studies in Am. Pol. Dev. 48. Although libertarian understandings of the late seventeenth-century constitutional compromises informed the drafting of the US Constitution, and government powers were limited by the formal separation of powers and federalism, sedition offences survived the passage of the Bill of Rights and the First Amendment. Jefferson's repeal of the 1798 federalist legislation limited federal jurisdiction over speech and the press beyond no prior restraint on the basis of state criminal law jurisdiction. The Bill of Rights did not apply to states until the Civil War period, and Jefferson's encouragement of seditious libel prosecutions was linked to a sustained campaign against political opponents that included his attempt to remove Justice Chase from the Supreme Court and to prosecute his former Vice President Burr for treason. See Stanley N. Katz, ed., *Brief Narrative of the Case and Trial of John Peter Zenger, Printer of the New York Weekly Journal* (Cambridge, MA: Harvard University Press, 1972); James Morton Smith, *Freedom's Fetters: The Alien and Sedition Law and American Civil Liberties* (Ithaca: Cornell University Press, 1956); Leonard W. Levy, *Freedom of Speech and the Press in Early American History: A Legacy of Suppression* (New York: Harper, 1963); Levy, *Jefferson and Civil Liberties: The Darker Side* (Cambridge, MA: Harvard University Press, 1963); and Levy, *Emergence of a Free Press* (New York: Oxford University Press, 1985). On the place of the press in widening American public engagement with politics, see Michael Warner, "The Mass Public and the Mass Subject" in Calhoun, ed., *supra* note 8, 82; and Warner, *The Letters of the Republic: Publication and the Public Sphere in Eighteenth-Century America* (Cambridge, MA: Harvard University Press, 1990).

11 See McLaren, *supra* note 2 at 179-81, 183-86 for a useful overview. See also Barry Wright, "The Gourlay Affair: Seditious Libel and the Sedition Act in Upper Canada, 1818-19," and Paul Romney, "Upper Canada in the 1820's: Criminal Prosecution and the Case of Francis Collins" both in F. Murray Greenwood and Barry Wright, eds., *supra* note 4, 487 and 505.

12 *New South Wales Act 1823,* 4 Geo. IV., c. 96. See McLaren, *supra* note 2 at 181, 187 for a useful overview. See also H.V. Evatt, *Rum Rebellion: A Study of the Overthrow*

of Governor Bligh by John Macarthur and the New South Wales Corps (Sydney: Angus and Robertson, 1938); and David Neal, *The Rule of Law in a Penal Colony: Law and Power in Early New South Wales* (Cambridge: Cambridge University Press, 1991) c. 1.

13 *Calvin's Case* (1608), 77 E.R. 377 attempted to clarify questions of allegiance and the legal rights of subjects where British sovereignty was asserted (although qualified by the view held in the American colonies, including Nova Scotia, that English law after 1497 was not applicable unless expressly adopted by charter or local legislative or judicial recognition) and formed the basis of what may be generally described as "informal" reception. English legal rights (and obligations) applied to subjects where local executives authorized by the British government found them feasible and reasonably applicable to the local circumstances of the colony. Once colonial settlement reached significant levels, there were demands for representative political institutions and colonial courts to regularly administer the law, the establishment of which marked the phase of "formal" reception. The full range of English common law and legislation in existence at that date became the foundation for that colony's laws, which could be amended by colonial legislation and the courts as local conditions required, subject to imperial supervision (see below) and Judicial Committee of the Privy Council appeals after 1833.

14 Geo. III., c. 1. *Fox's Act* was proclaimed before the provincial reception date, although there was uncertainty on this point during Gourlay's seditious libel prosecutions. See Wright, *supra* note 11.

15 *Australian Courts Act,* 9 Geo. IV., c. 83. *An Act for the Better Securing of this Province against All Seditious Attempts or Designs to Disturb the Tranquility Thereof* 1804 (U.C.) 44 Geo. III., c. 1. For a comparative look at similar temporary legislation passed in Britain (1793: 33 Geo. III., c. 27; 34 Geo. III., c. 54), Lower Canada (1794: 34 Geo. III., c. 5), and the United States (1798), see Wright, *supra* note 10.

16 Temporary enemy aliens legislation was passed in 1797 (37 Geo. III., c. 1), but the successor *Sedition Act,* introduced before elections and the emergence of an opposition party in the legislature, was wider ranging (extended from visiting "enemy" subjects to all foreigners and recently arrived British subjects) and permanent (only two members of the Assembly indicated preference for a temporary measure). See *Journals of the House of Assembly and Legislative Council* (February–March 1804) [*Journals*], reproduced in Archives of Ontario, *Sixth Report of the Archives for the Province of Ontario* (Toronto, 1911). William Weekes vigorously attacked the measure in his election broadside following its passage as an infringement on British liberties and an example of need of vigilant legislators to check executive and judicial abuses. See G.H. Paterson, *Dictionary of Canadian Biography,* vol. 5, ed. by Francess G. Halpenny and Jean Hamelin (Toronto: University of Toronto Press, 1983) *s.v.* "Weekes, William."

17 See Paul Romney and Barry Wright, "State Trials and Security Proceedings during the War of 1812" in F. Murray Greenwood and Barry Wright, eds., *supra* note 4, 379 at 380–82; and Wright, *supra* note 11 at 487.

18 Geo. IV., no. 2; 11 Geo. IV., no. 1. See Edgeworth, *supra* note 3 at 66–70, 79; and J.J. Spigelman, "Foundations of Freedom of the Press in Australia" (2003) 23 Austl. Bar Rev. 89 at 95–96.

19 Thompson noted the seeming paradox that formal claims around the rule of law limit the repressive potential of the criminal law and create possibilities to contest it: "For what we have observed is something more than the law as a pliant medium to be twisted this way and that by whichever interests already possess effective power ... If the law is evidently partial and unjust, then it will mask nothing, legitimize nothing ... [T]he essential precondition for the effectiveness of law, in its function as ideology, is that it shall display an independence from gross manipulation and shall seem to be just." Thompson, *Whigs and Hunters: The Origin of the Black Act* (Harmondsworth: Penguin, 1977) at 462-63; see also Thompson, "The Moral Economy of the English Crowd" (1971) 50 Past and Present 76.

20 See generally McLaren, *supra* note 2; Spigelman, *supra* note 18; Neal, *supra* note 12 at c. 4. On Forbes and tensions with Stephen in particular, see John M. Bennett, *Sir Francis Forbes: First Chief Justice of New South Wales, 1823-1837* (Sydney: Federation Press, 2001) at 60-72, 97-100 and *infra* note 49. On Robinson, see Patrick Brode, *Sir John Beverley Robinson: Bone and Sinew of the Compact* (Toronto: Osgoode Society for Canadian Legal History and University of Toronto Press, 1984) at 182-83, 209; Rainer Baehre, "Trying the Rebels: Emergency Legislation and the Colonial Executive's Overall Legal Strategy in the Upper Canadian Rebellion" in F. Murray Greenwood and Barry Wright, eds., *Canadian State Trials,* vol. 2: *Rebellion and Invasion in the Canadas, 1837-1839* (Toronto: Osgoode Society for Canadian Legal History and University of Toronto Press, 2002) 41 at 48.

21 See Paul Romney, *Mr Attorney: The Attorney General for Ontario in Court, Cabinet, and Legislature 1791-1899* (Toronto: Osgoode Society for Canadian Legal History and University of Toronto Press, 1986); and more generally Douglas Hay, "Controlling the English Prosecutor" (1983) 21 Osgoode Hall L.J. 165.

22 See *e.g.* Robert L. Fraser, "All the Privileges Which Englishmen Possess: Order, Rights, and Constitutionalism in Upper Canada" in Robert L. Fraser, ed., *Provincial Justice: Upper Canadian Legal Portraits from the Dictionary of Canadian Biography* (Toronto: Osgoode Society for Canadian Legal History and University of Toronto Press, 1992) xxi; Neal, *supra* note 12 at c. 5 and 6.

23 See Neal, *ibid.* at c. 7; Paul Romney, "From Constitutionalism to Legalism: Trial by Jury, Responsible Government and the Rule of Law in Canadian Political Culture" (1989) 7 L.H.R. 130; and more generally R. Blake Brown, "A Delusion, a Mockery, and a Snare: Array Challenges and Jury Selection in England and Ireland, 1800-1850" (2004) 39 Can. J. Hist. 1. Joseph Willcocks introduced (1811-12) the first of a series of bills to reform jury selection, which was again pursued in the 1820s. See also *Journals:* (16-22 November 1825) (defeated); (8 December 1826-27 February 1827) (passed in House by majority of fifteen); (18-28 January 1828) (passed in House by majority of twenty); and (23 February-17 March 1828). This defeat (along with controversies over prosecutorial power) helped to prompt an Assembly Select Committee on the administration of justice, but another bill (25 March 1828) was again defeated by the Legislative Council, and reform was achieved only in 1850.

24 See Barry Wright, "Sedition in Upper Canada: Contested Legality" (1992) 29 Labour/Le Travail 7. Most cases are recorded in "Court of King's Bench Assize Minutebook," Toronto, Archives of Ontario (RG 22, series 134). Examination of other King's Bench series (125, 136, and 138) and records associated with the War of 1812 (RG

22, series 143) reveals a dozen more cases than indicated in my 1992 article. This figure does not include summary deportations under the province's *Sedition Act*, private prosecutions for defamation and libel, and a number of other cases that the Crown did not pursue as indicated in the quarter sessions records of private informations or brought to the attention of the government by local justices of the peace and grand juries. The early records of the New South Wales Supreme Court are more accessible. See *infra* note 45.

25 Lieutenant-Governor Francis Gore, who played a leading role in the Irish repression after 1798, orchestrated government actions against leading opposition figures, including Thorpe's removal. The Willcocks indictment for seditious libel was converted into an *ex officio* information when the editor won a Niagara by-election, which enabled the Crown to change the venue to the capital and select a special jury. When Willcocks successfully challenged this and the trial was rescheduled for the Niagara assize, the government organized privilege proceedings for contempt for the libel still before the courts (a questionable use of such powers), resulting in his imprisonment for the duration of the session. See Greenwood and Wright, *supra* note 4 at 418-23.

26 Gourlay, who associated with Cobbett and Hunt in London, arrived in the province during a legislative crisis and organized local meetings to collect grievances under the guise of a "statistical accounting." The repeated premature proroguing of the legislature led to his call for the election of delegates for a constitutional convention. With the assistance of the former Attorney General of Massachusetts, Barnabas Bidwell, he defended himself successfully against two indictments for seditious libel resurrecting Erskine's arguments on the jury. The acquittals were met by the passage of a temporary *Seditious Meetings Act,* and Gourlay's response, "Gagg'd by Jingo," published in Ferguson's newspaper, prompted Attorney General Robinson to issue an *ex officio* information against Ferguson as a "hanging" threat and to submit the *Sedition Act* to the Court of King's Bench for an extrajudicial opinion as to its applicability to Gourlay. With every ambiguity resolved in the government's favour, Gourlay was imprisoned indefinitely for refusal to leave the province after a hearing declared him a seditious alien and ordered his banishment, and a later application for *habeas corpus* was turned down. Gourlay continued to write for Ferguson's paper, prompting the Attorney General to proceed on the information against Ferguson in August 1819. He secured a conviction with a packed jury (the sentence included the pillory, twelve months' imprisonment, and fines that proved ruinous to Ferguson's newspaper); at the same assize, Gourlay was convicted of disobeying a banishment order and sentenced to leave the province on pain of death. See Wright, *supra* note 11.

27 Jeffrey L. McNairn, *The Capacity to Judge: Public Opinion and Deliberative Democracy in Upper Canada, 1791-1854* (Toronto: University of Toronto Press, 2000) at 63-107, 116-33, 144-48.

28 See *Journals* (1823), *supra* note 16; H.P. Gundy, *Dictionary of Canadian Biography,* vol. 6, ed. by Francess G. Halpenny and Jean Hamelin (Toronto: University of Toronto Press, 1987) *s.v.* "Thomson, Hugh Christopher."

29 See Romney, *supra* notes 11 and 21. The reform-dominated committee used the expropriated Niagara hotelier William Forsyth's petition as the basis for a more

sweeping examination of the accumulated instances of partisan administration of justice and, in particular, the exercise of public prosecutions. See "Report of the Select Committee" in *Journals* (1828), *supra* note 16, Appendix.

30 See *Papers Relating to the Removal of the Honourable John Walpole Willis from the Office of One of His Majesty's Judges of the Court of King's Bench of Upper Canada* (N.p.: Printed by the British House of Commons, 1829) at 37-47, 216-20, London, UK, Public Record Office (PRO) (CO 42, vol. 386) [*Papers*]; R. Hett, "Judge Willis and the Court of King's Bench in Upper Canada" (1973) 65 Ontario History 19; and Romney, *supra* note 11.

31 Robinson to Maitland (10 May 1828), reproduced in *Papers, ibid.* at 24-25.

32 Robinson to Maitland, *ibid.* at 28-29. See also Robinson's report on the events surrounding the Collins Indictment at 154-57, PRO (CO 42, vol. 388). The grand jurors found a bill for a libel based on Mackenzie's "scandalous comments" about them in *Colonial Advocate* (10 April 1828).

33 Robinson missed the beginning of the session, and Willis allowed Collins to take his allegations before the grand jury just as the Attorney General arrived. When Willis reminded Robinson of his duty to prosecute the known offenders, he replied that he was not a "thief-taker" and that he was answerable to the government, not the bench. The grand jury returned true bills against Boulton and Small for Rideout's death in 1817 and against the pro-government rioters who destroyed Mackenzie's press in 1826, although the cases failed. Collins and Mackenzie were unable to have their indictments withdrawn as Robinson successfully held the charges over to the autumn assize. See Robinson to Maitland (10 and 20 May 1828), and Willis to Maitland (spring assize 1828), reproduced in *Papers, supra* note 30 at 16-23, 33, 211; *Canadian Freeman* (17 April 1828); *Upper Canada Observer* (5 May 1828); and *Canadian Freeman* (8 May 1828).

34 See note 30; and McLaren, *supra* note 2. Willis' objection called into question the validity of years of King's Bench decisions involving less than a full bench and, as Maitland reported to London, would cause "great public excitement." When King's Bench reconvened on 16 June, and Willis announced he would not preside until the bench was fully constituted, Maitland and the Executive Council suspended him.

35 *Upper Canada Herald* (1 July 1828). On constitutional meetings resulting in petitions to Britain in support of Willis, see *Canadian Freeman* (5 June-3 July 1828); Baldwin, Rolph, and Baldwin to Maitland (23 June 1838); Willis to Stephen (30 May 1828); Willis to Huskisson (31 May 1828); and Maitland to Huskisson (6 June 1828) in *Papers, supra* note 30 at 199, 189, 177, 187.

36 See *Canadian Freeman* (16 and 30 October 1828); "Statement of the case of Francis Collins Editor of the Canadian Freeman to be Laid Before His Excellency the Lieutenant Governor," Ottawa, Library and Archives Canada (LAC), (RG1 E3, vol. 15).

37 See "Statement," *ibid.;* and *Canadian Freeman* (16 October 1828). In this article, Collins drew another charge, writing: "The Attorney General, with a view of bringing us to trial unprepared, rose and stated a palpable falsehood in Court—namely, that we had been arraigned last assizes. When we contended to the contrary, to the satisfaction of the court, the Attorney, in his native malignancy, took till next day (yesterday) to look up authorities to see if he could force us to

trial without the privilege of traverse ... and our old customer Judge Hagerman was in favour of the measure."

38 See Sherwood to Colborne (5 December 1828), reproduced in *Papers, supra* note 30; Manuscript report of trial *The King v. Francis Collins* (25 October 1828), LAC (RG1 E3, vol. 15).

39 See *The King v. Francis Collins,* Manuscript report, *ibid.* The jurors deliberated for more than five hours on the limited evidence that did go to them, and their request for a dictionary was refused. See *Canadian Freeman* (30 October 1828).

40 The recently arrived Lieutenant-Governor Colborne was reluctant to act on the petitions, noting that though the Constitution supported "free and well-conducted press," it also bound him not to intervene in the verdict of juries or the opinion of judges. "Addresses to His Excellency, Sir John Colborne, Lieutenant Governor of Upper Canada," and "Reply," LAC (RG1 E3, vol. 15); "Report of the Select Committee on the Petition of Francis Collins" in *Journals* (1829), *supra* note 16, Appendix. The Collins petition was referred by the Colonial Office to the Crown law officers, who reported that the sentence was widely out of proportion to comparable English cases and recommended that it be halved. Scarlett and Sugden to Murray (30 June 1829), PRO (CO 42/390/49-50). Collins was released after forty-five weeks and his fines remitted.

41 The first repeal bill was brought in the Assembly in June 1819, and from March 1821 repeal bills were passed by majorities in the Assembly and repeatedly defeated by the upper house. See *Journals:* (8-17 June 1819); (26 February-8 March 1820); (3 February-8 March 1821); (28 November-4 December 1821); (15-21 January 1823); (17 November-3 December 1823); (10-21 November 1825); (19-27 December 1826) (Legislative Council returned this bill 9 February 1827 with extensive amendments that essentially preserved the Act); and (21-23 January and 17 March 1828) (the Assembly declared a constitutional crisis). The bill passed in January 1829 was petitioned directly to the British government. The British Government Committee on the Government of the Canadas, set up in late 1828, which recommended granting the petition, suggested that judges be removed from all governing councils and that ways be found to make the Legislative Councils more popularly representative and independent of executive control. On the jury, see note 23.

42 Executive Council Submissions, "Opinion of the Law Officers 16 March 1832," and "Executive Council 17 March 1832," LAC (RG1 E3, vol. 16). See also Greenwood and Wright, *supra* note 4 at 425.

43 *Christian Guardian* (7 December 1831), quoted in McNairn, *supra* note 27 at 143, 413.

44 This was by no means a secure advance, and the law continued to have repressive utility when governments perceived opinion to support it. Events in Upper Canada were closely followed by the 1835 case of Joseph Howe in Nova Scotia. The codification of criminal law by the Dominion of Canada (1892) left the definition of seditious intent to the common law, and the offence was used against labour leaders in the wake of the 1919 Winnipeg General Strike. It was only in 1951 that the Supreme Court of Canada adopted a restrictive definition of intent to incite violence or create public disorder for the purpose of resisting constitutional authority. See *Boucher v. R.,* [1951] 2 D.L.R. 369.

45 For the main official correspondence and newspaper extracts, see Australian Commonwealth Government, *Historical Records of Australia,* Series 1: *Governors' Dispatches to and from England,* vols. 9-16 (Sydney: Library Committee of the Commonwealth Parliament, 1914-25). The early records of the New South Wales Supreme Court are conveniently compiled and indexed in what Spigelman, *supra* note 18, calls the "Kercher Reports" (KR), a styling adopted here. See "Decisions of the Superior Courts of New South Wales, 1788-1899," online: Division of Law, Macquarie University, http://www.law.mq.edu.au/scnsw.

46 Edgeworth, *supra* note 3 at 69; see also 53-59, for his discussion of the emergence of a public sphere in New South Wales.

47 Edgeworth, *ibid.* at 53-54, 60-62; Spigelman, *supra* note 18 at 90-92.

48 Edgeworth, *ibid.* at 62-66; Spigelman, *supra* note 18 at 92-94; *R. v. Howe,* 20 October 1826 (KR).

49 See Bennett, *supra* note 20, particularly at 66-72. Bennett argues that exclusive representations to the British government mischaracterized Forbes' actions during the licensing controversies, resulting in unfair censure from Stephen and an inaccurate view perpetuated by later historians that Forbes was driven by legislative and political ambitions to usurp the Governor.

50 *Ibid.* at 83-87.

51 *Ibid.* at 92.

52 *Newspapers Act Opinion,* 16 April 1827 (KR).

53 *Ibid.;* Spigelman, *supra* note 18 at 95-96; Edgeworth, *supra* note 3 at 67.

54 Spigelman, *ibid.* at 97-98; Bennett, *supra* note 20 at 95-97.

55 Edgeworth, *supra* note 3 at 68.

56 Quoted in Bennett, *supra* note 20 at 93. Stephen's uncle was the other judge then on the New South Wales Supreme Court bench. Forbes and Stephen had common family connections and interests in Bermuda and the West Indies.

57 Edgeworth, *supra* note 3 at 72.

58 Spigelman, *supra* note 18 at 98; Edgeworth, *supra* note 3 at 70.

59 *R. v. Wardell* (no. 1), June 1827 (KR); *R. v. Wardell* (no. 2), September 1827 (KR); *R. v. Wardell* (no. 3), December 1827 (KR); Spigelman, *supra* note 18 at 99; Edgeworth, *supra* note 3 at 70-72.

60 Quoted in Spigelman, *ibid.* at 100.

61 *R. v. Hall* (no. 3), 7 July 1828 (KR); Spigelman, *supra* note 18 at 101.

62 See Bruce Kercher, "Establishment, Freedom of Speech and the Church of England: Pew Disputes in Early Nineteenth Century New South Wales and Newfoundland" (2000) 6 Austl. J. Legal Hist. 135. Dowling presided at each of the subsequent successful actions against the editors of the *Monitor* and the *Australian.* Edgeworth, *supra* note 3 at 72-73.

63 *R. v. Hall* (no. 2), 29 September 1828 (KR); Spigelman, *supra* note 18 at 103-4.

64 *R. v. Hayes,* 14 April 1829 (KR); Spigelman, *supra* note 18 at 105.

65 *R. v. Hall* (no. 4 & 5), 10 April 1829 (KR); *R. v. Hall* (no. 6), 21 December 1829 (KR), (no. 7), 23 December 1829 (KR), and (no. 8), 23 December 1829 (KR); Spigelman, *supra* note 18 at 106.

66 See Edgeworth, *supra* note 3 at 78.

67 Spigelman, *supra* note 18 at 107-8; Edgeworth, *supra* note 3 at 80-82.

68 As in Canada, this was a qualified advance. Later seditious libel prosecutions included the 1854 case of Henry Seekamp, editor of the *Ballarat Times,* in connection with Eureka Stockade. After Federation the common law doctrine continued to apply in many of the states, though codified jurisdictions such as Queensland adopted J.F. Stephen's 1880 Draft English Code rendition. Governments sensing compliant public opinion prosecuted anti-conscriptionists during the First World War and labour organizers in the 1930s. Although it had no direct jurisdiction over criminal law, the federal government developed sedition laws (s. 24 of the *Commonwealth Crimes Act*) within the scope of incidental powers (defence and executive jurisdiction to secure the nation from internal attack) used during the Cold War (*Burns v. Ransley* (1949), 79 C.L.R. 101; *R. v. Sharkey* (1949), 79 C.L.R. 121). Although related legislation that attempted to ban the Communist Party was defeated in 1951, controls over political expression were elaborated by the development of the D notice censorship system in 1952 and amendments to the *Crimes Act* in 1960. See Australian Law Reform Commission, *Fighting Words: A Review of Sedition Laws in Australia* (Canberra: Australian Law Reform Commission, 2006).

69 McLaren, *supra* note 2 at 191.

70 See Evatt, *supra* note 12.

71 See notes 68 and 44.

72 See note 19.

73 See notes 3 and 8.

CHAPTER 2: THE LIMITS OF DESPOTIC GOVERNMENT AT SEA

1 *Thompson v. Willet,* 1829, Supreme Court of New South Wales. Cases recorded solely by name and date are taken from "Decisions of the Superior Courts of New South Wales, 1788-1899" [NSW], online: Division of Law, Macquarie University, http://www.law.mq.edu.au/scnsw; and "Decisions of the Nineteenth Century Tasmanian Superior Courts" [VDL], online: Division of Law, Macquarie University, and School of History and Classics, University of Tasmania, http://www.law.mq.edu.au/sctas. Most quotations in this chapter are taken from these online cases.

2 Canadian colonial cases, not readily available online, were excluded from this study. See Judith Fingard, *Jack in Port: Sailortowns of Eastern Canada* (Toronto: University of Toronto Press, 1982) at 168-86, concentrating on litigation before the magistrates rather than on the superior courts.

3 *R. v. Dillon,* 1827 (VDL).

4 See George Steckley, "Collisions, Prohibitions, and the Admiralty Court in Seventeenth-Century London" (2003) 21 L.H.R. 41; Edward Roscoe, "Introduction" in *Edward Roscoe on the Admiralty Jurisdiction and Practice of the High Court of Justice,* 4th ed. (London: Stevens and Sons, 1920) 11; George Steckley, "Litigious Mariners: Wage Cases in the Seventeenth-Century Admiralty Court" (1999) 42 Historical Journal 315; C.W. O'Hare, "Admiralty Jurisdiction (Parts 1 and 2)" (1979-80) 6 Monash U.L. Rev. 91 and 195 at 91-99; M.J. Prichard, "Crime at Sea: Admiralty Sessions and the Background to Later Colonial Jurisdiction" (1984) 8 Dal. L.J. 43.

5   On admiralty jurisdiction in America, see O'Hare, *ibid.* at 99-104. Civil actions were also heard in some American common law courts: see Matthew Harrington, "The Legacy of the Colonial Vice-Admiralty Courts (Part II)" (1996) 27 J. Mar. L. & Com. 323 at 327, but see 348 on state admiralty courts regaining the jurisdiction.

6   (1828) 9 Geo. IV., c. 83, s. 24.

7   See O'Hare, *supra* note 4 at 109-21.

8   See Matthew Harrington, "The Legacy of the Colonial Vice-Admiralty Courts (Part I)" (1995) 26 J. Mar. L. & Com. 581; and Harrington, *supra* note 5.

9   See *e.g.* Robert Baker, "Creating Order in the Wilderness: Transplanting the English Law to Rupert's Land, 1835-51" (1999) 17 L.H.R. 209.

10 See *e.g.* Hamar Foster and John McLaren, eds., *Essays in the History of Canadian Law*, vol. 6: *British Columbia and the Yukon* (Toronto: Osgoode Society for Canadian Legal History and University of Toronto Press, 1995).

11 Peter Earle, *Sailors: English Merchant Seamen 1650-1775* (London: Methuen, 2007) at 43.

12 Douglas Hay and Paul Craven, "Introduction" in Douglas Hay and Paul Craven, eds., *Masters, Servants, and Magistrates in Britain and the Empire, 1562-1955* (Chapel Hill: University of North Carolina Press, 2004) 1 at 13; Paul Craven, "Canada, 1679-1935" in Hay and Craven, eds., *ibid.*, 217.

13 (1835) 5 & 6 Wm. IV., c. 19, s. 54.

14 See *e.g.* (1832) 2 Wm. IV., no. 10; and (1840) 4 Vict., no. 17 (NSW); and see the general theme in Hay and Craven, *supra* note 12.

15 See also Charles Abbott, *A Treatise of the Law Relative to Merchant Ships and Seamen* (London: Brooke and Rider, 1802) at 123, 126.

16 Marcus Rediker, *Between the Devil and the Deep Blue Sea: Merchant Seamen, Pirates, and the Anglo-American Maritime World, 1700-1750* (Cambridge: Cambridge University Press, 1989) at 207-8.

17 *Ibid.* at 213.

18 Pedder was referring to Abbott, *supra* note 15 at 125-26.

19 *R. v. Kellie,* 1826 (VDL).

20 *In re "Agincourt"* (1824), 1 Haggard 271, 166 E.R. 96; *Murray v. Moutrie* (1834), 6 Car. & P. 471, 172 E.R. 1324; and *R. v. Leggett and Nesbitt* (1838), 8 Car. & P. 191, 173 E. R. 456.

21 *King v. Franklin* (1858), 1 Foster and Finlason 360, 175 E.R. 764; and *Boyce v. Bayliffe* (1807), 1 Campbell 58, 170 E.R. 875 (battle).

22 See *e.g. Sheridan v. Furbur,* U.S. Dist. LEXIS 20, 21 F. Cas. 1266 (1834); *Gould v. Christianson,* U.S. Dist. LEXIS 20, 10 F. Cas. 857 (1836); and *Hutson v. Jordan,* U.S. Dist. LEXIS 13, 12 F. Cas. 1089 (1837).

23 See David Robertson, "Punitive Damages in American Maritime Law" (1997) 28 J. Mar. L. & Com. 73; see also *In re "Agincourt," supra* note 20.

24 Marie-Hélène Renaut, "L'Histoire par les Lois: Trois siècles d'évolution dans la repression des fautes disciplinaires de la marine marchande," trans. by Willya Waldburger (2002) 80 Revue Histoire Droit 23; and on German law, see Jann Witt, "'During the Voyage Every Captain Is Monarch of the Ship': The Merchant Captain from the Seventeenth to the Nineteenth Century" (2001) 13 Int'l J. Mar. Hist. 165.

25 *Maher v. Robinson*, 1833 (NSW).

26 *Solomon v. Bartlett*, 1841 (NSW).

27 *King v. Franklin, supra* note 21.

28 *Aldworth v. Stewart* (1866), 4 Foster and Finlason 957, 176 E.R. 865.

29 Don Charlwood, *The Long Farewell* (Ringwood: Penguin, 1993) at 177-78, and see 113.

30 See also Rediker, *supra* note 16 at 215-22, 224-25, outlining brutal cases heard in admiralty during the eighteenth century; and Earle, *supra* note 11 at c. 10, also on eighteenth-century discipline cases.

31 *Hart v. Hurst*, 1833 (VDL).

32 *Gunby v. Richards*, 1827 (VDL).

33 *Jay v. Almy*, 13 F. Cas. 387, 1746 U.S. App. LEXIS 528 (1846).

34 *In re "Agincourt," supra* note 20.

35 *Murray v. Moutrie, supra* note 20.

36 *Taylor v. Christie*, 1831 (NSW).

37 *Neal v. Brown*, 1833 (NSW).

38 *Gale v. Dalrymple* (1824), Ryan and Moody 118, 171 E.R. 963.

39 John Nicol, *Life and Adventures 1776-1801,* ed. by Tim Flannery (Melbourne: Text, 1997) at 47, 50, 108-9, 122-24. See also Charlwood, *supra* note 29 at 117, 231, 255; and Nathaniel Philbrick, *In the Heart of the Sea* (London: Flamingo, 2000) at 60-61, 75-76.

40 Greg Dening, *Mr Bligh's Bad Language* (Cambridge: Cambridge University Press, 1992) at 63-64, and see 114-16. Rediker, *supra* note 16 at 214-15 gives figures for the number of claims brought by ships' crews and remarks that numbers alone do not tell the full story.

41 See Michael Quinlan, "Industrial Relations before Unions: New South Wales Seamen 1810-1852" (1996) 38 J. Indus. Rel. 264. On piracy as a response to ill-treatment, see Marcus Rediker, *Villain of All Nations: Atlantic Pirates in the Golden Age* (London: Verso, 2004) at 25-26.

42 *R. v. Kellie*, 1826 (VDL). See also Jonathan S. Kitchen, *The Employment of Merchant Seamen* (London: Croom Helm, 1980) at 577.

43 *Lamb v. Burnett* (1831), 1 Crompton and Jervis 291, 148 E.R. 1430.

44 *R. v. Walton*, 1827 (NSW). On the customs of piracy, see Rediker, *supra* note 41 at c. 4 and 16-17, 42.

45 Craven, *supra* note 12 at 217; and see Michael Quinlan, "Making Labour Laws Fit for the Colonies: The Introduction of Laws Regulating Whalers in Three Australian Colonies 1835-1855" (1992) 62 Labour History 19 at 21, 25, 27. Hay and Craven, *supra* note 12. On the seamen's contracts, see Kitchen, *supra* note 42 at 328-32, 411-12.

46 Jerry Bannister, "Law and Labor in Eighteenth-Century Newfoundland" in Douglas Hay and Paul Craven, eds., *Masters, Servants, and Magistrates in Britain and the Empire, 1562-1955* (Chapel Hill: University of North Carolina Press, 2004) 153 at 154, 163. The statutes applying to seamen, described later, were more uniform than other master and servant legislation, due to imperial concern for uniformity: see Hay and Craven, *supra* note 12 at 13; Quinlan, *supra* note 41 at 265.

47 On the latter, see Quinlan, *supra* note 45 at 22.

48 Abbott, *supra* note 15 at 125; and see *Roberts v. Moncreif,* 1828 (NSW).

49 See (1700) 11 & 12 Wm. III., c. 7, s. 18; (1835) 5 & 6 Wm. IV., c. 19, s. 40 and ss. 41-44.

50 *R. v. Cape,* 1838 (NSW); *R. v. Northwood,* 1833 (NSW). For other abandonment cases, see Rediker, *supra* note 16 at 222.

51 See Douglas Hay, "England, 1562-1875" in Douglas Hay and Paul Craven, eds., *supra* note 12, 113 at 113-14; Abbott, *supra* note 15 at 124, 372; and Roscoe, *supra* note 4 at 255-56.

52 (1700) 11 & 12 Wm. III., c. 7, s. 17. See Rediker, *supra* note 41 at 26-28.

53 (1823) 4 Geo. IV., c. 25; (1835) 5 & 6 Wm. IV., c. 19, s. 9. In New South Wales, see (1832) 2 Wm. IV., no. 10, s. 3. On colonial anti-desertion statutes, see Fingard, *supra* note 2 at c. 4; Quinlan, *supra* note 41 at 270-71; Michael Quinlan, "Regulating Labour in a Colonial Context: Maritime Labour Legislation in the Australian Colonies, 1788-1850" (1998) 29 Austl. Hist. Stud. 303; and G.R. Henning, "Fourpenny Dark and Sixpenny Red" (1984) 46 Labour History 52.

54 *Geary v. Vivian,* 1830 (NSW); and see *Cassim v. MaryAnn,* 1831 (NSW).

55 (1835) 5 & 6 Wm. IV., c. 19, ss. 6, 7; (1835) 5 & 6 Wm. IV., c. 19, s. 7; and see (1832) 2 Wm. IV., no. 10, s. 5; Abbott, *supra* note 15 at 124-25, 373.

56 See the New South Wales statutes, (1832) 2 Wm. IV., no. 10; (1840) 4 Vict., no. 17, ss. 8 and 19; *Colonial Merchant Seamen's Act,* 14 Vict., no. 43 (interpreted in *Ex parte Towns* (1852), 1 Legge 708). On these Acts, see Quinlan, *supra* note 41 at 273-77, 281-88. Other colonies had similar laws: see Quinlan, *supra* note 45.

57 Quinlan, *supra* note 41 at 271; Quinlan, *supra* note 53 at 306.

58 Quinlan, *supra* note 53 at 316. For similar cases in Canada, see Fingard, *supra* note 2 at 159-60.

59 (1700) 11 & 12 Wm. III., c. 7, s. 9; on the extension, see (1700) 11 & 12 Wm. III., c. 7, s. 13 and accompanying side notes. See Kitchen, *supra* note 42 at 577-78.

60 *R. v. Anderson, Davis and others,* 1832 (NSW); for other New South Wales examples of revolt, see *R. v. Firth* (1832), N.S.W. Sel. Cas. (Dowling) 927; and *R. v. Taylor,* 1829 (NSW). For England, see *R. v. Hastings and Meharg* (1825), 1 Moody 82, 168 E.R. 1194; and *R. v. M'Gregor and Lambert* (1844), 1 Car. & K. 431, 174 E.R. 878.

61 See (1823) 4 Geo. IV., c. 48.

62 *R. v. Cam,* 1832 (VDL); *R. v. Walton,* 1827 (NSW); *R. v. Flanagan,* 1827 (NSW); and *R. v. Shiers,* 1837 (VDL).

63 *R. v. Smiley,* 1832 (VDL).

64 See also *R. v. Leggett and Nesbitt, supra* note 20; *R. v. Trigg,* 1839 (NSW); and *R. v. Skewes,* 1840 (NSW).

CHAPTER 3: ONE CHIEF, TWO CHIEFS, RED CHIEFS, BLUE CHIEFS

1 *Sawridge Band v. Canada* (1995), [1996] 1 F.C. 3 (T.D.) [*Sawridge*]. More specifically, the Sawridge (Treaty 8), Ermineskin (Treaty 6), and Sarcee (now Tsuu T'ina, Treaty 7) First Nations argued that changes to the *Indian Act,* R.S.C. 1985, c. I-5, restoring band membership to women who had married non-Indian men and to the children of these unions, violated their rights to control their memberships under s. 35 of

the *Constitution Act, 1982* and were contrary to long-standing customs whereby women's band membership followed that of their spouse.

2 *Ibid.* at para. 72.

3 *Sawridge Band v. Canada,* [1997] 3 F.C. 580 (C.A.). It is worth noting that the Court of Appeal found that Justice Muldoon did not appear to harbour negative views of Aboriginal people *per se,* but rather that a reasonable apprehension of bias arose due to comments that indicated his negative disposition toward the regime of distinctive rights for Aboriginal peoples enshrined in s. 35 of the Constitution (at paras. 15-16). In the aftermath of this decision, a new trial was commenced, and the matter remains hotly contested and unresolved. See *Sawridge Band v. Canada,* 2008 F.C. 322.

4 Justice Muldoon also considered evidence from Treaties 7 and 8, covering all of the treaties signed by the First Nations who brought the case. The choice to focus on Justice Muldoon's treatment of the evidence from Treaty 6 is one of convenience, and the interpretive exercise pursued in the chapter could undoubtedly be extended to his treatment of the evidence in the Treaty 7 and 8 records as well.

5 For discussions of the government's approach to treaties in this era, see *e.g.* John Leonard Taylor, "Canada's Northwest Indian Policy in the 1870s: Traditional Premises and Necessary Innovations" in Richard Price, ed., *The Spirit of the Alberta Indian Treaties* (Edmonton: Pica Pica Press, 1987; first published 1979) 3; and Olive Patricia Dickason, *Canada's First Nations: A History of Founding Peoples* (Toronto: McClelland and Stewart, 1992) at c. 17-19.

6 See Alexander Morris, *The Treaties of Canada with the Indians of Manitoba and the Northwest Territories, Including the Negotiations on Which They Were Based, and Other Information Relating Thereto* (Calgary: Fifth House, 1991; first published 1880) at 172-73.

7 *Ibid.* at 175, cited in *Sawridge, supra* note 1 at para. 85.

8 Morris, *supra* note 6 at 226, cited in *Sawridge, supra* note 1 at para. 83.

9 In the North American contexts of this chapter, see Toby Morantz, "Northern Algonquian Concepts of Status and Leadership Reviewed: A Case Study of the Eighteenth-Century Trading Captain System" (1982) 19 Canadian Review of Sociology and Anthropology 482 (regarding the institutions of indigenous peoples); Arthur J. Ray, "The Factor and the Trading Captain in the Hudson's Bay Company Fur Trade before 1763" in Jim Freedman and Jerome H. Barkow, eds., *Proceedings of the Second Congress, Canadian Ethnology Society,* vol. 1, Mercury Series, Ethnology Service Paper 28 (Ottawa: National Museum of Man, 1975) 586; and John E. Foster, "The Indian-Trader in the Hudson Bay Fur Trade Tradition" in Freedman and Barkow, eds., *ibid.,* 571 (regarding the institutions of the Hudson's Bay Company). For an excellent exploration of this thesis in colonial legal history more generally, see Lauren Benton, *Law and Colonial Cultures: Legal Regimes in World History, 1400-1900* (Cambridge: Cambridge University Press, 2002).

10 *Sawridge, supra* note 1 at 86.

11 Three recent examples include John McLaren, "Reflections on the Rule of Law: The Georgian Colonies of New South Wales and Upper Canada, 1788-1837" in Diane Kirkby and Catharine Coleborne, eds., *Law, History, Colonialism: The Reach of Empire* (Manchester: Manchester University Press, 2001); McLaren, Robert Menzies, and

Dorothy E. Chunn, eds., *Regulating Lives: Historical Essays on the State, Society, the Individual, and the Law* (Vancouver: UBC Press, 2002); and McLaren, A.R. Buck, and Nancy E. Wright, eds., *Despotic Dominion: Property Rights in British Settler Societies* (Vancouver: UBC Press, 2005).

12 See Theodore Binnema, *Contested and Common Ground: A Human and Environmental History of the Northwestern Plains* (Norman: University of Oklahoma Press, 2001) at 15.

13 Ethnohistory combines traditional historical methods with insights from other fields and sources, including ethnography, anthropology, archaeology, and oral traditions. The inclusion of such diverse sources is intended to allow for greater insight into peoples who did not participate in the creation of the written record. See Jennifer Brown and Elizabeth Vibert, eds., *Reading beyond Words: Contexts for Native History* (Peterborough, ON: Broadview Press, 1996) at xxii-xxiii.

14 See Janet E. Chute, "Ojibwa Leadership during the Fur Trade Era at Sault Ste. Marie" in Susan Sleeper-Smith, Jo-Anne Fiske, and William Wicken, eds., *New Faces of the Fur Trade: Selected Papers of the Seventh North American Fur Trade Conference, Halifax, Nova Scotia, 1995* (East Lansing: Michigan State University Press, 1998) 153 at 167. The Chief was Oshawano, also known as Cassaquadung, of the Crane dodem. Chute remarks that "[t]he Indian Affairs Department had so little idea of the composition of the Sault bands that it is doubtful they ever realized they had included an American Crane chief in their negotiations" (at 167). She also notes that the "error" was eventually corrected with the deletion of Oshawano's name from the Treaty text in 1859.

15 Evidence of Louis Norwegian, Proceedings of *Re Paulette,* vol. 2 at 149-52; Evidence of Phillip Lafferty, vol. 2 at 224-29; and Evidence of Charlie Cholo, vol. 2 at 237-38. Louis Norwegian's evidence is reproduced in René Fumoleau, *As Long as This Land Shall Last: A History of Treaty 8 and Treaty 11, 1870-1939,* rev. ed. (Calgary: University of Calgary Press, 2004; first published 1975) at 446. See also Fumoleau, *ibid.* at 98-101, for a description of events in the negotiation of Treaty 8 at Fort Resolution.

16 For a discussion of the some of the highlights of this history, see Val Napoleon, "Extinction by Number: Colonialism Made Easy" (2001) 16:1 C.J.L.S. 113. For recent case law, see *McIvor v. The Registrar, Indian and Northern Affairs Canada,* 2007 BCSC 827.

17 See *e.g. Paul v. Canada,* 2002 FCT 615 (the North Slave Métis Alliance failed in its application for an injunction to prevent the completion of the Dogrib Final Agreement, claiming that it had rights within the territory covered by the Agreement, that it had not been represented in its negotiation, and that the Dogrib Agreement would prejudice its rights); and *Gitanyow First Nation v. Canada,* [1998] 4 C.N.L.R. 47 (B.C.S.C.) (the Gitanyow First Nation sought declarations that, first, the Crown had a duty to negotiate with it in good faith (granted: (1999), 66 B.C.L.R. (3d) 165, leave to appeal granted 1999 BCCA 343), and, second, the completion of the Nisga'a Agreement prevented the Crown from negotiating with it in good faith because it claimed rights within the territory covered by the Agreement and the Agreement prejudiced its rights. The parties have since set aside the litigation and are seeking a resolution of these matters through negotiation).

18 See Daniel K. Richter, "Whose Indian History?" (1993) 50 Wm & Mary Q. 379.

19 See *e.g.* James Merrell, *Into the American Woods: Negotiators on the Pennsylvania Frontier* (New York: Norton, 1999).

20 See *e.g.* E.E. Rich, *Hudson's Bay Company, 1670-1870,* vol. 1 (New York: Macmillan, 1960). See generally Michael Payne, "Fur Trade Historiography" in Theodore Binnema, Gerhard J. Ens, and R.C. Macleod, eds., *From Rupert's Land to Canada: Essays in Honour of John E. Foster* (Edmonton: University of Alberta Press, 2001) 3; and Toby Morantz, "Old Texts, Old Questions: Another Look at the Issue of Continuity and the Early Fur-Trade Period" (1992) 58 Can. Hist. Rev. 166.

21 For the instructions, see "Letter to John Nixon, 21 May 1680" in E.E. Rich, ed., *Copy-book of Letters Outward &c. Begins 29th May, 1680 Ends 5 July, 1687* (Toronto: Champlain Society, 1948) at 9 and 12-13. For the company's claims, see Memorial prepared by James Hayes, undated [est., 1682] in Rich, *ibid.* at 70-71.

22 Canada, "Relation of the Voyage of Pierre Esprit Radisson to the North of America in the Years 1682 and 1683" by Pierre Esprit Radisson in "Report of the Minister of Agriculture for the Dominion of Canada, 1895," *Sessional Papers,* no. 8a (Ottawa, 1896). See also Gideon D. Scull, *Voyages of Peter Esprit Radisson* (New York: Burt Franklin, 1967). For descriptions of French-Indian diplomacy in the sixteenth and seventeenth centuries, see Richard White, *The Middle Ground: Indians, Empires, and Republics in the Great Lakes Regions, 1650-1815* (Cambridge: Cambridge University Press, 1991).

23 The Swampy Cree inhabited the swampy lowlands near the coast of Hudson Bay. They are distinct from the Woodland Cree, who lived inland from the bay in the surrounding boreal forest, and from the Plains Cree, who lived further inland still and hunted buffalo on the plains. In spite of their different homelands, these peoples spoke dialects of a common language. See Victor P. Lytwyn, *Muskekowuck Athinuwick: Original People of the Great Swampy Land* (Winnipeg: University of Manitoba Press, 2002) at c. 1.

24 Radisson, *supra* note 22 at 11, 13; Scull, *supra* note 22 at 262-64.

25 Radisson, *ibid.* at 11, 13, 77; Scull, *ibid.* at 262-64, 355.

26 Radisson, *ibid.* at 11; Scull, *ibid.* at 263.

27 Radisson, *ibid.* It is not clear from the record whether this elder was the Chief who had adopted Radisson as his son. It is perhaps worth considering whether this statement of anticipation was specific to Radisson, as, given his exploits and travels in the Great Lakes region, his reputation may have preceded him. Ultimately, however, this seems unlikely. Radisson's earlier travels took place in the 1650s and 1660s, and the speaker referred to the time in which their "fathers were born." This means that, were the anticipation specific to Radisson, the speaker would have to be quite young, a conclusion that is unlikely given Radisson's description of him as an elder.

28 Jean Baptiste Chouart, also known as Jean-Baptiste Des Groseilliers, was the son of Médard Chouart Des Groseilliers, the other famous French explorer who accompanied Radisson on his first mission on behalf of the HBC in 1667.

29 Radisson, *supra* note 22 at 67.

30 Radisson, *ibid.*

31 Radisson, *ibid.* at 71. According to the narrative, these detachments included more than four hundred men from the "Assinipoetes," who had come on the strength of alliances with Radisson that predated this mission along the Hudson Bay coast.

32 When the French merchants seemed uninterested in advancing or taking advantage of Radisson's explorations of Hudson Bay, Radisson sought greener pastures back with the English. See Rich, *supra* note 20 at 158-62.

33 *Radisson, supra* note 22 at 77.

34 In Lytwyn's interpretation, *supra* note 23 at 129, the man who sparked the conflict by demanding that the French recognize him as Chief is identified as The Bearded.

35 Radisson, *supra* note 22 at xxiii, identified this man as Captain "Gazer," but, as explained by Douglas Brymner, the archivist who compiled Radisson's narrative, Gazer was most probably Captain Geyer. See also Alice M. Johnson, *Dictionary of Canadian Biography Online*, vol. 1, ed. by John English and Réal Bélanger, *s.v.* "Geyer, George," online: Library and Archives Canada, http://www.biographi.ca/.

36 Radisson, *ibid.* at 77. In Scull, *supra* note 22 at 354-55, the "common Indian" in this passage is replaced with a "simple savage," a direct translation from the French.

37 For a recent biography of Radisson, see Martin Fournier, *Pierre-Esprit Radisson: Merchant Adventurer, 1636-1710* (Sillery, QC: Septentrion, 2002).

38 Radisson's hyperbole — he once infamously described himself and Des Groseilliers as "caesars" — has prompted historians to consider him untrustworthy. However, Germaine Warkentin explains that his style reflects the language of the court more than it does the overbearing ego often attributed to him. She also notes that hyperbole is less apparent in the accounts of his voyages from the 1680s — the source for this tale — which are written in a more plain style, aimed at the needs of merchants. Warkentin, "Discovering Radisson: A Renaissance Adventurer between Two Worlds" in Jennifer Brown and Elizabeth Vibert, eds., *Reading beyond Words: Contexts for Native History* (Peterborough, ON: Broadview Press, 1996) 43.

39 Regarding the conduct of the trade generally, see Arthur J. Ray and Don Freeman, *"Give Us Good Measure": An Economic Analysis of Relations between the Indians and the Hudson's Bay Company before 1763* (Toronto: University of Toronto Press, 1978). Regarding trading captains more specifically, see Morantz, *supra* note 9.

40 See Sylvia van Kirk, *"Many Tender Ties": Women in Fur-Trade Society in Western Canada, 1670-1870* (Winnipeg: Watson and Dwyer, 1980); Jennifer Brown, *Strangers in Blood: Fur Trade Company Families in Indian Country* (Vancouver: UBC Press, 1980); and Heather Rollanson Driscoll, "'A Most Important Chain of Connection': Marriage in the Hudson's Bay Company" in Theodore Binnema, Gerhard J. Ens, and R.C. Macleod, eds., *From Rupert's Land to Canada: Essays in Honour of John E. Foster* (Edmonton: University of Alberta Press, 2001) 81.

41 Ray and Freeman, *supra* note 39; and Glyndwr Williams, ed., *Andrew Graham's Observations on Hudson's Bay, 1767-91* (London: Hudson's Bay Record Society, 1969) at 317 [*Graham's Observations*].

42 See *e.g. Graham's Observations, ibid.* at 169-70; and Captain James Knight's observations in the York Factory Post Journal from 1717, Hudson's Bay Company Archives (HBCA) (B.239/a/3, 20 April 1717).

43 Ray and Freeman, *supra* note 39 at 68, remark that, according to a nineteenth-century source, the captains often gave away these coats, along with all the other gifts.

44 *Ibid.* at 69 and 241.

45 *Graham's Observations, supra* note 41.

46 Linguist Peter Bakker has noted the possibility that trade proceeded through interpreters and has remarked that "[g]iven that the HBC traded with Natives for such a long period, it is surprising that so few of their employees knew a Native language." Bakker, "Hudson Bay Trader's Cree: A Cree Pidgin?" in John D. Nichols and Arden C. Ogg, eds., *Nikotwâsik iskwâhtêm, pâskihtêpayih!: Studies in Honour of H.C. Wolfart* (Winnipeg: Algonquian and Iroquoian Linguistics, 1996) 1 at 4.

47 For discussions of the skill set of a trading post factor, see Ray, *supra* note 9; and Foster, *supra* note 9.

48 Daniel Francis and Toby Morantz, *Partners in Furs: A History of the Fur Trade in Eastern James Bay, 1600-1870* (Montreal and Kingston: McGill-Queen's University Press, 1983) at 44, quoting Fort Richmond Post Journal, HBCA (B.182/a/1:48d). See also Morantz, *supra* note 9 at 490.

49 Ethnographer David G. Mandelbaum writes that "[t]he Hudson's Bay Company disturbed the pattern of chieftainship in some degree." Mandelbaum, *The Plains Cree: An Ethnographic, Historical and Comparative Study* (Regina: Canadian Plains Research Center, University of Regina, 1979) at 108.

50 As Morantz, *supra* note 9 at 495, notes, "[t]he trading captain system may not have been extraordinary from the perspective of [northern Algonquian] social organization."

51 Arthur Ray notes that in spite of Simpson's intended reforms, trading practices "in the parkland area ... remained largely unchanged and at best the company managed to trim the excesses." Ray, *Indians in the Fur Trade: Their Role as Trappers, Hunters and Middlemen in the Lands Southwest of Hudson Bay, 1660-1870* (Toronto: University of Toronto Press, 1974) at 196.

52 See Arthur J. Ray, Jim Miller, and Frank J. Tough, *Bounty and Benevolence: A Documentary History of Saskatchewan Treaties* (Montreal and Kingston: McGill-Queen's University Press, 2000) at c. 1.

53 See Taylor, *supra* note 5.

54 Morris, *supra* note 6 at 174.

55 *Ibid.* The "Saulteaux" are known today as the Anishnabe or Ojibway people. Rudy Wiebe notes that in 1874, a year before Reverend McDougall's visit, the Hudson's Bay Company had recorded Big Bear's camp as consisting of sixty-five lodges, or approximately 520 people. By comparison, Sweet Grass, another prominent Plains Cree Chief who was named by the company as "Chief of the Country," had fifty-six lodges. See Wiebe, *Dictionary of Canadian Biography Online,* vol. 11, ed. by John English and Réal Bélanger, *s.v.* "Mistahimaskwa (Big Bear)," online: Library and Archives Canada, http://www.biographi.ca/.

56 See Binnema, *supra* note 12, who comments that, among the peoples of the northwestern plains, no necessary correspondence existed between ethnic groups/cultural units and social, political, and economic units; and Susan R. Sharrock, "Crees, Cree-Assiniboines, and Assiniboines: Interethnic Social Organization on the Far Northern

Plains" (1974) 21:2 Ethnohistory 95, who remarks that plains bands were often polyethnic in composition, either Cree-Assiniboine or Cree-Saulteaux, with fused ethnic identities emerging in the nineteenth century.

57 For example, Wiebe, *supra* note 55, notes that Big Bear's influence grew from approximately twelve tents (20 men) in 1862 to sixty-five lodges (520 people) in 1874 and then to 247 people in 1882. The waning of his influence in the latter years was tied to the starvation suffered by his people.

58 See Jean Friesen, *Dictionary of Canadian Biography Online,* vol. 11, ed. by John English and Réal Bélanger, *s.v.* "Morris, Alexander," online: Library and Archives Canada, http://www.biographi.ca/.

59 Morris, *supra* note 6 at 226.

60 *Ibid.* at 227.

61 *Ibid.* at 228.

62 *Ibid.* at 227.

CHAPTER 4: RHETORIC, REASON, AND THE RULE OF LAW

1 David Neal, *The Rule of Law in a Penal Colony: Law and Power in Early New South Wales* (Cambridge: Cambridge University Press, 1991) at 62, and reiterated in his Conclusion at 196.

2 Glenn Burgess, *The Politics of the Ancient Constitution: An Introduction to English Political Thought, 1603-1642* (University Park: Pennsylvania State University Press, 1992) at 3.

3 *Ibid.*

4 Neal, *supra* note 1 at 64.

5 This is broadly the position of the leading positivist legal philosopher, H.L.A. Hart. See *e.g.* Hart, "Positivism and the Separation of Law and Morals" (1958) 71 Harv. L. Rev. 593 at 608-12; and generally Hart, *The Concept of Law* (Oxford: Clarendon Press, 1961). Neal, *supra* note 1 at 66.

6 Neal, *ibid.* at 68, quoting E.P. Thompson, *Whigs and Hunters: The Origin of the Black Act* (New York: Pantheon, 1975).

7 See Thompson, *ibid.*; Douglas Hay, "Property, Authority, and the Criminal Law" in Douglas Hay *et al.,* eds., *Albion's Fatal Tree: Crime and Society in Eighteenth-Century England* (New York: Pantheon, 1975); and J. Langbein, "Albion's Fatal Flaws" (1983) 98 Past and Present 96.

8 This theme is developed in several essays contained in Suzanne Corcoran and Stephen Bottomley, eds., *Interpreting Statutes* (Annandale, NSW: Federation Press, 2005), especially c. 9, Stephen Bottomley, "A Framework for Understanding the Interpretation of Corporate Law in Australia" 147; and c. 12, Simon Bronitt, "Interpreting Law Enforcement Immunities: The Relationship between Judicial, Legislative and Administrative Models" 223.

9 See "Decisions of the Superior Courts of New South Wales, 1788-1899," online: Division of Law, Macquarie University, http://www.law.mq.edu.au/scnsw/html/Cable%20v%20Sinclair,%201788.htm. The New South Wales Court Records list the case as *Cable v. Sinclair* (July 1788), though the parties (who were illiterate) seemingly adopted the alternative spelling of Kable, which is applied here.

10 Neal, *supra* note 1 at c. 1; and Bruce Kercher, *An Unruly Child: A History of Law in Australia* (Sydney: Allen and Unwin, 1995) at 22-23.

11 V. Windeyer, "A Birthright and Inheritance: The Establishment of the Rule of Law in Australia" (1962) 1 Tasm. U.L. Rev. 635 at 662.

12 Neal, *supra* note 1 at 195.

13 John Braithwaite, "Crime in a Convict Republic" (2001) 64 Mod. L. Rev. 11 at 19.

14 *Ibid*. at 19-23. His thesis is reinforced by modern social psychological research on procedural justice that reveals that a strongly punitive criminal justice system can nevertheless deliver high levels of compliance with the law, when combined with the processes that are perceived to be fair to the accused. See Tom Tyler, *Why People Obey the Law* (New Haven: Yale University Press, 1990).

15 A.C. Castles, *An Australian Legal History* (Sydney: Law Book Company, 1982) at c. 18.

16 As Neal, *supra* note 1 at 78, noted, "[f]or the original inhabitants of the colony, the Aborigines, the rule of law provided cold comfort. For the white free settlers, convicts and emancipists, it provided a measure of protection against power from the top, and eventually was the instrument through which their claim to political status was realised; for the Aborigines, its authority stood behind their forceful dispossession, its protection proved largely illusory, its courts were closed to Aboriginal testimony, and its principles denied the existence of their own laws."

17 R. Hunter, "Australian Legal Histories in Context" (2003) 21:3 L.H.R. 607 at 612, pointing out that the challenge for legal historians extends beyond simply acknowledging the existence of the "gap" to exploring the "why," the "how," and the social and economic forces at work.

18 William Blackstone, *Commentaries on the Laws of England* (New York: Legal Classics Library, 1983) vol. 1 at 104.

19 Bruce Kercher, "Perish or Prosper: The Law and Convict Transportation in the British Empire 1700-1850" (2003) 21:3 L.H.R. 548.

20 It should be noted that these are distinct legal disabilities consequent upon attainder. Although it is clear that felons forfeited right to hold property and sue, it is not clear that the doctrine of "legal" or "civil death" meant that they were not *bound* by laws. See discussion at Neal, *supra* note 1 at 90, n. 15.

21 Indeed, this occurred subsequently in 1815 when one of the first legally qualified judges in the colony, Judge-Advocate Jeffrey Bent, denied Emancipist lawyers the rights of audience, the result of which effectively closed the Supreme Court for eighteen months. Neal, *ibid*. at 103.

22 Windeyer, *supra* note 11 at 660; and Neal, *supra* note 1 at 4-5.

23 In the century before, another legal fiction — benefit of clergy — operated to ameliorate the harshness of conviction for felony. It had emerged as a means of denying the jurisdiction of common law courts over clerics. By the eighteenth century, the benefit was no longer confined to religious orders, and any person who could read received it, subject to being branded on the thumb to prevent a second claim. The range of "clergyable crimes" was reduced, and from 1718 onward, a condition of the claim was that the offender submit to transportation for seven years. W.R. Cornish and G. Clarke, *Law and Society in England 1750–1950* (London: Sweet and Maxwell, 1989) at 558.

24 John Hirst, *Convict Society and Its Enemies* (Sydney: George Allen and Unwin, 1983) at 119.

25 *Ibid.*

26 Neal, *supra* note 1 at 178, Justice Field citing *Bullocks v. Dodds* (1819), 106 E.R. 361.

27 A.W.B. Simpson, *Legal Theory and Legal History—Essays on the Common Law* (London: Hambledon Press, 1987) at 362.

28 For a discussion of the relationship between formalism and the rule of law, see Stephen Bottomley and Simon Bronitt, *Law in Context,* 3d ed. (Annandale, NSW: Federation Press, 2006) at c. 3.

29 Geo. IV., c. 96 ("The Third Charter of Justice for New South Wales").

30 J.G.A. Pocock, *The Ancient Constitution and the Feudal Law,* 2d ed. (Cambridge: Cambridge University Press, 1987) at 38.

31 Burgess, *supra* note 2 at 19.

32 This discussion is, therefore, another beneficiary of Bruce Kercher's project to assemble the early law reports for New South Wales and Tasmania. Bruce is too modest a man to acknowledge this, but all of us interested in legal history owe him a great debt. It is not at all an exaggeration to say that for students of Australian legal history, he is the equivalent of the Selden Society. For the law reports, see "Decisions of the Superior Courts of New South Wales, 1788-1899" [NSW], online: Division of Law, Macquarie University, http://www.law.mq.edu.au/scnsw; and "Decisions of the Nineteenth Century Tasmanian Superior Courts," online: Division of Law, Macquarie University, and School of History and Classics, University of Tasmania, http://www.law.mq.edu.au/sctas.

33 Castles, *supra* note 15 at 24.

34 *Ibid.*

35 Blackstone, *supra* note 18 at 104-5 [emphasis added].

36 (1992), 175 C.L.R. 1 at 35.

37 (1889), 14 App. Cas. 286.

38 *Ibid.* at 291 (Lord Watson).

39 It is often claimed that, from this, the moment of "settlement," the laws and rights of indigenous peoples were definitively ousted by English law. But closer scrutiny of surviving historical material, some of it only recently uncovered through the research efforts of Bruce Kercher, reveals that the common law as received and applied in the early colonial period, consistent with practices in other British colonies, was far more pluralistic and fractured than conventional legal wisdom would have it. See Kercher, "Recognition of Indigenous Legal Autonomy in Nineteenth Century New South Wales" (1998) 4 Indigenous L. Bull. 7. See also Kercher, "Publication of Forgotten Case Law of the New South Wales Supreme Court" (1998) 72 Austl. L.J. 876.

40 Ian Holloway, "Sir Francis Forbes and the Earliest Australian Public Law Cases" (2004) 44 L.H.R. 209.

41 See C.H. Currey, *Sir Francis Forbes: The First Chief Justice of the Supreme Court of New South Wales* (Sydney: Angus and Robertson, 1968); and John M. Bennett, *Sir Francis Forbes: First Chief Justice of New South Wales, 1823-1837* (Sydney: Federation Press, 2001).

42 Bennett, *ibid.* at 102.

43 Kercher, "Publication," *supra* note 39 at 880.

44 Alex Castles, "The Judiciary and Political Questions: The First Australian Experience, 1824–1825" (1973–76) 5 Adel. L.R. 294 at 314.

45 Castles, *supra* note 15 at 185–86. The case is reported in *R. v. Magistrates,* [1824] N.S.W. Sup. C. 20 (14 October 1824).

46 On the "Forbes experiment" generally, see G.D. Woods, *A History of Criminal Law in New South Wales* (Sydney: Federation Press, 2002) at 56–61. On the Emancipist campaign to establish juries in New South Wales, see Neal, *supra* note 1 at c. 7.

47 Castles, *supra* note 44 at 296.

48 *Ibid.* at 294.

49 *R. v. Magistrates of Sydney* (NSW), *supra* note 32, http://www.law.mq.edu.au/scnsw/ html/r_v_magistrates_of_sydney__182.html.

50 Greg Marquis, "In Defence of Liberty: 17th Century England and 19th Century Maritime Political Culture" (1993) 42 U.N.B.L.J. 69.

51 *Ibid.* at 76-77.

52 Martin Loughlin, *Public Law and Political Theory* (Oxford: Clarendon Press, 1992) at 13-14.

53 Raia Prokhovnik, *Rhetoric and Philosophy in Hobbes' "Leviathan"* (New York: Garland, 1991).

54 Kercher, *supra* note 10 at 70.

55 Kercher, "Publication," *supra* note 39.

56 *Newspaper Acts Opinion* (NSW), *supra* note 32, http://www.law.mq.edu.au/scnsw/ Cases1827-28/html/newspaper_acts_opinion__1827.htm.

57 Currey, *supra* note 41 at 201-3.

58 John M. Bennett, *Sir John Pedder: First Chief Justice of Tasmania, 1824-1854* (Sydney: Federation Press, 2003) at 103.

59 *Ibid.* at 57.

60 *Newspaper Acts Opinion* (NSW), *supra* note 32.

61 *Ibid.* at n. 1 [emphasis added].

62 A report of the case can be found at (1831), 1 Legge 5 [Legge]. For Kercher's report, see NSW, *supra* note 32, http://www.law.mq.edu.au/scnsw/Cases1831-32/html/ r_v_farrell__dingle_and_woodwa.htm.

63 (1819), 106 E.R. 361. See also *Dugan v. Mirror Newspapers Ltd* (1978), 142 C.L.R. 583.

64 Legge, *supra* note 62 at 20.

65 A related argument was that if, in fact, a change to the rule were appropriate in New South Wales, it should not be made by the courts, for this would amount to judicial legislation. Any such change should be carried out by the legislature. Alternatively, the argument went, the Governor could grant a pardon to the proposed witness so as to rehabilitate him.

66 Legge, *supra* note 62 at 16.

67 *Ibid.* at 18.

68 *Ibid.* at 7.

69 *Ibid.* at 8.

70 *Ibid.* at 13.

71 Bennett, *supra* note 41 at 138-41.

72 Hirst, *supra* note 24 at 116.

73 A.V. Dicey, *Lectures on the Relation between Law and Opinion in England in the Nineteenth Century* (London: Macmillan, 1905) at 81.

74 A.C.V. Melbourne, *Early Constitutional Development in Australia* (St. Lucia: University of Queensland Press, 1963) at 116.

75 See Kercher, "Publication," *supra* note 39 at 880.

CHAPTER 5: SOMETIMES PERSUASIVE AUTHORITY

1 The term "Dominion" is chosen because no other convenient label is available. It is acknowledged to be inaccurate, given that South Africa ceased to be a Dominion in 1961, India and Pakistan (and later other states) became Dominions in 1947, and the Irish Free State, a Dominion from 1921 to 1949, is excluded from this study; Newfoundland has been included within Canada. The niceties of status were sometimes lost on the English — as late as 1948, counsel in a defamation suit could cite Canadian and South African decisions as "two colonial cases." See *Braddock v. Bevins*, [1948] 1 K.B. 580 at 584. For reasons that are far from clear and deserve further study, the courts of the Dominions made relatively little use of Scottish or Irish case law.

2 In 1953 the Incorporated Council began to publish the *Weekly Law Reports,* comprising the cases that would later be published in the *Law Reports* series together with a further volume (vol. 1 for each year) described by the publisher as containing "cases of value to practitioners which are not intended to be included in the Law Reports." These have not been included in the sample, because it is impossible to determine whether cases were first cited by counsel or by the judge, and because electronic searching was not possible. However, visual inspection suggests that only a very few Dominion references would have appeared in these volumes — there are only two in 1953 (the court indicated it had not seen the text of the cases), two in 1957, and one in 1962.

3 See *e.g. R. v. Lee Kun*, [1916] 1 K.B. 337; and *Lee v. Lau*, [1967] P. 14, where Hong Kong law was discussed; and *Rondel v. Worsley*, [1969] 1 A.C. 191, referring to a case from British Guiana.

4 *Conway v. Rimmer*, [1968] A.C. 910 at 929.

5 For the first known report, see *Chilton v. Progress Printing and Publishing Company,* [1895] 2 Ch. 29, where counsel cited *Wilson v. Luke* (1875), 1 Vict. L.R. 127, apparently drawn from Walter Arthur Copinger, *Law of Copyright in Works of Literature and Art: Including That of the Drama, Music, Engraving, Sculpture, Painting, Photography,* 3d ed. (London, 1893) at 64. See the structure of arguments in *Esso Petroleum Co Ltd v. Harper's Garage (Stourport) Ltd,* [1968] A.C. 269 at 281; *Conway v. Rimmer,* [1968] A.C. 910 at 917; and *Parry v. Cleaver,* [1970] A.C. 1 at 8.

6 See the reports of argument in *Weller and Co v. Foot and Mouth Disease Research Institute,* [1966] 1 Q.B. 569 at 575; and *Hewer v. Bryant,* [1970] 1 Q.B. 357 at 363; compare *Rondel v. Worsley,* [1967] 1 Q.B. 443 at 505.

7 Ten cases in the sample involved decisions that were reported separately at different stages; in others, two stages may have been reported separately. After we allow for

this, there were 257 individual pieces of litigation over this period. Each stage is counted separately in the total of decisions, but not in the total of matters litigated.

8   Some judges did list every case cited by counsel, though perhaps more as a matter of courtesy than because they took the citation seriously. Even so, in mentioning a Dominion precedent in their judgments, they could at least have entertained the possibility that it might be of real assistance.

9   The total counts separately each judgment in a case referring to any one Dominion decision. Multiple references by one judge to a case are counted as one; references by different judges in an appellate court are each counted separately.

10 See *e.g.* the citation in *Adler v. Dickson*, [1955] 1 Q.B. 158 at 182 of two Australian cases recorded in *Lloyd's Reports* (which dealt with cases on international trade and shipping law); and *R. v. Patents Appeal Tribunal, Ex parte Swift and Co*, [1962] 2 Q. B. 647 at 657, which cited an Australian and a New Zealand decision from the *Reports of Patent Cases,* which published a wide range of intellectual property decisions.

11 For *Bullock*, see [1959] Ch. 147 and successively [1959] Ch. 315 (C.A.), [1960] A.C. 351 (H.L.). For the Privy Council case, see *Union Corporation v. CIR*, [1952] 1 All E.R. 646. For *Koitaki*, see (1940), 64 C.L.R. 15 at 19.

12 In *Kelantan Government v. Duff Development Co*, [1923] A.C. 395 at 416, Lord Parmoor referred to *McRae and Co v. Lemay* (1890), 18 Can. S.C.R. 280, a case not cited by counsel but which had been canvassed in *Attorney-General for Manitoba v. Kelly*, [1922] 2 A.C. 268 at 281 (P.C.), a case in which Lord Parmoor sat.

13 *Hardwick Game Farm Ltd v. SAPPA*, [1969] 2 A.C. 31, adopting the view of Dixon J. in *Australian Knitting Mills Ltd v. Grant* (1933), 50 C.L.R. 387 rather than the Privy Council view at *Grant v. Australian Knitting Mills Ltd*, [1936] A.C. 85.

14 See *Societe Cooperative Sidmetal v. Titan International Ltd*, [1966] 1 Q.B. 829 at 834; *R. v. Aston University Senate ex p Roffey*, [1969] 2 Q.B. 538 at 554; and *Floydd v. Cheney*, [1970] Ch. 602 at 610. An English barrister recounts that in 1929, as a very junior pupil in chambers assisting with research in a case on insurance before arbitrators, he had discovered a directly applicable decision in the *British Columbia Law Reports* when all the other barristers involved (including a future chief justice of England) had concluded that no relevant case law authority existed on the point. See Alan King-Hamilton *And Nothing but the Truth* (London: Weidenfeld and Nicolson, 1982) at 18.

15 Minutes of the New Zealand Law Society Council (4 July 1905), New Zealand Law Society Archives, Wellington.

16 In *Midland Silicones Ltd v. Scruttons Ltd*, [1962] A.C. 446 at 472, Lord Simonds referred to an Australian case "which is fortunately reported also in Lloyd's Reports; fortunately, since the Commonwealth Law Reports are too seldom to be found in any counsel's chambers."

17 *R. v. McDonnell*, [1966] 1 Q.B. 233 at 244.

18 See the discussion of *Fawcett v. Star Car Sales Ltd*, [1960] N.Z.L.R. 406 in *Ingram v. Little*, [1961] 1 Q.B. 31 at 43; of *Skelton v. Collins* (1966), 39 A.L.J.R. 480 in *Andrews v. Freeborough*, [1967] 1 Q.B. 1 at 11; and of *Coulls v. Bagot's Executor and Trustee Co Ltd* (1967), 40 A.L.J.R. 471 in *Beswick v. Beswick*, [1968] A.C. 58 at 88, 90, and 101. See also *Gilbert v. Gilbert and Abdon*, [1958] P. 131 at 132, where Sachs J. referred to

the very recently reported *Mattina v. Mattina,* [1957] N.Z.L.R. 440. It is possible that judges were alerted to such developments by digests of as yet unreported decisions in Dominion journals, as occurred in *Herod v. Herod,* [1939] P. 11.

19 [1921] 1 K.B. 423 at 445.

20 Oddly, vol. 1 was the last volume issued!

21 For Salmond, see *Newstead v. London Express Newspaper Ltd,* [1939] 2 K.B. 317, aff'd [1940] 1 K.B. 377, citing *Lee v. Wilson* (1934), 51 C.L.R. 276; and *Burfitt v. A and E Kille,* [1939] 2 K.B. 743, citing *Fowell v. Grafton* (1910), 20 O.L.R. 639. Although Salmond was a New Zealander, later, posthumous, editions of his work were produced in England. For Fleming, see *e.g. Williams v. Williams,* [1964] A.C. 698 at 750-51; and *Imperial Chemical Industries Ltd v. Shatwell,* [1965] A.C. 656 at 683-84; compare counsel's reference to *Wynes on Legislation and Executive Powers in Australia* in *Belfast Corporation v. O D Cars Ltd,* [1960] A.C. 490 at 504. For the essay, Ivan A. Shearer, "Extradition in Australia" in D.P. O'Connell, ed., *International Law in Australia* (Sydney, 1965), see *R. v. Governor of Brixton Prison, ex p Armah,* [1968] A.C. 192 at 216.

22 Lord Chorley, "Edward Jenks 1861-1939" (1947) 1 J.S.P.T.L. (New Series) 114. Dominion law could sometimes be invisible, even to official eyes — the 1939 reports of the UK Law Revision Committee either omit mention of Dominion law or refer to it only in passing. Its post-war successor, the Law Reform Committee, made much more use of Dominion law.

23 For *Gold,* see [1942] 2 K.B. 293. For the article, see Arthur Lehman Goodhart, "Hospitals and Trained Nurses" (1938) 54 Law Q. Rev. 553 at 571, discussing *Nyberg v. Provost Municipal Hospital,* [1927] Can. S.C.R. 226, and *Logan v. Waitaki Hospital Board,* [1935] N.Z.L.R. 385.

24 See *e.g.* Harry Street, "Estoppel and Negligence" (1957) 73 Law Q. Rev. 359 at 371, discussing *Jackson v. Goldsmith* (1950), 81 C.L.R. 446, a case then cited in *Randolph v. Tuck,* [1962] 1 Q.B. 175 at 185 and 188.

25 For the reference to Dixon's address, see *Bratty v. Attorney-General for Northern Ireland,* [1963] A.C. 386 at 394, 412. For *Connelly,* see [1964] A.C. 1254 at 1262, 1274, and 1284, discussing Colin Howard, "Res Judicata in the Criminal Law" (1961) 3 Melbourne U.L. Rev. 101.

26 *Robinson-Scott v. Robinson-Scott,* [1958] P. 71, where an article by Erwin Griswold, "Divorce Jurisdiction and Recognition of Divorce Decrees — A Comparative Study" (1951) 65 Harv. L. Rev. 193, seems to have been the source for a reference to *Worth v. Worth,* [1931] N.Z.L.R. 1109.

27 A note, by "BS," the editor of the *Australian Law Journal,* on *Wright v. Cedzich* (1930), 43 C.L.R. 493, appears at (1932) 48 Law Q. Rev. 323 at 324. *Wright v. Cedzich* and another case cited by BS, *Johnson v. The Commonwealth* (1927), 27 S.R. 133 (N.S.W.), are cited and discussed in *Best v. Samuel Fox and Co Ltd,* [1951] 2 K.B. 639 at 658 and on appeal, [1952] A.C. 716 at 727 and 732.

28 For the misprision case, see *R. v. Sykes,* [1961] 2 Q.B. 9, aff'd *Sykes v. DPP,* [1962] A.C. 528. See *R. v. Crimmins,* [1959] V.R. 270; *R. v. Semenick* (1955), 15 W.W.R. 333 (N.S.); Norval Morris, "An Australian Letter" [1955] Crim. L. Rev. 290; and Colin Howard, "Misprisions, Compoundings and Compromises" [1959] Crim. L. Rev. 750. A further Australian case, *R. v. Hosking* (unreported N.S.W.D.C.), noted

by Morris in "An Australian Letter" [1955] Crim. L. Rev. 290 at 292, was also cited in the Court of Appeal.

29 [1970] A.C. 132, discussing Colin Howard, "Strict Responsibility in the High Court of Australia" (1960) 76 Law Q. Rev. 547.

30 The use of "his" and "he" reflects the fact that, although there was one female High Court Judge (Dame Elizabeth Lane, appointed 1965) in our period of study, none of her judgments in the law reports of the period include Dominion authority.

31 See *e.g. Bourne v. Keane*, [1919] 1 A.C. 815 at 831; and *In re Hastings (No. 2)*, [1959] 1 Q.B. 358. Curiously, eight of the eleven cases in which such views were stated date from the 1950s.

32 See *e.g. Staffs Motor Guarantee Ltd v. British Wagon Co Ltd*, [1934] 2 K.B. 305 *(Sale of Goods Act);* and *Charter v. Sullivan*, [1957] 2 Q.B. 117 *(Limitation Act).* Contrast the approach in *Edwards v. Porter*, [1925] A.C. 1.

33 [1963] 1 Q.B. 773; [1963] 2 Q.B. 477.

34 (1940), 63 C.L.R. 73.

35 *The Amerika*, [1914] P. 167, aff'd [1917] A.C. 38, applying *Monaghan v. Horn* (1882), 7 Can. S.C.R. 409.

36 *Arbon v. Anderson*, [1943] 1 K.B. 252 at 255, citing *Gibson v. Young* (1900), 21 N.S.W.L.R. 7.

37 See *Blyth v. Blyth*, [1966] A.C. 643, preferring *Wright v. Wright* (1948), 77 C.L.R. 191 to *Ginesi v. Ginesi*, [1948] P. 179. See also *Bater v. Bater*, [1951] P. 35 at 38; and Anon., "The Standard of Proof in Adultery" (1950) 66 Law Q. Rev. 36.

38 See *Bourke v. Butterfield and Lewis Ltd* (1926), 38 C.L.R. 354, not followed in *Flower v. Ebbw Vale Steel, Iron and Coal Co Ltd.*, [1934] 2 K.B. 132 at 139, aff'd on appeal *Flower v. Ebbw Vale Steel, Iron and Coal Co Ltd*, [1936] A.C. 206. See also *Caswell v. Powell Duffryn Associated Collieries Ltd*, [1940] A.C. 152; and *Lewis v. Denye*, [1940] A.C. 921.

39 For *In re Callaway*, see [1956] Ch. 559 at 563; *In re Jane Tucker, decd* (1921), 21 S.R. 175 (N.S.W.).

40 See *e.g. Best v. Samuel Fox and Co Ltd*, [1952] A.C. 716 at 727, 736.

41 *Whitaker v. Minister of Pensions and National Insurance*, [1967] 1 Q.B. 156 at 168. As mentioned earlier, in *Ingram v. Little, supra* note 18, the Court referred to *Fawcett v. Star Car Sales Ltd*, [1960] N.Z.L.R. 406, a decision that had been noted by Anthony Hugh Hudson, "Mistake of Identity in Contract" (1960) 23 Mod. L. Rev. 567.

42 [1965] A.C. 1175 at 1240, 1258.

43 This was contrary to a majority, though not universal, expectation among the Law Lords that cases should be decided solely on the basis of the points and authorities argued by counsel. Alan Paterson, *The Law Lords* (London: Macmillan, 1982) at 38ff.

44 [1965] 1 Q.B. 232 at 245, applying *Kruber v. Grzesiak*, [1963] 2 V.R. 621, a decision cited by counsel and expressly applied by Denning and Diplock L.JJ.

45 Cited in Philip Ayres, *Owen Dixon* (Melbourne: Miegunyah Press, 2003) at 231.

46 *Attorney-General v. Clough*, [1963] 1 Q.B. 773 at 791, Lord Parker C.J., applying *Mc-Guinness v. Attorney-General of Victoria* (1940), 63 C.L.R. 73.

47 *R. v. Gould,* [1968] 2 Q.B. 65 at 73, per Diplock L.J.

48 For these contacts, see Ayres, *supra* note 45 at 240, 269-70.

49 See *Compania Naviera Maropan S/A v. Bowaters Lloyd Pulp and Paper Mills Ltd,* [1955] 2 Q.B. 68, relying on Dixon C.J.'s dissent in *Reardon Smith Line Ltd. v. Australian Wheat Board,* [1954] 2 Ll. Rep. 148.

50 An address by Owen Dixon, published as "A Legacy of Hadfield M'Naghten and Maclean" (1957) 31 A.L.J. 255, was cited in *Bratty v. Attorney-General for Northern Ireland,* [1963] A.C. 386 at 394 (by counsel) and 412 (by Lord Denning).

CHAPTER 6: COURTS, COMMUNITIES, AND COMMUNICATION

1 *Supreme Court Circuit Act,* S.N.S. 1774, c. 6.

2 *Supreme Court Circuit Acts,* S.N.S. 1781, c. 6; 1802, c. 1; 1805, c. 13.

3 *Supreme Court Circuit Act,* S.N.S. 1816, c. 2. As of 1816 annual visits were made to Cumberland, Lunenburg, Queens, Shelburne, and Sydney Counties. The Court went twice a year to Annapolis, Hants, and Kings Counties, and to Colchester and Pictou Districts of Halifax County.

4 *Cape Breton Laws Act,* S.N.S. 1820-21, c. 5.

5 *Supreme Court Circuit Act,* S.N.S. 1834, c. 4.

6 *Judiciary Act,* S.N.S. 1841, c. 3, s. 22.

7 *County of Cape Breton Act,* S.N.S. 1851, c. 4, s. 7.

8 See John McLaren, "The Early British Columbia Judges, the Rule of Law and the 'Chinese Question': The California and Oregon Connection" in John McLaren, Hamar Foster, and Chet Orloff, eds., *Law for the Elephant, Law for the Beaver: Essays in the Legal History of the North American West* (Regina and Pasadena: Canadian Plains Research Center/Ninth Judicial Circuit Historical Society, 1992) 233.

9 Before Confederation circuits operated in New Brunswick (subject to interruption by the judges' refusal to undertake them), Upper and Lower Canada, Newfoundland, and British Columbia. See variously K. Donovan, "The Origin and Establishment of the New Brunswick Courts" (1980) J. N.B. Museum 57; N.J. Goudie, "The Supreme Court on Circuit: Northern District, 1826-1833" in C. English, ed., *Essays in the History of Canadian Law,* vol. 9: *Two Islands, Newfoundland and Prince Edward Island* (Toronto: Osgoode Society for Canadian Legal History and University of Toronto Press, 2005) 115; Margaret A. Banks, "The Evolution of the Ontario Courts, 1788-1981" in D. Flaherty, ed., *Essays in the History of Canadian Law,* vol. 2 (Toronto: Osgoode Society for Canadian Legal History and University of Toronto Press, 1983) 502; D. Fyson, *The Court Structure of Quebec and Lower Canada, 1760-1860* (Montreal: Montreal History Group, 1994); Hamar Foster, "The Struggle for the Supreme Court: Law and Politics in British Columbia, 1871-1885" in Louis A. Knafla, ed., *Law and Justice in a New Land: Essays in Western Canadian Legal History* (Toronto: Carswell, 1986) 167; Foster, "The Kamloops Outlaws and Commissions of Assize in Nineteenth-Century British Columbia" in David H. Flaherty, ed., *Essays in the History of Canadian Law,* vol. 2 (Toronto: Osgoode Society for Canadian Legal History and University of Toronto Press, 1983) 308; and David Ricardo Williams, *"The Man for a New Country": Sir Matthew Baillie Begbie* (Sidney, BC: Gray's,

1977). Of the American colonies, only North Carolina, Pennsylvania, Maryland, and New York had a circuit system, but such courts were fairly widely used during the territorial expansion of an independent United States. See variously E.C. Surrency, "The Courts in the American Colonies" (1967) 11 Am. J. Legal Hist. 347; W.W. Blume and E.G. Brown, "Territorial Courts and Law—Unifying Factors in the Development of American Legal Institutions" (1962) 61 Mich. L. Rev. 467; and Larry Bakken, *Justice in the Wilderness: A Study of Frontier Courts in Canada and the United States, 1670-1870* (Littleton, CO: Fred B. Rothman, 1986). On the English assizes, see J.S. Cockburn, *A History of English Assizes, 1558-1714* (Cambridge: Cambridge University Press, 1972).

10 A system of Federal Court circuits was established in the early nineteenth century, but no judges were appointed to them. Rather, each Supreme Court judge was assigned a circuit, which he travelled in company with a district judge from the locality. On circuit, the Court dealt only with a limited class of cases. See principally G.E. White, "The Working Life of the Marshall Court, 1815-1835" (1984) 70 Va. L. Rev. 1; K. Newmeyer, "Justice Joseph Story on Circuit and a Neglected Phase of American Legal History" (1970) 14 Am. J. Legal Hist. 112; and Joshua Glick, "On the Road: The Supreme Court and the History of Circuit Riding" (2003) 24 Cardozo L. Rev. 1753.

11 See generally Williams, *supra* note 9.

12 Douglas Hay, "Property, Authority, and the Criminal Law" in Douglas Hay *et al., Albion's Fatal Tree: Crime and Society in Eighteenth-Century England* (London: Allen Lane, 1975) 17, especially at 27 and 30-31.

13 See J. Phillips, "'High above the Generality of the People': The Origins of the Nova Scotia Supreme Court Circuit" in J. Phillips, R.R. McMurtry, and J. Saywell, eds., *Essays in the History of Canadian Law,* vol. 10: *A Tribute to Peter Oliver* (Toronto: Osgoode Society for Canadian Legal History and University of Toronto Press, 2008) 200 at 200-21.

14 See Foster, "The Struggle," *supra* note 9.

15 For the early Court see Barry Cahill and Jim Phillips, "The Supreme Court of Nova Scotia: Origins to Confederation" in Philip Girard, Jim Phillips, and Barry Cahill, eds., *The Supreme Court of Nova Scotia, 1754-2004: From Imperial Bastion to Provincial Oracle* (Toronto: Osgoode Society for Canadian Legal History and University of Toronto Press, 2004) 53 at 64-67; and, for a fuller account of this argument, Phillips, *supra* note 13. For later developments see Lieutenant-Governor John Wentworth's comment on the 1806 Act to extend the circuit to Lunenburg and Pictou, that "the Supreme Court sitting in these places, gives great information to the courts of common pleas, and magistrates, and establishes decorum and respectability toward all the functions of justice, and impresses the minds of the people with deference to the laws." Wentworth to Windham (14 November 1806), Halifax, Nova Scotia Archives and Records Management (NSARM), Selections from the Files of Government Officials [Selections] (RG 1, vol. 54, 134-35).

16 For reports on JPs, see *e.g.* Halliburton and Stewart to Provincial Secretary (5 November 1822), Selections (RG 1, vol. 230, no. 109), regarding the need for more JPs in the eastern districts; Wilkins to Lieutenant-Governor (5 August 1828), *ibid.*

(vol. 235, no. 43), concerning the need to remove a JP from the commission; and Council Minutes (21 August and 1 October 1829), *ibid.* (vol. 214.5B), on asking the judges for a general report. For the ICCPs see *inter alia* Council Minutes (25 April 1835), *ibid.* (vol. 214.5C). For bridges, see *Journals of the Nova Scotia House of Assembly* [*Assembly Journals*] (3 April 1830) at 738–39 — £1,250 to be granted for a bridge over the Cornwallis River "when it shall be certified by one of the Judges of the Supreme Court that the said Bridge is completed." For sheriffs see *Sheriffs Act,* S.N.S. 1795, c. 1, s. 1. The Chief Justice or, in his absence, the senior Puisne Judge, drew up a list of three people from each county, and the Lieutenant-Governor selected one.

17 See the many reports from divisional chief justices in Selections (RG 1, vols. 236, 237, and 242).

18 David Graham Bell, "Maritime Legal Institutions under the 'Ancien Regime'" (1996) 23 Man. L.J. 103 at 110.

19 For a full discussion, albeit one about the majesty of the law generally and not about circuits, see D. Fyson, *Magistrates, Police and People: Everyday Criminal Justice in Quebec and Lower Canada, 1764-1837* (Toronto: Osgoode Society for Canadian Legal History and University of Toronto Press, 2006) at c. 8.

20 This discussion of the courthouses is based on C.A. Hale, *Early Court Houses of Nova Scotia,* 2 vols. (N.p.: Parks Canada, 1977).

21 Two exceptions were the courthouse at Tusket, built between 1801 and 1805 and said to be the oldest courthouse extant in Canada, albeit not used as such since the 1920s, and the one at Annapolis Royal, erected in 1837 when the existing courthouse burned down. This "expensive and magnificent" edifice was considered "the best in the province" before the erection of Halifax's new courthouse in 1860 and is still in use as a courthouse: Hale, *ibid.* at 23. It features a granite first floor, initially used as a jail, and a wooden upper floor constructed on a symmetrical Palladian plan, with the second-floor entrance covered by an impressive pediment supported by four large Tuscan columns.

22 Thomas Chandler Haliburton, *The Old Judge, or Life in a Colony* (Toronto: Clarke, Irwin, 1968; first published 1849) at 10-11.

23 *Novascotian* (28 October 1841).

24 Stewart to Wiswall (21 March 1825), NSARM, Wiswall Papers (MG 1, vol. 980, no. 100).

25 Stewart to Wiswall (3 August 1829), *ibid.* (no. 150).

26 NSARM, Assembly Papers (RG 5, Series P, vol. 3, no. 30).

27 *Supreme Court Circuit Act,* S.N.S. 1839, c. 30; *Assembly Journals* (16 February and 6 March 1839), *supra* note 16 at 525, 557-58.

28 See *e.g.* the various petitions for the move of the Court from Windsor to Newport in Hants County: NSARM, Assembly Papers (RG 5, Series P, vol. 2, nos. 45B, 46, 51, 58, 61, 64-66, and 90-93). One suspects that whatever the merits of this campaign it would never have been successful, because the aged Chief Justice Blowers lived at Windsor and restricted his circuit duty to that town only: see below. For petitions to move the Sydney Court to Ship Harbour, see *Assembly Journals* (16 March 1830), *supra* note 16 at 680.

29 *Supreme Court Act,* S.N.S. 1816, c. 2, s. 1; and *Cumberland Circuit Act,* S.N.S. 1830, c. 4. For the petitions see NSARM, Assembly Papers (RG 5, Series P, vol. 1, no. 75; vol. 2, no. 62; vol. 3, nos. 1, 2, 7-10, 13, 15, 19, 21, 25, 26, 33, 34, and 72; and vol. 4, nos. 2, 6, and 16A).

30 Assembly Papers, *ibid.* (vol. 7, no. 26).

31 For a full discussion of this problem, see R.B. Brown, *The Jury, Politics and the State in British North America: Reforms to Jury Systems in Nova Scotia and Upper Canada, 1825-1867* (Ph.D. diss., Dalhousie University, 2005) [unpublished] especially c. 2; and R. Blake Brown, "Storms, Roads and Harvest Time: Criticisms of Jury Service in Pre-Confederation Nova Scotia" (2006) 36 Acadiensis 93.

32 For comments on the Court being busy, see, *inter alia,* Wiswall to his wife (28 May 1830), NSARM, Wiswall Papers (MG 1, vol. 980, no. 40); and Stewart to Wiswall (5 November 1827), *ibid.* (no. 124).

33 The reasons for the almost equivalent civil jurisdiction in the two levels of courts are discussed in Cahill and Phillips, *supra* note 15 at 58-59. In 1823 the position of a First Justice of the Common Pleas and President of the Courts of Sessions was created for Cape Breton. The appointee was to preside at all county and district courts, a kind of circuit judge for the lower courts. *Cape Breton Courts Act,* S.N.S. 1823, c. 36. A year later the same arrangement was made for the mainland, with three "divisional chief justices" appointed to preside in the lower courts, which were organized into middle, eastern, and western divisions. *Equal Administration of Justice Act,* S.N.S. 1824, c. 38, ss. 1-2.

34 Stewart to Wiswall (3 August 1829), NSARM, Wiswall Papers (MG 1, vol. 980, no. 150).

35 Stewart to Wiswall (28 August 1826), *ibid.* (no. 110).

36 Stewart to Wiswall (23 August 1824), *ibid.* (no. 94).

37 Marshall to Lord Stanley (3 January 1842), NSARM, J.G. Marshall Papers (MG 1, vol. 1282, no. 10).

38 The information here is from *Assembly Journals* (1838), *supra* note 16, Appendices 12 and 39; and (1841) Appendix 22. The criminal circuit caseload was very light also. Between 1835 and 1839 inclusive, the NSSC on circuit conducted only 50 criminal trials throughout the colony, whereas the circuit and the ICCPs saw a total of 548 civil trials.

39 *Assembly Journals* (22 and 26 December 1834 and 21 January 1835), *ibid.* at 742, 752, and 803-4. There were a good number of other similar proposals in the years leading up to 1841. See generally J. Phillips and B. Miller, "The Judiciary and the Judicial System in Nova Scotia Politics, c. 1830 — 1848" (2008) [unpublished].

40 Memorandum on the Courts (n.d., probably by Murdoch 1828 or 1829), NSARM, Brenton Halliburton Papers (MG 1, vol. 334, no. 77). For Beamish Murdoch's belief that the divisional chief justices had brought a considerable degree of professionalism to the ICCPs see his *Epitome of the Laws of Nova Scotia,* 4 vols. (Halifax, 1832-34) vol. 3 at 60-61.

41 *Assembly Journals* (12 March 1836), *supra* note 16 at 1016-17.

42 For a detailed account see Phillips and Miller, *supra* note 39.

43 *Assembly Journals* (12 March 1836), *supra* note 16 at 1016-17.

44 As John Morton, MHA for Cornwallis Township, insisted in an Assembly debate on judicial reform, "the Magistrates were often consulted by the first Justice of the Sessions. They were not men made of straw, as lawyers sometimes attempted to make them in the House of Assembly." *Novascotian* (19 March 1834).

45 See *e.g.* the *Sydney Supreme Court Act,* S.N.S. 1844 (2d Sess.), c. 3, which removed all proceedings from the May to the September term of that year because the judge had not been able to reach Sydney.

46 Bliss to Henry Bliss (4 August 1841), NSARM, Bliss Papers (MG 1, vol. 1599, no. 55); Halliburton, Wilkins, Hill, Bliss, and Haliburton to Lieutenant-Governor Falkland (29 April 1842) in *Assembly Journals* (1843), *supra* note 16, Appendix 63.

47 Bliss to Henry Bliss (5 July 1850), NSARM, Bliss Papers (MG 1, vol. 1599, no. 135).

48 Bliss to Henry Bliss (28 September 1850 and 2 October 1859), *ibid.* (nos. 138 and 152).

49 When the mainland circuit was completed in 1816, the Assembly also provided an additional judge to the four in place, known as the "Associate Circuit Judge," who had a lower salary than the full NSSC judges and a jurisdiction limited to the circuit. The appointee, Peleg Wiswall, died in 1836 and was not replaced. In 1841, with the abolition of the ICCPs, a fifth full judge was added.

50 See White, *supra* note 10, especially at 8-9.

51 The figures given here are compiled from public accounts. From 1805 the Assembly granted the judges one pound and three shillings and fourpence a day in circuit travelling expenses. *Supreme Court Circuit Act,* S.N.S. 1805, c. 14, s. 4. The amounts claimed can be located in the appendices to the *Assembly Journals* for most years after 1834, and in the public accounts prior to 1834, at NSARM, Public Accounts (RG 1, vols. 399 and 400). From the total claimed one can calculate the number of days.

52 Memorial from Judge Haliburton to Provincial Secretary Joseph Howe (21 July 1848), Selections (RG 1, vol. 257, no. 132); William Bliss to Henry Bliss (18 April [c. 1840]), NSARM, Bliss Papers (MG 1, vol. 1599, no. 203).

53 See especially the correspondence between Peleg Wiswall and his colleagues in NSARM, Wiswall Papers (MG 1, vols. 979 and 980). For Bliss' description of Halliburton's claim to decide his own circuits, see Bliss to Henry Bliss (16 May 1836), NSARM, Bliss Papers (MG 1, vol. 1599, no. 29).

54 Again, there are frequent references in the Wiswall correspondence (MG 1, vol. 980).

55 P.R. Blakeley, *Dictionary of Canadian Biography Online,* vol. 7, ed. by John English and Réal Bélanger, *s.v.* "Blowers, Sampson Salter," online: Library and Archives Canada, http://www.biographi.ca/. For Blowers at Windsor see *inter alia* Stewart to Wiswall (7 May 1827 and 12 May 1828), NSARM, Wiswall Papers (MG 1, vol. 980, nos. 118 and 134).

56 Halliburton to Wiswall (26 May 1833), *ibid.* (vol. 979, folder 5, no. 11).

57 This had been part of the original circuit arrangements in 1774. The rule was altered in 1806, allowing court to be held with one NSSC judge and one other person, either a lawyer or a judge of the local ICCP. This permissive regimen seems quickly

to have become the norm, but the Assembly equally quickly reverted to the two-judge system in 1809. See *Supreme Court Circuit Acts,* S.N.S. 1805, c. 14, s. 5; 1809, c. 15, s. 3.

58 The legislation is *Supreme Court Circuit Act,* S.N.S. 1834, c. 4, s. 1. For its passage and the other issues discussed in this paragraph, see Phillips and Miller, *supra* note 39.

59 *Supreme Court Circuit Act,* S.N.S. 1809, c. 15, s. 4.

60 Stewart to Wiswall (23 August 1824), NSARM, Wiswall Papers (MG 1, vol. 980, no. 94).

61 Wilkins to Wiswall (22 May 1828), *ibid.* (vol. 979, folder 7, no. 13).

62 Wilkins to Wiswall (10 May 1831), *ibid.* (no. 15) [emphasis in original].

63 This paragraph on the road system summarizes R. Mackinnon, "Roads, Cart Tracks, and Bridle Paths: Land Transportation and the Domestic Economy of Mid-Nineteenth Century Eastern British North America" (2003) 84 Can. Hist. Rev. 177; R. Evans, *Transportation and Communication in Nova Scotia, 1815-1850* (M.A. thesis, Dalhousie University, 1936) [unpublished]; and Evans, "Stage Coaches in Nova Scotia, 1815-1867" (1938) 24 Collections of the Nova Scotia Historical Society 107.

64 Bliss to Henry Bliss (8 October 1831), NSARM, Bliss Papers (MG 1, vol. 1598, no. 292); Stewart to Wiswall (21 August 1818), NSARM, Wiswall Papers (MG 1, vol. 980, no. 66).

65 Bliss to Lieutenant-Governor (30 January 1836), Selections (RG 1, vol. 241, no. 15).

66 White, *supra* note 10 at 7.

67 Wilkins to Wiswall (4 August 1831), NSARM, Wiswall Papers (MG 1, vol. 979, folder 7, no. 19); and Stewart to Wiswall (23 August 1824), *ibid.* (vol. 980, no. 94).

68 Stewart to Wiswall (23 August 1824), *ibid.* (vol. 980, no. 94).

69 Bliss to Henry Bliss (17 July 1839), NSARM, Bliss Papers (MG 1, vol. 1599, no. 47).

70 Stewart to Wiswall (20 December 1820), NSARM, Wiswall Papers (MG 1, vol. 980, no. 76).

71 Council Minutes (6 February 1822 and 23 February 1823), Selections (RG 1, vol. 214.5, at 110-12 and 173-74).

72 Wilkins to Wiswall (5 August 1823), NSARM, Wiswall Papers (MG 1, vol. 979, folder 6, no. 13).

73 *Assembly Journals* (2 April 1830), *supra* note 16 at 732. The grant was continued annually until 1840.

74 Halliburton to Lieutenant-Governor Campbell (11 February 1836), Selections (RG 1, vol. 241, no. 27).

75 *Judiciary Act,* S.N.S. 1841, c. 3, s. 44.

76 Halliburton, Bliss, Wilkins, Hill, and Haliburton to Lieutenant-Governor Falkland (29 April 1842) in *Assembly Journals* (1842), *supra* note 16, Appendix 63.

77 Stewart to Wiswall (29 January 1822 and 20 April 1829), NSARM, Wiswall Papers (MG 1, vol. 980, nos. 80 and 146).

78 Bliss to Henry Bliss (17 March 1834), NSARM, Bliss Papers (MG 1, vol. 1599, no. 16); Halliburton to Wiswall (13 July 1825), NSARM, Wiswall Papers (MG 1, vol. 979, folder 5, no. 3).

79 Stewart to Wiswall (25 July 1825, 28 August 1826, 16 February 1827, and 26 August 1827), NSARN, Wiswall Papers (MG 1, vol. 980, nos. 102, 110, 114, and 120).

80 Halliburton to Wiswall (13 July 1825), *ibid.* (vol. 979, folder 5, no. 3).

81 Bliss to Henry Bliss (17 December 1844), NSARM, Bliss Papers (MG 1, vol. 1599, no. 93).

82 Philip V. Girard, *Patriot Jurist: Beamish Murdoch of Halifax, 1800-1876* (Ph.D. thesis, Dalhousie University, 1998) at 117-53 [unpublished].

83 King to Halli Fraser (n.d. [1830 or 1831]), quoted in A.T. Marion, *Harry King's Courtship Letters, 1829-1831* (M.A. thesis, Acadia University, 1986) at 329 [unpublished].

84 Bliss to Henry Bliss (18 May 1824), NSARM, Bliss Papers (MG 1, vol. 1598, no. 246).

85 Bliss to Henry Bliss (24 June 1829), *ibid.* (no. 274).

86 Bliss to Henry Bliss (8 October 1831), *ibid.* (no. 292).

87 See, ironically, Bliss' pleasure after his elevation to the bench at noting when he opened the September 1847 term of the Court at Yarmouth that no trial of any kind had occurred in the town for four years. *Yarmouth Herald and Western Adviser* (30 September 1847).

88 NSARM, William Young Papers (MG 2, vol. 760), and *ibid.*, Daybook 1834-42 (vol. 766). We thank Bill Laurence for these references. Young had extensive mercantile connections, and it is possible that some of the sums recorded represent either non-legal work or the collection of debts for legal work done at other times.

89 Bliss to Henry Bliss (17 June 1823), NSARM, Bliss Papers (MG 1, vol. 1598, no. 239).

90 King to Fraser (30 May 1830), quoted in Marion, *supra* note 83 at 208. On the social and regulatory role of the circuit messes in England, see Raymond Cocks, *Foundations of the Modern Bar* (London: Sweet and Maxwell, 1983); and J.R. Lewis, *The Victorian Bar* (London: Robert Hale, 1982). It is clear that the custom of the mess was reproduced on the Nova Scotia circuits, although much of its regulatory role was unnecessary in the New World as a result of the combination of barristerial and solicitorial roles. On the role of the circuit in affirming the masculine ideals of the bar, see Michael Grossberg, "Institutionalizing Masculinity: The Law as a Masculine Profession" in Mark C. Carnes and Clyde Griffen, eds., *Meanings for Manhood: Constructions of Masculinity in Victorian America* (Chicago: University of Chicago Press, 1990) 133.

91 King to Fraser (8 June 1830), quoted in Marion, *ibid.* at 211.

92 King to Fraser (19 October 1830), quoted in Marion, *ibid.* at 270.

93 King to Fraser (12 June 1831), quoted in Marion, *ibid.* at 412.

94 The phrase is from Julian Gwyn, *Excessive Expectations: Maritime Commerce and the Economic Development of Nova Scotia, 1740-1870* (Montreal and Kingston: McGill-Queen's University Press, 1998).

95 See "The Decline of Circuit Life" (1881) Can. L.J. 77.

96 Although this point might be overly speculative, there is also architectural evidence for the decline of the circuit as a highly visible event. Courthouses built before mid-century all had spectators' galleries, but only two of the seven built between 1888 and 1914, those in Truro and Digby, contain such a feature, and Pictou closed up its gallery in 1887. This change in design was probably a recognition of the

declining importance of the circuit. See P. Girard, "Historic Courthouses of Nova Scotia" (2005) [unpublished].

CHAPTER 7: FAME AND INFAMY

1 *Salmond Symposium* (18-19 August 2006), online:Victoria University of Wellington, http://www.victoria.ac.nz/law/events/event_details/event_TemplatePage-Salmond.aspx.

2 John William Salmond, *First Principles of Jurisprudence* (London: Stevens and Haynes, 1893); and Salmond, *Jurisprudence: Or the Theory of the Law* (London: Stevens and Haynes, 1902).

3 The building housing the University of Victoria Law Faculty is now known as the Murray and Anne Fraser Building. "UVic Buildings," online: University of Victoria, http://www.uvic.ca/buildings/fra.html.

4 David Ricardo Williams, *Dictionary of Canadian Biography Online,* vol. 12, ed. by John English and Réal Bélanger, *s.v.* "Begbie, Sir Matthew Baillie," online: Library and Archives Canada, http://www.biographi.ca/. See also Williams, *"The Man for a New Country": Sir Matthew Baillie Begbie* (Sidney, BC: Gray's, 1977); Williams, *Matthew Baillie Begbie* (Don Mills: Fitzhenry and Whiteside, 1980); and Hamar Foster, "The Queen's Law Is Better Than Yours: International Homicide in Early British Columbia" in J. Phillips *et al.,* eds., *Essays in the History of Canadian Law,* vol. 5: *Crime and Criminal Justice in Canadian History* (Toronto: Osgoode Society for Canadian Legal History and University of Toronto Press, 1994) 41.

5 Jacinta Ruru, ed., *"In Good Faith": Symposium Proceedings Marking the 20th Anniversary of the Lands Case* (Wellington/Dunedin, NZ: New Zealand Law Foundation/University of Otago, 2008).

6 *Wi Parata v. Bishop of Wellington* (1877), 3 N.Z. Jurist Reports (New Series) 72 [*Wi Parata*].

7 A. Frame, *Dictionary of New Zealand Biography,* vol. 3 (Wellington, NZ: Auckland University Press in association with the Department of Internal Affairs, 1996) *s.v.* "Salmond, John William 1862-1924," online: http://www.dnzb.govt.nz/dnzb/.

8 A. Frame, *Salmond: Southern Jurist* (Wellington, NZ: Victoria University Press, 1995). Appendix A at 243-46 contains a full list of Salmond's publications and of those books published under his name by subsequent scholarly editors of the calibre of Glanville Williams, W.T.S. Stallybrass, Percy Winfield, and R.F.V. Heuston.

9 J. Bassett and J.G.H. Hannan, *Dictionary of New Zealand Biography,* vol. 1 (Wellington, NZ: Auckland University Press in association with the Department of Internal Affairs, 1990) *s.v.* "Prendergast, James 1826-1921."

10 P. Spiller, "The Courts and the Judiciary" in P. Spiller, J. Finn, and R. Boast, eds., *A New Zealand Legal History* (Wellington, NZ: Brookers, 1995) 174 at 194. *Wi Parata, supra* note 6 at 76.

11 See Claudia Orange, *The Treaty of Waitangi* (Wellington, NZ: Allen and Unwin, 1987).

12 For the Treaty as "founding document," see Te Puni Kokiri [Ministry of Maori Development], *He Tirohanga o Kawa ki te Tiriti o Waitangi: A Guide to the Principles of*

the Treaty of Waitangi (Wellington, NZ: Te Puni Kokiri, 2001) at 14. Another government publication is "Paths to Nationhood—Ngâ Ara Ki Te Whenuatanga," online: http://www.archives.govt.nz/. Scholarly contributions on the legal and constitutional status of the Treaty include B.V. Harris, "The Constitutional Future of New Zealand" [2004] N.Z.L. Rev. 269; Philip A. Joseph, *Constitutional and Administrative Law in New Zealand,* 3d ed. (Wellington, NZ: Brookers, 2007) at 45-91; F.M. Brookfield, *Waitangi and Indigenous Rights* (Auckland: Auckland University Press, 2006); Morag McDowell and Duncan Webb, *The New Zealand Legal System,* 2d ed. (Wellington, NZ: Butterworths, 1998) at 189-233; and P.G. McHugh, *The Maori Magna Carta: New Zealand Law and the Treaty of Waitangi* (Auckland: Oxford University Press, 1991). For the Treaty as "constitutional document," see G.W.R. Palmer, *Constitutional Conversations* (Wellington, NZ: Victoria University Press, 2002) at 22. For the Treaty as "most important document," see R. Cooke, "Introduction" (1990) 14:1 N.Z.U.L. Rev. 1 at 1; see also S. Elias, "The Treaty of Waitangi and Separation of Powers in New Zealand" in B.D. Gray and R.B. McClintock, eds., *Courts and Policy: Checking the Balance* (Wellington, NZ: Brookers, 1995) 206 at 206. See also articles by D.V. Williams, "The Constitutional Status of the Treaty of Waitangi: An Historical Perspective" (1990) 14 N.Z.U.L. Rev. 9; K.J. Keith, "The Treaty of Waitangi in the Courts" (1990) 14 N.Z.U.L. Rev. 37; E.T. Durie and G.S. Orr, "The Role of the Waitangi Tribunal and the Development of a Bicultural Jurisprudence" (1990) 14 N.Z.U.L. Rev. 62; A. Frame, "A State Servant Looks at the Treaty" (1990) 14 N.Z.U.L. Rev. 82; and A. Mikaere, "Book Review" (1990) 14 N.Z.U.L. Rev. 97 in the special sesquicentennial issue on the Treaty of Waitangi and constitutional issues. For the Treaty as "essential to the foundation of New Zealand," see *Huakina Development Trust v. Waikato Valley Authority,* [1987] 2 N.Z.L.R. 188 at 210 (H.C.), per Chilwell J. For the Treaty as "of the greatest constitutional importance," see *New Zealand Maori Council v. Attorney-General,* [1994] 1 N.Z.L.R. 513 at 516 (P.C.), per Lord Woolf.

13 *New Zealand History online: Treaty of Waitangi,* online: http://www.nzhistory.net.nz/category/tid/133.

14 G. Morris, *Chief Justice James Prendergast and the Administration of New Zealand Colonial Justice 1862-1899* (Ph.D. thesis, University of Waikato, Hamilton, 2001) [unpublished]. See also G. Morris, "James Prendergast and the Treaty of Waitangi: Judicial Attitudes to the Treaty during the Latter Half of the Nineteenth Century" (2004) 35 V.U.W.L.R. 117; and Morris, "James Prendergast and the New Zealand Parliament: Issues in the Legislative Council during the 1860s" (2005) 3 New Zealand Journal of Public and International Law 177.

15 Bassett and Hannan, *supra* note 9 at 354.

16 J.W. Tate, "*Hohepa Wi Neera:* Native Title and the Privy Council Challenge" (2004) 35 V.U.W.L.R. 73; and Tate, "The Privy Council and Native Title: A Requiem for *Wi Parata*" (2004) 12 Waikato L. Rev. 101; and Tate, "*Tamihana Korokai* and Native Title: Healing the Imperial Breach" (2005) 13 Waikato L. Rev. 108.

17 John McLaren, "'The Judicial Office ... Bowing to No Power but the Supremacy of the Law': Judges and the Rule of Law in Colonial Australia and Canada, 1788-1840" (2003) 7 Austl. J. Legal Hist. 177. See also McLaren, "The Tribulations of Judges in 'Anomalous' Colonial Societies: Were Boulton of Newfoundland and

Montagu of Van Diemen's Land Framed?" (Paper presented to Law's Empire, Canadian Law and Society Association Conference, Harrison Hot Springs, BC, June 2005) [unpublished]; McLaren, "Men of Principle or Judicial Ratbags? The Trials and Tribulations of Maverick Judges in British Colonies in the Nineteenth Century" (Public lecture, University of Auckland, 15 March 2006) [unpublished].

18 This Act is sometimes known as the *Act of Settlement 1700,* but not because it predated England's change from the Julian to the Gregorian calendar in 1752. The Act was passed in June 1701, but, before the *Acts of Parliament (Commencement) Act 1793,* statutes were deemed to have come into force on the first sitting day of the session of Parliament—which in this instance commenced in 1700.

19 R. Jones, *An Encyclopaedia of New Zealand,* ed. by A.H. McLintock (Wellington, NZ: Government Printer, 1966), *s.v.* "Prendergast, Sir James (1826-1921)," online: http://www.teara.govt.nz/1966/.

20 *In re the Ninety-Mile Beach,* [1963] N.Z.L.R. 461 at 467-68.

21 Michael Belgrave, *Historical Frictions: Maori Claims and Reinvented Histories* (Auckland: Auckland University Press, 2005) at c. 2.

22 On tuku whenua, see Waitangi Tribunal, *Muriwhenua Land Report* (Wellington, NZ: GP Publications, 1997); and (for a somewhat different perspective) Waitangi Tribunal, *The Hauraki Report,* vol. 1 (Wellington, NZ: Legislation Direct, 2006); on tuku rangatira, see the preamble to the Agreed Historical Account in "Agreement in Principle between the Crown and Ngati Whatua o Orakei, for the Settlement of the Historical Treaty Claims of Ngati Whatua o Orakei" (9 June 2006), online: Office of Treaty Settlements, http://www.ots.govt.nz/.

23 *Wi Parata, supra* note 6 at 72-73, 76.

24 *Ibid.* at 78.

25 *Ibid.* at 79.

26 *Ibid.* at 77-78.

27 *Ibid.* at 83.

28 Most reported cases in the early colonial period involving Maori litigants included all names of the litigant in the citation of the case. Furthermore, cases were indexed by reference to the first letter of the Christian name rather than the first letter of the surname as is customary in relation to European names. This is doubtless accounted for by the ignorance of New Zealand law reporters as to names in the Maori language.

29 Te Rangitaki of Te Atiawa was baptized and better known as Wiremu Kingi (William King). See A. Parsonson, *Dictionary of New Zealand Biography,* vol. 1 (Wellington, NZ: Auckland University Press in association with the Department of Internal Affairs, 1990) *s.v.* "Te Rangitaki, Wiremu Kingi, ?-1882," online: http://www.dnzb.govt.nz/dnzb/.

30 See Waitangi Tribunal, *The Taranaki Report: Kaupapa Tuatahi* (Wellington, NZ: GP Publications, 1996) at 67-87.

31 J. Starke, *Dictionary of New Zealand Biography,* vol. 1 (Wellington, NZ: Auckland University Press in association with the Department of Internal Affairs, 1990) *s.v.* "Hadfield, Octavius 1814?-1904," online: http://www.dnzb.govt.nz/dnzb/.

32 *Wi Parata, supra* note 6 at 79, 75, and 76.

33 For a North American perspective on this issue, see John Philip Reid, *Patterns of Vengeance: Crosscultural Homicide in the North American Fur Trade* (Pasadena: Ninth Circuit Historical Society, 1999).

34 A. Griffiths, "Legal Pluralism" in R. Banakar and M. Travers, eds., *An Introduction to Law and Social Theory* (Oxford: Hart, 2002) 289. See also Harry Arthurs, *Without the Law: Administrative Justice and Legal Pluralism in Nineteenth Century England* (Toronto: University of Toronto Press, 1985) at 1-3.

35 D.V. Williams, "Unique Treaty-Based Relationships Remain Elusive" in M. Belgrave, M. Kawharu, and D.V. Williams, eds., *Waitangi Revisited: Perspectives on the Treaty of Waitangi* (Melbourne: Oxford University Press, 2005) 366. See also Williams, "Te Taha Maori Recognised" (1983) 9 Recent Law 378; Williams, "The Recognition of 'Native Custom' in Tanganyika and New Zealand: Legal Pluralism or Mono-cultural Imposition" in P. Sack and E. Minchin, eds., *Legal Pluralism* (Canberra: Australian National University, 1986) 145; Williams, "Te Tiriti o Waitangi — Unique Relationship between Crown and Tangata Whenua?" in I.H. Kawharu, ed., *Waitangi: Maori and Pakeha Perspectives of the Treaty of Waitangi* (Auckland: Oxford University Press, 1989) 64; and Williams, "The Waitangi Tribunal and Legal Pluralism: A Re-assessment" (1994) 10 Austl. J.L. Soc. 195.

36 *Wi Parata, supra* note 6 at 78.

37 Texts and translations of the Treaty are compiled in Belgrave, Kawharu, and Williams, eds., *supra* note 35 at 388-93.

38 P.G. McHugh, *Aboriginal Societies and the Common Law* (Oxford: Oxford University Press, 2004) at 506, nn. 333-36; and McHugh, "New Dawn to Cold Light: Courts and Common Law Aboriginal Rights" [2005] N.Z.L. Rev. 485 at 506, n. 61.

39 *Wi Parata, supra* note 6 at 73, 79.

40 *Te Heuheu Tukino v. Aotea District Maori Land Board,* [1941] N.Z.L.R. 590, [1941] A.C. 308.

41 Anglo-American Arbitral Tribunal, "Award of 12 December 1925" (1926) 20 A.J.I.L. 391, cited by B. Kingsbury, "The Treaty of Waitangi: Some International Law Aspects" in I.H. Kawharu, ed., *Waitangi: Maori and Pakeha Perspectives of the Treaty of Waitangi* (Auckland: Oxford University Press, 1989) 121 at 125, n. 23.

42 *New Zealand Maori Council v. Attorney-General,* [1987] 1 N.Z.L.R. 641 at 667-68 (C.A.); and Cooke, *supra* note 12.

43 *New Zealand Maori Council v. Attorney-General,* [1994] 1 N.Z.L.R. 513 (P.C.).

44 Te Puni Kokiri, *supra* note 12.

45 Williams, "Te Tiriti o Waitangi," *supra* note 35 at 76-84; and Williams, "Unique Treaty-Based," *supra* note 35 at 369-70.

46 *Ngati Apa v. Attorney-General,* [2003] 3 N.Z.L.R 643 (C.A.) [*Ngati Apa*]; M. Chen, "A Public Law Assessment of the Treaty of Waitangi's Constitutional Future" (Paper presented to the 8th Annual Public Law Forum, Wellington, NZ, 21 March 2006) [unpublished].

47 J. Salmond, "Memorandum. Notes on the History of Native-Land Legislation," Native Land Bill, House of Representatives, *Bills Books, no. 87-3* (Wellington, NZ: Government Printer, 1909) 1.

48 *Wi Parata, supra* note 6 at 78.

49 *Nireaha Tamaki v. Baker* (1894), 12 N.Z.L.R. 483.

50 *Ibid.* at 488.

51 Salmond, *supra* note 47 at 1.

52 *Ibid.*

53 *Nireaha Tamaki v. Baker,* [1901] A.C. 561 at 577-78.

54 *Ngati Apa, supra* note 46.

55 Salmond, *supra* note 47 at 1.

56 The input of Maori lawyers in the drafting of *Te Ture Whenua Maori/Maori Land Act 1993* finally led to the repeal of Salmond's Crown-sourced definition of customary land and its replacement in s. 129(2)(a) by a definition based on Maori customary law: "[L]and that is held by Maori in accordance with tikanga Maori shall have the status of Maori customary land."

57 *Native Land Claims Adjustment and Laws Amendment Act 1901,* s. 27.

58 *New Zealand Parliamentary Debates* (1902), vol. 122 at 374-92, 641-54, and 686-92.

59 *Maori Land Claims and Adjustment and Laws Amendment Act 1904,* s. 4.

60 M.P.K. Sorrenson, *Dictionary of New Zealand Biography,* vol. 3 (Wellington, NZ: Auckland University Press in association with the Department of Internal Affairs, 1996) *s.v.* "Ngata, Apirana Turupa 1874-1950," online: http://www.dnzb.govt.nz/dnzb/.

61 Salmond to Ngata (22 December 1909), Crown Law Office, Wellington, "Case File 84," quoted in Frame, *supra* note 8 at 114.

CHAPTER 8: MOVING IN AN "ECCENTRIC ORBIT"

1 John P.S. McLaren, "'The Judicial Office ... Bowing to No Power but the Supremacy of the Law': Judges and the Rule of Law in Colonial Australia and Canada, 1788-1840" (2003) 7:2 Austl. J. Legal Hist. 177 at 178; see also David Neal, *The Rule of Law in a Penal Colony: Law and Power in Early New South Wales* (Cambridge: Cambridge University Press, 1991) at c. 4.

2 Robert Stevens, "The Act of Settlement and the Questionable History of Judicial Independence" (2001) 1 O.U.C.L.J. 253.

3 McLaren, *supra* note 1 at 187-88.

4 *Ibid.* at 191-92.

5 D.M. Klerman and P.C. Mahoney, "The Value of Judicial Independence: Evidence from Eighteenth-Century England" in P. Brand, K. Costello, and W.N. Osborough, eds., *Adventures of the Law: Proceedings of the Sixteenth British Legal History Conference* (Dublin: Four Courts Press, 2005) 139 at 144.

6 Stevens, *supra* note 2 at 264; Neal, *supra* note 1 at 87.

7 Alex Castles, *An Australian Legal History* (Sydney: Law Book Company, 1982) at 239-43, 276-79, and 407-8.

8 *Hobart Town Courier* (5 January 1848) 1 at 2.

9 *Launceston Advertiser* (16 August 1844) 1 at 3 [emphasis in original].

10 For a critique of "essentialist biographies," see R.A. Posner, "Objectivity and Hagiography in Judicial Biography" (1995) 70 N.Y.U.L. Rev. 503.

11 *Colonial Times* (28 December 1847) 1 at 2.

12 *Colonial Times* (27 December 1842) 1 at 2.

13 The mutual "antipathy" between the judges was well known. See John M. Bennett, *Sir John Pedder: First Chief Justice of Tasmania, 1824-1854* (Sydney: Federation Press, 2003) at 76.

14 *Colonial Times* (2 May 1843) 1 at 2.

15 The major works on Montagu are Robert Baker, "The Early Judges of Tasmania" (1960) 8 Tasmanian Historical Research Association Papers and Proceedings 71 at 78-80; P.A. Howell, "The Van Diemen's Land Judge Storm" (1966) 2 U. Tasm. L. Rev. 253; Howell, "Of Ships and Sealing Wax: The Montagus, the Navy and the Law" (1966) 13 Tasmanian Historical Research Association Papers and Proceedings 101; B.A. Keon-Cohen, "Mad Judge Montagu: A Misnomer" (1975) 2 Monash U.L. Rev. 50; and Richard Ely, ed., *Carrel Inglis Clark: The Supreme Court of Tasmania: Its First Century, 1824-1924* (Hobart: University of Tasmania Law Press, 1995).

16 Howell, "Of Ships," *ibid.* at 101-13.

17 Michael Charles Ivan Levy, *Governor George Arthur: A Colonial Benevolent Despot* (Melbourne: Georgian House, 1953) at 63.

18 *Colonial Times* (20 May 1834) 1 at 5.

19 Montagu to Arthur (29 August 1836), Hobart, Archives Office of Tasmania (AOT), (Executive Council [EC]) 2/3.

20 *Colonial Times* (14 September 1831) 1 at 2.

21 *Colonial Times* (2 October 1832) 1 at 2.

22 Arthur to Goderich (28 October 1831), Australian Joint Copying Project (AJCP), (Colonial Office [CO]) 280/30 at 238, D. 60.

23 *Australian Dictionary of Biography*, vol. 1, ed. by Douglas Pike (Melbourne: Melbourne University Press, 1966) *s.v.* "Baxter, Alexander Macduff (1798-1836?)."

24 Arthur to Goderich (25 March 1833) AJCP (CO 280/41, D. 21); Arthur to Hanley (19 December 1833) AJCP (CO 280/43 at 462, D. 60).

25 For an account of the newspapers, see Edmund Morris Miller, *Pressmen and Governors: Australian Editors and Writers in Early Tasmania* (Sydney: Sydney University Press, 1973).

26 *Colonist* (8 February 1833) 1 at 2.

27 *Colonial Times* (5 February 1833) 1 at 2.

28 *Colonial Times* (13 August 1833) 1 at 2.

29 *Colonial Times* (14 July 1835) 1 at 5 [emphasis in original]; for Robertson's defence, see Robertson, Letter to the Editor, *True Colonist* (24 July 1835) 1 at 2.

30 *Colonial Times* (7 February 1837) 1 at 7.

31 *Ibid.*

32 *Hobart Town Courier* (11 June 1841) 1 at 2.

33 *Colonial Times* (7 February 1837) 1 at 4 [emphasis in original]; *True Colonist* (7 April 1837) 1 at 4.

34 C. Graig, *Australian Dictionary of Biography*, vol. 2, ed. by A.G.L. Shaw and C.M.H. Clark (Melbourne: Melbourne University Press, 1967) *s.v.* "Lyttleton, William Thomas (1786?-1839)" at 143; Levy, *supra* note 17 at 351; and Bennett, *supra* note 13 at 91. An assigned convict was a convict assigned as a labourer to a free settler by the Convict Department.

35 Arthur to Stanley (25 October 1834), Colonial Office to Arthur (10 July 1835) AJCP (CO 280/50 at 301, D. 63); Arthur to Stanley (17 December 1834) AJCP (CO 280/52 at 118, D. 79); *Colonial Times* (3 May 1836) 1 at 4; Keon-Cohen, *supra* note 15 at 59-61.

36 For Jeffreys, see H. Montgomery Hyde, *Judge Jeffreys,* 2d ed. (London: Butterworths, 1948).

37 Arthur to Stanley (25 October 1834), Colonial Office to Arthur (10 July 1835) AJCP (CO 280/50 at 301, D. 63); *Colonial Times* (29 December 1835) 1 at 4.

38 The Executive Council, modelled on the Privy Council, comprised the Lieutenant-Governor and heads of bureaucratic departments as well as the Chief Justice of the colony. Alex Castles, *Lawless Harvests or God Save the Judges: Van Diemen's Land 1803-1853, A Legal History* (Melbourne: Australian Scholarly Publishing, 2007) at 102.

39 Colonial Office to Arthur (10 July 1835) AJCP (CO 280/50 at 301, D. 63); Law officers to Glenelg (17 January 1837) AOT, (Governor's Office [GO]) 1/26 at 483, D. 159.

40 *Colonial Times* (10 July 1838) 1 at 4; Normanby to Franklin (30 March 1839) AOT (GO 1/33 at 341, D. 36).

41 *Colonist* (27 May 1834) 1 at 2.

42 *Independent* (17 May 1834) 1 at 3.

43 *Colonial Times* (29 December 1835, 24 July 1838) 1 at 4 and 1 at 4.

44 Howell, "Of Ships," *supra* note 15 at 116.

45 See also the case of T.G. Gregson, who was fined £200 and imprisoned for three months but ultimately released by Franklin. See *Colonial Times* (7 February 1837) 1 at 4; and Kathleen Fitzpatrick, *Sir John Franklin in Tasmania 1837-1843* (Melbourne: Melbourne University Press, 1949) at 119-20.

46 *Colonial Times* (18 May 1841, 27 December 1842) 1 at 2 and 1 at 3; Alfred Stephen, Letter to the Editor, *Colonial Times* (17 April 1849) 1 at 3; *Launceston Advertiser* (16 August 1844) 1 at 3; Ely, *supra* note 15 at 204-5.

47 *Colonial Times* (17 April 1849) 1 at 2-3; *A Dictionary of New Zealand Biography,* vol. 2, ed. by G.H. Scholefield (Wellington, NZ: Department of Internal Affairs, 1940) *s.v.* "Stephen, Sidney (1797-1858)."

48 *Colonist* (6 May 1834) 1 at 2.

49 *Colonist* (20 May 1834) 1 at 2.

50 See also the case of Samuel Yates. Stephen to Arthur (30 September 1836) AOT (EC 2/3).

51 *Hobart Town Courier* (9 August 1844) 1 at 2.

52 *Hobart Town Advertiser* (31 May 1842) 1 at 2; *Tasmanian and Austral-Asiatic Review* (21 October 1842) 1 at 3.

53 *Hobart Town Advertiser* (31 May 1842) 1 at 2; *Colonial Times* (13 June 1843) 1 at 3.

54 *Hobart Town Courier* (9 August 1844) 1 at 2.

55 Bennett, *supra* note 13 at 80-81.

56 *Hobart Town Courier* (19 February 1841) 1 at 2.

57 Montagu to Colonial Secretary (24 July 1840) AOT (GO 39/3 at 127); Pedder found it difficult to resist the desire to "compromise opinions." Bennett, *supra* note 13 at 81.

58 See also the very strong views expressed in the *True Colonist* (16 February 1844) 1 at 2; *Launceston Advertiser* (16 August 1844) 1 at 3; and *Hobart Town Advertiser* (5 August 1845) 1 at 2.

59 Franklin to Russell (15 October 1840) AJCP (CO 280/121 at 240, D. 131); Eardley-Wilmot to Stanley (8 December 1843) AOT (GO 33/46 at 846, D. 39, petition at 856); for an analysis of the first six occasions, see Ross to Colonial Secretary (13 August 1840) AJCP (CO 280/121 at 292).

60 Eardley-Wilmot to Stanley (5 March 1844), and Eardley-Wilmot to petitioners (5 March 1844) AOT (GO 33/47 at 598, D. 57); Stanley to Eardley-Wilmot (5 May 1845) AOT (GO 1/71 at 49, D. 430).

61 *Colonial Times* (10 November 1840) 1 at 4.

62 Bennett, *supra* note 13 at 76.

63 *Hobart Town Advertiser* (10 December 1841) 1 at 2; in a letter of 24 July 1840, Montagu had written at length on the need to reform the constitution of the Supreme Court. Van Diemen's Land was "too young for the application of the system which is in motion and which in England has grown to its present perplexity through a series of centuries." He went on to argue for a number of reforms, including that of equity. Montagu to Forster (24 July 1840) AJCP (CO 280/121 at 271).

64 Castles, *supra* note 7 at 405-6.

65 Fitzpatrick, *supra* note 45 at 97.

66 *Austral-Asiatic Review* (18 December 1838, 8 January 1839) 1 at 4 and 1 at 4.

67 *Bent's News* (17 August 1838) 1 at 2.

68 *Bent's News, ibid.* 1 at 2.

69 Franklin to Russell (6 January 1841) AJCP (CO 280/129 at 53, D. 6); *Hobart Town Courier* (8 December 1840) 1 at 2; *Austral-Asiatic Review* (15 December 1840) 1 at 4.

70 *Hobart Town Courier* (8 December 1840) 1 at 2.

71 Franklin to Russell (6 February 1841) AJCP (CO 280/129 at 374, D. 70).

72 Stanley to Franklin (27 September 1842) AOT (GO 1/47 at 569, D.159).

73 Stephen to Arthur (9 July 1836) AOT (EC 2/3); see also Stephen to Arthur (5 September and 30 September 1836), *ibid.*

74 Stephen to Arthur (9 July 1836) AOT (EC 2/3) [emphasis in original]; see also Stephen to Arthur (5 September and 30 September 1836), *ibid.*

75 Castles, *supra* note 38 at 112.

76 Stephen to Arthur (11 August 1836) AOT (EC 2/3).

77 Montagu to Arthur (29 August 1836) AOT (EC 2/3) [emphasis in original].

78 *Ibid.*

79 Montagu to Arthur (19 September 1836) AOT (EC 2/3) [emphasis in original].

80 *Colonial Times* (7 June 1836) 1 at 6.

81 Arthur to Glenelg (26 October 1836) AJCP (CO 280/74 at 3, D. 100) [emphasis in original].

82 Glenelg to Franklin (7 August 1837) AOT (GO 1/26 at 627, D. 171).

83 *Launceston Advertiser* (25 January, 1 February 1838) 1 at 2 and 1 at 2.

84 *True Colonist* (10 July 1844) 1 at 2; John West, *The History of Tasmania,* ed. by A.G.L. Shaw (Sydney: Angus and Robertson, 1971) at 178; Keon-Cohen, *supra* note 15 at 63.

85 *Hobart Town Courier* (28 June 1844) 1 at 2.

86 *Ibid.;* death recorded meant a formal sentence of death, without an intention that the sentence would be carried out. Under (1823) 4 Geo. IV., c. 48, s. 1, except in cases of murder, the Judge had considerable discretion where an offender was convicted of a felony punishable by death. If the Judge thought that the circumstances made the offender fit for the exercise of royal mercy, then, instead of sentencing the offender to death, he could order that judgment of death be recorded. The effect was the same as if judgment of death had been ordered and the offender reprieved (s. 2).

87 *Hobart Town Courier* (28 June 1844) 1 at 2.

88 *True Colonist* (10 July 1844) 1 at 2; Ely, *supra* note 15 at 32-33.

89 *Hobarton Guardian* (28 August 1847) 1 at 2.

90 Montagu to Denison (28 December 1847) AJCP (CO 280/223 at 501).

91 The ending of the assignment system also meant that Montagu lost the benefit of convict servants to work his land. Howell, "The Van Diemen's Land," *supra* note 15 at 255.

92 *Ibid.* at 501. Soon after his appointment as Judge, Montagu sought leave to return to England, claiming that, were the leave denied, he would suffer "a very heavy pecuniary sacrifice." The leave was granted and he sold his law library, but for reasons that are obscure did not take his leave. Arthur to Glenelg (10 September 1835), Colonial Office to Arthur (22 March 1836), Montagu to Arthur (4 August 1835) AJCP (CO 280/59 at 67, D. 66); Howell, "The Van Diemen's Land," *supra* note 15 at 267.

93 *True Colonist* (7 October 1836) 1 at 10; Keon-Cohen, *supra* note 15 at 56.

94 Stanley to Eardley-Wilmot (17 July 1843) AOT (GO 1/51 at 123, D. 57).

95 Stanley to Eardley-Wilmot (26 June 1844) AOT (GO 1/54 at 414, D. 225).

96 Eardley-Wilmot to Stanley (18 December 1844) AJCP (CO 280/173 at 437, D. 265).

97 Denison to Grey (17 January 1848) AJCP (CO 280/223 at 405, D. 19).

98 *Colonial Times* (30 November 1847) 1 at 3; Keon-Cohen, *supra* note 15 at 67-72; Bennett, *supra* note 13 at 96-102.

99 Howell, "The Van Diemen's Land," *supra* note 15 at 258; the Solicitor General estimated that four-fifths of the colony's revenue was at risk. Howell, *ibid.* at 264.

100 Denison to Grey (17 January 1848), Young to Bicheno (3 December 1847), Minute by Denison (6 December 1847), AJCP (CO 280/223 at 405, D. 19); *Hobart Town Advertiser* (12 December 1848) 1 at 2.

101 Denison to Grey (17 January 1848), Young to Bicheno (3 December 1847), Minute by Denison (6 December 1847), AJCP (CO 280/223 at 405, D. 19).

102 In Young to Bicheno, *ibid.,* Young referred to Montagu's mistreatment of Sidney Stephen, and this might have been a motive for seeking his removal. Moreover, Montagu had used strong language against Young in an assault case and shown partiality to his attacker Rowlands. Young complained to Franklin. Franklin to Glenelg (21 February 1839) AOT (GO 33/31 at 1138, D. 38).

103 Montagu to Denison (28 December 1847) AJCP (CO 280/223 at 501).

104 Denison to Grey (17 January 1848) AJCP (CO 280/223 at 405, D. 19).

105 Denison to Grey (23 January 1848) AJCP (CO 280/223 at 617, Separate Dispatch).

106 Minute by Merivale (2 June 1848), AJCP (CO 280/223 at 622); see also Minute by Merivale (19 June 1848), AJCP (CO 280/224 at 261), where Merivale questioned "whether 'amoval' was the proper course"; Howell, "Of Ships," *supra* note 15 at 122.

107 Minute by Merivale (19 June 1848), AJCP (CO 280/224 at 50); Grey to Denison (30 June 1848) AOT (GO 1/69 at 161, D. 105).

108 Minute by Merivale (19 June 1848), AJCP (CO 280/224 at 141).

109 For criticism of Montagu, see *Hobart Town Courier* (1 December 1847) 1 at 2; *Colonial Times* (26 November 1847) 1 at 3; and *Hobart Town Advertiser* (4 January 1848) 1 at 2.

110 *Hobart Town Courier* (8 January 1848) 1 at 2.

111 *Hobart Town Courier* (15 January 1848) 1 at 2; Howell, "The Van Diemen's Land," *supra* note 15 at 256.

112 *Examiner* (8 January 1848) 1 at 5 [capitals in original].

113 *Hobart Town Courier* (19 January 1848) 1 at 3; Howell, "The Van Diemen's Land," *supra* note 15 at 265 ignores Brewer's speech.

114 *Colonial Times* (1 February 1848) 1 at 2.

115 One smaller creditor did demand his money, and this was paid by Charles Rowlands, son of one of Montagu's old friends. *Ibid.*

116 Greville to Merivale (18 July 1849) AOT (GO 1/74 at 89).

117 Colonial Office to Denison (10 November 1849) AJCP (CO 280/223 at 565, D. 23). In a dispatch dated 6 September 1849 that was marked "cancelled," the Colonial Office expressed concern that Horne also suffered from "pecuniary difficulties" that might "affect his independence" and that this would further weaken "public confidence" in the judiciary. *Colonial Times* (7 January 1848) 1 at 2; Howell, "The Van Diemen's Land," *supra* note 15 at 267.

118 *Hansard's Parliamentary Debates,* 3d ser., vol. 107, cols. 251-61 at col. 256 (12 July 1849).

119 W. Denison and C. Denison, *Varieties of Vice-Regal Life (Van Diemen's Land Section),* ed. by Richard Davis and Stefan Petrow (Hobart: Tasmanian Historical Research Association, 2004) at 98-99.

120 See London's *Daily News* (2 August 1848), as cited in the *Examiner* (16 December 1848) 1 at 3.

121 P.A. Howell, *Australian Dictionary of Biography,* vol. 2, ed. by A.G.L. Shaw and C.M.H. Clark (Melbourne: Melbourne University Press, 1967) *s.v.* "Montagu, Algernon Sidney (1802-1880)."

CHAPTER 9:
"NOT IN KEEPING WITH THE TRADITIONS OF THE CARIBOO COURTS"

1 Cyril Hare, *Tragedy at Law* (London: Pan Books, 1999; first published 1942) at 5-9. Thanks to John McLaren, whose keen interest in judges and English police procedurals compelled him to bring Hare's novel to my attention.

2 Douglas Hay, "Property, Authority, and the Criminal Law" in Douglas Hay *et al.,* eds., *Albion's Fatal Tree: Crime and Society in Eighteenth-Century England* (London: Penguin Books, 1977) 17.

3 On the politicized assessment of character for potential judges, see Jonathan Swainger, *The Canadian Department of Justice and the Completion of Confederation, 1867-78* (Vancouver: UBC Press, 2000) at 98-110.

4 John McLaren wrote in 1986 that the extension of legal traditions and institutions from the more settled parts of the nation "to what was at first a sparsely populated, racially sensitive frontier society, and later to a swelling expectant multiracial populace is in itself cause for a careful and extensive study." Although he was referring to the central and southern portions of the Canadian West, his perspective is well suited for the Peace country of northeastern British Columbia. See John McLaren, "Preface" in Louis A. Knafla, ed., *Law and Justice in a New Land: Essays in Western Canadian Legal History* (Calgary: Carswell, 1986) at xiiv-xiv.

5 See Benedict Anderson, *Imagined Communities: Reflections on the Origin and Spread of Nationalism,* rev. ed. (London: Verso, 2002).

6 Although the "Cariboo" typically refers to the central interior region of British Columbia, the northeastern portion of the province was included in the Cariboo administrative district. The revised statutes of 1924 made specific reference to the Peace River watershed as being part of the Cariboo district. See *An Act Respecting the Territorial Division of British Columbia for Judicial and Other Purposes,* R.S.B.C. 1924, c. 50, s. 2(1). The Peace region remained within the Cariboo judicial district until at least 1960.

7 See Kenneth Coates and William Morrison, *The Alaska Highway in World War II: The US Army Occupation in Canada's Northwest* (Toronto: University of Toronto Press, 1992); and Heath Twichell, *Northwest Epic: The Building of the Alaska Highway* (New York: St. Martin's Press, 1992).

8 See "Dawson Creek Explosion and Investigation," Victoria, BC Archives (BCA) (GR 1723, reel B7472); *Rex v. Miller Construction Company Incorporated,* BCA (GR 2235, box 2, file 53/43); and "Explosion at Dawson Creek" *Peace River Record [PRR]* (19 February 1943) 1.

9 "Dawson Creek Village Commissioners Resign" *Peace River Block News [PRBN]* (22 April 1943) 1. On increasing disorder, see the *PRBN* columns throughout 1944 and 1945.

10 [Margaret Murray], "Ho Hum—There's No Crime Wave Here Anyhow!" *Alaska Highway News [AHN]* (6 December 1945) at 1.

11 [Margaret Murray], "Crime-Free St. John Leaves Cops Time for Community Betterment" *AHN* (12 September 1946) 1.

12 For coverage of the Weigner case, see [Margaret Murray], "Murder Charge Follows Discovery of Body on Alcan Highway; Self Confessed Slayer Will Come Here for Hearing; Coroners Jury Adjourned—BC Police Will Seek Protection of Justice for Travellers on Highway" *AHN* (2 September 1948) 1; [Murray], "Wiegner's Guilty Conscience Was His Undoing; Trigger Finger Pulled Him into Confession of Fatal Shooting" *AHN* (9 September 1948) 1; [Murray], "Highway Murder Case to Higher Court" *AHN* (9 September 1948) 1; [Murray], "'I Like Him—I Like Him!' I Still Like Him Says Victim's Daughter" *AHN* (9 September 1948) 3.

13   *R. v. Gustav Weigner,* BCA (GR 2036, box 1, file 58/48). For newspaper coverage, see the *Prince George Citizen* [*PGC*] of 30 September and 14 October 1948. The spelling of Weigner's name varies in all sources on the case.

14   [Margaret Murray], "Sordid Shooting Case Ends; Weigner Gets Two Years" *AHN* (14 October 1948) at 1. On the Potter case, see *R. v. Byron Bruce Potter,* BCA (GR 2036, box 1, file 27/45); and *R. v. Byron Bruce Potter,* Ottawa, Library and Archives Canada (RG 13, box 1650, file CC 584).

15   Jonathan Swainger, "Breaking the Peace: Fictions of the Law-Abiding Peace River Country, 1930-50" (Autumn 1998) 119 BC Studies 5.

16   Report on William E. Innes, suicide, 7 June 1926, Dawson Creek Court House, pre-1930 estate files and Inquest on the body of William Innes, BCA (MSS 1134, box 8, file 18). See also "Confessed Double Murder Before Committing Suicide" *PRR* (6 May 1926) 1.

17   Author interview with "Short" Tompkins, Fort St. John, BC, 15 April 1999.

18   Author interview with Jeanne Clelland, Fort St. John, BC, 2 August 2000.

19   Author interview with [name withheld], Prince George, BC, 22 March 2003. See Jonathan Swainger, "Creating the Peace: Crime and Community Identity in North-eastern British Columbia, 1930-1950" in Louis A. Knafla, ed., *Violent Crime in North America* (Westport: Praeger, 2003) 131.

20   Inquisition upon the body of Morely Reid Kier, 9 December 1937, BCA (GR 1327, reel B2445, file 329/37); *Rex v. Belo Mathews,* BCA (GR 2239, box 3, file 14/38); and "Inquest Held on Death of Morley Reid Kier" *PRBN* (17 December 1937) 3.

21   "Pouce Coupé Park Maliciously Damaged" *PRBN* (27 October 1938) at 1.

22   C.A. Dawson assisted by R.W. Murchie, *The Settlement of the Peace River Country—A Study of a Pioneer Area* (Toronto: Macmillan, 1934) at 35.

23   See "Editorial" *PRBN* (30 May 1940) 2, for a commentary on the gas and oil prospects in the Peace region. The column had been inspired by an editorial authored by George Murray, MLA, and owner of the *Bridge River-Lillooet News.* Both George and Margaret Murray would move to Fort St. John to establish the *Alaska Highway News* in 1944.

24   Jonathan Swainger, "'Ordinary Duty' in the Peace and Police Culture in British Columbia, 1910-1939" in Jonathan Swainger and Constance Backhouse, eds., *People and Place: Historical Influences on Legal Culture* (Vancouver: UBC Press, 2003) 198.

25   This section's subheading is, of course, a reference to David Ricardo Williams, "*The Man for a New Country": Sir Matthew Baillie Begbie* (Sidney, BC: Gray's, 1977). Hamar Foster, "The Struggle for the Supreme Court: Law and Politics in British Columbia, 1871-1885" in Louis A. Knafla, ed., *Law and Justice in a New Land: Essays in Western Canadian Legal History* (Calgary: Carswell, 1986) 167.

26   *An Act Respecting the Jurisdiction and Procedure of County Courts,* S.B.C. 1905, c. 14, s. 62. Legislative attempts to create a County Court system in British Columbia date from September 1867, but it took the better part of two decades to fashion a working system.

27   *Ibid.* at s. 29.

28   David R. Verchere, *A Progression of Judges: A History of the Supreme Court of British Columbia* (Vancouver: UBC Press, 1988) at 154; and T.M. Eastwood and Paul

Williamson, *Dictionary of Canadian Biography*, vol. 11, ed. by Francess G. Halpenny and Jean Hamelin (Toronto: University of Toronto Press, 1982) *s.v.* "Robertson, Alexander Rocke."

29 Foster, *supra* note 25 at 181-83.

30 "Of Provincial and General Interest" *Kamloops Standard Sentinel* (6 October 1916) at 3.

31 See Hamar Foster, "The Kamloops Outlaws and Commissions of Assize in Nineteenth-Century British Columbia" in David H. Flaherty, ed., *Essays in the History of Canadian Law,* vol. 2 (Toronto: University of Toronto Press for the Osgoode Society for Canadian Legal History, 1983) 308; Foster, *supra* note 25; and Williams, *supra* note 25.

32 See "'Bob' Fry Accompanies Judge Robertson to Pouce Coupé" *PRBN* (29 September 1938) 1; and "Local and Personal" *PRBN* (21 September 1939) 2.

33 "Judge Robertson Returns from North" *Prince George Star* (3 November 1916) at 3.

34 *Ibid.*

35 Daily Provincial Police Report [Police Report], October 1917, BCA (GR 445, box 41, file 5); Police Report, September 1918, BCA (GR 445, box 45, file 3); Police Report, September 1919, BCA (GR 445, box 54, file 15); and Police Report, September 1920, BCA (GR 445, box 59, file 3). The arrival of Robertson's daughters was noted in the police report for 24 September 1919.

36 On the notion of duty, see Modris Ecksteins, *Rites of Spring—The Great War and the Birth of the Modern Age* (Toronto: Lester and Orpen Dennys, 1989) at 175-91.

37 "Judge Struggled in River's Icy Waters When Boat Capsized" *PRR* (30 September 1926) 1.

38 *Ibid.*

39 Monica Storrs diary, entry for September 1936 at 6, Fort St. John, North Peace Museum; and "Local and Personal" *PRBN* (25 September 1936) 4.

40 See Police Report, September 1918, BCA (GR 445, box 45, file 3); Police Report, September 1919, BCA (GR 445, box 54, file 15); and Police Report, September 1920, BCA (GR 445, box 59, file 3).

41 Esme Tuck, *A Brief History of Pouce Coupé Village and District* (Dawson Creek: Pouce Coupé Women's Institute, n.d.) at 6.

42 "Local and Personal" *PRBN* (11 June 1937) at 4; and "Local School Wins Judge Robertson Cup" *PRBN* (18 June 1937) 1.

43 See "Pouce Coupe News" *PRBN* (26 January 1932) 1.

44 See "George Hart" in Lillian York, ed., *Lure of the South Peace: Tales of the Early Pioneers to 1945* (Dawson Creek: Peace River Block News, 1981) 177; private conversation with author.

45 Georgina Keddell, *The Newspapering Murrays* (Toronto: McClelland and Stewart, 1967) at 176.

46 "Final Rites Observed for Judge Robertson, Veteran Cariboo Jurist" *PGC* (7 May 1942) at 1.

47 See generally Dawson and Murchie, *supra* note 22.

48 "Sentenced to Five Month Imprisonment" *PRBN* (21 April 1931) 1; and *R. v. Dan Lawson,* BCA (GR 2235, file 19/31).

49 "Heavy Sentences Issued to Men for Breaking and Entering" *PRBN* (13 October 1931) at 1.

50 *Ibid.*

51 "Judge Robertson Issues Warning" *PRBN* (16 January 1934) 1.

52 "Pouce Coupé Assize," BCA (GR 1723, reel B7426).

53 "Pouce Coupé News" *PRBN* (16 June 1938) 4.

54 "Pouce Coupé Assize," BCA (GR 1723, reel B7426).

55 *Rex v. Moody,* BCA (GR 2036, box 1, file 119/44). See also "Burt Miller Acquitted Manslaughter Charge" *PRBN* (21 June 1945) 1.

56 R.R. Earle, K.C., Dawson Creek, to W.R. Colvin, Assistant Departmental Solicitor, Victoria (14 June 1945), "Pouce Coupé Assize," BCA (GR 1723, reel B7426). On Mohammed Slyman, see Earle, "A Man Who Knew Furs" in Marguerite Davies and Cora Ventress, eds., *Fort St. John Pioneer Profiles* (Fort St. John: Fort St. John Centennial Committee, 1971) 32.

57 R.R. Earle, K.C., Dawson Creek, to W.R. Colvin, Assistant Departmental Solicitor, Victoria (14 June 1945), "Pouce Coupé Assize," BCA (GR 1723, reel B7426). According to the *PRBN*, the jury was censured and dismissed for the balance of the assize. See "Burt Miller Acquitted Manslaughter Charge" *PRBN* (21 June 1945) 1.

58 See "Pouce Coupé Assize," BCA (GR 1723, reel B7426).

59 W.B. Farris, C.J., Supreme Court, Vancouver, to Colonel Eric Pepler, K.C., Deputy Attorney General, Victoria (2 April 1948), *ibid.*

60 See "Report Condition of Judge Robertson as Still Serious" *PGC* (19 March 1942) 8; "Local and Personal" *PRBN* (26 March 1942) 4; "Report Condition of Judge Robertson Still Serious" *PRBN* (2 April 1942) 2; "Judge Robertson Goes to Victoria" *PGC* (7 April 1942) 8; "Judge Robertson Flown to Victoria" *PRBN* (9 April 1942) 4; "Judge Robertson Retires from Cariboo County Bench" *PRBN* (16 April 1942) 1; "Judge Robertson Dies at Victoria" *PRBN* (14 May 1942) 1.

61 "New Cariboo Judge Arrives via Plane" *AHN* (18 May 1944) at 4.

62 Author interview with Mary Humphries, Fort St. John, BC, 9 January 2001.

63 "US Army Handing Salvage on Alaska Road to Dominion" *Edmonton Journal* (25 July 1944), in "Investigation—Destruction of US Equipment," Library and Archives Canada (RG 36/7, vol. 36, file 11-16). See generally "At Police Court: Vagrancy, Thefts, Weapons and Dogs on the Police Blotter" *AHN* (27 June 1946) 1; "Thieves Steal Jail at 'Alcan,' Report—Fort Alcan 'Brig' Lined with Wallboard Not Steel" *AHN* (9 May 1946) 1; and "More Scandal on the Dumphead" *AHN* (31 July 1947) 2.

64 Taking items from army dumps was considered theft, for, according to Constable Bill Lumsden of the BCPP, "It makes no difference what local citizens think of War assets or surplus government property. The point is, any intrusion on these properties is an offence—and theft is theft, whether from the government or from widows and orphans—and we intend to prosecute all offenders to the limit." See "At Police Court: Vagrancy, Thefts, Weapons and Dogs on the Police Blotter" *AHN* (27 June 1946) at 1.

65 "Tompkins Brothers 'Rolled Out the Barrels' but Got No Barrel of Fun—Theft and Manslaughter Charges Fill Assize Docket. Soldier Gets Off; Truckers, Not Guilty" *AHN* (26 May 1949) 1. See *R. v. James McNish Tompkins,* BCA (GR 2235,

box 3, file 97/48); and *R. v. William David Tompkins,* BCA (GR 2036, box 1, file 98/48).

CHAPTER 10: STARKIE'S ADVENTURES IN NORTH AMERICA

1 See John McLaren, "Recalculating the Wages of Sin: The Social and Legal Construction of Prostitution, 1850-1920" (1996) 23 Man. L.J. 524; and McLaren, "The Despicable Crime of Nudity: Law, the State, and Civil Protest among the Sons of Freedom Sect of Doukhobors, 1899-1935" (1999) 38:3 J. West 2.

2 Notable texts describing these trials include Leonard W. Levy, *Emergence of a Free Press* (New York: Oxford University Press, 1985); Levy, *Blasphemy: Verbal Offense against the Sacred, from Moses to Salman Rushdie* (New York: Knopf, 1993); Donald Thomas, *A Long Time Burning: The History of Literary Censorship in England* (New York: Praeger, 1969); and Joss Marsh, *Word Crimes: Blasphemy, Culture, and Literature in Nineteenth-Century England* (Chicago: University of Chicago Press, 1998).

3 See *e.g.* Anthony Highmore, *Reflections on the Distinction Usually Adopted in Criminal Libel Prosecutions for Libel* (London, 1791); and George Dyer, *An Address to the People of Great Britain, on the Doctrine of Libels, and the Office of Juror* (London, 1799).

4 Francis Ludlow Holt, *The Law of Libel* [etc.] (London, 1812); Thomas Starkie, *A Treatise on the Law of Slander, Libel, Scandalum Magnatum, and False Rumors* [etc.] (London, 1813). A third, more modest text that left no lasting mark was John George's *Treatise on the Offence of Libel* [etc.] (London, 1812).

5 Francis Ludlow Holt, *The Law of Libel* [etc.], 2d ed. (London, 1816); Holt, *The Law of Libel* [etc.], 1st Amer. ed., ed. by Anthony Bleecker (New York, 1818).

6 Thomas Starkie, *A Treatise on the Law of Slander, Libel, Scandalum Magnatum, and False Rumours* [etc.], 1st Amer. ed., ed. by Edward D. Ingraham (New York, 1826) [*Starkie 1826*]; Starkie, *A Treatise on the Law of Slander, Libel, Scandalum Magnatum, and False Rumours* [etc.], 2d Amer. ed., ed. by Thomas Huntington (New York, 1832) [*Starkie 1832*]; and Starkie, *A Treatise on the Law of Slander and Libel, and Incidentally of Malicious Prosecutions,* 2d ed. (London, 1830) [*Starkie 1830*].

7 See Jeffrey L. Pasley, *"The Tyranny of Printers": Newspaper Politics in the Early American Republic* (Charlottesville: University Press of Virginia, 2001).

8 See Levy, *Emergence, supra* note 2 at c. 8 and 9; Norman L. Rosenberg, *Protecting the Best Men: An Interpretive History of the Law of Libel* (Chapel Hill: University of North Carolina Press, 1986) at c. 4 and 5; and Pasley, *supra* note 7.

9 See Ernest Clarke, "The Cumberland Glebe Dispute and the Background to the American Revolution in Nova Scotia, 1771-1774" (1993) 42 U.N.B.L.J. 95; Ernest A. Clarke and Jim Phillips, "Rebellion and Repression in Nova Scotia in the Era of the American Revolution" in F. Murray Greenwood and Barry Wright, eds., *Canadian State Trials,* vol. 1: *Law, Politics, and Security Measures, 1608-1837* (Toronto: University of Osgoode Society for Canadian Legal History and University of Toronto Press, 1996) 172; Barry Cahill, "The Treason of the Merchants: Dissent and Repression in Halifax in the Era of the American Revolution" (1996) 26 Acadiensis 52; and David Graham Bell, "Sedition among the Loyalists: The Case of Saint John, 1784-1786" (1995) 44 U.N.B.L.J. 163.

10   Jim Phillips has been working on this affair. See Barry Cahill and Jim Phillips, "The Supreme Court of Nova Scotia: Origins to Confederation" in Philip Girard, Jim Phillips, and Barry Cahill, eds., *The Supreme Court of Nova Scotia, 1754-2004: From Imperial Bastion to Provincial Oracle* (Toronto: Osgoode Society for Canadian Legal History and University of Toronto Press, 2004) 53 at 67-71.

11   *R. v. Wilkie*. Barry Cahill says that *Wilkie* was "almost certainly the first prosecution for 'public' or 'political' libel." Cahill, "Sedition in Nova Scotia: *R. v. Wilkie* (1820) and the Incontestable Illegality of Seditious Libel before *R. v. Howe* (1835)" (1994) 17 Dal. L.J. 458 at 461.

12   The editors of the *Acadian Recorder* and *Free Press* were disciplined by the House of Assembly for their roles in promulgating assemblyman John Barry's allegations that certain fellow assemblymen were engaging in smuggling. See the newspapers of late April and early May 1829. The newspapers also indicate that the next year, although the House shook its sabres, Joseph Howe was ultimately not disciplined for reporting the Attorney General's address to the House during the Brandy Dispute.

13   No libel texts appear in the 1814 estate catalogues of the libraries of Samuel Sewall and Theophilus Parsons. See Samuel Sewall, *Catalogue of the Library of the Late Chief Justice Sewall, to be Sold at Auction Sep. 2, 1814* (Cambridge, MA: Hilliard and Metcalf, 1814); *Catalogue of the Library of the Hon. Theophilus Parsons. To be Sold by Auction March 1st 1814* (Boston, 1814). An 1823 Boston book catalogue lacked any law books but Blackstone's *Commentaries*. See *Catalogue of Books to be Sold at Auction on Thursday, March 13th, 1823*.

14   *Catalogue of the Library of the Law School of Harvard University* (Cambridge, MA, 1826) [*Harvard Catalogue 1826*].

15   One book auction catalogue of 1827 lacks any libel books, but thirty copies of "Starkie on Slander" were available in the Boston Trade Sale the same year. Joseph Cunningham, *Catalogue of Law Books to be Sold on Thursday, June 13, 1827;* and *Boston Trade Sale. Catalog of Books to be Sold to Booksellers Only, on Tuesday, August 7, 1827* [*1827 Trade Sale Catalog*]. (The American trade sale catalogues survive in the holdings of the American Antiquarian Society in Worcester, MA.)

16   Starkie did not appear in the Harvard law library catalogue until 1841. The 1834 catalogue had the 1816 second English edition of Holt but no longer the 1818 American edition and no Starkie. The 1830 second English edition of Starkie appeared in the 1841 catalogue as did the 1832 second American edition and the 1816 English edition of Holt. *Harvard Catalogue 1826, supra* note 14; *A Catalogue of the Law Library of Harvard University in Cambridge, Massachusetts* (Cambridge, MA, 1834) [*Harvard Catalogue 1834*]; *A Catalogue of the Law Library of Harvard University in Cambridge, Massachusetts* (Cambridge, MA, 1841) [*Harvard Catalogue 1841*]. Hilliard, Gray and Co. was marketing "Holt on Libel" in 1831 and 1832 but not Starkie. *Catalogue of Law Books for Sale by Hilliard, Gray and Co.— Boston* (Boston, 1831, 1832). By 1837, Boston's Little and Brown was marketing both the 1818 American edition of Holt and the 1832 second American edition of Starkie. *A Catalogue of Law Books Published and For Sale by Charles C. Little and James Brown* (Boston, 1837). In 1834, Simon Greenleaf recommended "Starkie on Slander" to law students for

private reading, but it was not part of the regular curriculum. *A Sketch of the Law School at Cambridge* (Cambridge: James Munroe, 1834), as published in (January 1835) 13 Amer. Jur. at 122-23. The *American Jurist's* comprehensive 1834 review of law books did not mention any libel texts. "Characters of Law Books and Judges" (1834) 12 Amer. Jur. 5.

17 I examined twenty-five reported civil and criminal speech cases from 1820 to 1840. The first citation of Holt, from *Comm. v. Buckingham* (Boston Mun. Ct. December term 1822), appears in *Maffit's Trial; or, Buckingham Acquitted, on a Charge of Slander against the Character of John N. Maffit* (New York, 1831) at 19. Responding to that case, H.G. Otis also cited Holt. See A Member of the Suffolk Bar [Otis], *A Letter to the Hon. Josiah Quincy, Judge of the Municipal Court, in the City of Boston, on the Law of Libel, as Laid Down by Him in the Case of Commonwealth vs. Buckingham* (Boston, 1823) at 13. The sole judicial reference to one of these treatises was by Peter Thacher in *Comm. v. Buckingham*, Thach. Crim. Cas. 29 at 32 (Boston Mun. Ct. 1824). I cannot determine which edition(s) of Holt was cited in these three instances. The 1825 citation appears in *Comm. v. Blanding*, 20 Mass. 304 (S.J.Ct. 1825) [Blanding]. Counsel cited both a British review of the 1816 text and Holt's text itself. The review was "Liberty of the Press and Its Abuses: Rev. of Francis Ludlow Holt, *The Law of Libel*" (1816) 27 Edin. Rev. 102.

18 *Blanding, ibid.* at 315. The citations to Starkie in earlier published cases are the work of later editors.

19 Three 1830s cases mention Holt. See *Comm. v. Guild*, Thach. Crim. Cas. 329 at 331 (Boston Mun. Ct. 1833); *Comm. v. Kneeland*, Thach. Crim. Cas. 346 at 353 (Boston Mun. Ct. 1834); and *Carter v. Andrews*, 33 Mass. 1 (S.J.Ct. 1834). Starkie was cited in *Gay v. Homer*, 30 Mass. 535 (S.J.Ct. 1833); *Carter v. Andrews; Comm. v. Snelling*, 32 Mass. 321 (S.J.Ct. 1834) [*Snelling 1*]; *Comm. v. Snelling*, 32 Mass. 337 (S.J.Ct. 1834) [*Snelling 2*]; and *Comm. v. Kneeland*.

20 Conveniently, the 1830 edition of Starkie came in two volumes. References to the American editions therefore do not indicate "volume 1" or "volume 2," and they often cite page numbers higher than any that appear in the 1830 edition. See *Comm. v. Kneeland, ibid.* at 353; and *Snelling 1, supra* note 19. The American edition of Holt appears in the 1837 Little and Brown catalogue, *supra* note 16, was cited in "Judge Thacher's Charge in Relation to Publications Tending to Excite the Slaves of Other States to Insurrection" (1832) 8 Amer. Jur. 213 at 214-15, and was used in *Comm. v. Child* (Mass. S.J.Ct. Middlesex October term 1828). See John W. Whitman, *Trial of the Case of the Commonwealth versus David Lee Child, for Publishing in the Massachusetts Journal a Libel on the Honorable John Keyes* (Boston, 1829) at 9-10. Further proceedings are at 27 Mass. 252 (S.J.Ct. 1830); and 30 Mass. 198 (S.J.Ct. 1832).

21 Thirty copies of "Starkie on Slander" were listed in the *1827 Trade Sale Catalog*, *supra* note 15. Ten copies were listed in 1828 and five in 1829. See *Second Boston Trade Sale. Catalogue of Books to be Sold to Booksellers Only on Tuesday, July 22, 1828*; and *Third Boston Trade Sale. Catalogue of Books to be Sold to Booksellers Only on Tuesday, July 21, 1829*.

22 Only the 1832 American edition of Starkie appeared in *A Catalogue of Law Books Published and For Sale by Charles C. Little and James Brown* (Boston, 1837). William

H. Laurence has likewise noted that Americans became less receptive to foreign law books as their own publishing industry developed. Laurence, "Acquiring the Law: The Personal Law Library of William Young, Halifax, Nova Scotia, 1835" (1998) 21 Dal. L.J. 490 at 513.

23 Philip V. Girard, *Patriot Jurist: Beamish Murdoch of Halifax, 1800-1876* (Ph.D. thesis, Dalhousie University, 1998) at 133-36 [unpublished]. According to Gerard Wilfred Gawalt, *Massachusetts Lawyers: A Historical Analysis of the Process of Professionalization, 1760-1840* (Ph.D. diss., Clark University, Worcester, MA, 1969) at 225 [unpublished], there were, in 1820, 489 lawyers in the Massachusetts counties that did not become part of Maine. Ten years later, there were 582. In 1820, there were 47 in Middlesex, 135 in Suffolk, and 41 in nearby Essex. In 1830, there were 65 in Middlesex, 146 in Suffolk, and 55 in Essex. The Boston area was the largest market for legal texts, with Worcester being second (63 lawyers in 1820 and 77 in 1830). Boston's market for legal texts would therefore have been several times the size of Halifax's in both 1820 and 1830.

24 C.H. Belcher, *Catalogue of Books, for Sale by C.H. Belcher, July, 1837, Halifax, Nova-Scotia.* This catalogue survives at Nova Scotia Archives and Records Management (NSARM) in Halifax.

25 Laurence, *supra* note 22, says William Young employed these methods to stock his library. Attorney General R.J. Uniacke used similar strategies. See John Macleod, "The Library of Richard John Uniacke" in Patricia Lockhart Fleming, Gilles Gallichan, and Yvan Lamond, eds., *History of the Book in Canada,* vol. 1: *Beginnings to 1840* (Toronto: University of Toronto Press, 2004) 209.

26 Macleod, *ibid.*

27 *List of Books Belonging to the Estate of the Late Hon. R.J. Uniacke to be sold THIS DAY, Monday at 11 o'clock, by W.M. Allan* [Uniacke Library] (available at NSARM); *Catalogue of Books, in the Law Library at Halifax. Michaelmas Term, 1835* (Halifax, 1835) [*Barristers' Library Catalogue*].

28 Laurence, *supra* note 22 at 495.

29 *Harvard Catalogue 1834, supra* note 16.

30 *Barristers' Library Catalogue, supra* note 27.

31 William Laurence, personal communication concerning Young's library, 28 January 2006; Joseph Howe, *The Speeches and Public Letters of Joseph Howe,* ed. by J.A. Chisholm (Halifax: Chronicle, 1909) vol. 1 at 36 [Howe, *Speeches*].

32 The first Massachusetts citation of this text that I have found is in the *Harvard Catalogue 1841, supra* note 16.

33 *Uniacke Library, supra* note 27; Laurence, *supra* note 22; Howe, *Speeches, supra* note 31, vol. 1 at 64-65, citing *Starkie 1830, supra* note 6, vol. 1 at xcviii-xcix, ci, cxl, cxli-cxlii, and 210-11.

34 Michael Lobban has noted Starkie's political shift from Tory to liberal some time during this period. Lobban, *Oxford Dictionary of National Biography,* ed. by Lawrence Goldman, *s.v.* "Starkie, Thomas," online: http://www.oxforddnb.com.

35 *Starkie 1832, supra* note 6 at 147. Cf. *Starkie 1826, supra* note 6 at 201.

36 *Starkie 1830, supra* note 6, vol. 2 at 256.

37 See Howe, *Speeches, supra* note 31, vol. 1 at 64-65, citing *Starkie 1830, supra* note 6, vol. 1 at xcviii-xcix, ci, cxl, cxli-cxlii, and 210-11.

38 *Fraser v. Holland* (Easter term 1821, N.S. S.Ct. Halifax); "The Press" *Acadian Recorder* (5 May 1821) 1.

39 On *Zenger*, see Rosenberg, *supra* note 8 at 35-40; and James Alexander, *A Brief Narrative of the Case and Trial of John Peter Zenger, Printer of the New York Weekly Journal*, ed. by Stanley N. Katz (Cambridge, MA: Belknap Press, 1963).

40 *People v. Croswell*, 3 Johns. Cas. 337 (N.Y. Sup. Ct. 1804).

41 *Comm. v. Clap*, 4 Mass. 163 (S.J.Ct. 1808).

42 *Clap, ibid.* at 169.

43 *Trial: Commonwealth vs. J. T. Buckingham, On an Indictment for a Libel, Before the Municipal Court of the City of Boston, December 1822* (Boston, 1823) at 5.

44 See Otis, *supra* note 17; Edmund Kimball, *Reflections upon the Law of Libel in a Letter Addressed to "A Member of the Suffolk Bar"* (Boston, 1823).

45 *Blanding, supra* note 17.

46 *Blanding, ibid.* at 312-13.

47 *An Act Relating to Prosecutions for Libel, and to Pleadings in Actions for Libel and Slander*, St. 1826, c. 107, s. 1 [Rev. St., c. 133, s. 6].

48 I have examined all the reported cases on libel and slander. For the unreported cases, I went through the record books for the Supreme Judicial Court for Worcester and Suffolk Counties for 1820-40, the record books for the Boston Municipal Court for 1820, 1830, and part of 1840, and the record books for the Worcester County Court of Common Pleas for 1825, 1830, 1835, and 1840. I found fourteen criminal prosecutions for defamatory libel addressed by courts after the 1826 statute was passed. It is possible to determine whether or not truth was pleaded in twelve of these. Truth was pleaded in six, and of these, the prosecution ended in favour of the defendant in four, including two *nolles*.

49 *Snelling 1, supra* note 19.

50 Charles H. Locke, *Trial of Moore and Sevey for a Libel on Samuel D. Greene, in the Municipal Court, Boston, July Term, 1833* (Boston, 1833) at 58.

51 *Review, of the Report of the Case of the Commonwealth versus David Lee Child: For Publishing in the Massachusetts Journal a Libel on the Honorable John Keyes* (Boston, 1829) at 5.

52 *Ibid.* at 4.

53 This argument is contained in the Bill of Exceptions in the case file for *Comm. v. Snelling* (S.J.Ct., Suffolk November term 1833). See also S.J.Ct. Suffolk Record Book, v. 21, pt. 2, 484v. (Both are available at the Massachusetts Judicial Archives in Boston.)

54 *Snelling 2, supra* note 19.

55 *Ibid.*

56 See George B. Cheever, *Defence in Abatement of Judgment for an Alleged Libel in the Story Entitled "Inquire at Amos Giles' Distillery"* (New York, 1836) at 14-19, citing Thomas Starkie, *A Practical Treatise of the Law of Evidence and Digest of Proofs in Civil and Criminal Proceedings* (London, 1824) at 863, 881. Regarding Cheever's trial, see also Robert M. York, *George B. Cheever, Religious and Social Reformer 1807-1890* (Orono, ME: University Press, 1955) at 72-78.

57 Before the trial, critical, politically oriented letters to the newspapers very often began with a reminder to readers of the writer's right to express his (or perhaps

her) opinions freely. These cautious claims of right basically disappeared after the trial, a suggestion that they were no longer perceived as necessary. It is hard to be entirely certain from the newspaper report, but an argument that echoed Howe's assertions about intention and qualified privilege seems to have been made as well in *Ward v. English and Blackadar* (N.S. S.C. Halifax, May 1840), reported in "Supreme Court. Libel Case" *Pearl* (9 May 1840) 150.

CHAPTER 11:
THE LAW OF DOWER IN NEW SOUTH WALES AND THE UNITED STATES

1 "Select Committee on the Real Property and Dower Bills" (1850) 2 Votes and Proceedings of the New South Wales Legislative Council ["Select Committee 1850"]: G.K. Holden, in evidence, 18 August 1850.

2 "Select Committee 1850," *ibid.*, Robert Johnson, in evidence, 13 August 1850.

3 "Select Committee 1850," *ibid.*, G.K. Holden, in evidence, 18 August 1850.

4 Nancy E. Wright and A.R. Buck, "The Transformation of Colonial Property: A Study of Dower in New South Wales, 1836-1863" (2004) 23 U. Tasm. L. Rev. 98.

5 However, for two excellent comparative studies of property rights in the eighteenth and nineteenth centuries that deal with both colonial Australia and the United States, see Peter Karsten, *Between Law and Custom: "High" and "Low" Legal Cultures in the Lands of the British Diaspora—The United States, Canada, Australia and New Zealand, 1600-1900* (Cambridge: Cambridge University Press, 2002); and John C. Weaver, *The Great Land Rush and the Making of the Modern World, 1650-1900* (Montreal and Kingston: McGill-Queen's University Press, 2003).

6 *Southern Courier* (2 August 1861).

7 Peter Gay, *The Cultivation of Hatred* (New York: Norton, 1993) at 218, has argued, with reference to nineteenth-century Europe, that, "[f]or the middle classes, the prospect of power was more enticing than the prospect of democracy. Their ambivalence about the looming triumph of popular politics, the supreme issue of the age, was perfectly understandable; it presented them with dangers no less than opportunities." The same was true of colonial Australia.

8 The land question in New South Wales—indeed, in Australia generally—still awaits its historian. However, for an introduction, see Stuart Macintyre, *Winners and Losers: The Pursuit of Social Justice in Australian History* (Sydney: Allen and Unwin, 1985) at 19-39.

9 Nancy E. Wright and A.R. Buck, "Property Rights and the Discourse of Improvement in Nineteenth-Century New South Wales" in A.R. Buck, John McLaren, and Nancy E. Wright, eds., *Land and Freedom: Law, Property Rights and the British Diaspora* (Aldershot: Ashgate, 2001) 103. See also Weaver, *supra* note 5 passim.

10 See *e.g.* the opinions given in evidence before the Select Committee on the Upset Price of Land in 1847 in (1847) 2 Votes and Proceedings of the New South Wales Legislative Council, Appendix.

11 See A.R. Buck, "'The Poor Man': Rhetoric and Political Culture in Mid Nineteenth-Century New South Wales" (1996) 43 Austl. J. Pol. & Hist. 200.

12 In the United States, the term "squatter" referred to a poor man who established a homestead without any claim. In New South Wales, in contrast, the term

colloquially referred to wealthy pastoralists who grazed stock on substantial runs to which they held no title. See Stephen H. Roberts, *History of Australian Land Settlement 1788-1920* (Melbourne: Macmillan, 1968) at 187-88; and C.J. King, *An Outline of Closer Settlement in New South Wales* (Sydney: Government Printer, 1957) at 80. Concerning popular debate about free selectors in New South Wales, see Nancy E. Wright, "Reading the Past: The Dispossession of the Poor and Aborigines in Colonial New South Wales" in Peter Farrugia, ed., *The River of History* (Calgary: University of Calgary Press, 2005) 103.

13   Quoted in Charles C. Geisler, "A History of Land Reform in the United States: Old Wine, New Bottles" in Charles C. Geisler and Frank J. Popper, eds., *Land Reform, American Style* (Totowa, NJ: Rowman and Allanheld, 1984) 1 at 11.

14   *Homestead Act, Statutes at Large* (1862), vol. 12, c. 75. The law also allowed that those taking up a homestead could bypass the full five-year qualification period if they could pay the minimum price after six months' residency and cultivation on a quarter section of the land.

15   Michael L. Lanza, *Agrarianism and Reconstruction Politics: The Southern Homestead Act* (Baton Rouge: Louisiana State University Press, 1990) at 10.

16   John F. Hart, "Land Use Law in the Early Republic and the Original Meaning of the Takings Clause" (2000) 94 Nw. U.L. Rev. 1099; and Hart, "Colonial Land Use Law and Its Significance for Modern Takings Doctrine" (1996) 109 Harv. L. Rev. 1252.

17   See *e.g. Attorney General v. Brown* (1847), 1 Legge 312. The significance of this case is discussed in A.R. Buck, *The Making of Australian Property Law* (Sydney: Federation Press, 2006) at 1-10.

18   N.G. Butlin, "Colonial Socialism in Australia, 1860-1900" in H.G.J. Aitken, ed., *The State and Economic Growth* (New York: Social Science Research Council, 1959) 26. This interpretation, though designated "colonial socialism" by N.G. Butlin, lies embedded in the argument of William Pember Reeves, *State Experiments in Australia and New Zealand,* 2 vols. (London, 1902).

19   Andro Linklater, *Measuring America: How the United States Was Shaped by the Greatest Land Sale in History* (New York: Plume, 2003) at 248.

20   3 & 4 Wm. IV., c. 105.

21   7 Wm. IV., no. 8.

22   26 Vict., no. 9.

23   14 Vict., no. 27.

24   54 Vict., no. 25.

25   On the history of community property laws with particular reference to dower, see Richard A. Ballinger, *A Treatise on the Property Rights of Husband and Wife, Under the Community or Ganancial System* (Seattle: Bancroft-Whitney, 1895). On the history of dower in the United States generally, see Chester G. Vernier, *American Family Laws* (Stanford: Stanford University Press, 1935) vol. 3 at 345-527. See also Charles H. Scribner, *A Treatise on the Law of Dower,* 2d ed. (Philadelphia, 1883).

26   Carol Shammas, Marylynn Salmon, and Michel Dahlin, *Inheritance in America from Colonial Times to the Present* (New Brunswick, NJ: Rutgers University Press, 1987) at 83.

27 It should be noted that this chapter does not engage with the history of dower or women's property rights in the American colonies in the seventeenth or eighteenth centuries, or in the early republic, as its purpose is to find a logical point of comparison to nineteenth-century Australia. For this topic during those earlier years, see Marylynn Salmon, *Women and the Law of Property in Early America* (Chapel Hill: University of North Carolina Press, 1986). See also George L. Haskins, "Reception of the Common Law in Seventeenth-Century Massachusetts: Case Study [of Dower Rights]" in George Athan Billias, ed., *Selected Essays: Law and Authority in Colonial America* (Barre, MA: Barre, 1965) 24.

28 Norma Basch, *In the Eyes of the Law: Women, Marriage and Property in Nineteenth-Century New York* (Ithaca: Cornell University Press, 1982); Peggy A. Rabkin, *Fathers to Daughters: The Legal Foundations of Female Emancipation* (Westport: Greenwood Press, 1980); Elisabeth Bowles Warbasse, *The Changing Legal Rights of Married Women, 1800-1861* (New York: Garland, 1987); and Kathleen Elizabeth Lazarou, *Concealed under Petticoats: Married Women's Property and the Law of Texas, 1840-1913* (New York: Garland, 1986).

29 Isador Loeb, *The Legal Relations of Married Persons: A Study in Comparative Legislation* (New York: Columbia University Press, 1900) at 138-39.

30 George L. Haskins, "Estates Arising from the Marriage Relationship and Their Characteristics" in A. James Casner, ed., *American Law of Property: A Treatise on the Law of Property in the United States,* vol. 1 (Boston: Little, Brown, 1952) 632 at 632.

31 See Nancy E. Wright, "'The Lady Vanishes': Women and Property Rights in Nineteenth-Century New South Wales" in John McLaren, A.R. Buck, and Nancy E. Wright, eds., *Despotic Dominion: Property Rights in British Settler Societies* (Vancouver: UBC Press, 2005) 190.

32 14 Vict., no. 27. "Select Committee 1850," *supra* note 1, James Norton, in evidence, 5 November 1850.

33 "Select Committee on the Real Property Law Bill" (1849) 2 Votes and Proceedings of the New South Wales Legislative Council: Robert Johnson, in evidence, 24 July 1849 ["Real Property Law Bill"].

34 "Real Property Law Bill," *ibid.,* G.K. Holden, in evidence, 24 July 1849.

35 The system of registration of title (or system of registered conveyancing) developed by Sir Robert Richard Torrens (1814-84) was enacted in the six states of Australia and other British colonies. As James Edward Hogg remarks, "[a]daptations and modifications of the Australian system are also known as 'Torrens' systems. Thus, there is now an English Torrens system, a Canadian Torrens system, and an American Torrens system." See Hogg, *The Australian Torrens System* (London: William Clowes and Sons, 1905) at 1. See also A.R. Buck, "Torrens Title, Intestate Estates and the Origins of Australian Property Law" (1996) 4:2 Austl. Prop. L.J. 89.

36 Robert R. Torrens, *The South Australian System of Conveyancing by Registration of Title* (Adelaide, 1859) at 6-7.

37 *Sydney Morning Herald* (23 June 1859).

38 John Stuart Mill, *Principles of Political Economy* (Harmondsworth: Penguin Books, 1970) at 367.

39 Torrens, *supra* note 36 at 44.

40 "Royal Commission to Inquire into and Report on the Workings of the Real
Property Acts" (1879-80) 5 Votes and Proceedings of the New South Wales Legislative Assembly: Alfred Cape, in evidence, 6 May 1879 ["Royal Commission"].

41 *Real Property Act, 1862,* 26 Vict., no. 9 came into operation on 1 January 1863.

42 "Royal Commission," *supra* note 40, Alfred Cape, in evidence, 6 May 1879.

43 "Royal Commission," *ibid.,* Edward Ward, in evidence, 14 March 1879.

44 7 Wm. IV., no. 8, ss. 2 and 12, respectively.

45 The following section draws on John M. Bennett, *Equity Law in New South Wales
1788-1902* (Sydney: University of Sydney Legal Research Project, 1962) at 333-36.

46 Bennett, *ibid.* at 334 [emphasis in original].

47 *Ex parte Murphy* (1867), 6 S.C.R. Eq. 63.

48 *Merriman v. The Perpetual Trustee Co. Ltd.* (1896), 17 N.S.W.R. Eq. 325.

49 "Select Committee on Intestacy" (1858) 2 Votes and Proceedings of the New South
Wales Legislative Council 33 at 33.

50 This argument is developed in Buck, *supra* note 17.

51 See *e.g.* A.R. Buck, "Property Law and the Origins of Australian Egalitarianism"
(1995) 1 Austl. J. Legal Hist. 145.

52 *Underwood v. Underwood* (1879), 1 N.S.W.R. Eq. 16.

53 Joan Hoff, *Law, Gender and Injustice: A Legal History of U.S. Women* (New York: New
York University Press, 1991) at 106-16.

54 *Flynn v. Flynn et al.,* 171 Mass. 312 (1898).

CHAPTER 12: CONTESTING PROHIBITION AND THE CONSTITUTION

1 James K. Chapman, "The Mid-Nineteenth Century Temperance Movement in
New Brunswick and Maine" (1954) 35 Can. Hist. Rev. 43; T.W. Acheson, *Saint John:
A Colonial Urban Community* (Toronto: University of Toronto Press, 1984) at c. 3;
Jan Noel, *Canada Dry: Temperance Crusades before Confederation* (Toronto: University
of Toronto Press, 1995) at c. 3.

2 John McLaren and John Lowman, "Enforcing Canada's Prostitution Laws, 1892-
1920: Rhetoric and Practice" in Martin L. Freidland, ed., *Securing Compliance: Seven
Case Studies* (Toronto: University of Toronto Press, 1990) 21.

3 New Brunswick, *Journal of the House of Assembly of the Province of New Brunswick
from the Seventeenth to the Twenty-Sixth Day of July, 1856, Being the First Session of the
Seventeenth General Assembly* (Fredericton: John Simpson, 1856) at 7; W. Stewart
MacNutt, *New Brunswick: A History, 1784-1867* (Toronto: Macmillan, 1963).

4 Chapman, *supra* note 1.

5 Acheson, *supra* note 1 at c. 3; Noel, *supra* note 1 at c. 3. For an overview of nineteenth-century temperance and drinking practices, see Craig Heron, *Booze: A Distilled History* (Toronto: Between the Lines, 2003) at c. 2 and 3.

6 Acheson, *ibid.* at c. 3; Noel, *ibid.* at c. 3.

7 Gail G. Campbell, "Disenfranchised but Not Quiescent: Women Petitioners in New
Brunswick in the Mid Nineteenth Century" (Spring 1989) 18:2 Acadiensis 22.

8 Acheson, *supra* note 1 at c. 3.

9 Head to Newcastle (9 September 1852), Fredericton, Provincial Archives of New
Brunswick (PANB) (CO 188/120). For an overview of the US, see Ian Tyrrell,

Sobering Up: From Temperance to Prohibition in Antebellum America, 1800-1860 (Westport: Greenwood Press, 1979).

10 "Report of the Medical Superintendent for 1852" in *Journal of the House of Assembly of the Province of New Brunswick from the Seventh Day of January to the Seventh Day of April, 1852, being the Second Session of the Fifteenth General Assembly* (Fredericton: John Simpson, 1852) Appendix; *Saint John Morning News* (19 March 1854); Saint John Police Court Records, August 1849 to December 1852, Saint John, Saint John Public Library.

11 Acheson, *supra* note 1 at 159; Anne Marie E. Szymanski, *Pathways to Prohibition: Radicals, Moderates and Social Movement Outcomes* (Durham: Duke University Press, 2002).

12 MacNutt, *supra* note 3 at 350.

13 *Miramichi Gleaner* (2 February 1856). The rise of the Sons of Temperance coincided with the spread of another fraternal organization, the Loyal Orange Association (LOA), which was popular in Protestant rural parishes. Scholars have not attempted to compare and contrast the two movements for the mid-Victorian period, although in Upper Canada temperance has been interpreted as a protective device for American settlers who wanted to prove their loyalty in the face of a growing Orange movement by the 1830s. Many individual Orange lodges were temperance lodges, but the LOA was not a temperance organization. See Glen Lockwood, "Temperance in Upper Canada as Ethnic Subterfuge" in Cheryl Krasnick Warsh, ed., *Drink in Canada: Historical Essays* (Montreal and Kingston: McGill-Queen's University Press, 1993) 43.

14 Chapman, *supra* note 1 at 52-53. Ernest J. Dick makes this same point for Nova Scotia. See Dick, "From Temperance to Prohibition in 19th Century Nova Scotia" (Autumn 1981) 61:3 Dalhousie Rev. 530 at 533-34.

15 F.L. Barron, *The Genesis of Temperance in Ontario, 1828-1850* (M.A. thesis, University of Guelph, 1976) [unpublished].

16 Noel, *supra* note 1 at 152-53.

17 *New Brunswick Courier* (7 April 1849).

18 Acheson, *supra* note 1 at 155.

19 *Rapport du comité spécial de l'assemblée législative, chargé de rechercher des measures législative pour remedier aux maux que résultant de l'intemperence* (Montreal: Lovell and Gibson, 1849).

20 Jon Sterngass, *Alcohol and Temperance in Modern History: An International Encyclopedia,* vol. 2, ed. by Jack Blocker Jr., David M. Fahey, and Ian R. Tyrrell (Denver: ABC-CLIO, 2003) *s.v.* "Maine Law."

21 Gail G. Campbell, "'Smashers' and 'Rummies': Voters and the Rise of Parties in Charlotte County, New Brunswick, 1846-1857" (1986) 21:1 Historical Papers 86.

22 *Journal of the House of Assembly* (1852) at 31, 136, and 31-15; New Brunswick, "An Act to Prevent the Traffic in Intoxicating Liquors," 1852, *The Revised Statutes of New Brunswick,* vol. 2: *The Public Statutes of New Brunswick, Passed in the year 1854: Together with Those Unrepealed by the Revised Statutes* (Fredericton: J. Simpson, 1855) 99. See also *Headquarters* (3 May 1854).

23 William M. Baker, *Timothy Warren Anglin, 1822-96: Irish Catholic Canadian* (Toronto: University of Toronto Press, 1977) at 267, n. 93; Acheson, *supra* note 1 at 227-28;

Greg Marquis, "'A Machine of Oppression under the Guise of the Law': The Saint John Police Establishment, 1860-1890" (1986) 16:1 Acadiensis 58.

24 *New Brunswick Courier* (18 March 1854).

25 *Morning News* (4 March 1853); *Headquarters* (3 May 1854); *Weekly Chronicle* (20 January 1854); MacNutt, *supra* note 3 at 350-51. In the United States, the legality of selling stocks of liquor that had been purchased prior to a prohibition statute taking effect was decided in the New York Court of Appeal case *Wynehamer v. the People* (1856). See Edward Keynes, *Liberty, Property and Privacy: Towards a Jurisprudence of Substantive Due Process* (Pittsburgh: Pennsylvania State University Press, 1996) at 24-25.

26 Head to John Pakington (8 April 1852), PANB (CO 188/116).

27 In 1853, Head was concerned that legislation was being passed for local and particularistic reasons, not the greater good of the colony. In the recent legislative session, only thirteen out of sixty-nine laws had been "public." The rest had been private or local. See Head to Newcastle (6 May 1853), PANB (CO 188/119).

28 *Headquarters* (3 May 1854); MacNutt, *supra* note 3 at 351; C.M. Wallace, *Dictionary of Canadian Biography Online* [*DCB*], vol. 12, ed. by John English and Réal Bélanger, *s.v.* "Wallace, Lemuel Allen," online: Library and Archives Canada, http://www.biographi.ca/.

29 Phillip A. Buckner, *The Transition to Responsible Government: British Policy in British North America, 1815-1850* (Westport: Greenwood Press, 1985) at 308.

30 New Brunswick, "An Act to Regulate the Sale of Spiritous Liquors" c. 15 in *Journal of the House of Assembly of the Province of New Brunswick from the Ninth day of February to the First day of May, 1854, being the Fifth Session of the Fifteenth General Assembly* (Fredericton: John Simpson, 1854) 450; *Morning Freeman* (14 July 1855); James A. Gibson, "Head, Sir Edmund Walker," *DCB*, vol. 9, *supra* note 28.

31 Campbell, *supra* note 21; C.M. Wallace, "Fisher, Charles," *DCB*, vol. 10, *supra* note 28.

32 Richard Wilbur, "Manners-Sutton, John Henry Thomas," *DCB*, vol. 10, *supra* note 28; *Morning News* (16 June 1854).

33 Manners-Sutton to Colonial Secretary (January 1855), PANB (CO 188/124); *Morning News* (22 May 1854); C.M. Wallace, "Tilley, Samuel Leonard," *DCB*, vol. 12, *supra* note 28; T. Jason Soderstrum, *Alcohol and Temperance in Modern History: An International Encyclopedia*, vol. 2, ed. by Jack Blocker Jr., David M. Fahey, and Ian R. Tyrrell (Denver: ABC-CLIO, 2003) *s.v.* "Tilley, Samuel Leonard" (1818-1896).

34 MacNutt, *supra* note 3 at 351.

35 *Morning News* (29 June 1854).

36 *Headquarters* (11 April 1855); *Morning News* (19 March 1855); C.M. Wallace, "Smith, Sir Albert James," *DCB*, vol. 11, *supra* note 28.

37 James Hannay, *Sir Leonard Tilley* (Toronto: Morang, 1910) at 35. Hannay opposed prohibition. See his "Prohibition in New Brunswick" (April 1905) 3 New Brunswick Magazine 149.

38 James Hannay, *History of New Brunswick,* vol. 2 (Saint John: J.A. Bowes, 1909) 175-76; Wallace, "Tilley, Samuel Leonard," *supra* note 33.

39 Manners-Sutton to Russell (4 July 1855), PANB (CO 188/125).

40 MacNutt, *supra* note 3 at 359; Manners-Sutton to Russell (4 July 1855), PANB (CO 188/125).

41 Minutes of Council Committee (29 October 1855), PANB (CO 188/125); William Menzies Whitelaw, *The Maritimes and Canada before Confederation* (Toronto: Oxford University Press, 1934) at 118. The same arguments about investment and railways were made in Nova Scotia. See Dick, *supra* note 14 at 540-41.

42 *Morning News* (10, 15, 17 May 1854); *Weekly Chronicle* (14 April 1854).

43 New Brunswick, "An Act to Prevent the Importation, Manufacture and Traffic in Intoxicating Liquors" (1855) c. 36 in *Acts of the General Assembly of Her Majesty's Province of New Brunswick 1854-1860* (Fredericton: James Simpson, 1860) 113. See also *Morning Freeman* (20 December 1855).

44 Observations by the Attorney General on the 58 Acts passed by the Legislature of New Brunswick in the Month of April, 1855, PANB (CO 188/124).

45 Between 1836 and 1864, 341 bills from the British North American colonies were either reserved by governors or suspended in operation, pending review by the imperial authorities. The British government refused only 13.7 percent of the bills. See Alpheus Todd, *Parliamentary Government in the Colonies,* 2d ed. (London: Longmans, Green, 1894) at 173-74.

46 Petition of Magistrates, Merchants, Freeholders, and Others, Inhabitants of the City and County of Saint John, to J.H.T. Manners-Sutton (n.d.), PANB (CO 188/124); Petition of Magistrates, Merchants, Freeholders and other Inhabitants of the County of Charlotte (n.d.); Petition of Magistrates and other Residents of Restigouche, 10 July 1855, PANB (CO 188/125); *Morning News* (23, 25 January, 8, 13 February 1856); *Miramichi Gleaner* (11, 26 January 1856). The relevant Colonial Office memos, 8 October and 1 November 1855, including marginal notations, are found in Minutes of the Board of Trade, NB Act No. 2409 (26 October 1855) PANB (CO 188/126).

47 *Weekly Chronicle* (25 April 1855); *New Brunswick Reporter* (25 January 1856).

48 Marquis, *supra* note 23.

49 Tyrrell, *supra* note 9 at c. 11.

50 Scott See, *Riots in New Brunswick: Orange Nativism and Social Violence in the 1840s* (Toronto: University of Toronto Press, 1993) at 54.

51 *Morning News* (25 January, 8, 13 February 1856).

52 *Miramichi Gleaner* (2 February 1856); *New Brunswick Reporter* (25 January 1856).

53 *Miramichi Gleaner* (2 February 1856).

54 *Weekly Chronicle* (4 January 1856); *Morning News* (18 June 1856).

55 *Miramichi Gleaner* (2 February 1856).

56 New Brunswick, *Journal of the House of Assembly* (1856) at 290-95.

57 *Morning News* (12, 19 March, 14 April 1856).

58 Acheson, *supra* note 1 at 158.

59 Memorandum to Council, 21 May 1856, PANB (CO 188/127); C.M. Wallace, "Gray, John Hamilton," *DCB, supra* note 28.

60 The comment is found in notations on Manners-Sutton to Labouchere (31 May 1856), PANB (CO 188/127).

61 Hannay, *supra* note 38, vol. 2 at 181; Chapman, *supra* note 1 at 54. Chapman noted that the anti-prohibition *New Brunswick Courier* criticized Manners-Sutton, as did

the *New Brunswick Reporter* and the *Miramichi Gleaner*. The *New Brunswicker* and the *Saint John Freeman* supported the Governor.

62 *Morning Freeman* (14 July 1855); Baker, *supra* note 23 at 32-33.

63 Quoted in *Morning News* (19 March 1855).

64 *Morning News* (1 February 1856); W.A. Spray, "Wilmot, Robert Duncan," *DCB*, *supra* note 28. Chapman, *supra* note 1 at 57, judged the new Assembly to consist of twenty-one Conservatives, sixteen or seventeen Liberals (most of them anti-prohibitionists), and three or four anti-Conservative independents.

65 New Brunswick, "An Act to Repeal the Act to Prevent the Importation, Manufacture and Traffic in Intoxicating Liquors, and to Regulate the Sale Thereof" (1856) c. 1 in *Acts of the General Assembly of Her Majesty's Province of New Brunswick 1854-1860* (Fredericton: James Simpson, 1860) 1.

66 New Brunswick, *ibid.* at 35, who was more of a Whig historian, regarded the Governor's actions as "astounding."

67 Manners-Sutton to Labouchere (25 July 1856), PANB (CO 188/127).

68 Manners-Sutton to Labouchere (25 July, 30 July 1856), PANB (CO 188/127).

69 *New Brunswick Reporter* (13 June 1856); *Miramichi Gleaner* (7, 14 June 1856); *Weekly Chronicle* (1 August 1856).

70 Baker, *supra* note 23 at 35; Wallace, "Fisher, Charles," *supra* note 31.

71 Manners-Sutton to Labouchere (26 April 1857), PANB (CO 188/128).

72 *Morning Freeman* (15 July 1858); Wilbur, "Manners-Sutton, John Henry Thomas," *supra* note 32; P.B. Waite, "The Fall and Rise of the Smashers: Some Private Letters of Manners-Sutton" (Autumn 1976) 2:1 Acadiensis 65. In 1859 the Nova Scotia Assembly passed a Bill authorizing a prohibition plebiscite; the Legislative Council blocked it as unconstitutional. See Dick, *supra* note 14 at 542.

73 Todd, *supra* note 45 at 660-61. For an overview of the power of dissolution, see Eugene A. Forsey, *The Royal Power of Dissolution of Parliament in the British Commonwealth* (Toronto: Oxford University Press, 1943).

74 J.M.S. Careless, *Brown of the Globe*, vol. 1: *The Voice of Upper Canada, 1818-1859* (Toronto: Macmillan, 1959) at 265-76, 278-91; Donald Creighton, *John A. Macdonald: The Young Politician* (Toronto: Macmillan, 1952) at c. 10.

75 John Herd Thompson with Allen Seager, *Canada 1922-1939: Decades of Discord* (Toronto: McClelland and Stewart, 1985) at 122-25. See also Arthur Lower, *Colony to Nation* (Toronto: Longmans Canada, 1946) at 503-5; William Lewis Morton, *The Kingdom of Canada* (Toronto: McClelland and Stewart, 1963) at 451-52; and Eugene A. Forsey, *Freedom and Order* (Toronto: McClelland and Stewart, 1974) at 35, 87-88, and 105-9.

76 Peter Hogg, *Constitutional Law of Canada*, 4th ed. (Toronto: Carswell, 1997) at 9.6(d); Ronald I. Cheffins, "The Royal Prerogative and the Office of the Lieutenant Governor" (Spring 2000) 23 Canadian Parliamentary Review, online: http://www. parl.gc.ca/Infoparl/english/issue.htm?param=74&art=163.

77 Buckner, *supra* note 29 at 303.

78 Robert E. Popham and Wolfgang Schmidt, *Statistics of Alcohol Use and Alcoholism in Canada, 1871-1956* (Toronto: University of Toronto Press, 1957) at Table II-1.

79 *Morning Freeman* (6 June 1871).

80 F.S. Spence, *The Royal Commission on the Liquor Traffic: The Facts of the Case* (Toronto, 1896) at 154-57. For the operation of the CTA, see Jacques Paul Couturier, "Prohibition or Regulation? The Enforcement of the Canada Temperance Act in Moncton, 1881-1896" in Cheryl Krasnick Warsh, ed., *Drink in Canada: Historical Essays* (Montreal and Kingston: McGill-Queen's University Press, 1993) 144.

81 C. Mark Davis, *Prohibition in New Brunswick, 1917-1927* (M.A. thesis, University of New Brunswick, 1978) [unpublished]; Greg Marquis, "Civilized Drinking: Alcohol and Society in New Brunswick, 1945-1975" (2000) 11 J. Can. Hist. Ass'n (New Series) 173.

Chapter 13: From Humble Prayers to Legal Demands

1 *Haida Nation v. British Columbia (Minister of Forests)*, [2004] 3 S.C.R. 511 is a recent example.

2 See Hamar Foster and Alan Grove, "'Trespassers on the Soil': *United States v. Tom* and a New Perspective on the Short History of Treaty Making in Nineteenth-Century British Columbia" (2003) 138-39 BC Studies 51.

3 The doctrine of sovereign immunity meant, in effect, that the sole legal obligations of the government were those to which it consented: a lawsuit against the Crown required the Crown's permission, which was granted by way of a *fiat* (an abbreviation of *fiat justicia,* or "let right be done," the phrase endorsed on petitions seeking permission). See *Young v. SS. "Scotia,"* [1903] A.C. 501 at 505. British Columbia was the last Canadian jurisdiction to abolish the doctrine, in 1974.

4 The phrase "British Columbia Indian land question" dates from the 1870s, and BC did not finally acquiesce in a renewed treaty process until the early 1990s.

5 *Calder v. British Columbia (Attorney-General)*, [1973] S.C.R. 313, in which six of the seven Supreme Court Justices stated that Aboriginal title was a part of Canadian law, and three of these six were of the view that Nisga'a title had never been legally extinguished.

6 For a compendium of reasons why this is so, see Hamar Foster, Heather Raven, and Jeremy Webber, eds., *Let Right Be Done: Aboriginal Title, the Calder Case, and the Future of Indigenous Rights* (Vancouver: UBC Press, 2007).

7 See Hamar Foster, "We Are Not O'Meara's Children: Law, Lawyers and the First Campaign for Aboriginal Title in British Columbia" in Hamar Foster, Heather Raven, and Jeremy Webber, eds., *Let Right Be Done: Aboriginal Title, the Calder Case, and the Future of Indigenous Rights* (Vancouver: UBC Press, 2007) 61.

8 Copies of the Cowichan Petition are in Vancouver at the Vancouver City Archives (VCA) (Add MSS 44, vol. 18, file 9) and in Victoria at the BC Archives (BCA) (F/52/C83). Neil J. Sterritt *et al., Tribal Boundaries in the Nass Watershed* (Vancouver: UBC Press, 1998) at 140 anticipated the thesis we hope to prove in this essay by noting that it is likely that the Cowichan Petition "helped to spread knowledge of the Royal Proclamation of 1763 and formed a model for the Nisga'a Petition." Robert Galois also gives the Cowichan Petition some attention in his "The Indian Rights Association, Native Protest Activity and the 'Land Question' in British Columbia, 1903-1916" (1992) 8:2 Native Stud. Rev. 1 at 8-9. But there is little else. Even

Daniel Marshall gives it only a paragraph in a book that devotes a whole chapter to the Cowichan in the first decade of the twentieth century. See Marshall, *Those Who Fell from the Sky: A History of the Cowichan Peoples* (Duncan, BC: Cultural and Education Centre, Cowichan Tribes, 1999) at 158. However, Dr. Marshall has done a great deal of research on this topic and is hoping to do a second volume on the Cowichan contribution to the land question. He has been of great assistance to us with some of our research questions and for this we thank him.

9   See *e.g.* John McLaren, "The Early British Columbia Judges, the Rule of Law and the 'Chinese Question': The California and Oregon Connection" in John McLaren, Hamar Foster, and Chet Orloff, eds., *Law for the Elephant, Law for the Beaver: Essays in the Legal History of the North American West* (Regina and Pasadena: Canadian Plains Research Center/Ninth Judicial Circuit Historical Society, 1992) 237; McLaren, "'The Judicial Office ... Bowing to No Power but the Supremacy of the Law': Judges and the Rule of Law in Colonial Australia and Canada, 1788-1840" (2003) 7:2 Austl. J. Legal Hist. 177; and McLaren, "Reflections on the Rule of Law: The Georgian Colonies of New South Wales and Upper Canada, 1788-1837" in Diane Kirkby and Catharine Coleborne, eds., *Law, History, Colonialism: The Reach of Empire* (Manchester: Manchester University Press, 2001) 46.

10   From an edited transcript of an interview with BC's Executive Council, 3 March 1911, BCA (GR 3074, file 1/1).

11   See *infra* nn. 75-76 and 78, and accompanying text.

12   For the history of indigenous disenfranchisement in New Zealand, see Andrew Geddis, "A Dual Track Democracy? The Symbolic Role of the Mâori Seats in New Zealand's Electoral System" (2006) 5:4 Election L.J. 347; and Neil Atkinson, *Adventures in Democracy: A History of the Vote in New Zealand* (Dunedin, NZ: University of Otago Press, 2003). For a discussion of the voting rights of indigenous Australians since 1902, see Will Sanders, "Delivering Democracy to Indigenous Australians: Aborigines, Torres Strait Islanders and Commonwealth Electoral Administration" in Marian Sawer, ed., *Elections Full, Free and Fair* (Sydney: Federation Press, 2001) 158. See also Pat Stretton and Christine Finnimore, "Black Fellow Citizens: Aborigines and the Commonwealth Franchise" (2003) 23 Austl. Hist. Stud. 521 at 521.

13   Because British Columbia did not abolish Crown immunity until 1974, *Calder* (*supra* note 5) was disposed of at the Supreme Court of Canada in 1973 on the basis of that doctrine. See *supra* note 3 and the *Crown Proceeding Act,* S.B.C. 1974, c. 24, now R.S.B.C. 1979, c. 86.

14   Provincially, the prohibition on Indians voting in provincial elections was removed with the *Act to Amend the Provincial Elections Act,* S.B.C. 1949, c. 19. It was only in 1960, with the *Act to Amend the Canada Elections Act,* S.C. 1960, c. 7, that the federal franchise was fully and unconditionally extended to Aboriginal people in Canada.

15   See *Act to Amend the Indian Act,* S.C. 1927, c. 32, s. 6, which was dropped from the Act in 1951. At that time the *Criminal Code* made it a crime to incite or "stir up" any three or more Indians or "half breeds" to riotous or disorderly behaviour. Indeed, it was enough simply to incite them "to make any request or demand of govern-

ment in a disorderly manner." This provision became s. 109 in 1906 and was in force until the *Criminal Code* was revised in 1954 (S.C. 1953-54, c. 51).

16 For information about indigenous petitions in Australian legal history, see Robert Tickner, *Taking a Stand: Land Rights to Reconciliation* (Sydney: Allen and Unwin, 2001). On the history of these appeals in New Zealand, see Claudia Orange, *The Treaty of Waitangi* (Wellington, NZ: Allen and Unwin, 1987) at 205–25.

17 T.R.E. McInnes, *Report on the Indian Title,* quoted in Hamar Foster, "A Romance of the Lost: The Role of Tom MacInnes in the History of the British Columbia Indian Land Question" in G. Blaine Baker and Jim Phillips, eds., *Essays in the History of Canadian Law,* vol. 8: *In Honour of RCB Risk* (Toronto: Osgoode Society for Canadian Legal History and University of Toronto Press, 1999) 171 at 171.

18 In 1881, Aboriginal people constituted 51.9 percent of the provincial population. By 1891, this figure had dropped to 26.0 percent and by 1901, to 14.3 percent. In 1911, two years after the Cowichan Petition was filed, they were only 5.1 percent and still falling. Census of Canada, cited in Galois, *supra* note 8 at 2.

19 A pertinent example for our purposes involves a delegation from Cowichan, discussed later, that went to England in 1906. As quoted in Marshall, *supra* note 8 at 151-53, the *Cowichan Leader* referred to their petition as "rot" and a "farce." Although the Cowichan had been bitterly protesting government land policy since at least the 1860s, the newspaper charged that it was not the Indians who were complaining but "those who, instead of following the teachings of Christ, go about stirring up strife. In all the years that we have lived here we have never yet heard an Indian complain of not having land enough." In referring to those who stirred up strife, the paper clearly had missionary C.M. Tate in mind; he too is discussed later.

20 In the 1880s BC's Attorney General wanted to have missionary William Duncan arrested and charged with sedition. Patricia Roy, "Law and Order in British Columbia in the 1880s: Images and Realities" in R.C. MacLeod, ed., *Swords and Ploughshares: War and Agriculture in Western Canada* (Edmonton: University of Alberta Press, 1993) 55 at 63.

21 Philip Drucker, *The Native Brotherhoods: Modern Intertribal Organizations on the Northwest Coast,* Smithsonian Institution Bureau of American Ethnology Bulletin 168 (Washington DC: Government Printing Office, 1958) at 81.

22 Although sometimes they did take pains to conceal their involvement. See Lynn A. Blake, "Oblate Missionaries and the 'Indian Land Question'" (1998) 119 BC Studies 27.

23 Governor Douglas, for example, believed that because the Indians of Vancouver Island had "distinct ideas of property in land, and mutually recognize their several exclusive possessory rights in certain districts, they would not fail to regard the occupation of [these territories] by white settlers, unless with the full consent of the proprietary tribes, as national wrongs." Douglas to Newcastle (25 March 1861), in *British Columbia: Papers Connected with the Indian Land Question 1850-1875* (Victoria, 1875) at 19.

24 Protestants were more active than Roman Catholics, but of course generalizations are tricky. As Blake, *supra* note 22, has pointed out, some Roman Catholic priests were land claims advocates.

25 Jean Usher, *William Duncan of Metlakatla: A Victorian Missionary in British Columbia,*
Publications in History No. 5 (Ottawa: National Museum of Man, 1974) at 128.

26 "Indians' Petition to King Edward: Full Text of Appeal Which Will Be Laid at Foot
of the Throne" *Victoria Daily Colonist* (6 July 1906) at 8. On the 1906 delegation,
see Keith Thor Carlson, "Rethinking Dialogue and History: The King's Promise
and the 1906 Aboriginal Delegation to London" (2005) 16:2 Native Stud. Rev. 1.

27 See *e.g.* Father Charles Grandidier's letter of 28 August 1874 to the *Victoria Standard,*
reproduced in *British Columbia: Papers Connected, supra* note 23 at 145-48, and Blake,
supra note 22 at 34-44. Grandidier was an Oblate priest at Kamloops.

28 In the opinion he rendered to the Dominion government in 1909, McInnes, *supra*
note 17 at 192, notes that the ordinary lawyer "looks askance at the Indian title"
because it does not fit well with what he has been taught about land tenure.

29 "In White Man's Way Indians Fight Case" *Victoria Daily Colonist* (19 June 1910) 11
at 15.

30 Even those who did speak English did so in a way unlikely to impress power. For
example, a 1910 notice that the Kitwanga and Kitwancool Chiefs posted in their
territories read, in part, as follows: "This land belongs to our forefathers and King
George 3 tell this land belong to Indian. We never fight for this land. No pay us
any money ... Take away land and we got no place to live on." Quoted in Robert
Galois, "A History of the Upper Skeena Region, 1850 to 1927" (1993-94) 9:2 Native
Stud. Rev. 113 at 152. The contrast with the language of the Cowichan Petition is
striking, and the reference to King George is clearly a reference to the Proclamation, revealing how quickly word of that document had spread.

31 For a detailed example of this, see Brett Christophers, *Positioning the Missionary:
John Booth Good and the Confluence of Culture in Nineteenth Century British Columbia*
(Vancouver: UBC Press, 1998). Reserve Commissioner Gilbert Malcolm Sproat
wrote that even in the 1870s some missionaries in the southern Interior were not
allowed to attend meetings with the commission because "the Indians did not want
them. It was a Queen's matter from their point of view, not a church matter."
Letter to the editor, *Colonist* (n.d.) BCA (Add MSS 257, file 11).

32 Kelly attended the Coqualeetza Institute, the Methodist residential school at Sardis,
from 1900 to 1903, and Columbian College from 1913 to 1916, after which he was
ordained a Methodist minister. See Alan Morley, *Roar of the Breakers* (Toronto:
Ryerson Press, 1967) at 58-59 and 86, 90. Paull went to the Roman Catholic school
at the Mission Reserve between 1899 and 1907, and then spent a number of years
working in the law office of Hugh Cayley. See E. Palmer Patterson II, "Andrew
Paull (1892-1959): Finding a Voice for the 'New Indian'" (1976) 6 Western Can. J.
of Anthropology 63 at 63, 64.

33 On Aboriginal participation in the workforce, see Rolf Knight, *Indians at Work: An
Informal History of Native Labour in British Columbia 1858-1930,* 2d ed. (Vancouver:
New Star Books, 1996). In April of 1911, the lawyer for the Nisga'a told Prime
Minister Laurier that he had recently been to the Land Office in Victoria and had
been astonished at the "scores of applications for purchase" of land in Nisga'a territory: *Report of Deputation before Sir Wilfrid Laurier, 26th April 1911,* BCA (F/52/C
16) 35 at 43.

34 Galois, *supra* note 8 at 6-7 and 27, n. 25. Galois, *ibid.* at 6-7, states that it is unclear whether the Chiefs met the King but that they did meet with Pope Leo XIII. However, Leo died in 1903, so either they met Pius X, his successor, or the trip was in 1903. Joanne Drake-Terry, *The Same as Yesterday: The Lillooet Chronicle the Theft of Their Land and Resources* (Lillooet: Lillooet Tribal Council, 1989) at 222, says that they also met with King Edward.

35 "Indians' Petition," *supra* note 26 at 8.

36 Marshall, *supra* note 8 at 146-50. That same year the Interior tribes—the Lillooet, the Nlaka'pamux, the Shuswap, the Okanagan, and others—began to meet together to discuss strategy. See Drake-Terry, *supra* note 34 at 231. Eventually, these groups coalesced into a loose organization known as the Interior Tribes of British Columbia, which in turn was, more or less, absorbed by the Allied Indian Tribes of British Columbia in 1916.

37 The wording of the 1907 petitions suggests that, although missionaries may have had some involvement, they did not write them. See *e.g.* the one reproduced in Douglas Sanders, "Aboriginal Rights: The Search for Recognition in International Law" in Menno Boldt and J. Anthony Long, eds., *The Quest for Justice: Aboriginal Peoples and Aboriginal Rights* (Toronto: University of Toronto Press, 1985) 292 at 294.

38 The events in the Nass and Skeena regions are ably set out by Galois, *supra* note 30.

39 The case was adjourned *sine die* when the Dominion refused to participate. It is discussed in Hamar Foster, "Roadblocks and Legal History, Part II: Aboriginal Title and S. 91(24)" (1996) 54 Advocate 531 at 539.

40 On O'Meara, see E. Palmer Patterson II, "Arthur E. O'Meara, Friend of the Indians" (1967) 58 Pacific Northwest Quarterly 90, and two much more recent studies: Mary Haig-Brown, "Arthur Eugene O'Meara: Servant, Advocate, Seeker of Justice" in David A. Nock and Celia Haig-Brown, eds., *With Good Intentions: Euro-Canadian and Aboriginal Relations in Colonial Canada* (Vancouver: UBC Press, 2006) 258, and Foster, *supra* note 7.

41 On Wade, see the effusive entry in E.O.S. Scholefield, *British Columbia from the Earliest Times to the Present* (Vancouver: S.J. Clark, 1914) vol. 4 at 1149-50. Wade was retained by the Dominion when BC announced its intention to refer the Indian land issue to the provincial courts, but (as mentioned in note 39) Ottawa then decided not to participate. O'Meara to Wade (12 March 1913), VCA (Add MSS 44, vol. 18, file 9).

42 On Clark, see the even more effusive entry in Hector Charlesworth, ed., *A Cyclopedia of Canadian Biography* (Toronto: Hunter-Ross, 1919) at 78-79, which is almost as long as the one on Prime Minister Robert Borden. On the BC Indian Rights Association, see Galois, *supra* note 8.

43 On McInnes and his report, see Foster, *supra* note 17.

44 *St. Catherine's Lumber and Milling Company v. The Queen* (1888), 14 A.C. 46 [*St. Catherine's*], discussed in the text accompanying note 63 in this chapter.

45 In this opinion, Télésphore Fournier and his deputy quoted liberally from the Royal Proclamation and other legal authorities to argue that Indian title was "an interest in the lands of British Columbia" to which the title of the province was subject. The recently enacted *Crown Land Act* was therefore "objectionable, as tending to

deal with lands which are assumed to be the absolute property of the province, an assumption which completely ignores, as applicable to the Indians of British Columbia, the honour and good faith [of the] Crown." "Report of the Honourable the Minister of Justice, approved by His Excellency the Governor General in Council on the 23rd January 1875" reproduced as Appendix B in *House of Commons: Special Committees of the Senate and House of Commons Meeting in Joint Session to Inquire into the Claims of the Allied Indian Tribes of British Columbia, as Set Forth in Their Petition Submitted to Parliament in June 1926: Proceedings, Reports and the Evidence* (Ottawa, 1927) 39 at 43 [*Report of the Special Committees*].

46 *St. Catherine's, supra* note 44. The trial decision was in 1885, and the case went to the Ontario Court of Appeal and the Supreme Court of Canada before reaching the Judicial Committee of the Privy Council.

47 See Dara Culhane, *The Pleasure of the Crown: Anthropology, Law and First Nations* (Burnaby: Talonbooks, 1998) at 217. In an endnote, Culhane refers to an unnamed article by Doug Sanders and to Paul Tennant's *Aboriginal People and Politics* but cites no page numbers for either. Our search uncovered nothing in Sanders' work or Tennant's book that directly supports her assertion.

48 Paul Tennant, *Aboriginal People and Politics: The Indian Land Question in British Columbia, 1849-1989* (Vancouver: UBC Press, 1990) at 71.

49 *Ibid.* at 90.

50 *Ibid.* at 86. Barton was also the interpreter for the Chiefs at their 1887 meeting with Premier Smithe in Victoria.

51 Although it does not appear to have been mentioned in what some refer to as the Nisga'a Petition of 1908: see *infra* note 69. For the historical and contemporary importance of the Royal Proclamation to how First Nations, in particular in the southern Great Lakes region, have conceived of Aboriginal-settler legal relations, see John Borrows, "Constitutional Law from a First Nation Perspective: Self-Government and the Royal Proclamation" (1994) 28:1 U.B.C. L. Rev. 1.

52 Although Galois, *supra* note 8 at 27, also indicates that the Chiefs visited Ottawa, we are grateful to Dr. Dan Marshall (*supra* note 8) for the information about the reserve stay. Dr. Marshall also points out that the chiefs met poetess Pauline Johnson on this trip, who became a good friend of Chief Capilano and re-located to Vancouver. Even earlier, missionary Tate had accompanied a Cowichan fisherman's union delegation to a labour convention in Berlin (now Kitchener), Ontario, in 1902, where they may have learned about the Proclamation.

53 O'Meara to Bishop Stringer, Yukon (1 December 1908), BCA (Add MSS 1950, box 141, file 7). O'Meara also wrote to the Reverend A.E. Green, inquiring about the clause in the Terms of Union dealing with Indian lands and asking Green's help in getting permission to see books and papers "relating to the Indian title" that were in another clergyman's possession. See O'Meara to Green (25 January 1909), BCA (H/D/R57/OM2).

54 Tate went by train from Duncan to Victoria "to confer with Mr. O'Meara, of the Yukon Episcopal Indian Mission ... [W]e spent an hour discussing the condition of the Indians, and planning a course to ask for a treaty." Diary of C.M. Tate, entry for 1 February 1909, BCA (Add MSS 303, box 3, file 1). They talked again on 5

February, and then, on 29 May, they met with the Cowichan at Kokahsilah, near Duncan. See Galois, *supra* note 8 at 9.

55 O'Meara to Bishop Perrin, Victoria (15 March 1909), BCA (Add MSS 1950, box 141, file 5).

56 Clark was counsel in *Ontario Mining Co. v. Seybold*, [1903] A.C. 73. Charlesworth, *supra* note 42 at 78, wrote in 1919 that Clark's efforts in *Seybold* had "excited the attention of the legal profession and the public, both because the case had decided the Indian title question [in Ontario] and because a similar situation is becoming acute in British Columbia."

57 See *e.g.* the Gitksan notice described in note 30. In November 1909 Chief Simadeeks of Kitwanga wired Clark to advise that a letter in support of the Cowichan Petition had been sent. Sterritt *et al.*, *supra* note 8 at 276, n. 5. By 1910 a number of tribes were referring to Clark as their lawyer.

58 For copies of the petition, see *supra* note 8. See also Appendix 13.1 to the present discussion.

59 The resolution, dated 30 September 1909, is at BCA (F/52/C16) at 4-6 and has twenty-nine signatories, five of whom are Cowichan. The remainder (spelled as they appear in the document) are other Coast Salish tribes (Songish, Saanich, Nanaimo, Squamish, Sechalt, and Bella Coola), Haida (Skidegate, Masset), Nisga'a (Naas River), Tsimshian (Port Simpson, Kitkahta), Wakashan (Laquilto, Nimpkish, Quaqult, Cloyquet, Kilsomaht, and Bella Bella), and "several other tribes which were represented by letters, as they were not able to be present" at the Vancouver meeting that produced the memorandum. This meeting was widely reported in the press. See "Indians Are Out on Legal Warpath: Declare They Are Entitled to Interest in All Provincial Lands and Want Privy Council Decision" *Vancouver Province* (30 September 1909) at 1; "B.C. Indians Appeal to King: Want Claims to Lands in Province Adjudicated by Privy Council" *Victoria Daily Colonist* (2 October 1909) at 3; and "Indians Send Petition to King: Drafted at Meeting of Representatives of Tribes at Vancouver" *Victoria Times* (2 October 1909) at 18. Clark's "Statement" is at BCA (NWp, 970.5, C593s and H/D/R57/OM2).

60 "Indians Are Out on Legal Warpath," *ibid.* The second quoted phrase is taken, verbatim, from the memorandum.

61 Clark sent a copy of the petition to F.C. Wade, adding that he was "especially pleased to note your decided opinion that the Proclamation of 1763 applied to British Columbia." Clark to Wade (4 May 1910), VCA (Add MSS 44, vol. 18, file 9).

62 *Calder et al. v. Attorney General of British Columbia* (1971), 13 D.L.R. (3d) 64. This issue has generated a substantial literature, which, because the Supreme Court of Canada has ruled that the Proclamation simply confirmed pre-existing Aboriginal rights that were already recognized at common law, need not detain us here. See *Guerin v. The Queen*, [1984] 2 S.C.R. 335. There was a similar, albeit very short-lived, debate in the US about the applicability of the *Indian Trade and Intercourse Act* to the Oregon Territory. See Foster and Grove, *supra* note 2.

63 As the Judicial Committee put it in *St. Catherine's*, *supra* note 44 at 59, Dominion legislative power over lands reserved for Indians was not "inconsistent with the right of the Province to a beneficial interest" in those same lands. However, this

interest was "available to [the province] as a source of revenue *whenever the estate of the Crown is disencumbered of the Indian title*" [emphasis added].

64 *British Columbia Terms of Union (U.K.) (1871)*, R.S.C. 1985, App. II, no. 10. The original title for this document, "Order of Her Majesty in Council Admitting British Columbia into the Union," was changed to its current form with the *Constitution Act, 1982*, being Schedule B to the *Canada Act 1982* (U.K.), 1982, c. 11, s. 53, Schedule, item 4.

65 Order-in-Council 1036 (1938). Ottawa's view that the McKenna-McBride Agreement of 1912 removed the jurisdictional basis for imperial intervention prevailed, notwithstanding its fragile and unstable nature: it required two revisions and even then it took twenty-six years to complete.

66 See Appendix 13.1 for these references. A number of them can also be found in the 1875 Dominion Order-in-Council recommending disallowance of BC's Crown lands legislation, which became an important part of the argument for title as it developed after 1909.

67 See text accompanying "Indians' Petition," *supra* note 26.

68 O'Meara came in for particularly severe criticism. See Foster, *supra* note 7; Patterson, *supra* note 40; and Haig-Brown, *supra* note 40.

69 The original of the Nisga'a Petition is in the Public Record Office, London, UK (PRO) (PC 8/1240), and is reproduced as an appendix in Foster, Raven, and Webber, *supra* note 6. There was an earlier Nisga'a petition in 1908, but it appears to have been confined to a description of the lands claimed and "extensive quotations 'from the scriptures.'" Sterritt *et al., supra* note 8 at 139, quoting the *Vancouver Province* for 28 March 1908. It was not submitted to the imperial Privy Council.

70 But see Sterritt *et al., ibid.,* demonstrating that these maps are contested, even today.

71 Foster, *supra* note 17 at 173 and the text accompanying note 43.

72 Bowser to H.A. McLean (16 April 1909), BCA (GR 429, box 16, file 03, folio 1837/09).

73 A copy of the questions is at BCA (F/52/C16) at 91-95.

74 "Action Taken by Moral and Social Reform Council of Canada," BCA (F/52/C16) at 14 and 15-21 (the latter is comprised of letters and an interview report).

75 Correspondence, a transcript of this meeting and McBride's formal reply are at BCA (F/52/C16) at 53-84.

76 For the government record of this meeting, see BCA (F/52/C16) at 29-34; there is another at BCA (GR-3074).

77 *Report of Deputation before Sir Wilfrid Laurier, 26th April 1911*, BCA (F/52/C16) 35 at 51.

78 McBride believed that a court decision in favour of the Indians "would affect title to all land on the mainland ... and more than half of the land ... on Vancouver Island, and would have a most disastrous effect on our financial standing and would jeopardize the very large sums of money already invested in the province by English and other investors. I think you will agree with me that this is too serious a matter to be submitted to the determination of any court, however competent from a legal point of view. In other words, the considerations in this matter are political considerations and not legal questions." Draft letter from McBride to Laurier (19

November 1910), BCA (GR 441, box 149), quoted in Jeannie L. Kanakos, *The Negotiations to Relocate the Songhees Indians, 1843-1911* (M.A. thesis, Simon Fraser University, 1974) at 71 [unpublished].

79 S.C. 1910, c. 28, s. 1 and S.C. 1911, c. 14, s. 4 provided for an action in the Exchequer Court, with an appeal to the Supreme Court of Canada, if the claim was for Indian reserve land or land in respect of which Indians claimed "possession or any right of possession." This was necessary because litigation concerning land in a province was ordinarily within the exclusive jurisdiction of the province's superior court.

80 Reproduced in *Report of the Special Committees, supra* note 45, as Appendix E at 52.

81 McKenna to McBride (29 July 1912), excerpted in the testimony of Duncan Campbell Scott in *Report of the Special Committees, supra* note 45 at 8-9.

82 For the Agreement, see *Report of the Royal Commission on Indian Affairs for the Province of British Columbia* (Victoria: Acme Press, 1916) vol. 1 at 10-11.

83 In 1915 the Deputy Minister of Justice advised the Indian Department in Ottawa that it would be "inconsistent with the [McKenna-McBride] agreement" to involve the Colonial Secretary. Article 13 applied only "in case of disagreement" and did not "contemplate an appeal as against the agreement of the two Governments." E.L. Newcombe to D.C. Scott (26 April 1915), PRO (PC 8/1240).

84 Contrary to what many lawyers believed at the time (and even today), the Privy Council had statutory authority to refer a legal question to the Judicial Committee even if it had not been heard first in the colonial courts. See *An Act for the Better Administration of Justice in His Majesty's Privy Council, 1833* (U.K.), 3 & 4 Wm. IV., c. 41 (U.K.), s. 4. Indeed, the important Native title case of *In re Southern Rhodesia,* [1919] A.C. 211 came before the Judicial Committee pursuant to this provision and at the same time that the Nisga'a were pressing for their case to be heard with it.

85 For example, when the Privy Council was considering whether to refer the Nisga'a Petition to the Judicial Committee in 1913, it did not do so partly because the Dominion had assured the Colonial Office that Indian title was within the mandate of the Royal Commission of 1913 (McKenna-McBride Commission). This was of course not true, and when it came to light five years later, it caused that body to hesitate before once again deciding not to refer the petition to the Judicial Committee. See the documentation at PRO (PC 8/1240).

AFTERWORD: LOOKING FROM THE PAST INTO THE FUTURE

1 K.J.M. Smith and John McLaren, "History's Living Legacy: An Outline of 'Modern' Historiography of the Common Law" (2001) 21 L.S. 251 at 310.

2 Graham Parker, "Canadian Legal Culture" in Louis A. Knafla, ed., *Law and Justice in a New Land: Essays in Western Canadian Legal History* (Calgary: Carswell, 1986) 3 at 18.

3 A.G.L. Shaw, "Colonial Office" in Graeme Davison, John Hirst, and Stuart MacIntyre, eds., *Oxford Companion to Australian History* (Melbourne: Oxford University Press, 1998) 138; Martin Wight, *The Development of the Legislative Council 1606-1945* (London: Faber and Faber, 1946) at 53-56; and David B. Swinfen, *Imperial Control of Colonial Legislation, 1813-1865: A Study of British Policy towards Colonial Legislative Powers* (Oxford: Clarendon Press, 1970).

4 Cole Harris, *Making Native Space: Colonialism, Resistance, and Reserves in British Columbia* (Vancouver: UBC Press, 2002) at 4-15; Russell Smandych, "'To Soften the Extreme Rigor of Their Bondage': James Stephen's Attempt to Reform the Criminal Slave Laws of the West Indies, 1813-1833" (2005) 23 Law and History 537; and Smandych, "Contemplating the Testimony of 'Others': James Stephen, the Colonial Office, and the Fate of Australian Aboriginal Evidence Acts, circa 1839-1849" (2004) 8 Austl. J. Legal Hist. 237.

5 See in the context of racial discrimination, John McLaren, "The Burdens of Empire and the Legalization of White Supremacy in Canada" in W. Gordon and T. Ferguson, eds., *Legal History in the Making* (London: Hambledon Press, 1991) 187.

6 For two older but remarkably informative books on the Privy Council's control of imperial policy and law in earlier eras, see Leonard Woods Larabee, *Royal Government in America: A Study of the British Colonial System before 1783* (New Haven: Yale University Press, 1930); and Helen Taft Manning, *British Colonial Government after the American Revolution 1782-1820* (Hamden, CT: Archon Books, 1966).

7 P.A. Howell, *The Judicial Committee of the Privy Council 1833-1876: Its Origins, Structure and Development* (Cambridge: Cambridge University Press, 1979); David P. Swinfen, *Imperial Appeal: The Debate on the Appeal to the Privy Council, 1833-1986* (Manchester: Manchester University Press, 1987).

8 Bruce Kercher, "Unreported Privy Council Appeals from the Australian Colonies before 1850" (2003) 77 Austl. L.J. 309.

9 See *e.g.* Michael Belgrave, Merata Kawharu, and David Williams, *Waitangi Revisited: Perspectives on the Treaty of Waitangi* (Oxford: Oxford University Press, 2005); John Borrows, *Recovering Canada: The Resurgence of Indigenous Law* (Toronto: University of Toronto Press, 2002); Jan Crichett, *A Distant Field of Murder: Western District Frontiers 1834-1848* (Melbourne: University of Melbourne Press, 1990); Sid Harring, *White Man's Law: Native People in Nineteenth Century Canadian Jurisprudence* (Toronto: University of Toronto Press for the Osgoode Society for Canadian Legal History, 1998); Roger Milliss, *Waterloo Creek: The Australia Day Massacre of 1838, George Gipps and the British Conquest of New South Wales* (Sydney: University of New South Wales Press, 1992); Peter Russell, *Recognizing Aboriginal Title: The Mabo Case and Indigenous Resistance to English-Settler Colonialism* (Toronto: University of Toronto Press, 2005); Brian Titley, *A Narrow Vision: Duncan Campbell Scott and the Administration of Indian Affairs in Canada* (Vancouver: UBC Press, 1986); Alan Ward, *A Show of Justice: Racial "Amalgamation" in Nineteenth Century New Zealand* (Toronto: University of Toronto Press, 1974); and Ward, *An Unsettled History: Treaty Claims in New Zealand Today* (Wellington, NZ: Bridget Williams Books, 2000).

10 See *e.g.* Constance Backhouse, *Colour-Coded: A Legal History of Racism in Canada, 1900-1950* (Toronto: University of Toronto Press for the Osgoode Society for Canadian Legal History, 1999); Kathryn Cronin, *Colonial Casualties: Chinese in Early Victoria* (Melbourne: University of Melbourne Press, 1982); Richard Huttenback, *Racism and Empire: White Settlers and Coloured Immigrants in the British Self-Governing Colonies, 1830-1910* (Ithaca: Cornell University Press, 1976); Andrew Markus, *Fear and Hatred: Purifying Australia and California 1850-1901* (Sydney: Hale and Iremonger, 1979); Charles Price, *The Great Walls Are Built: Restrictive Immigration to North America and Australasia 1836-1888* (Canberra: Australian National University Press, 1974);

Patricia Roy, *A White Man's Province: British Columbia Politicians and Chinese and Japanese Immigrants, 1858-1914* (Vancouver: UBC Press, 1989); Peter Ward, *White Canada Forever: Popular Attitudes towards Orientals in British Columbia*, 2d ed. (Montreal and Kingston: McGill-Queen's University Press, 1990); Patricia Roy, *The Oriental Question: Consolidating a White Man's Province, 1914-41* (Vancouver: UBC Press, 2003); and James St. J. Walker, *"Race," Rights and the Law in the Supreme Court of Canada* (Toronto: University of Toronto Press for the Osgoode Society for Canadian Legal History, 1997).

11 Paul Romney, *Mr. Attorney: The Attorney General for Ontario in Court, Cabinet, and Legislature, 1791-1899* (Toronto: University of Toronto Press for the Osgoode Society for Canadian Legal History, 1986); Jonathan Swainger, *The Canadian Department of Justice and the Completion of Confederation, 1867-78* (Vancouver: UBC Press, 2000).

12 Rande Kostal, *A Jurisprudence of Power: Victorian Empire and the Rule of Law* (Oxford: Oxford University Press, 2005). For a recent study of Eyre as an icon of British colonialist culture, see Julie Evans, *Edward Eyre: Race and Colonial Governance* (Dunedin, NZ: University of Otago Press, 2005).

13 John Philip Reid, *Law for the Elephant: Property and Social Behavior on the Overland Trail* (San Marino, CA: Huntington Library, 1980).

14 Peter Karsten, *Between Law and Custom: "High" and "Low" Legal Cultures in the Lands of the British Diaspora—The United States, Canada, Australia and New Zealand, 1600-1900* (Cambridge: Cambridge University Press, 2002).

15 Jerry Bannister, *The Rule of the Admirals: Law, Custom and Government in Newfoundland, 1699-1832* (Toronto: University of Toronto Press for the Osgoode Society for Canadian Legal History, 2003).

16 Among examples are Paula Byrne, *Criminal Law and the Colonial Subject: New South Wales 1810-1830* (Cambridge: Cambridge University Press, 1993); F. Murray Greenwood and Barry Wright, *Canadian State Trials*, vol. 1: *Law, Politics, and Security Measures, 1608-1837* (Toronto: University of Toronto Press for the Osgoode Society for Canadian Legal History, 1996); Greenwood and Wright, *Canadian State Trials*, vol. 2: *Rebellion and Invasion in the Canadas, 1837-1839* (Toronto: University of Toronto Press for the Osgoode Society for Canadian Legal History, 2002); David Neal, *The Rule of Law in a Penal Colony: Law and Power in Early New South Wales* (Cambridge: Cambridge University Press, 1991); and Jim Phillips, Tina Loo, and Susan Lewthwaite, eds., *Essays in the History of Canadian Law*, vol. 5: *Crime and Criminal Justice in Canadian History* (Toronto: University of Toronto Press for the Osgoode Society for Canadian History, 1994).

17 A.R. Buck, John McLaren, and Nancy E. Wright, *Land and Freedom: Law, Property Rights and the British Diaspora* (Aldershot: Ashgate, 2001); and John McLaren, A.R. Buck, and Nancy E. Wright, eds., *Despotic Dominion: Property Rights in British Settler Societies* (Vancouver: UBC Press, 2005). John C. Weaver, *The Great Land Rush and the Making of the Modern World, 1650-1900* (Montreal and Kingston: McGill-Queen's University Press, 2003); Stuart Banner, *How the Indians Lost Their Land: Law and Power on the Frontier* (Cambridge: Cambridge University Press, 2005) and *Possessing the Pacific: Land, Settlers, and Indigenous People from Australia to Alaska* (Cambridge, MA: Harvard University Press, 2007); and Lindsay G. Robertson, *Conquest by Law:*

How the Discovery of America Dispossessed Indigenous Peoples of Their Lands (Oxford: Oxford University Press, 2005).

18 R.C.B. Risk, "The Nineteenth Century Foundations of the Business Corporation in Ontario" (1973) 23 U.T.L.J. 307; Risk, "The Golden Age: The Law about the Market in Nineteenth-Century Ontario" (1976) 26 U.T.L.J. 307; Risk, "The Last Golden Age: Property and the Allocation of Losses in Ontario in the Nineteenth-Century" (1977) 27 U.T.L.J. 199; and Risk, "Law and the Economy in Mid-nineteenth Century Ontario: A Perspective" (1977) 27 U.T.L.J. 403. Bruce Kercher, *Debt, Seduction and Other Disasters: The Birth of Civil Law in Convict New South Wales* (Sydney: Federation Press, 1996).

19 Karsten, *supra* note 14. Under the editorship of Andrew Buck, the *Australian Journal of Legal History* (recently renamed *Legal History*) has been attracting articles in some of these fields. See *e.g.* Thomas G.W. Telfer, "A Canadian 'World without Bankruptcy': The Failure of Bankruptcy Reform in Canada, 1880 to 1903" (2004) 8 Austl. J. Legal Hist. 83; and John C. Weaver, "A Pathology of Insolvents: Melbourne, 1871-1915" (2004) 8 Austl. J. Legal Hist. 109.

20 Jeremy Finn, "Australasian Law and Canadian Statutes in the Nineteenth Century: A Study of the Movement of Colonial Legislation between Jurisdictions" (2002) 25 Dal. L.J. 169.

21 John Bennett, *Sir Francis Forbes: First Chief Justice of New South Wales, 1823-1837* (Sydney: Federation Press, 2001); Bennett, *Sir James Dowling: Second Chief Justice of New South Wales, 1837-1844* (Sydney: Federation Press, 2001); Bennett, *Sir William a'Becket: First Chief Justice of Victoria, 1852-1857* (Sydney: Federation Press, 2001); Bennett, *Sir Charles Cooper: First Chief Justice of South Australia, 1856-1861* (Sydney: Federation Press, 2002); Bennett, *Sir Archibald Burt: First Chief Justice of Western Australia, 1861-1879* (Sydney: Federation Press, 2002); Bennett, *Sir John Pedder: First Chief Justice of Tasmania, 1824-1854* (Sydney: Federation Press, 2003); Bennett, *Sir James Cockle: First Chief Justice of Queensland, 1863-1879* (Sydney: Federation Press, 2003); Bennett, *Sir Henry Wrensfordley: Second Chief Justice of Western Australia, 1880-1883* (Sydney: Federation Press, 2004); Bennett, *Sir William Stawell: Second Chief Justice of Victoria, 1857-1886* (Sydney: Federation Press, 2004); Bennett, *Sir James Martin: Fourth Chief Justice of New South Wales, 1873-1886* (Sydney: Federation Press, 2005); and Bennett, *Sir George Higginbotham: Third Chief Justice of Victoria* (Sydney: Federation Press, 2007). Among impressive Canadian judicial biographies of colonial and early provincial judges are Patrick Brode, *Sir John Beverley Robinson: Bone and Sinew of the Compact* (Toronto: University of Toronto Press for the Osgoode Society for Canadian Legal History, 1984); David Ricardo Williams, *"The Man for a New Country": Sir Matthew Baillie Begbie* (Sidney, BC: Gray's, 1977); and Peter Oliver, ed., *The Conventional Man: The Diaries of Ontario Chief Justice Robert A. Harrison 1856-1878* (Toronto: University of Toronto Press for the Osgoode Society for Canadian Legal History, 2003). For an intriguing biography of one of the peripatetic judges of the late nineteenth-century British Empire, see Bridget Brereton, *Law, Justice and Empire: The Colonial Career of John Gorrie, 1829-1892* (Kingston, Jamaica: University Press of the West Indies, 1997). On the challenges of judicial biography, see Philip V. Girard, "Judging Lives: Judicial Biography from Hale to Holmes" (2003) 7 Austl. J. Legal Hist. 87.

22 Neal, *supra* note 16; Romney, *supra* note 11; F. Murray Greenwood, *Legacies of Fear: Law and Policies in Quebec in the Era of the French Revolution* (Toronto: University of Toronto Press for the Osgoode Society for Canadian Legal History, 1993); and Diane Kirkby and Catharine Coleborne, eds., *Law, History, Colonialism: The Reach of Empire* (Manchester: Manchester University Press, 2001).

23 The connections between British interpretations of liberty and the rule of law and the colonial experience are touched upon in John McLaren, "Reflections on the Rule of Law: The Georgian Colonies of New South Wales and Upper Canada, 1788-1837" in Diane Kirkby and Catharine Coleborne, eds., *Law, History, Colonialism: The Reach of Empire* (Manchester: Manchester University Press, 2001) 46; and McLaren, "'The Judicial Office ... Bowing to No Power but the Supremacy of the Law': Judges and the Rule of Law in Colonial Australia and Canada, 1788-1840" (2003) 7:2 Austl. J. Legal Hist. 177. Irish Whig influence on law and politics in Upper Canada is addressed in John McLaren, "The Rule of Law and Irish Whig Constitutionalism in Upper Canada: William Warren Baldwin, the 'Irish Opposition' and the Volunteer Connection" in Jim Phillips and John Saywell, eds., *Essays in the History of Canadian Law*, vol. 11: *In Honour of Peter Oliver* (Toronto: University of Toronto Press for the Osgoode Society for Canadian Legal History, 2007) 11.

24 Lauren Benton, *Law and Colonial Cultures: Legal Regimes in World History, 1400-1900* (Cambridge: Cambridge University Press, 2002).

25 Alex Castles, *Annotated Bibliography of Printed Materials on Australian Law, 1788-1900* (Sydney: Law Book Company, 1994).

26 See "Decisions of the Superior Courts of New South Wales, 1788-1899," online: Division of Law, Macquarie University, http://www.law.mq.edu.au/scnsw; and "Decisions of the Nineteenth Century Tasmanian Superior Courts," online: Division of Law, Macquarie University, and School of History and Classics, University of Tasmania, http://www.law.mq.edu.au/sctas.

27 In the dedication of Karsten, *supra* note 14, to Bruce Kercher and attributed to Ian Holloway. Bruce Kercher has recently added further weight to this description by editing, with T.D. Castle, *Dowling's Select Cases 1828 to 1844: Decisions of the Supreme Court of New South Wales* (Sydney: Francis Forbes Society for Legal History, 2005).

28 See for Australia and New Zealand, respectively, Bruce Kercher, *An Unruly Child: A History of Law in Australia* (Sydney: Allen and Unwin, 1995); and Peter Spiller, Jeremy Finn, and Richard Boast, *A New Zealand Legal History*, 2d ed. (Wellington, NZ: Brookers, 2001). In Canada, in which European legal history straddles the period from the sixteenth century on, the emphasis has been on regional studies. See the Osgoode Society for Canadian Legal History's Essays in the History of Canadian Law Series; Louis A. Knafla, ed., *Law and Justice in a New Land: Essays in Western Canadian Legal History* (Calgary: Carswell, 1986); and Louis A. Knafla and Jonathan Swainger, eds., *Laws and Societies in the Canadian Prairie West, 1670-1940* (Vancouver: UBC Press, 2005).

SELECTED BIBLIOGRAPHY

Abbott, Charles. *A Treatise of the Law Relative to Merchant Ships and Seamen* (London: Brooke and Rider, 1802).

Acheson, T.W. *Saint John: A Colonial Urban Community* (Toronto: University of Toronto Press, 1984).

Alexander, James. *A Brief Narrative of the Case and Trial of John Peter Zenger, Printer of the New York Weekly Journal,* ed. by Stanley N. Katz (Cambridge, MA: Belknap Press, 1963).

Allan, T.R.S. *Constitutional Justice: A Liberal Theory of the Rule of Law* (Oxford and New York: Oxford University Press, 2001).

Anderson, Benedict. *Imagined Communities: Reflections on the Origin and Spread of Nationalism,* rev. ed. (London: Verso, 2002).

Arthurs, Harry. *Without the Law: Administrative Justice and Legal Pluralism in Nineteenth Century England* (Toronto: University of Toronto Press, 1985).

Atkinson, Neil. *Adventures in Democracy: A History of the Vote in New Zealand* (Dunedin, NZ: University of Otago Press, 2003).

Australian Dictionary of Biography. Vol. 1, ed. by Douglas Pike (Melbourne: Melbourne University Press, 1966) *s.v.* "Baxter, Alexander Macduff (1798-1836?)."

Ayres, Philip. *Owen Dixon* (Melbourne: Miegunyah Press, 2003).

Backhouse, Constance. *Colour-Coded: A Legal History of Racism in Canada, 1900-1950* (Toronto: Osgoode Society for Canadian Legal History and University of Toronto Press, 1999).

Baehre, Rainer. "Trying the Rebels: Emergency Legislation and the Colonial Executive's Overall Legal Strategy in the Upper Canadian Rebellion" in F. Murray Greenwood and Barry Wright, eds. *Canadian State Trials.* Vol. 2: *Rebellion and Invasion in the Canadas, 1837-1839* (Toronto: Osgoode Society for Canadian Legal History and University of Toronto Press, 2002) 41.

Baker, Robert. "Creating Order in the Wilderness: Transplanting the English Law to Rupert's Land, 1835-51" (1999) 17 L.H.R. 209.

—. "The Early Judges of Tasmania" (1960) 8 Tasmanian Historical Research Association Papers and Proceedings 71.

Baker, William M. *Timothy Warren Anglin, 1822-96: Irish Catholic Canadian* (Toronto: University of Toronto Press, 1977).

Bakken, Larry. *Justice in the Wilderness: A Study of Frontier Courts in Canada and the United States, 1670-1870* (Littleton, CO: Fred B. Rothman, 1986).

Bakker, Peter. "Hudson Bay Trader's Cree: A Cree Pidgin?" in John D. Nichols and Arden C. Ogg, eds. *Nikotwâsik iskwâhtêm, pâskihtêpayih!: Studies in Honour of H.C. Wolfart* (Winnipeg: Algonquian and Iroquoian Linguistics, 1996) 1.

Ballinger, Richard A. *A Treatise on the Property Rights of Husband and Wife, Under the Community or Ganancial System* (Seattle: Bancroft-Whitney, 1895).

Banks, Margaret A. "The Evolution of the Ontario Courts, 1788-1981" in D. Flaherty, ed. *Essays in the History of Canadian Law.* Vol. 2 (Toronto: University of Toronto Press, 1983) 502.

Banner, Stuart. *How the Indians Lost Their Land: Law and Power on the Frontier* (Cambridge: Cambridge University Press, 2005).

—. *Possessing the Pacific: Land, Settlers, and Indigenous People from Australia to Alaska* (Cambridge, MA: Harvard University Press, 2007).

Bannister, Jerry. "Law and Labor in Eighteenth-Century Newfoundland" in Douglas Hay and Paul Craven, eds. *Masters, Servants, and Magistrates in Britain and the Empire, 1562-1955* (Chapel Hill: University of North Carolina Press, 2004) 153.

—. *The Rule of the Admirals: Law, Custom and Government in Newfoundland, 1699-1832* (Toronto: Osgoode Society for Canadian Legal History and University of Toronto Press, 2003).

Barrell, John. *Imagining the King's Death: Figurative Treason, Fantasies of Regicide, 1793-1796* (Oxford: Oxford University Press, 2000).

Barron, F.L. *The Genesis of Temperance in Ontario, 1828-1850* (M.A. thesis, University of Guelph, 1976) [unpublished].

Basch, Norma. *In the Eyes of the Law: Women, Marriage and Property in Nineteenth-Century New York* (Ithaca: Cornell University Press, 1982).

Bassett, J., and J.G.H. Hannan. *Dictionary of New Zealand Biography.* Vol. 1, ed. by W.H. Oliver (Wellington/Auckland, NZ: Auckland University Press with Bridget Williams Books and the Department of Internal Affairs, 1998) *s.v.* "Prendergast, James 1826-1921," online: http://www.dnzb.govt.nz/dnzb/.

Beatty, David. *The Ultimate Rule of Law* (Oxford and New York: Oxford University Press, 2004).

Belgrave, Michael. *Historical Frictions: Maori Claims and Reinvented Histories* (Auckland: Auckland University Press, 2005).

Belgrave, Michael, Merata Kawharu, and David Williams, eds. *Waitangi Revisited: Perspectives on the Treaty of Waitangi* (Oxford: Oxford University Press, 2005).

Bell, David Graham. "Maritime Legal Institutions under the 'Ancien Regime'" (1996) 23 Man. L.J. 103.

—. "Sedition among the Loyalists: The Case of Saint John, 1784-1786" (1995) 44 U. N.B.L.J. 163.

Bennett, John M. *Equity Law in New South Wales 1788-1902* (Sydney: University of Sydney Legal Research Project, 1962).

—. *Sir Archibald Burt: First Chief Justice of Western Australia, 1861-1879* (Sydney: Federation Press, 2002).

—. *Sir Charles Cooper: First Chief Justice of South Australia, 1856-1861* (Sydney: Federation Press, 2002).

—. *Sir Francis Forbes: First Chief Justice of New South Wales, 1823-1837* (Sydney: Federation Press, 2001).

—. *Sir George Higginbotham: Third Chief Justice of Victoria* (Sydney: Federation Press, 2007).

—. *Sir Henry Wrensfordley: Second Chief Justice of Western Australia, 1880-1883* (Sydney: Federation Press, 2004).

—. *Sir James Cockle: First Chief Justice of Queensland, 1863-1879* (Sydney: Federation Press, 2003).

—. *Sir James Dowling: Second Chief Justice of New South Wales, 1837-1844* (Sydney: Federation Press, 2001).

—. *Sir James Martin: Fourth Chief Justice of New South Wales, 1873-1886* (Sydney: Federation Press, 2005).

—. *Sir John Pedder: First Chief Justice of Tasmania, 1824-1854* (Sydney: Federation Press, 2003).

—. *Sir William a'Becket: First Chief Justice of Victoria, 1852-1857* (Sydney: Federation Press, 2001).

—. *Sir William Stawell: Second Chief Justice of Victoria, 1857-1886* (Sydney: Federation Press, 2004).

Benton, Lauren. *Law and Colonial Cultures: Legal Regimes in World History, 1400-1900* (Cambridge: Cambridge University Press, 2002).

Binnema, Theodore. *Contested and Common Ground: A Human and Environmental History of the Northwestern Plains* (Norman: University of Oklahoma Press, 2001).

Blackstone, William. *Commentaries on the Laws of England*. Vol. 1 (New York: Legal Classics Library, 1983).

Blake, Lynn A. "Oblate Missionaries and the 'Indian Land Question'" (1998) 119 BC Studies 27.

Blume, W.W., and E.G. Brown. "Territorial Courts and Law—Unifying Factors in the Development of American Legal Institutions" (1962) 61 Mich. L. Rev. 467.

Borrows, John. "Constitutional Law from a First Nation Perspective: Self-Government and the Royal Proclamation" (1994) 28:1 U.B.C. L. Rev. 1.

—. *Recovering Canada: The Resurgence of Indigenous Law* (Toronto: University of Toronto Press, 2002).

Bottomley, Stephen. "A Framework for Understanding the Interpretation of Corporate Law in Australia" in Suzanne Corcoran and Stephen Bottomley, eds. *Interpreting Statutes* (Annandale, NSW: Federation Press, 2005) 147.

Bottomley, Stephen, and Simon Bronitt. *Law in Context*, 3d ed. (Annandale, NSW: Federation Press, 2006).

Braithwaite, John. "Crime in a Convict Republic" (2001) 64 Mod. L. Rev. 11.

Brereton, Bridget. *Law, Justice and Empire: The Colonial Career of John Gorrie, 1829-1892* (Kingston, Jamaica: University Press of the West Indies, 1997).

Brode, Patrick. *Sir John Beverley Robinson: Bone and Sinew of the Compact* (Toronto: Osgoode Society for Canadian Legal History and University of Toronto Press, 1984).

Bronitt, Simon. "Interpreting Law Enforcement Immunities: The Relationship between Judicial, Legislative and Administrative Models" in Suzanne Corcoran and Stephen Bottomley, eds. *Interpreting Statutes* (Annandale, NSW: Federation Press, 2005) 223.

Brookfield, F.M. *Waitangi and Indigenous Rights* (Auckland: Auckland University Press, 2006).

Brown, Jennifer. *Strangers in Blood: Fur Trade Company Families in Indian Country* (Vancouver: UBC Press, 1980).

Brown, Jennifer, and Elizabeth Vibert, eds. *Reading beyond Words: Contexts for Native History* (Peterborough, ON: Broadview Press, 1996).

Brown, R. Blake. "A Delusion, a Mockery, and a Snare: Array Challenges and Jury Selection in England and Ireland, 1800-1850" (2004) 39 Can. J. Hist. 1.

—. *The Jury, Politics and the State in British North America: Reforms to Jury Systems in Nova Scotia and Upper Canada, 1825-1867* (Ph.D. diss., Dalhousie University, 2005) [unpublished].

—. "Storms, Roads and Harvest Time: Criticisms of Jury Service in Pre-Confederation Nova Scotia" (2006) 36 Acadiensis 93.

Buck, A.R. *The Making of Australian Property Law* (Sydney: Federation Press, 2006).

—. "'The Poor Man': Rhetoric and Political Culture in Mid Nineteenth-Century New South Wales" (1996) 43 Austl. J. Pol. & Hist. 200.

—. "Property Law and the Origins of Australian Egalitarianism" (1995) 1 Austl. J. Legal Hist. 145.

—. "Torrens Title, Intestate Estates and the Origins of Australian Property Law" (1996) 4:2 Austl. Prop. L.J. 89.

Buck, A.R., John McLaren, and Nancy E. Wright. *Land and Freedom: Law, Property Rights and the British Diaspora* (Aldershot: Ashgate, 2001).

Buckner, Phillip A. *The Transition to Responsible Government: British Policy in British North America, 1815-1850* (Westport: Greenwood Press, 1985).

Burgess, Glenn. *The Politics of the Ancient Constitution: An Introduction to English Political Thought, 1603-1642* (University Park: Pennsylvania State University Press, 1992).

Butlin, N.G. "Colonial Socialism in Australia, 1860-1900" in H.G.J. Aitken, ed. *The State and Economic Growth* (New York: Social Science Research Council, 1959) 26.

Byrne, Paula. *Criminal Law and the Colonial Subject: New South Wales 1810-1830* (Cambridge: Cambridge University Press, 1993).

Cahill, Barry. "Sedition in Nova Scotia: *R. v. Wilkie* (1820) and the Incontestable Illegality of Seditious Libel before *R. v. Howe* (1835)" (1994) 17 Dal. L.J. 458.

—. "The Treason of the Merchants: Dissent and Repression in Halifax in the Era of the American Revolution" (1996) 26 Acadiensis 52.

Cahill, Barry, and Jim Phillips. "The Supreme Court of Nova Scotia: Origins to Confederation" in Philip Girard, Jim Phillips, and Barry Cahill, eds. *The Supreme Court of Nova Scotia, 1754-2004: From Imperial Bastion to Provincial Oracle* (Toronto: Osgoode Society for Canadian Legal History and University of Toronto Press, 2004) 53.

Calhoun, Craig, ed. *Habermas and the Public Sphere* (Cambridge, MA: MIT Press, 1992).

Campbell, Gail G. "Disenfranchised but Not Quiescent: Women Petitioners in New Brunswick in the Mid Nineteenth Century" (Spring 1989) 18:2 Acadiensis 22.

—. "'Smashers' and 'Rummies': Voters and the Rise of Parties in Charlotte County, New Brunswick, 1846-1857" (1986) 21:1 Historical Papers 86.

Careless, J.M.S. *Brown of the Globe.* Vol. 1: *The Voice of Upper Canada, 1818-1859* (Toronto: Macmillan, 1959).

Carlson, Keith Thor. "Rethinking Dialogue and History: The King's Promise and the 1906 Aboriginal Delegation to London" (2005) 16:2 Native Stud. Rev. 1.

Castles, Alex. *Annotated Bibliography of Printed Materials on Australian Law, 1788-1900* (Sydney: Law Book Company, 1994).

—. *An Australian Legal History* (Sydney: Law Book Company, 1982).

—. *Lawless Harvests or God Save the Judges: Van Diemen's Land 1803-1853, A Legal History* (Melbourne: Australian Scholarly Publishing, 2007).

Chapman, James K. "The Mid-Nineteenth Century Temperance Movement in New Brunswick and Maine" (1954) 35 Can. Hist. Rev. 43.

Charlesworth, Hector, ed. *A Cyclopedia of Canadian Biography* (Toronto: Hunter-Ross, 1919).

Charlwood, Don. *The Long Farewell* (Ringwood: Penguin, 1993).

Cheever, George B. *Defence in Abatement of Judgment for an Alleged Libel in the Story Entitled "Inquire at Amos Giles' Distillery"* (New York, 1836).

Cheffins, Ronald I. "The Royal Prerogative and the Office of the Lieutenant Governor" (Spring 2000) 23 Canadian Parliamentary Review, online: http://www.parl.gc.ca/Infoparl/english/issue.htm?param=74&art=163.

Chorley, Lord. "Edward Jenks 1861-1939" (1947) 1 J.S.P.T.L. (New Series) 114.

Christophers, Brett. *Positioning the Missionary: John Booth Good and the Confluence of Culture in Nineteenth-Century British Columbia* (Vancouver: UBC Press, 1998).

Chute, Janet E. "Ojibwa Leadership during the Fur Trade Era at Sault Ste. Marie" in Susan Sleeper-Smith, Jo-Anne Fiske, and William Wicken, eds. *New Faces of the Fur Trade: Selected Papers of the Seventh North American Fur Trade Conference, Halifax, Nova Scotia, 1995* (East Lansing: Michigan State University Press, 1998) 153.

Clarke, Ernest. "The Cumberland Glebe Dispute and the Background to the American Revolution in Nova Scotia, 1771-1774" (1993) 42 U.N.B.L.J. 95.

Clarke, Ernest A., and Jim Phillips. "Rebellion and Repression in Nova Scotia in the Era of the American Revolution" in F. Murray Greenwood and Barry Wright, eds. *Canadian State Trials.* Vol. 1: *Law, Politics, and Security Measures, 1608-1837* (Toronto: Osgoode Society for Canadian Legal History and University of Toronto Press, 1996) 172.

Coates, Kenneth, and William Morrison. *The Alaska Highway in World War II: The US Army Occupation in Canada's Northwest* (Toronto: University of Toronto Press, 1992).

Cockburn, J.S. *A History of English Assizes, 1558-1714* (Cambridge: Cambridge University Press, 1972).

Cocks, Raymond. *Foundations of the Modern Bar* (London: Sweet and Maxwell, 1983).

Cooke, R. "Introduction" (1990) 14:1 N.Z.U.L. Rev. 1.

Corcoran, Suzanne, and Stephen Bottomley, eds. *Interpreting Statutes* (Annandale, NSW: Federation Press, 2005).

Couturier, Jacques Paul. "Prohibition or Regulation? The Enforcement of the Canada Temperance Act in Moncton, 1881-1896" in Cheryl Krasnick Warsh, ed. *Drink in Canada: Historical Essays* (Montreal and Kingston: McGill-Queen's University Press, 1993) 144.

Creighton, Donald. *John A. Macdonald: The Young Politician* (Toronto: Macmillan, 1952).

Crichett, Jan. *A Distant Field of Murder: Western District Frontiers 1834-1848* (Melbourne: University of Melbourne Press, 1990).

Cronin, Kathryn. *Colonial Casualties: Chinese in Early Victoria* (Melbourne: University of Melbourne Press, 1982).

Culhane, Dara. *The Pleasure of the Crown: Anthropology, Law and First Nations* (Burnaby: Talonbooks, 1998).

Currey, C.H. *Sir Francis Forbes: The First Chief Justice of the Supreme Court of New South Wales* (Sydney: Angus and Robertson, 1968).

Dawson, C.A., assisted by R.W. Murchie. *The Settlement of the Peace River Country—A Study of a Pioneer Area* (Toronto: Macmillan, 1934).

"The Decline of Circuit Life" (1881) Can. L.J. 77.

Dening, Greg. *Mr Bligh's Bad Language* (Cambridge: Cambridge University Press, 1992).

Denison, W., and C. Denison. *Varieties of Vice-Regal Life (Van Diemen's Land Section),* ed. by Richard Davis and Stefan Petrow (Hobart: Tasmanian Historical Research Association, 2004).

Dicey, A.V. *Introduction to the Study of the Law of the Constitution* (Indianapolis: Liberty Classics, 1982; first published 1915).

—. *Lectures on the Relation between Law and Opinion in England in the Nineteenth Century* (London: Macmillan, 1905).

Dick, Ernest J. "From Temperance to Prohibition in 19th Century Nova Scotia" (Autumn 1981) 61:3 Dalhousie Rev. 530.

Dickason, Olive Patricia. *Canada's First Nations: A History of Founding Peoples* (Toronto: McClelland and Stewart, 1992).

Donovan, K. "The Origin and Establishment of the New Brunswick Courts" (1980) Journal of the New Brunswick Museum 57.

Drake-Terry, Joanne. *The Same as Yesterday: The Lillooet Chronicle the Theft of Their Land and Resources* (Lillooet: Lillooet Tribal Council, 1989).

Driscoll, Heather Rollanson. "'A Most Important Chain of Connection': Marriage in the Hudson's Bay Company" in Theodore Binnema, Gerhard J. Ens, and R.C. Macleod, eds. *From Rupert's Land to Canada: Essays in Honour of John E. Foster* (Edmonton: University of Alberta Press, 2001) 81.

Drucker, Philip. *The Native Brotherhoods: Modern Intertribal Organizations on the Northwest Coast.* Smithsonian Institution Bureau of American Ethnology Bulletin 168 (Washington DC: Government Printing Office, 1958).

Durie, E.T., and G.S. Orr. "The Role of the Waitangi Tribunal and the Development of a Bicultural Jurisprudence" (1990) 14 N.Z.U.L. Rev. 62.

Dyer, George. *An Address to the People of Great Britain, on the Doctrine of Libels, and the Office of Juror* (London, 1799).

Earle, Peter. *Sailors: English Merchant Seamen 1650-1775* (London: Methuen, 2007).

Earle, R.R. "A Man Who Knew Furs" in Marguerite Davies and Cora Ventress, eds. *Fort St. John Pioneer Profiles* (Fort St. John: Fort St. John Centennial Committee, 1971) 32.

Eastwood, T.M., and Paul Williamson. *Dictionary of Canadian Biography.* Vol. 11, ed. by Francess G. Halpenny and Jean Hamelin (Toronto: University of Toronto Press, 1982) *s.v.* "Robertson, Alexander Rocke."

Ecksteins, Modris. *Rites of Spring—The Great War and the Birth of the Modern Age* (Toronto: Lester and Orpen Dennys, 1989).

Edgeworth, Brendan. "Defamation Law and the Emergence of a Critical Press in Colonial New South Wales, 1824-1831" (1990) 6 Austl. J. L. & Soc. 50.

Elias, S. "The Treaty of Waitangi and Separation of Powers in New Zealand" in B.D. Gray and R.B. McClintock, eds. *Courts and Policy: Checking the Balance* (Wellington, NZ: Brookers, 1995) 206.

Ely, Richard, ed. *Carrel Inglis Clark: The Supreme Court of Tasmania: Its First Century, 1824-1924* (Hobart: University of Tasmania Law Press, 1995).

Emsley, C. "An Aspect of Pitt's 'Terror': Prosecutions for Sedition during the 1790's" (1981) 6 Social History 155.

Evans, Julie. *Edward Eyre: Race and Colonial Governance* (Dunedin, NZ: University of Otago Press, 2005).

Evans, R. "Stage Coaches in Nova Scotia, 1815-1867" (1938) 24 Collections of the Nova Scotia Historical Society 107.

—. *Transportation and Communication in Nova Scotia, 1815-1850* (M.A. thesis, Dalhousie University, 1936) [unpublished].

Evatt, H.V. *Rum Rebellion: A Study of the Overthrow of Governor Bligh by John Macarthur and the New South Wales Corps* (Sydney: Angus and Robertson, 1938).

Faulkner, William. *Requiem for a Nun* (New York: Random House, 1951).

Ferguson, Niall. *Empire: The Rise and Demise of the British World Order and the Lessons for Global Power* (New York: Basic Books, 2004).

Fingard, Judith. *Jack in Port: Sailortowns of Eastern Canada* (Toronto: University of Toronto Press, 1982).

Finn, Jeremy. "Australasian Law and Canadian Statutes in the Nineteenth Century: A Study of the Movement of Colonial Legislation between Jurisdictions" (2002) 25 Dal. L.J. 169.

Fitzpatrick, Kathleen. *Sir John Franklin in Tasmania 1837-1843* (Melbourne: Melbourne University Press, 1949).

Forsey, Eugene A. *Freedom and Order* (Toronto: McClelland and Stewart, 1974).

—. *The Royal Power of Dissolution of Parliament in the British Commonwealth* (Toronto: Oxford University Press, 1943).

Foster, Hamar. "The Kamloops Outlaws and Commissions of Assize in Nineteenth-Century British Columbia" in David H. Flaherty, ed. *Essays in the History of Canadian Law*. Vol. 2 (Toronto: Osgoode Society for Canadian Legal History and University of Toronto Press, 1983) 308.

—. "Mutiny on the Beaver: Law and Authority in the Fur Trade 'Navy' on the Northwest Coast, 1836-1839" (1991) 20 Man. L.J. 15.

—. "The Queen's Law Is Better than Yours: International Homicide in Early British Columbia" in J. Phillips, Tina Loo, and Susan Lewthwaite, eds. *Essays in the History of Canadian Law*. Vol. 5: *Crime and Criminal Justice in Canadian History* (Toronto: Osgoode Society for Canadian Legal History and University of Toronto Press, 1994) 41.

—. "Roadblocks and Legal History, Part II: Aboriginal Title and S. 91(24)" (1996) 54 Advocate 531.

—. "A Romance of the Lost: The Role of Tom MacInnes in the History of the British Columbia Indian Land Question" in G. Blaine Baker and Jim Phillips, eds. *Essays in the History of Canadian Law*. Vol. 8: *In Honour of RCB Risk* (Toronto: Osgoode Society for Canadian Legal History and University of Toronto Press, 1999) 171.

—. "Shooting the Elephant: Historians and the Problem of Frontier Lawlessness" in Richard Eales and David Sullivan, eds. *The Political Context of Law* (London: Hambledon Press, 1987) 135.

—. "The Struggle for the Supreme Court: Law and Politics in British Columbia, 1871–1885" in Louis A. Knafla, ed. *Law and Justice in a New Land: Essays in Western Canadian Legal History* (Toronto: Carswell, 1986) 167.

—. "We Are Not O'Meara's Children: Law, Lawyers and the First Campaign for Aboriginal Title in British Columbia" in Hamar Foster, Heather Raven, and Jeremy Webber, eds. *Let Right Be Done: Aboriginal Title, the Calder Case, and the Future of Indigenous Rights* (Vancouver: UBC Press, 2007) 61.

Foster, Hamar, and Alan Grove. "'Trespassers on the Soil': *United States v. Tom* and a New Perspective on the Short History of Treaty Making in Nineteenth-Century British Columbia" (2003) 138–39 BC Studies 51.

Foster, Hamar, Heather Raven, and Jeremy Webber, eds. *Let Right Be Done: Aboriginal Title, the Calder Case, and the Future of Indigenous Rights* (Vancouver: UBC Press, 2007).

Foster, Hamar, and John McLaren, eds. *Essays in the History of Canadian Law.* Vol. 6: *British Columbia and the Yukon* (Toronto: Osgoode Society for Canadian Legal History and University of Toronto Press, 1995).

Foster, John E. "The Indian-Trader in the Hudson Bay Fur Trade Tradition" in Jim Freedman and Jerome H. Barkow, eds. *Proceedings of the Second Congress, Canadian Ethnology Society.* Mercury Series, Ethnology Service Paper 28 (Ottawa: National Museum of Man, 1975) 571.

Frame, A. "A State Servant Looks at the Treaty" (1990) 14 N.Z.U.L. Rev. 82.

Fraser, Robert L. "All the Privileges Which Englishmen Possess: Order, Rights, and Constitutionalism in Upper Canada" in Robert L. Fraser, ed. *Provincial Justice: Upper Canadian Legal Portraits from the Dictionary of Canadian Biography* (Toronto: Osgoode Society for Canadian Legal History and University of Toronto Press, 1992) xxi.

Friesen, Jean. *Dictionary of Canadian Biography Online.* Vol. 11, ed. by John English and Réal Bélanger, *s.v.* "Morris, Alexander," online: Library and Archives Canada, http://www.biographi.ca/.

Galois, Robert. "A History of the Upper Skeena Region, 1850 to 1927" (1993-94) 9:2 Native Stud. Rev. 113.

—. "The Indian Rights Association, Native Protest Activity and the 'Land Question' in British Columbia, 1903-1916" (1992) 8:2 Native Stud. Rev. 1.

Gawalt, Gerard Wilfred. *Massachusetts Lawyers: A Historical Analysis of the Process of Professionalization, 1760-1840* (Ph.D. diss., Clark University, Worcester, MA, 1969) [unpublished].

Gay, Peter. *The Cultivation of Hatred* (New York: Norton, 1993).

Geddis, Andrew. "A Dual Track Democracy? The Symbolic Role of the Mâori Seats in New Zealand's Electoral System" (2006) 5:4 Election L.J. 347.

Geertz, Clifford. *Local Knowledge: Further Essays in Interpretive Anthropology* (New York: Basic Books, 1983).

Geisler, Charles C. "A History of Land Reform in the United States: Old Wine, New Bottles" in Charles C. Geisler and Frank J. Popper, eds. *Land Reform, American Style* (Totowa, NJ: Rowman and Allanheld, 1984) 1.

George, John. *Treatise on the Offence of Libel* [etc.] (London, 1812).

"George Hart" in Lillian York, ed. *Lure of the South Peace: Tales of the Early Pioneers to 1945* (Dawson Creek: Peace River Block News, 1981) 177.

Gibson, Dale, and W. Wesley Pue, eds. *Glimpses of Canadian Legal History* (Winnipeg: Legal Research Institute, University of Manitoba, 1991).

Gibson, James A. *Dictionary of Canadian Biography Online.* Vol. 9, ed. by John English and Réal Bélanger, *s.v.* "Head, Sir Edmund Walker," online: Library and Archives Canada http://www.biographi.ca/.

Gilmartin, Kevin. *Print Politics: The Press and Radical Opposition in Early Nineteenth Century England* (Cambridge: Cambridge University Press, 1996).

Girard, Philip V. "Judging Lives: Judicial Biography from Hale to Holmes" (2003) 7 Austl. J. Legal Hist. 87.

—. *Patriot Jurist: Beamish Murdoch of Halifax, 1800-1876* (Ph.D. thesis, Dalhousie University, 1998) [unpublished].

Glick, Joshua. "On the Road: The Supreme Court and the History of Circuit Riding" (2003) 24 Cardozo L. Rev. 1753.

Goudie, N.J. "The Supreme Court on Circuit: Northern District, 1826-1833" in C. English, ed. *Essays in the History of Canadian Law.* Vol. 9: *Two Islands, Newfoundland and Prince Edward Island* (Toronto: Osgoode Society for Canadian Legal History and University of Toronto Press, 2005) 115.

Graig, C. *Australian Dictionary of Biography.* Vol. 2, ed. by A.G.L. Shaw and C.M.H. Clark (Melbourne: Melbourne University Press, 1967) *s.v.* "Lyttleton, William Thomas (1786?-1839)."

Green, Thomas Andrew. *Verdict According to Conscience: Perspectives on the English Criminal Trial Jury 1200-1800* (Chicago: University of Chicago Press, 1985).

Greenwood, F. Murray. *Legacies of Fear: Law and Policies in Quebec in the Era of the French Revolution* (Toronto: Osgoode Society for Canadian Legal History and University of Toronto Press, 1993).

Greenwood, F. Murray, and Barry Wright. *Canadian State Trials.* Vol. 1: *Law, Politics, and Security Measures, 1608-1837* (Toronto: Osgoode Society for Canadian Legal History and University of Toronto Press, 1996).

—. *Canadian State Trials.* Vol. 2: *Rebellion and Invasion in the Canadas, 1837-1839* (Toronto: Osgoode Society for Canadian Legal History and University of Toronto Press, 2002).

—. "Parliamentary Privilege and the Repression of Dissent in the Canadas" in F. Murray Greenwood and Barry Wright, eds. *Canadian State Trials.* Vol. 1: *Law, Politics, and Security Measures, 1608-1837* (Toronto: Osgoode Society for Canadian Legal History and University of Toronto Press, 1996) 409.

Griffiths, A. "Legal Pluralism" in R. Banakar and M. Travers, eds. *An Introduction to Law and Social Theory* (Oxford: Hart, 2002) 289.

Grossberg, Michael. "Institutionalizing Masculinity: The Law as a Masculine Profession" in Mark C. Carnes and Clyde Griffen, eds. *Meanings for Manhood: Constructions of Masculinity in Victorian America* (Chicago: University of Chicago Press, 1990) 133.

Gundy, H.P. *Dictionary of Canadian Biography.* Vol. 6, ed. by Francess G. Halpenny and Jean Hamelin (Toronto: University of Toronto Press, 1987) *s.v.* "Thomson, Hugh Christopher."

Gwyn, Julian. *Excessive Expectations: Maritime Commerce and the Economic Development of Nova Scotia, 1740-1870* (Montreal and Kingston: McGill-Queen's University Press, 1998).

Habermas, Jürgen. *The Structural Transformation of the Public Sphere: An Inquiry into a Category of Bourgeois Society,* trans. by Thomas Burger (Cambridge, MA: MIT Press, 1992).

Haig-Brown, Mary. "Arthur Eugene O'Meara: Servant, Advocate, Seeker of Justice" in David A. Nock and Celia Haig-Brown, eds. *With Good Intentions: Euro-Canadian and Aboriginal Relations in Colonial Canada* (Vancouver: UBC Press, 2006) 258.

Hale, C.A. *Early Court Houses of Nova Scotia.* 2 vols. (N.p.: Parks Canada, 1977).

Haliburton, Thomas Chandler. *The Old Judge, or Life in a Colony* (Toronto: Clarke, Irwin, 1968; first published 1849).

Hamburger, P. "The Development of the Law of Seditious Libel and Control of the Press" (1985) 37 Stan. L. Rev. 727.

Hannay, James. *History of New Brunswick.* Vol. 2 (Saint John: J.A. Bowes, 1909).

—. *Sir Leonard Tilley* (Toronto: Morang, 1910).

Hare, Cyril. *Tragedy at Law* (London: Pan Books, 1999; first published 1942).

Harring, Sid. *White Man's Law: Native People in Nineteenth Century Canadian Jurisprudence* (Toronto: Osgoode Society for Canadian Legal History and University of Toronto Press, 1998).

Harrington, Matthew. "The Legacy of the Colonial Vice-Admiralty Courts (Part I)" (1995) 26 J. Mar. L. & Com. 581.

—. "The Legacy of the Colonial Vice-Admiralty Courts (Part II)" (1996) 27 J. Mar. L. & Com. 323.

Harris, B.V. "The Constitutional Future of New Zealand" [2004] N.Z.L. Rev. 269.

Harris, Cole. *Making Native Space: Colonialism, Resistance, and Reserves in British Columbia* (Vancouver: UBC Press, 2002).

Hart, H.L.A. *The Concept of Law* (Oxford: Clarendon Press, 1961).

—. "Positivism and the Separation of Law and Morals" (1958) 71 Harv. L. Rev. 593.

Hart, John F. "Colonial Land Use Law and Its Significance for Modern Takings Doctrine" (1996) 109 Harv. L. Rev. 1252.

—. "Land Use Law in the Early Republic and the Original Meaning of the Takings Clause" (2000) 94 Nw. U.L. Rev. 1099.

Haskins, George L. "Estates Arising from the Marriage Relationship and Their Characteristics" in A. James Casner, ed. *American Law of Property: A Treatise on the Law of Property in the United States.* Vol. 1 (Boston: Little, Brown, 1952) 632.

—. "Reception of the Common Law in Seventeenth-Century Massachusetts: Case Study [of Dower Rights]" in George Athan Billias, ed. *Selected Essays: Law and Authority in Colonial America* (Barre, MA: Barre, 1965) 24.

Hay, Douglas. "Controlling the English Prosecutor" (1983) 21 Osgoode Hall L.J. 165.

—. "England, 1562–1875" in Douglas Hay and Paul Craven, eds. *Masters, Servants, and Magistrates in Britain and the Empire, 1562-1955* (Chapel Hill: University of North Carolina Press, 2004) 113.

—. "Property, Authority, and the Criminal Law" in Douglas Hay, Peter Linebaugh, John Rule, E.P. Thompson, and Cal Winslow, eds. *Albion's Fatal Tree: Crime and Society in Eighteenth-Century England* (London: Penguin Books, 1977) 17.

Hay, Douglas, and Paul Craven, eds. *Masters, Servants, and Magistrates in Britain and the Empire, 1562-1955* (Chapel Hill: University of North Carolina Press, 2004).

Henning, G.R. "Fourpenny Dark and Sixpenny Red" (1984) 46 Labour History 52.

Heron, Craig. *Booze: A Distilled History* (Toronto: Between the Lines, 2003).

Hett, R. "Judge Willis and the Court of King's Bench in Upper Canada" (1973) 65 Ontario History 19.

Hewart, Lord. *The New Despotism* (London: Ernest Bean, 1929).

Highmore, Anthony. *Reflections on the Distinction Usually Adopted in Criminal Libel Prosecutions for Libel* (London, 1791).

Hirst, John. *Convict Society and Its Enemies* (Sydney: George Allen and Unwin, 1983).

Hoff, Joan. *Law, Gender and Injustice: A Legal History of U.S. Women* (New York: New York University Press, 1991).

Hogg, James Edward. *The Australian Torrens System* (London: William Clowes and Sons, 1905).

Hogg, Peter. *Constitutional Law of Canada,* 4th ed. (Toronto: Carswell, 1997).

Holloway, Ian. "Sir Francis Forbes and the Earliest Australian Public Law Cases" (2004) 44 L.H.R. 209.

Holt, Francis Ludlow. *The Law of Libel* [etc.] (London, 1812).

—. *The Law of Libel* [etc.], 1st Amer. ed., ed. by Anthony Bleecker (New York, 1818).

—. *The Law of Libel* [etc.], 2d ed. (London, 1816).

Howard, Colin. "Res Judicata in the Criminal Law" (1961) 3 Melbourne U.L. Rev. 101.

—. "Strict Responsibility in the High Court of Australia" (1960) 76 Law Q. Rev. 547.

Howe, Joseph. *The Speeches and Public Letters of Joseph Howe,* ed. by J.A. Chisholm (Halifax: Chronicle, 1909).

Howell, P.A. *Australian Dictionary of Biography.* Vol. 2, ed. by A.G.L. Shaw and C.M.H. Clark (Melbourne: Melbourne University Press, 1967) *s.v.* "Montagu, Algernon Sidney (1802-1880)."

—. *The Judicial Committee of the Privy Council 1833-1876: Its Origins, Structure and Development* (Cambridge: Cambridge University Press, 1979).

—. "Of Ships and Sealing Wax: The Montagus, the Navy and the Law" (1966) 13 Tasmanian Historical Research Association Papers and Proceedings 101.

—. "The Van Diemen's Land Judge Storm" (1966) 2 U. Tasm. L. Rev. 253.

Hunter, R. "Australian Legal Histories in Context" (2003) 21:3 L.H.R. 607.

Huttenback, Richard. *Racism and Empire: White Settlers and Coloured Immigrants in the British Self-Governing Colonies, 1830-1910* (Ithaca: Cornell University Press, 1976).

Hyde, H. Montgomery. *Judge Jeffreys,* 2d ed. (London: Butterworths, 1948).

Johnson, Alice M. *Dictionary of Canadian Biography Online.* Vol. 1, ed. by John English and Réal Bélanger, *s.v.* "Geyer, George," online: Library and Archives Canada, http://www.biographi.ca/.

Jones, R. *An Encyclopaedia of New Zealand, s.v.* "Prendergast, Sir James (1826-1921)," online: http://www.teara.govt.nz/1966/.

Joseph, Philip A. *Constitutional and Administrative Law in New Zealand,* 3d ed. (Wellington, NZ: Brookers, 2007).

"Judge Thacher's Charge in Relation to Publications Tending to Excite the Slaves of Other States to Insurrection" (1832) 8 A.J. 213.

Kahn, Paul W. *The Cultural Study of Law: Reconstructing Legal Scholarship* (Chicago and London: University of Chicago Press, 1999).

Kanakos, Jeannie L. *The Negotiations to Relocate the Songhees Indians, 1843-1911* (M.A. thesis, Simon Fraser University, 1974) [unpublished].

Karsten, Peter. *Between Law and Custom: "High" and "Low" Legal Cultures in the Lands of the British Diaspora—The United States, Canada, Australia and New Zealand, 1600-1900* (Cambridge: Cambridge University Press, 2002).

Katz, Stanley N., ed. *Brief Narrative of the Case and Trial of John Peter Zenger, Printer of the New York Weekly Journal* (Cambridge, MA: Harvard University Press, 1972).

Keddell, Georgina. *The Newspapering Murrays* (Toronto: McClelland and Stewart, 1967).

Keith, K.J. "The Treaty of Waitangi in the Courts" (1990) 14 N.Z.U.L. Rev. 37.

Keon-Cohen, B.A. "Mad Judge Montagu: A Misnomer" (1975) 2 Monash U.L. Rev. 50.

Kercher, Bruce. *Debt, Seduction and Other Disasters: The Birth of Civil Law in Convict New South Wales* (Sydney: Federation Press, 1996).

—. "Establishment, Freedom of Speech and the Church of England: Pew Disputes in Early Nineteenth Century New South Wales and Newfoundland" (2000) 6 Austl. J. Legal Hist. 135.

—. "Perish or Prosper: The Law and Convict Transportation in the British Empire 1700-1850" (2003) 21:3 L.H.R. 548.

—. "Publication of Forgotten Case Law of the New South Wales Supreme Court" (1998) 72 Austl. L.J. 876.

—. "Recognition of Indigenous Legal Autonomy in Nineteenth Century New South Wales" (1998) 4 Indigenous L. Bull. 7.

—. "Unreported Privy Council Appeals from the Australian Colonies before 1850" (2003) 77 Austl. L.J. 309.

—. *An Unruly Child: A History of Law in Australia* (Sydney: Allen and Unwin, 1995).

Kercher, Bruce, and T.D. Castle, eds. *Dowling's Select Cases 1828 to 1844: Decisions of the Supreme Court of New South Wales* (Sydney: Francis Forbes Society for Legal History, 2005).

Keynes, Edward. *Liberty, Property and Privacy: Towards a Jurisprudence of Substantive Due Process* (Pittsburgh: Pennsylvania State University Press, 1996).

Kimball, Edmund. *Reflections upon the Law of Libel in a Letter Addressed to "A Member of the Suffolk Bar"* (Boston, 1823).

King, C.J. *An Outline of Closer Settlement in New South Wales* (Sydney: Government Printer, 1957).

King-Hamilton, Alan. *And Nothing but the Truth* (London: Weidenfeld and Nicolson, 1982).

Kirkby, Diane, and Catharine Coleborne, eds. *Law, History, Colonialism: The Reach of Empire* (Manchester: Manchester University Press, 2001).

Kitchen, Jonathan S. *The Employment of Merchant Seamen* (London: Croom Helm, 1980).

Klerman, D.M., and P.C. Mahoney. "The Value of Judicial Independence: Evidence from Eighteenth-Century England" in P. Brand, K. Costello, and W.N. Osborough, eds. *Adventures of the Law: Proceedings of the Sixteenth British Legal History Conference* (Dublin: Four Courts Press, 2005) 139.

Knafla, Louis A., and Jonathan Swainger, eds. *Laws and Societies in the Canadian Prairie West, 1670-1940* (Vancouver: UBC Press, 2005).

Knight, Rolf. *Indians at Work: An Informal History of Native Labour in British Columbia 1858-1930*, 2d ed. (Vancouver: New Star Books, 1996).

Kostal, Rande. *A Jurisprudence of Power: Victorian Empire and the Rule of Law* (Oxford: Oxford University Press, 2005).

Lanza, Michael L. *Agrarianism and Reconstruction Politics: The Southern Homestead Act* (Baton Rouge: Louisiana State University Press, 1990).

Larabee, Leonard Woods. *Royal Government in America: A Study of the British Colonial System before 1783* (New Haven: Yale University Press, 1930).

Laurence, William H. "Acquiring the Law: The Personal Law Library of William Young, Halifax, Nova Scotia, 1835" (1998) 21 Dal. L.J. 490.

Lazarou, Kathleen Elizabeth. *Concealed under Petticoats: Married Women's Property and the Law of Texas, 1840-1913* (New York: Garland, 1986).

Lear, Jonathan. *Radical Hope: Ethics in the Face of Cultural Devastation* (Cambridge, MA: Harvard University Press, 2006).

Levy, Leonard W. *Blasphemy: Verbal Offense against the Sacred, from Moses to Salman Rushdie* (New York: Knopf, 1993).

—. *Emergence of a Free Press* (New York: Oxford University Press, 1985).

—. *Freedom of Speech and the Press in Early American History: A Legacy of Suppression* (New York: Harper, 1963).

—. *Jefferson and Civil Liberties: The Darker Side* (Cambridge, MA: Harvard University Press, 1963).

Levy, Michael Charles Ivan. *Governor George Arthur: A Colonial Benevolent Despot* (Melbourne: Georgian House, 1953).

Lewis, J.R. *The Victorian Bar* (London: Robert Hale, 1982).

Linklater, Andro. *Measuring America: How the United States Was Shaped by the Greatest Land Sale in History* (New York: Plume, 2003).

Llewellyn, Karl. "The Constitution as Institution" (1934) 34 Colum. L. Rev. 1.

Lobban, Michael. "From Seditious Libel to Unlawful Assembly: Peterloo and the Changing Face of Political Crime c. 1770-1820" (1990) 10 Oxford J. Legal Stud. 307.

—. *Oxford Dictionary of National Biography* (Oxford: Oxford University Press) *s.v.* "Starkie, Thomas," online: http://www.oxforddnb.com.

Locke, Charles H. *Trial of Moore and Sevey for a Libel on Samuel D. Greene, in the Municipal Court, Boston, July Term, 1833* (Boston, 1833).

Lockwood, Glen. "Temperance in Upper Canada as Ethnic Subterfuge" in Cheryl Krasnick Warsh, ed. *Drink in Canada: Historical Essays* (Montreal and Kingston: McGill-Queen's University Press, 1993) 43.

Loeb, Isador. *The Legal Relations of Married Persons: A Study in Comparative Legislation* (New York: Columbia University Press, 1900).

Loo, Tina. *Making Law, Order, and Authority in British Columbia, 1821-1871* (Toronto: University of Toronto Press, 1994).

Lower, Arthur. *Colony to Nation* (Toronto: Longmans Canada, 1946).

Lytwyn, Victor P. *Muskekowuck Athinuwick: Original People of the Great Swampy Land* (Winnipeg: University of Manitoba Press, 2002).

Mackinnon, R. "Roads, Cart Tracks, and Bridle Paths: Land Transportation and the Domestic Economy of Mid-Nineteenth Century Eastern British North America" (2003) 84 Can. Hist. Rev. 177.

Macleod, John. "The Library of Richard John Uniacke" in Patricia Lockhart Fleming, Gilles Gallichan, and Yvan Lamond, eds. *History of the Book in Canada*. Vol. 1: *Beginnings to 1840* (Toronto: University of Toronto Press, 2004) 209.

MacNutt, W. Stewart. *New Brunswick: A History, 1784-1867* (Toronto: Macmillan, 1963).

Maitland, Frederic William. "Why the History of English Law Is Not Written" in H.A.L. Fisher, ed. *The Collected Papers of Frederic William Maitland*. Vol. 1 (Cambridge: Cambridge University Press, 1911) 480.

Mandelbaum, David G. *The Plains Cree: An Ethnographic, Historical and Comparative Study* (Regina: Canadian Plains Research Center, University of Regina, 1979).

Manning, Helen Taft. *British Colonial Government after the American Revolution 1782-1820* (Hamden, CT: Archon Books, 1966).

Marion, A.T. *Harry King's Courtship Letters, 1829-1831* (M.A. thesis, Acadia University, 1986) [unpublished].

Markus, Andrew. *Fear and Hatred: Purifying Australia and California 1850-1901* (Sydney: Hale and Iremonger, 1979).

Marquis, Greg. "Civilized Drinking: Alcohol and Society in New Brunswick, 1945-1975" (2000) 11 J. Can. Hist. Ass'n (New Series) 173.

—. "In Defence of Liberty: 17th Century England and 19th Century Maritime Political Culture" (1993) 42 U.N.B.L.J. 69.

—. "'A Machine of Oppression under the Guise of the Law': The Saint John Police Establishment, 1860-1890" (1986) 16:1 Acadiensis 58.

Marsh, Joss. *Word Crimes: Blasphemy, Culture, and Literature in Nineteenth-Century England* (Chicago: University of Chicago Press, 1998).

Marshall, Daniel Patrick. *Those Who Fell from the Sky: A History of the Cowichan Peoples* (Duncan, BC: Cultural and Education Centre, Cowichan Tribes, 1999).

McDowell, Morag, and Duncan Webb. *The New Zealand Legal System,* 2d ed. (Wellington, NZ: Butterworths, 1998).

McHugh, P.G. *Aboriginal Societies and the Common Law* (Oxford: Oxford University Press, 2004).

—. *The Maori Magna Carta: New Zealand Law and the Treaty of Waitangi* (Auckland: Oxford University Press, 1991).

—. "New Dawn to Cold Light: Courts and Common Law Aboriginal Rights" [2005] N.Z.L. Rev. 485.

McLaren, John. "The Burdens of Empire and the Legalization of White Supremacy in Canada" in W. Gordon and T. Ferguson, eds. *Legal History in the Making* (London: Hambledon Press, 1991) 187.

—. "The Despicable Crime of Nudity: Law, the State, and Civil Protest among the Sons of Freedom Sect of Doukhobors, 1899-1935" (1999) 38:3 J. West 2.

—. "The Doukhobor Belief in Individual Faith and Conscience and the Demands of the Secular State" in H. Coward and J. McLaren, eds. *Religious Conscience, the State and the Law: Historical Contexts and Contemporary Significance* (Albany: SUNY Press, 1998) 117.

—. "The Early British Columbia Judges, the Rule of Law and the 'Chinese Question': The California and Oregon Connection" in John McLaren, Hamar Foster, and Chet Orloff, eds. *Law for the Elephant, Law for the Beaver: Essays in the Legal History of the North American West* (Regina and Pasadena: Canadian Plains Research Center/Ninth Judicial Circuit Historical Society, 1992) 233.

—. "The Early British Columbia Supreme Court and the 'Chinese Question': Echoes of the Rule of Law" (1991) 20 Man. L.J. 107.

—. "'The Judicial Office ... Bowing to No Power but the Supremacy of the Law': Judges and the Rule of Law in Colonial Australia and Canada, 1788-1840" (2003) 7:2 Austl. J. Legal Hist. 177.

—. "The King, the People, the Law ... and the Constitution: Justice Robert Thorpe and the Roots of Irish Whig Ideology in Early Upper Canada" in Jonathan Swainger and Constance Backhouse, eds. *People and Place: Historical Influences on Legal Culture* (Vancouver: UBC Press, 2003) 11.

—. "Maternal Feminism in Action—Emily Murphy P.M." (1989) 8 Windsor Y.B. Access Just. 234.

—. "Preface" in Louis A. Knafla, ed. *Law and Justice in a New Land: Essays in Western Canadian Legal History* (Calgary: Carswell, 1986) xiiv.

—. "Recalculating the Wages of Sin: The Social and Legal Construction of Prostitution, 1850-1920" (1996) 23 Man. L.J. 524.

—. "Reflections on the Rule of Law: The Georgian Colonies of New South Wales and Upper Canada, 1788-1837" in Diane Kirkby and Catharine Coleborne, eds. *Law, History, Colonialism: The Reach of Empire* (Manchester: Manchester University Press, 2001) 46.

—. "The Rule of Law and Irish Whig Constitutionalism in Upper Canada: William Warren Baldwin, the 'Irish Opposition' and the Volunteer Connection" in Jim Phillips and John Saywell, eds. *Essays in the History of Canadian Law.* Vol. 11: *In Honour of Peter Oliver* (Toronto: Osgoode Society for Canadian Legal History and University of Toronto Press, 2007) 11.

—. "The State, Child Snatching and the Law: The Seizure and Indoctrination of Sons of Freedom Children in British Columbia" in John McLaren, Robert Menzies, and Dorothy E. Chunn, eds. *Regulating Lives: Historical Essays on the State, Society, the Individual, and the Law* (Vancouver: UBC Press, 2002) 259.

McLaren, John, A.R. Buck, and Nancy E. Wright, eds. *Despotic Dominion: Property Rights in British Settler Societies* (Vancouver: UBC Press, 2005).

—. "Property Rights in the Colonial Imagination and Experience" in John McLaren, A.R. Buck, and Nancy E. Wright, eds. *Despotic Dominion: Property Rights in British Settler Societies* (Vancouver: UBC Press, 2005) 1.

McLaren, John, and Hamar Foster. "Hard Choices and Sharp Edges: The Legal History of British Columbia and the Yukon" in Hamar Foster and John McLaren, eds. *Essays in the History of Canadian Law.* Vol. 6: *British Columbia and the Yukon* (Toronto: Osgoode Society for Canadian Legal History and University of Toronto Press, 1995) 3.

McLaren, John, and John Lowman. "Enforcing Canada's Prostitution Laws, 1892-1920: Rhetoric and Practice" in Martin L. Freidland, ed. *Securing Compliance: Seven Case Studies* (Toronto: University of Toronto Press, 1990) 21.

McLaren, John, Robert Menzies, and Dorothy E. Chunn, eds. *Regulating Lives: Historical Essays on the State, Society, the Individual, and the Law* (Vancouver: UBC Press, 2002).

McNairn, Jeffrey L. *The Capacity to Judge: Public Opinion and Deliberative Democracy in Upper Canada, 1791-1854* (Toronto: University of Toronto Press, 2000).

Melbourne, A.C.V. *Early Constitutional Development in Australia* (St. Lucia: University of Queensland Press, 1963).

Merrell, James. *Into the American Woods: Negotiators on the Pennsylvania Frontier* (New York: Norton, 1999).

Mikaere, A. "Book Review" (1990) 14 N.Z.U.L. Rev. 97.

Mill, John Stuart. *Principles of Political Economy* (Harmondsworth: Penguin Books, 1970).

Miller, Edmund Morris. *Pressmen and Governors: Australian Editors and Writers in Early Tasmania* (Sydney: Sydney University Press, 1973).

Milliss, Roger. *Waterloo Creek: The Australia Day Massacre of 1838, George Gipps and the British Conquest of New South Wales* (Sydney: University of New South Wales Press, 1992).

Morantz, Toby. "Northern Algonquian Concepts of Status and Leadership Reviewed: A Case Study of the Eighteenth-Century Trading Captain System" (1982) 19 Can. Rev. Soc. & Anthropology 482.

—. "Old Texts, Old Questions: Another Look at the Issue of Continuity and the Early Fur-Trade Period" (1992) 58 Can. Hist. Rev. 166.

Morley, Alan. *Roar of the Breakers* (Toronto: Ryerson Press, 1967).

Morris, Alexander. *The Treaties of Canada with the Indians of Manitoba and the Northwest Territories, Including the Negotiations on Which They Were Based, and Other Information Relating Thereto* (Calgary: Fifth House, 1991; first published 1880).

Morris, G. *Chief Justice James Prendergast and the Administration of New Zealand Colonial Justice 1862-1899* (Ph.D. thesis, University of Waikato, Hamilton, 2001) [unpublished].

—. "James Prendergast and the Treaty of Waitangi: Judicial Attitudes to the Treaty during the Latter Half of the Nineteenth Century" (2004) 35 V.U.W.L.R. 117.

Morton, Arthur S. *A History of the Canadian West,* 2d ed. (Toronto: University of Toronto Press, 1973).

Morton, William Lewis. *The Kingdom of Canada* (Toronto: McClelland and Stewart, 1963).

Murdoch, Beamish. *Epitome of the Laws of Nova Scotia.* 4 vols. (Halifax, 1832-34).

Napoleon, Val. "Extinction by Number: Colonialism Made Easy" (2001) 16:1 C.J.L.S. 113.

Neal, David. *The Rule of Law in a Penal Colony: Law and Power in Early New South Wales* (Cambridge: Cambridge University Press, 1991).

New Brunswick. *Acts of the General Assembly of Her Majesty's Province of New Brunswick 1854-1860* (Fredericton: James Simpson, 1860).

—. *Journal of the House of Assembly of the Province of New Brunswick from the Seventh Day of January to the Seventh Day of April, 1852, being the Second Session of the Fifteenth General Assembly* (Fredericton: John Simpson, 1852).

—. *Journal of the House of Assembly of the Province of New Brunswick from the Ninth day of February to the First day of May, 1854, being the Fifth Session of the Fifteenth General Assembly* (Fredericton: John Simpson, 1854).

—. *Journal of the House of Assembly of the Province of New Brunswick from the Seventeenth to the Twenty-Sixth Day of July, 1856, Being the First Session of the Seventeenth General Assembly* (Fredericton: John Simpson, 1856).

—. *The Revised Statutes of New Brunswick*. Vol. 2: *The Public Statutes of New Brunswick, Passed in the year 1854: Together with Those Unrepealed by the Revised Statutes* (Fredericton: J. Simpson, 1855).

Newmeyer, K. "Justice Joseph Story on Circuit and a Neglected Phase of American Legal History" (1970) 14 Am. J. Legal Hist. 112.

Nicol, John. *Life and Adventures 1776-1801,* ed. by Tim Flannery (Melbourne: Text, 1997).

Noel, Jan. *Canada Dry: Temperance Crusades before Confederation* (Toronto: University of Toronto Press, 1995).

O'Hare, C.W. "Admiralty Jurisdiction (Parts 1 and 2)" (1979-80) 6 Monash U.L. Rev. 91 and 195.

Oliver, Peter, ed. *The Conventional Man: The Diaries of Ontario Chief Justice Robert A. Harrison 1856-1878* (Toronto: Osgoode Society for Canadian Legal History and University of Toronto Press, 2003).

Orange, Claudia. *The Treaty of Waitangi* (Wellington, NZ: Allen and Unwin, 1987).

Orwell, George. "Shooting an Elephant" in *Shooting an Elephant and Other Essays* (London: Secker and Warburg, 1950) 1.

Palmer, G.W.R. *Constitutional Conversations* (Wellington, NZ: Victoria University Press, 2002).

Parker, Graham. "Canadian Legal Culture" in Louis A. Knafla, ed. *Law and Justice in a New Land: Essays in Western Canadian Legal History* (Calgary: Carswell, 1986) 3.

Parsonson, A. *Dictionary of New Zealand Biography.* Vol. 1, ed. by W.H. Oliver (Wellington/Auckland, NZ: Auckland University Press with Bridget Williams Books and the Department of Internal Affairs, 1998) *s.v.* "Te Rangitaki, Wiremu Kingi, ?-1882," online: http://www.dnzb.govt.nz/dnzb/.

Pasley, Jeffrey L. *"The Tyranny of Printers": Newspaper Politics in the Early American Republic* (Charlottesville: University Press of Virginia, 2001).

Paterson, Alan. *The Law Lords* (London: Macmillan, 1982).

Paterson, G.H. *Dictionary of Canadian Biography.* Vol. 5, ed. by Francess G. Halpenny and Jean Hamelin (Toronto: University of Toronto Press, 1983) *s.v.* "Weekes, William."

Patterson, E. Palmer, II. "Andrew Paull (1892-1959): Finding a Voice for the 'New Indian'" (1976) 6 Western Can. J. Anthropology 63.

—. "Arthur E. O'Meara, Friend of the Indians" (1967) 58 Pacific Northwest Quarterly 90.

Payne, Michael. "Fur Trade Historiography" in Theodore Binnema, Gerhard J. Ens, and R.C. Macleod, eds. *From Rupert's Land to Canada: Essays in Honour of John E. Foster* (Edmonton: University of Alberta Press, 2001) 3.

Phillips, J. "'High above the Generality of the People': The Origins of the Nova Scotia Supreme Court Circuit" in J. Phillips, R.R. McMurtry, and J. Saywell, eds. *Essays in the History of Canadian Law.* Vol. 10: *A Tribute to Peter Oliver* (Toronto: Osgoode Society for Canadian Legal History and University of Toronto Press, 2008.

Phillips, Jim, Tina Loo, and Susan Lewthwaite, eds. *Essays in the History of Canadian Law.* Vol. 5: *Crime and Criminal Justice in Canadian History* (Toronto: Osgoode Society for Canadian Legal History and University of Toronto Press, 1994).

Pocock, J.G.A. *The Ancient Constitution and the Feudal Law,* 2d. ed. (Cambridge: Cambridge University Press, 1987).

Pollock, Sir Frederick, and Frederic William Maitland. *The History of English Law before the Time of Edward I.* 2 vols. (Birmingham: Legal Classics Library, 1982; 2d ed. first published 1899).

Popham, Robert E., and Wolfgang Schmidt. *Statistics of Alcohol Use and Alcoholism in Canada, 1871-1956* (Toronto: University of Toronto Press, 1957).

Posner, R.A. "Objectivity and Hagiography in Judicial Biography" (1995) 70 N.Y.U.L. Rev. 503.

Price, Charles. *The Great Walls Are Built: Restrictive Immigration to North America and Australasia 1836-1888* (Canberra: Australian National University Press, 1974).

Prichard, M.J. "Crime at Sea: Admiralty Sessions and the Background to Later Colonial Jurisdiction" (1984) 8 Dal. L.J. 43.

Prochaska, F.K. "English State Trials in the 1790s: A Case Study" (1973) 17 J. Brit. Stud. 63.

Prokhovnik, Raia. *Rhetoric and Philosophy in Hobbes' "Leviathan"* (New York: Garland, 1991).

Quinlan, Michael. "Industrial Relations before Unions: New South Wales Seamen 1810-1852" (1996) 38 J. Indus. Rel. 264.

—. "Making Labour Laws Fit for the Colonies: The Introduction of Laws Regulating Whalers in Three Australian Colonies 1835-1855" (1992) 62 Labour History 19.

—. "Regulating Labour in a Colonial Context: Maritime Labour Legislation in the Australian Colonies, 1788-1850" (1998) 29 Austl. Hist. Stud. 303.

Rabkin, Peggy A. *Fathers to Daughters: The Legal Foundations of Female Emancipation* (Westport: Greenwood Press, 1980).

Ray, Arthur J. "The Factor and the Trading Captain in the Hudson's Bay Company Fur Trade before 1763" in Jim Freedman and Jerome H. Barkow, eds. *Proceedings of the Second Congress, Canadian Ethnology Society.* Mercury Series, Ethnology Service Paper 28 (Ottawa: National Museum of Man, 1975) 586.

—. *Indians in the Fur Trade: Their Role as Trappers, Hunters and Middlemen in the Lands Southwest of Hudson Bay, 1660-1870* (Toronto: University of Toronto Press, 1974).

Ray, Arthur J., and Don Freeman. *"Give Us Good Measure": An Economic Analysis of Relations between the Indians and the Hudson's Bay Company before 1763* (Toronto: University of Toronto Press, 1978).

Ray, Arthur J., Jim Miller, and Frank J. Tough. *Bounty and Benevolence: A Documentary History of Saskatchewan Treaties* (Montreal and Kingston: McGill-Queen's University Press, 2000).

Rediker, Marcus. *Between the Devil and the Deep Blue Sea: Merchant Seamen, Pirates, and the Anglo-American Maritime World, 1700-1750* (Cambridge: Cambridge University Press, 1989).

—. *Villain of All Nations: Atlantic Pirates in the Golden Age* (London: Verso, 2004).

Reeves, William Pember. *State Experiments in Australia and New Zealand.* 2 vols. (London, 1902).

Reid, John Philip. *Law for the Elephant: Property and Social Behavior on the Overland Trail* (San Marino, CA: Huntington Library, 1980).

—. *Patterns of Vengeance: Crosscultural Homicide in the North American Fur Trade* (Pasadena: Ninth Circuit Historical Society, 1999).

Renaut, Marie-Hélène. "L'Histoire par les Lois: Trois siècles d'évolution dans la repression des fautes disciplinaires de la marine marchande" (2002) 80 Revue Histoire Droit 23.

Rich, E.E., ed. *Copy-book of Letters Outward &c. Begins 29th May, 1680 Ends 5 July, 1687* (Toronto: Champlain Society, 1948).

—. *Hudson's Bay Company, 1670-1870.* Vol. 1 (New York: Macmillan, 1960).

Richter, Daniel K. "Whose Indian History?" (1993) 50 Wm. & Mary Q. 379.

Risk, R.C.B. "The Golden Age: The Law about the Market in Nineteenth-Century Ontario" (1976) 26 U.T.L.J. 307.

—. "The Last Golden Age: Property and the Allocation of Losses in Ontario in the Nineteenth-Century" (1977) 27 U.T.L.J. 199.

—. "Law and the Economy in Mid-nineteenth Century Ontario: A Perspective" (1977) 27 U.T.L.J. 403.

—. "The Nineteenth Century Foundations of the Business Corporation in Ontario" (1973) 23 U.T.L.J. 307.

Roberts, Stephen H. *History of Australian Land Settlement 1788-1920* (Melbourne: Macmillan, 1968).

Robertson, David. "Punitive Damages in American Maritime Law" (1997) 28 J. Mar. L. & Com. 73.

Robertson, Lindsay G. *Conquest by Law: How the Discovery of America Dispossessed Indigenous Peoples of Their Lands* (Oxford: Oxford University Press, 2005).

Romney, Paul. "From Constitutionalism to Legalism: Trial by Jury, Responsible Government and the Rule of Law in Canadian Political Culture" (1989) 7 L.H.R. 130.

—. *Mr. Attorney: The Attorney General for Ontario in Court, Cabinet, and Legislature, 1791-1899* (Toronto: Osgoode Society for Canadian Legal History and University of Toronto Press, 1986).

—. "Upper Canada in the 1820's: Criminal Prosecution and the Case of Francis Collins" in F. Murray Greenwood and Barry Wright, eds. *Canadian State Trials.* Vol. 1: *Law, Politics, and Security Measures, 1608-1837* (Toronto: Osgoode Society for Canadian Legal History and University of Toronto Press, 1996) 505.

Romney, Paul, and Barry Wright. "State Trials and Security Proceedings during the War of 1812" in F. Murray Greenwood and Barry Wright, eds. *Canadian State Trials.* Vol. 1: *Law, Politics, and Security Measures, 1608-1837* (Toronto: Osgoode Society for Canadian Legal History and University of Toronto Press, 1996) 379.

Roscoe, Edward. "Introduction" in *Edward Roscoe on the Admiralty Jurisdiction and Practice of the High Court of Justice,* 4th ed. (London: Stevens and Sons, 1920) 11.

Rosenberg, Norman L. *Protecting the Best Men: An Interpretive History of the Law of Libel* (Chapel Hill: University of North Carolina Press, 1986).

Roy, Patricia. "Law and Order in British Columbia in the 1880s: Images and Realities" in R.C. MacLeod, ed. *Swords and Ploughshares: War and Agriculture in Western Canada* (Edmonton: University of Alberta Press, 1993) 55.

—. *The Oriental Question: Consolidating a White Man's Province, 1914-41* (Vancouver: UBC Press, 2003).

—. *A White Man's Province: British Columbia Politicians and Chinese and Japanese Immigrants, 1858-1914* (Vancouver: UBC Press, 1989).

Russell, Peter. *Recognizing Aboriginal Title: The Mabo Case and Indigenous Resistance to English-Settler Colonialism* (Toronto: University of Toronto Press, 2005).

Salmon, Marylynn. *Women and the Law of Property in Early America* (Chapel Hill: University of North Carolina Press, 1986).

Salmond, John William. *First Principles of Jurisprudence* (London: Stevens and Haynes, 1893).

—. *Jurisprudence: Or the Theory of the Law* (London: Stevens and Haynes, 1902).

Sanders, Douglas. "Aboriginal Rights: The Search for Recognition in International Law" in Menno Boldt and J. Anthony Long, eds. *The Quest for Justice: Aboriginal Peoples and Aboriginal Rights* (Toronto: University of Toronto Press, 1985) 292.

Sanders, Will. "Delivering Democracy to Indigenous Australians: Aborigines, Torres Strait Islanders and Commonwealth Electoral Administration" in Marian Sawer, ed. *Elections Full, Free and Fair* (Sydney: Federation Press, 2001) 158.

Scholefield, E.O.S. *British Columbia from the Earliest Times to the Present*. Vol. 4 (Vancouver: S.J. Clark, 1914).

Scholefield, G.H., ed. *A Dictionary of New Zealand Biography* (Wellington, NZ: Department of Internal Affairs, 1940).

Scribner, Charles H. *A Treatise on the Law of Dower,* 2d ed. (Philadelphia, 1883).

Scull, Gideon D. *Voyages of Peter Esprit Radisson* (New York: Burt Franklin, 1967).

See, Scott. *Riots in New Brunswick: Orange Nativism and Social Violence in the 1840s* (Toronto: University of Toronto Press, 1993).

Sewall, Samuel. *Catalogue of the Library of the Late Chief Justice Sewall, to be Sold at Auction Sep. 2, 1814* (Cambridge, MA: Hilliard and Metcalf, 1814).

Shammas, Carol, Marylynn Salmon, and Michel Dahlin. *Inheritance in America from Colonial Times to the Present* (New Brunswick, NJ: Rutgers University Press, 1987).

Sharrock, Susan R. "Crees, Cree-Assiniboines, and Assiniboines: Interethnic Social Organization on the Far Northern Plains" (1974) 21:2 Ethnohistory 95.

Shaw, A.G.L. "Colonial Office" in Graeme Davison, John Hirst, and Stuart MacIntyre, eds. *Oxford Companion to Australian History* (Melbourne: Oxford University Press, 1998) 138.

Simpson, A.W.B. *Legal Theory and Legal History—Essays on the Common Law* (London: Hambledon Press, 1987).

Smandych, Russell. "Contemplating the Testimony of 'Others': James Stephen, the Colonial Office, and the Fate of Australian Aboriginal Evidence Acts, circa 1839-1849" (2004) 8 Austl. J. Legal Hist. 237.

—. "'To Soften the Extreme Rigor of Their Bondage': James Stephen's Attempt to Reform the Criminal Slave Laws of the West Indies, 1813-1833" (2005) 23 Law and History 537.

Smith, James Morton. *Freedom's Fetters: The Alien and Sedition Law and American Civil Liberties* (Ithaca: Cornell University Press, 1956).

Smith, K.J.M., and John McLaren. "History's Living Legacy: An Outline of 'Modern' Historiography of the Common Law" (2001) 21 L.S. 251.

Soderstrum, T. Jason. *Alcohol and Temperance in Modern History: An International Encyclopedia*. Vol. 2, ed. by Jack Blocker Jr., David M. Fahey, and Ian R. Tyrrell (Denver: ABC-CLIO, 2003) *s.v.* "Tilley, Samuel Leonard (1818-1896)."

Sorrenson, M.P.K. *Dictionary of New Zealand Biography.* Vol. 3, ed. by C. Orange (Wellington, NZ: Auckland University Press with Bridget Williams Books and the Department of Internal Affairs, 1996) *s.v.* "Ngata, Apirana Turupa 1874-1950," online: http://www.dnzb.govt.nz/dnzb/.

Spence, F.S. *The Royal Commission on the Liquor Traffic: The Facts of the Case* (Toronto, 1896).

Spigelman, J.J. "Foundations of Freedom of the Press in Australia" (2003) 23 Austl. Bar Rev. 89.

Spiller, P. "Courts and the Judiciary" in P. Spiller, J. Finn, and R. Boast, eds. *A New Zealand Legal History* (Wellington, NZ: Brookers, 1995) 194.

Spiller, Peter, Jeremy Finn, and Richard Boast. *A New Zealand Legal History,* 2d ed. (Wellington, NZ: Brookers, 2001).

Spray, W.A. *Dictionary of Canadian Biography Online.* Vol. 1, ed. by John English and Réal Bélanger, *s.v.* "Wilmot, Robert Duncan," online: Library and Archives Canada, http://www.biographi.ca/.

Starke, J. *Dictionary of New Zealand Biography.* Vol. 1 (Wellington, NZ: Auckland University Press in association with the Department of Internal Affairs, 1990) *s.v.* "Hadfield, Octavius 1814?-1904," online: http://www.dnzb.govt.nz/dnzb/.

Starkie, Thomas. *A Practical Treatise of the Law of Evidence and Digest of Proofs in Civil and Criminal Proceedings* (London, 1824).

—. *A Treatise on the Law of Slander and Libel, and Incidentally of Malicious Prosecutions,* 2d ed. (London, 1830).

—. *A Treatise on the Law of Slander, Libel, Scandalum Magnatum, and False Rumors* [etc.] (London, 1813).

—. *A Treatise on the Law of Slander, Libel, Scandalum Magnatum, and False Rumours* [etc.], 1st Amer. ed., ed. by Edward D. Ingraham (New York, 1826).

—. *A Treatise on the Law of Slander, Libel, Scandalum Magnatum, and False Rumours* [etc.], 2d Amer. ed., ed. by Thomas Huntington (New York, 1832).

Steckley, George. "Collisions, Prohibitions, and the Admiralty Court in Seventeenth-Century London" (2003) 21 L.H.R. 41.

—. "Litigious Mariners: Wage Cases in the Seventeenth-Century Admiralty Court" (1999) 42 Historical Journal 315.

Stephen, James Fitzjames. *A History of Criminal Law.* Vol. 2 (London, 1883).

Sterngass, Jon. *Alcohol and Temperance in Modern History: An International Encyclopedia.* Vol. 2, ed. by Jack Blocker Jr., David M. Fahey, and Ian R. Tyrrell (Denver: ABC-CLIO, 2003) *s.v.* "Maine Law."

Sterritt, Neil J., Susan Marsden, Robert Galois, Peter R. Grant, and Richard Overstall. *Tribal Boundaries in the Nass Watershed* (Vancouver: UBC Press, 1998).

Stevens, Robert. "The Act of Settlement and the Questionable History of Judicial Independence" (2001) 1 O.U.C.L.J. 253.

Street, Harry. "Estoppel and Negligence" (1957) 73 Law Q. Rev. 359.

Stretton, Pat, and Christine Finnimore. "Black Fellow Citizens: Aborigines and the Commonwealth Franchise" (2003) 23 Austl. Hist. Stud. 521.

Surrency, E.C. "The Courts in the American Colonies" (1967) 11 Am. J. Legal Hist. 347.

Swainger, Jonathan. "Breaking the Peace: Fictions of the Law-Abiding Peace River Country, 1930-50" (Autumn 1998) 119 BC Studies 5.

—. *The Canadian Department of Justice and the Completion of Confederation, 1867-78* (Vancouver: UBC Press, 2000).

—. "Creating the Peace: Crime and Community Identity in Northeastern British Columbia, 1930-1950" in Louis A. Knafla, ed. *Violent Crime in North America* (Westport: Praeger, 2003) 131.

—. "'Ordinary Duty' in the Peace and Police Culture in British Columbia, 1910-1939" in Jonathan Swainger and Constance Backhouse, eds. *People and Place: Historical Influences on Legal Culture* (Vancouver: UBC Press, 2003) 198.

Swinfen, David B. *Imperial Appeal: The Debate on the Appeal to the Privy Council, 1833-1986* (Manchester: Manchester University Press, 1987).

—. *Imperial Control of Colonial Legislation, 1813-1865: A Study of British Policy towards Colonial Legislative Powers* (Oxford: Clarendon Press, 1970).

Szymanski, Anne Marie E. *Pathways to Prohibition: Radicals, Moderates and Social Movement Outcomes* (Durham: Duke University Press, 2002).

Tate, J.W. "*Hohepa Wi Neera*: Native Title and the Privy Council Challenge" (2004) 35 V.U.W.L.R. 73.

—. "The Privy Council and Native Title: A Requiem for *Wi Parata*" (2004) 12 Waikato L. Rev. 101.

—. "*Tamihana Korokai* and Native Title: Healing the Imperial Breach" (2005) 13 Waikato L. Rev. 108.

Taylor, John Leonard. "Canada's Northwest Indian Policy in the 1870s: Traditional Premises and Necessary Innovations" in Richard Price, ed. *The Spirit of the Alberta Indian Treaties* (Edmonton: Pica Pica Press, 1987; first published 1979) 3.

Telfer, Thomas G.W. "A Canadian 'World without Bankruptcy': The Failure of Bankruptcy Reform in Canada, 1880 to 1903" (2004) 8 Austl. J. Legal Hist. 83.

Tennant, Paul. *Aboriginal People and Politics: The Indian Land Question in British Columbia, 1849-1989* (Vancouver: UBC Press, 1990).

Thompson, John Herd, with Allen Seager. *Canada 1922-1939: Decades of Discord* (Toronto: McClelland and Stewart, 1985).

Thomson, E.P. "The Moral Economy of the English Crowd" (1971) 50 Past and Present 76.

Tickner, Robert. *Taking a Stand: Land Rights to Reconciliation* (Sydney: Allen and Unwin, 2001).

Titley, Brian. *A Narrow Vision: Duncan Campbell Scott and the Administration of Indian Affairs in Canada* (Vancouver: UBC Press, 1986).

Todd, Alpheus. *Parliamentary Government in the Colonies,* 2d ed. (London: Longmans, Green, 1894).

Torrens, Robert R. *The South Australian System of Conveyancing by Registration of Title* (Adelaide, 1859).

Tuck, Esme. *A Brief History of Pouce Coupé Village and District* (Dawson Creek: Pouce Coupé Women's Institute, n.d.).

Twichell, Heath. *Northwest Epic: The Building of the Alaska Highway* (New York: St. Martin's Press, 1992).

Tyler, Tom. *Why People Obey the Law* (New Haven: Yale University Press, 1990).

Tyrrell, Ian. *Sobering Up: From Temperance to Prohibition in Antebellum America, 1800-1860* (Westport: Greenwood Press, 1979).

Usher, Jean. *William Duncan of Metlakatla: A Victorian Missionary in British Columbia.* Publications in History No. 5 (Ottawa: National Museum of Man, 1974).

van Kirk, Sylvia. *"Many Tender Ties":Women in Fur-Trade Society in Western Canada, 1670-1870* (Winnipeg:Watson and Dwyer, 1980).

Verchere, David R. *A Progression of Judges:A History of the Supreme Court of British Columbia* (Vancouver: UBC Press, 1988).

Vernier, Chester G. *American Family Laws.* Vol. 3 (Stanford: Stanford University Press, 1935).

Waite, P.B. "The Fall and Rise of the Smashers: Some Private Letters of Manners–Sutton" (Autumn 1976) 2:1 Acadiensis 65.

Walker, James St. J. *"Race," Rights and the Law in the Supreme Court of Canada* (Toronto: Osgoode Society for Canadian Legal History and University of Toronto Press, 1997).

Wallace, C.M. *Dictionary of Canadian Biography Online.* Vol. 10, ed. by John English and Réal Bélanger, *s.v.* "Fisher, Charles," online: Library and Archives Canada, http://www.biographi.ca/.

—. *Dictionary of Canadian Biography Online.* Vol. 11, ed. by John English and Réal Bélanger, *s.v.* "Smith, Sir Albert James," online: Library and Archives Canada, http://www.biographi.ca/.

—. *Dictionary of Canadian Biography Online.* Vol. 12, ed. by John English and Réal Bélanger, *s.v.* "Tilley, Samuel Leonard," online: Library and Archives Canada, http://www.biographi.ca/.

—. *Dictionary of Canadian Biography Online.* Vol. 12, ed. by John English and Réal Bélanger, *s.v.* "Wallace, Lemuel Allen," online: Library and Archives Canada, http://www.biographi.ca/.

Warbasse, Elisabeth Bowles. *The Changing Legal Rights of Married Women, 1800-1861* (New York: Garland, 1987).

Ward, Alan. *A Show of Justice: Racial "Amalgamation" in Nineteenth Century New Zealand* (Toronto: University of Toronto Press, 1974).

—. *An Unsettled History: Treaty Claims in New Zealand Today* (Wellington, NZ: Bridget Williams Books, 2000).

Ward, Peter. *White Canada Forever: Popular Attitudes towards Orientals in British Columbia,* 2d ed. (Montreal and Kingston: McGill-Queen's University Press, 1990).

Warner, Michael. *The Letters of the Republic: Publication and the Public Sphere in Eighteenth-Century America* (Cambridge, MA: Harvard University Press, 1990).

—. "The Mass Public and the Mass Subject" in Craig Calhoun, ed. *Habermas and the Public Sphere* (Cambridge, MA: MIT Press, 1992) 379.

Weaver, John C. *The Great Land Rush and the Making of the Modern World, 1650-1900* (Montreal and Kingston: McGill-Queen's University Press, 2003).

—. "A Pathology of Insolvents: Melbourne, 1871-1915" (2004) 8 Austl. J. Legal Hist. 109.

West, John. *The History of Tasmania,* ed. by A.G.L. Shaw (Sydney:Angus and Robertson, 1971).

White, G.E. "The Working Life of the Marshall Court, 1815-1835" (1984) 70 Va. L. Rev. 1.

White, Richard. *The Middle Ground: Indians, Empires, and Republics in the Great Lakes Regions, 1650-1815* (Cambridge: Cambridge University Press, 1991).

Whitelaw, William Menzies. *The Maritimes and Canada before Confederation* (Toronto: Oxford University Press, 1934).

Wiebe, Rudy. *Dictionary of Canadian Biography Online.* Vol. 11, ed. by John English and Réal Bélanger, *s.v.* "Mistahimaskwa (Big Bear)," online: Library and Archives Canada, http://www.biographi.ca/.

Wight, Martin. *The Development of the Legislative Council 1606-1945* (London: Faber and Faber, 1946).

Wilbur, Richard. *Dictionary of Canadian Biography Online.* Vol. 10, ed. by John English and Réal Bélanger, *s.v.* "Manners-Sutton, John Henry Thomas," online: Library and Archives Canada, http://www.biographi.ca/.

Williams, D.V. "The Constitutional Status of the Treaty of Waitangi: An Historical Perspective" (1990) 14 N.Z.U.L. Rev. 9.

—. "The Recognition of 'Native Custom' in Tanganyika and New Zealand: Legal Pluralism or Monocultural Imposition" in P. Sack and E. Minchin, eds. *Legal Pluralism* (Canberra: Australian National University, 1986) 145.

—. "Te Taha Maori Recognised" (1983) 9 Recent Law 378.

—. "Te Tiriti o Waitangi — Unique Relationship between Crown and Tangata Whenua?" in I.H. Kawharu, ed. *Waitangi: Maori and Pakeha Perspectives of the Treaty of Waitangi* (Auckland: Oxford University Press, 1989) 64.

—. "Unique Treaty-Based Relationships Remain Elusive" in M. Belgrave, M. Kawharu, and D.V. Williams, eds. *Waitangi Revisited: Perspectives on the Treaty of Waitangi* (Melbourne: Oxford University Press, 2005) 366.

—. "The Waitangi Tribunal and Legal Pluralism: A Reassessment" (1994) 10 Austl. J.L. Soc. 195.

Williams, David Ricardo. *Dictionary of Canadian Biography Online.* Vol. 12, ed. by John English and Réal Bélanger, *s.v.* "Begbie, Sir Matthew Baillie," online: Library and Archives Canada, http://www.biographi.ca/.

—. *"The Man for a New Country": Sir Matthew Baillie Begbie* (Sidney, BC: Gray's, 1977).

—. *Matthew Baillie Begbie* (Don Mills: Fitzhenry and Whiteside, 1980).

Williams, Glyndwr, ed. *Andrew Graham's Observations on Hudson's Bay, 1767-91* (London: Hudson's Bay Record Society, 1969).

Windeyer, V. "A Birthright and Inheritance: The Establishment of the Rule of Law in Australia" (1962) 1 Tasm. U.L. Rev. 635.

Witt, Jann. "'During the Voyage Every Captain Is Monarch of the Ship': The Merchant Captain from the Seventeenth to the Nineteenth Century" (2001) 13 Int'l J. Mar. Hist. 165.

Woods, G.D. *A History of Criminal Law in New South Wales* (Sydney: Federation Press, 2002).

Wright, Barry. "The Gourlay Affair: Seditious Libel and the Sedition Act in Upper Canada, 1818-19" in F. Murray Greenwood and Barry Wright, eds. *Canadian State Trials.* Vol. 1: *Law, Politics, and Security Measures, 1608-1837* (Toronto: Osgoode Society for Canadian Legal History and University of Toronto Press, 1996) 487.

—. "Migration, Radicalism and State Security: Legislative Initiatives in the Canadas and the United States c. 1794-1804" (2002) 16 Studies in American Political Development 48.

—. "Sedition in Upper Canada: Contested Legality" (1992) 29 Labour/Le Travail 7.

Wright, Nancy E. "'The Lady Vanishes': Women and Property Rights in Nineteenth-Century New South Wales" in John McLaren, A.R. Buck, and Nancy E. Wright, eds. *Despotic Dominion: Property Rights in British Settler Societies* (Vancouver: UBC Press, 2005) 190.

—. "Reading the Past: The Dispossession of the Poor and Aborigines in Colonial New South Wales" in Peter Farrugia, ed. *The River of History* (Calgary: University of Calgary Press, 2005) 103.

Wright, Nancy E., and A.R. Buck. "Property Rights and the Discourse of Improvement in Nineteenth-Century New South Wales" in A.R. Buck, John McLaren, and Nancy E. Wright, eds. *Land and Freedom: Law, Property Rights and the British Diaspora* (Aldershot: Ashgate, 2001) 103.

—. "The Transformation of Colonial Property: A Study of Dower in New South Wales, 1836-1863" (2004) 23 U. Tasm. L. Rev. 98.

York, Robert M. *George B. Cheever, Religious and Social Reformer 1807-1890* (Orono, ME: University Press, 1955).

Ziff, Bruce. "Warm Reception in a Cold Climate: English Property Law and the Suppression of Canadian Legal Identity" in John McLaren, A.R. Buck, and Nancy E. Wright, eds. *Despotic Dominion: Property Rights in British Settler Societies* (Vancouver: UBC Press, 2005) 103.

CONTRIBUTORS

Benjamin L. Berger is an Assistant Professor in the Faculty of Law, University of Victoria. His principal areas of research and teaching are law and religion and constitutional and criminal law and theory.

Simon Bronitt is a Professor in the College of Law, and Director, National Europe Centre, Research School of Humanities at the Australian National University. His scholarly interests extend across the fields of criminal law, law and society, legal history, and comparative law. Recent books include *Law in Context* (co-edited with S. Bottomley) and *Principles of Criminal Law* (co-edited with B. McSherry).

A.R. Buck is a Professor of Law and Co-Director of the Centre for Comparative Law, History and Governance at Macquarie University, Australia, where he also edits the journal *Legal History*. He is the author of *The Making of Australian Property Law* and the co-editor, most recently, of *The Poor Man: Law and Satire in 19th Century New South Wales* and *Despotic Dominion: Property Rights in British Settler Societies*.

Lyndsay M. Campbell is putting the finishing touches on a Ph.D. in Jurisprudence and Social Policy at the University of California, Berkeley. Her dissertation compares the legal and extra-legal regulation of controversial expression in Nova Scotia and Massachusetts in the 1820s and 1830s.

Jeremy Finn is a Professor of Law at the University of Canterbury, where he has taught since 1978. He has a particular interest in the legal history of New

Zealand and of other components of the former British Empire. He also researches and teaches criminal law, contract law, and intellectual property law.

Hamar Foster is a Professor of Law at the University of Victoria. Most of his research and writing has focused on the legal history of British Columbia, of Aboriginal/non-Aboriginal relations in western and northern Canada, and on comparative Canadian-US criminal law. His most recent publication, with Heather Raven and Jeremy Webber, is *Let Right Be Done: Aboriginal Title, the Calder Case, and the Future of Indigenous Rights.*

Philip Girard is a Professor of Law, History, and Canadian Studies at Dalhousie University. He is the author of *Bora Laskin: Bringing Law to Life* and edits the *Dalhousie Law Journal.*

Ian Holloway, Q.C., is a Professor and Dean of Law at the University of Western Ontario. Formerly, he was Associate Dean of Law at the Australian National University. His teaching and research interests are in the areas of administrative law and legal history

Bruce Kercher is Emeritus Professor of Law at Macquarie University, Australia. He has published a number of books and articles about the Australian colonies' place in the British legal empire, including *An Unruly Child: A History of Law in Australia* and *Outsiders: Tales from the Supreme Court of NSW, 1824-1836.*

Greg Marquis teaches Canadian history at the University of New Brunswick Saint John. He is the author of two books and of a number of articles and chapters on Canadian legal and criminal justice history. His current interests are the history of alcohol control and urban history.

John McLaren is Emeritus Professor of Law at the University of Victoria, British Columbia. His research interests lie in comparative colonial legal history and, most especially, in contested interpretations of the rule of law in, and the accountability and tenure of judges appointed to, British colonies.

Stefan Petrow is a Senior Lecturer in Australian History in the School of History and Classics at the University of Tasmania, Hobart. His research focuses on Tasmanian legal and urban planning history and the history of policing.

Jim Phillips is a Professor of Law and History at the University of Toronto. He has co-edited five volumes published by the Osgoode Society for Canadian Legal History and is the author or editor of three other books, including *Murdering Holiness: The Trials of Franz Creffield and George Mitchell* (with Rosemary Gartner). He is editor-in-chief of the Osgoode Society.

Janna Promislow teaches public law and the history and theory of law and indigenous peoples at Osgoode Hall Law School, York University. She is also completing a Ph.D. on law, history, and treaties, exploring normative continuities in indigenous-settler relations in the Canadian northwest.

Jonathan Swainger is an Associate Professor and Chair of the History program at the University of Northern British Columbia, where he has published a number of articles and book chapters on the history of the bench in Quebec and Ontario and the criminal history of central Alberta and northeastern British Columbia. He has also published a book on the Canadian Department of Justice and edited three essay collections on western Canadian legal history.

David V. Williams is a Professor of Law at the University of Auckland in New Zealand. He has qualifications in law, history, and theology, and he teaches law and society and legal history courses. His research writings focus on colonial legal history and responses by indigenous peoples, especially the Maori of Aotearoa (New Zealand), to law and government policies in colonial states.

John Williams is a Professor in the Law School at the University of Adelaide. His research is in the areas of Australian constitutional law and legal history. He is the author of *The Australian Constitution: A Documentary History.*

Barry Wright is a Professor of Law and Criminology at Carleton University. He edited, with Murray Greenwood, the first two volumes of *Canadian State Trials;* Volume 3 (1840-1914), edited with Susan Binnie, is currently in submission. He has also published comparative work on the late nineteenth-century self-governing British jurisdiction codifications of criminal law.

Nancy E. Wright is a Professor and Head of the School of Humanities and Languages at the University of Western Sydney, Australia. Her recent books include *The Poor Man: Law and Satire in 19th Century New South Wales* and the co-edited collections *Despotic Dominion: Property Rights in British Settler Societies* and *Women, Property, and the Letters of the Law in Early Modern England.*

INDEX

Note: "(m)" after a page reference indicates a map; "(p)," a photograph; "(t)," a table. "BC" stands for British Columbia; "NB," for New Brunswick; "NS," for Nova Scotia; "NSW," for New South Wales; "NZ," for New Zealand; "UC," for Upper Canada; "VDL," for Van Diemen's Land

Aboriginal title in British Columbia: BC's refusal to allow adjudication, 240, 257-58, 346n78; *Calder* case (1973), 240-41, 254, 260, 339n5; Cowichan Petition (1909), 241-42, 246, 254-56, 257-59, 261-67; delegation to King (1906), 246, 248(p), 249-50, 249(p); delegation to Ottawa (1908), 250; end of jurisdiction of Colonial Office, 259-60; impact of Aboriginal education on claims, 245-46; impact of Dominion 1911 election, 258-59; lawyers' involvement in claims, 250-51, 254-56; missionary appeals/petitions, 243-45; Nisga'a Petition (1913), 241, 242, 254, 256, 259-60; petitions the only method for Aboriginal protests, 241, 242-43; reference to federal courts (1911), 257-58; reserve process, 250, 255, 259; Royal Proclamation of 1763 and, 245, 251-53, 254, 256; threat during economic boom (early 1900s), 246, 247(p)

Act to amend the Law of Dower in certain respects (NSW, 1850), 215

Act to Prevent the Traffic in Intoxicating Liquors (NB, 1853), 225-27

Act to Regulate the Sale of Spiritous Liquors (NB, 1854), 227

Addison, John, 171-72

Admiralty Courts, 40

admiralty law, 39-40. *See also* discipline at sea

Alaska Highway News (AHN), 180, 190

All England Law Reports, 105-6

Allied Indian Tribes of British Columbia, 246, 250, 259, 260

"ancient constitution," 78, 85-86, 90

Anglin, T.W., 234

Archibald, S.G., 201-2

Arnold, Samuel, 160

Arthur, George: appointment of Montagu, 158-59; licensing and stamp duty legislation, 30, 31, 92-93; Montagu-Stephen dispute and, 166, 167-68; Thomas Lewis case and, 160-61

attainder doctrine, 82-83, 94-97

Attorney-General v. Clough, 110-11

Attorney-General v. Mulholland, 110-11

Austral-Asiatic Review, 164

New South Wales: attempts to license
newspapers, 16, 30, 32-33, 92-93;
British disallowance of repressive
colonial laws, 16-17, 32, 35; centrality
of courts, 16, 20, 23-24, 33-34, 36;
constitution *(see New South Wales
Act);* control over jury trials, 24;
discipline at sea, case law, 41, 42, 44-
45, 48, 49; discipline at sea, statute
law and judicial application, 50-52;
dower in *(see* dower in New South
Wales); executive domination of
justice, 16-17, 23-24, 29-31, 33-35, 36,
87, 156; land policies, 210, 211-12;
political and legal context, 21; property and democracy intertwined,
209-10, 212-13; property titles and
transfers, 215-16; reception of British
law, 22-23, 40, 79, 82, 85-86, 88-90,
91, 92, 282n13; status as settled colony,
86-87. *See also* Forbes, Francis; rule
of law in New South Wales; seditious
libel in New South Wales
New South Wales Act (NSW, 1823), 21, 22,
24, 88, 91-92
New Zealand: Crown grants non-
contestable on grounds of non-
extinguished native title, 135, 139-40,
145, 152-53; Crown's radical title to
land *(Native Land Act 1909),* 139-40,
153; *Wi Parata* case, 135, 144-47, 151-
53. *See also* Maori of New Zealand;
Prendergast, James; Salmond, John
William; Treaty of Waitangi
New Zealand Law Reports, 108
*New Zealand Maori Council v. Attorney-
General* (1987), 138
Newspaper Acts Opinion (NSW, 1827),
92-94
Ngata, Apirana, 154
Nicol, John, 46
Nireaha Tamaki v. Baker (1894), 152-54,
155
Nisga'a: *Calder* case (1973), 240-41, 254,
260, 339n5; Nisga'a Land Commit-
tee, 245, 250, 252

Nisga'a Petition of 1913, 241, 242, 254,
256, 259-60. *See also* Aboriginal title
in British Columbia
North-West Territories. *See* Hudson's
Bay Company; indigenous peoples,
Rupert's Land; Rupert's Land
Nova Scotia Supreme Court (NSSC):
benefits of circuits for communities,
121-22, 134; Cape Breton circuit, 117,
118(m), 130-31; circuits (1816-50),
117-18; communities' preference for
lower courts, 119, 123-25; cost of
judicial system, 124; courtroom
facilities, 121; drawbacks of circuits
for communities, 123-24; duties of
circuit judges, 120; impact of abolish-
ment of inferior civil courts, 117,
125-26; lawyers on circuits, 131-33,
134; more "professional" system than
local courts, 120, 124; role in colonial
governance, 119-20, 133-34; travelling
conditions, 129-31; two-judge vs
one-judge rule, 127-29; workload of
circuit judges, 126-28

Olive, James, 230
O'Meara, Arthur Eugene, 250, 251, 252-
53, 257
Ontario, 251
Ordinances of the Colony of Sierra Leone
(Montagu), 175
Orwell, George, 5

Palmerston, Lord, 231
Parker, Graham, 8, 268
pastoralists (NSW), 210
Paull, Andy, 245-46
Peace River Block News (PRBN), 182
Peace River Record, 187
Peace River region (BC): Cariboo court
traditions, 179-83; description, 177,
178(m); impact of Second World War,
179-81, 190-91; positive view of legal
system due to judge's affinity for
country, 177, 179, 183; practical and
common sense approach, 190-91;

PUBLICATIONS OF THE OSGOODE
SOCIETY FOR CANADIAN LEGAL HISTORY

2008 Constance Backhouse, *Carnal Crimes: Sexual Assault Law in Canada, 1900-1975*

Jim Phillips, R. Roy McMurtry, and John Saywell, eds., *Essays in the History of Canadian Law, Vol. X: A Tribute to Peter N. Oliver*

Gregory Taylor, *The Law of the Land: Canada's Receptions of the Torrens System*

Hamar Foster, Benjamin Berger, and A.R. Buck, eds., *The Grand Experiment: Law and Legal Culture in British Settler Societies*

2007 Robert Sharpe and Patricia McMahon, *The Persons Case: The Origins and Legacy of the Fight for Legal Personhood*

Lori Chambers, *Misconceptions: Unmarried Motherhood and the Ontario Children of Unmarried Parents Act, 1921-1969*

Jonathan Swainger, ed., *The Alberta Supreme Court at 100: History and Authority*

Martin Friedland, *My Life in Crime and Other Academic Adventures*

2006 Donald Fyson, *Magistrates, Police and People: Everyday Criminal Justice in Quebec and Lower Canada, 1764-1837*

Dale Brawn, *The Court of Queen's Bench of Manitoba 1870-1950: A Biographical History*

R.C.B. Risk, *A History of Canadian Legal Thought: Collected Essays*, edited and introduced by G. Blaine Baker and Jim Phillips

2005 Philip Girard, *Bora Laskin: Bringing Law to Life*

Christopher English, ed., *Essays in the History of Canadian Law, Vol. IX: Two Islands, Newfoundland and Prince Edward Island*

Fred Kaufman, *Searching for Justice: An Autobiography*

2004 John D. Honsberger, *Osgoode Hall: An Illustrated History*

Frederick Vaughan, *Aggressive in Pursuit: The Life of Justice Emmett Hall*

Constance Backhouse and Nancy Backhouse, *The Heiress versus the Establishment: Mrs. Campbell's Campaign for Legal Justice*

Philip Girard, Jim Phillips, and Barry Cahill, eds., *The Supreme Court of Nova Scotia, 1754-2004: From Imperial Bastion to Provincial Oracle*

2003 Robert Sharpe and Kent Roach, *Brian Dickson: A Judge's Journey*

George Finlayson, *John J. Robinette: Peerless Mentor*

Peter Oliver, *The Conventional Man: The Diaries of Ontario Chief Justice Robert A. Harrison, 1856-1878*

Jerry Bannister, *The Rule of the Admirals: Law, Custom and Naval Government in Newfoundland, 1699-1832*

2002   John T. Saywell, *The Law Makers: Judicial Power and the Shaping of Canadian Federalism*

David Murray, *Colonial Justice: Justice, Morality and Crime in the Niagara District, 1791-1849*

F. Murray Greenwood and Barry Wright, eds., *Canadian State Trials, Volume Two: Rebellion and Invasion in the Canadas, 1837-8*

Patrick Brode, *Courted and Abandoned: Seduction in Canadian Law*

2001   Ellen Anderson, *Judging Bertha Wilson: Law as Large as Life*

Judy Fudge and Eric Tucker, *Labour Before the Law: Collective Action in Canada, 1900-1948*

Laurel Sefton MacDowell, *Renegade Lawyer: The Life of J.L. Cohen*

2000   Barry Cahill, *"The Thousandth Man": A Biography of James McGregor Stewart*

A.B. McKillop, *The Spinster and the Prophet: Florence Deeks, H.G. Wells, and the Mystery of the Purloined Past*

Beverley Boissery and F. Murray Greenwood, *Uncertain Justice: Canadian Women and Capital Punishment*

Bruce Ziff, *Unforeseen Legacies: Reuben Wells Leonard and the Leonard Foundation Trust*

1999   Constance Backhouse, *Colour-Coded: A Legal History of Racism in Canada, 1900-1950*

G. Blaine Baker and Jim Phillips, eds., *Essays in the History of Canadian Law, Vol. VIII: In Honour of R.C.B. Risk*

Richard W. Pound, *Chief Justice W.R. Jackett: By the Law of the Land*

David Vanek, *Fulfilment: Memoirs of a Criminal Court Judge*

1998   Sidney Harring, *White Man's Law: Native People in Nineteenth-Century Canadian Jurisprudence*

Peter Oliver, *"Terror to Evil-Doers": Prisons and Punishments in Nineteenth-Century Ontario*

1997   James W. St. G. Walker, *"Race," Rights and the Law in the Supreme Court of Canada: Historical Case Studies*

Lori Chambers, *Married Women and Property Law in Victorian Ontario*

Patrick Brode, *Casual Slaughters and Accidental Judgments: Canadian War Crimes and Prosecutions, 1944-1948*

Ian Bushnell, *The Federal Court of Canada: A History, 1875-1992*

1996   Carol Wilton, ed., *Essays in the History of Canadian Law, Vol. VII: Inside the Law—Canadian Law Firms in Historical Perspective*

William Kaplan, *Bad Judgment: The Case of Mr. Justice Leo A. Landreville*

Murray Greenwood and Barry Wright, eds., *Canadian State Trials, Volume I: Law, Politics and Security Measures, 1608-1837*

1995 David Williams, *Just Lawyers: Seven Portraits*

Hamar Foster and John McLaren, eds., *Essays in the History of Canadian Law, Vol. VI: British Columbia and the Yukon*

W.H. Morrow, ed., *Northern Justice: The Memoirs of Mr. Justice William G. Morrow*

Beverley Boissery, *A Deep Sense of Wrong: The Treason, Trials and Transportation to New South Wales of Lower Canadian Rebels after the 1838 Rebellion*

1994 Patrick Boyer, *A Passion for Justice: The Legacy of James Chalmers McRuer*

Charles Pullen, *The Life and Times of Arthur Maloney: The Last of the Tribunes*

Jim Phillips, Tina Loo, and Susan Lewthwaite, eds., *Essays in the History of Canadian Law, Vol. V: Crime and Criminal Justice*

Brian Young, *The Politics of Codification: The Lower Canadian Civil Code of 1866*

1993 Greg Marquis, *Policing Canada's Century: A History of the Canadian Association of Chiefs of Police*

Murray Greenwood, *Legacies of Fear: Law and Politics in Quebec in the Era of the French Revolution*

1992 Brendan O'Brien, *Speedy Justice: The Tragic Last Voyage of His Majesty's Vessel Speedy*

Robert Fraser, ed., *Provincial Justice: Upper Canadian Legal Portraits from the Dictionary of Canadian Biography*

1991 Constance Backhouse, *Petticoats and Prejudice: Women and Law in Nineteenth-Century Canada*

1990 Philip Girard and Jim Phillips, eds., *Essays in the History of Canadian Law, Vol. III: Nova Scotia*

Carol Wilton, ed., *Essays in the History of Canadian Law, Vol. IV: Beyond the Law — Lawyers and Business in Canada 1830-1930*

1989 Desmond Brown, *The Genesis of the Canadian Criminal Code of 1892*

Patrick Brode, *The Odyssey of John Anderson*

1988 Robert Sharpe, *The Last Day, the Last Hour: The Currie Libel Trial*

John D. Arnup, *Middleton: The Beloved Judge*

1987 C. Ian Kyer and Jerome Bickenbach, *The Fiercest Debate: Cecil A. Wright, the Benchers and Legal Education in Ontario, 1923-1957*

1986   Paul Romney, *Mr. Attorney: The Attorney General for Ontario in Court, Cabinet and Legislature, 1791-1899*

Martin Friedland, *The Case of Valentine Shortis: A True Story of Crime and Politics in Canada*

1985   James Snell and Frederick Vaughan, *The Supreme Court of Canada: History of the Institution*

1984   Patrick Brode, *Sir John Beverley Robinson: Bone and Sinew of the Compact*

David Williams, *Duff: A Life in the Law*

1983   David H. Flaherty, ed., *Essays in the History of Canadian Law, Vol. II*

1982   Marion MacRae and Anthony Adamson, *Cornerstones of Order: Courthouses and Town Halls of Ontario, 1784-1914*

1981   David H. Flaherty, ed., *Essays in the History of Canadian Law, Vol. I*

LAW AND
SOCIETY

2008   Catherine E. Bell and Robert K. Paterson, eds., *Protection of First Nations Cultural Heritage: Laws, Policy, and Reform*

Richard J. Moon, ed., *Law and Religious Pluralism in Canada*

Catherine E. Bell and Val Napoleon, eds., *First Nations Cultural Heritage and Law: Case Studies, Voices, and Perspectives*

Douglas C. Harris, *Landing Native Fisheries: Indian Reserves and Fishing Rights in British Columbia, 1849-1925*

Peggy J. Blair, *Lament for a First Nation: The Williams Treaties in Southern Ontario*

2007   Lori G. Beaman, *Defining Harm: Religious Freedom and the Limits of the Law*

Stephen Tierney, ed., *Multiculturalism and the Canadian Constitution*

Julie Macfarlane, *The New Lawyer: How Settlement Is Transforming the Practice of Law*

Kimberley White, *Negotiating Responsibility: Law, Murder, and States of Mind*

Dawn Moore, *Criminal Artefacts: Governing Drugs and Users*

Hamar Foster, Heather Raven, and Jeremy Webber, eds., *Let Right Be Done: Aboriginal Title, the Calder Case, and the Future of Indigenous Rights*

Dorothy E. Chunn, Susan B. Boyd, and Hester Lessard, eds., *Reaction and Resistance: Feminism, Law, and Social Change*

Margot Young, Susan B. Boyd, Gwen Brodsky, and Shelagh Day, eds., *Poverty: Rights, Social Citizenship, and Legal Activism*

Rosanna L. Langer, *Defining Rights and Wrongs: Bureaucracy, Human Rights, and Public Accountability*

C.L. Ostberg and Matthew E. Wetstein, *Attitudinal Decision Making in the Supreme Court of Canada*

Chris Clarkson, *Domestic Reforms: Political Visions and Family Regulation in British Columbia, 1862-1940*

2006   Jean McKenzie Leiper, *Bar Codes: Women in the Legal Profession*

Gerald Baier, *Courts and Federalism: Judicial Doctrine in the United States, Australia, and Canada*

Avigail Eisenberg, ed., *Diversity and Equality: The Changing Framework of Freedom in Canada*

2005 Randy K. Lippert, *Sanctuary, Sovereignty, Sacrifice: Canadian Sanctuary Incidents, Power, and Law*

James B. Kelly, *Governing with the Charter: Legislative and Judicial Activism and Framers' Intent*

Dianne Pothier and Richard Devlin, eds., *Critical Disability Theory: Essays in Philosophy, Politics, Policy, and Law*

Susan G. Drummond, *Mapping Marriage Law in Spanish Gitano Communities*

Louis A. Knafla and Jonathan Swainger, eds., *Laws and Societies in the Canadian Prairie West, 1670-1940*

Ikechi Mgbeoji, *Global Biopiracy: Patents, Plants, and Indigenous Knowledge*

Florian Sauvageau, David Schneiderman, and David Taras, with Ruth Klinkhammer and Pierre Trudel, *The Last Word: Media Coverage of the Supreme Court of Canada*

Gerald Kernerman, *Multicultural Nationalism: Civilizing Difference, Constituting Community*

Pamela A. Jordan, *Defending Rights in Russia: Lawyers, the State, and Legal Reform in the Post-Soviet Era*

Anna Pratt, *Securing Borders: Detention and Deportation in Canada*

Kirsten Johnson Kramar, *Unwilling Mothers, Unwanted Babies: Infanticide in Canada*

W.A. Bogart, *Good Government? Good Citizens? Courts, Politics, and Markets in a Changing Canada*

Catherine Dauvergne, *Humanitarianism, Identity, and Nation: Migration Laws in Canada and Australia*

Michael Lee Ross, *First Nations Sacred Sites in Canada's Courts*

Andrew Woolford, *Between Justice and Certainty: Treaty Making in British Columbia*

2004 John McLaren, Andrew Buck, and Nancy Wright, eds., *Despotic Dominion: Property Rights in British Settler Societies*

Georges Campeau, *From UI to EI: Waging War on the Welfare State*

Alvin J. Esau, *The Courts and the Colonies: The Litigation of Hutterite Church Disputes*

Christopher N. Kendall, *Gay Male Pornography: An Issue of Sex Discrimination*

Roy B. Flemming, *Tournament of Appeals: Granting Judicial Review in Canada*

Constance Backhouse and Nancy L. Backhouse, *The Heiress vs the Establishment: Mrs. Campbell's Campaign for Legal Justice*

Christopher P. Manfredi, *Feminist Activism in the Supreme Court: Legal Mobilization and the Women's Legal Education and Action Fund*

Annalise Acorn, *Compulsory Compassion: A Critique of Restorative Justice*

2003 Jonathan Swainger and Constance Backhouse, eds., *People and Place: Historical Influences on Legal Culture*

Jim Phillips and Rosemary Gartner, *Murdering Holiness: The Trials of Franz Creffield and George Mitchell*

David R. Boyd, *Unnatural Law: Rethinking Canadian Environmental Law and Policy*

Ikechi Mgbeoji, *Collective Insecurity: The Liberian Crisis, Unilateralism, and Global Order*

2002 Rebecca Johnson, *Taxing Choices: The Intersection of Class, Gender, Parenthood, and the Law*

John McLaren, Robert Menzies, and Dorothy E. Chunn, eds., *Regulating Lives: Historical Essays on the State, Society, the Individual, and the Law*

2001 Joan Brockman, *Gender in the Legal Profession: Fitting or Breaking the Mould*

Printed and bound in Canada by Friesens
Set in Bembo by Artegraphica Design Co. Ltd.
Copy editor: Deborah Kerr
Proofreader: Stacy Belden
Cartographer: Eric Leinberger
Indexer: Patricia Buchanan